KISS FAQ

Series Editor: Robert Rodriguez

KISS FAQ

All That's Left to Know About the Hottest Band in the Land

Dale Sherman

Backbeat
Books

An Imprint of Hal Leonard Corporation

Published in 2012 by Backbeat Books
An Imprint of Hal Leonard Corporation
7777 West Bluemound Road
Milwaukee, WI 53213

Trade Book Division Editorial Offices
33 Plymouth St., Montclair, NJ 07042

The FAQ series was conceived by Robert Rodriguez and developed with Stuart Shea.

Marvel and Archie comic book covers used by permission.

Book design by Snow Creative Services

Printed in the United States of America

Library of Congress Cataloging-in-Publication Data is available upon request.

ISBN 978-1-61713-091-5

www.backbeatbooks.com

Contents

Foreword

by Bill Starkey, Founder of the KISS Army

W hen I look back on my early years as a KISS fan, I sometimes wonder how people tolerated the overbearing attitude of a teenager who couldn't see beyond the makeup and the flash pots. I would've killed for those guys, which thankfully, and to the band's credit, never got past anything other than an Army and/or references to one's "love gun." So what can inspire someone to such levels of irrational behavior?

We KISS fans are a proud lot and very tight-knit group. Yet I've never seen such an eclectic group of people, all motivated to share in their devotion to KISS, to one another, or to those who don't subscribe to our love to "rock and roll all nite and party every day." By no means do I consider myself at the top of the KISS hierarchy either. Not even close. I was just an innocent messenger who led a group whose escapades were heard from Indiana all the way to New York City. Many times at KISS expos or concerts I've been introduced to KISS fans who have dedicated their homes as a shrine, invested all of their money, made permanent artwork on their bodies, lost spouses, lost friends, maybe even lost some of their hearing and/or named their children after their favorite rock band. That is real devotion.

We relish debating about our favorite members, albums, album covers, songs, tours, opening acts, eras, merchandise, collectibles, and on and on. The conversations might be about the hidden meanings in *"The Elder,"* or the drumming styles of Criss or Carr or Singer, or the styles of Ace or Bruce or Tommy. Whatever, KISS fans will find something to discuss and debate to the wee hours of the morning. All will have an opinion and not be swayed by the other.

The band has only added to the debates with promises to never do a ballad let alone perform one live, to never get the original group back together, or to put the makeup back on or take it off. Thankfully, other promises like "The Final Farwell Tour" to never do any new material due to the current state of music piracy haven't materialized, to our delight—they continue to tour and add to an already great catalogue of music.

I must say it is amazing to see new fans at shows and expos, fans from abroad, and to share KISS experiences with people I've met along the way. Many of us have grown up with the band, and some might say we've "never grown up" when it comes to watching Paul jump with his platform shoes while throwing around his Flying V or squeal when Gene vomits blood. Why don't we ever tire of it? We just don't.

To others, KISS is a religion. A way to approach one's life. A way to overcome obstacles or a way to reach out to someone who needs your support. We love sharing our KISS experiences and enrolling new troops in the KISS Army. So when I was approached by Dale Sherman—a man I met many years ago, whose books I proudly keep in my modest KISS collection —to add to one of his latest endeavors, I was flattered, to say the least. Because I'm not the greatest KISS fan nor have I ever claimed to be. I'm not sure who that might be.

I believe that the greatest KISS fans are actually Paul, Gene, Eric, and Tommy. I can honestly say that, based on the brief conversations that I was lucky enough to have with them, their OWN love and dedication to KISS is greater than we might imagine. Proof being that the band continues to endure and endure in such a noble way, while many acts with similar proud accomplishments fail to live up to their past reputations.

So here is my KISS Army salute to all of you rock soldiers in the mighty KISS Army. May you continue to shout out loud your devotion to the hottest band in the land—KISS!

KISS Army: The True Story

Legends and tall tales have a way of changing over time. Maybe that is good, because if the story is interesting, then I guess people will continue to talk about it over and over. Unfortunately, when things are passed on from one to another, the story might change from its true origin. Sometimes by accident, other times by convenience. My experiences as the commander-in-chief of the KISS Army, the international fan club by which all KISS fans are known, have gone through some revisions as well.

The mid-'70s were a fun time to be a rock 'n' roller. Concert tickets were cheap, and bands would often tour even through small Midwest cites like Terre Haute, Indiana. The home of Indiana State University. Live concerts were valued, and the only way to actually see one's favorite bands live was usually in a concert setting. The other way was on late-night television. Rock bands, especially hard-rock bands, were relegated to late night/midnight concert shows so as to not offend anyone.

Eating my breakfast cereal one morning and leafing through the TV section of our newspaper, I spotted a picture of some "unusual thing" playing a guitar. The caption read that the band "KISS" would be playing on *Don Kirshner's Rock Concert* on ABC that Friday night. That "thing" was Gene Simmons, but I was reading that Foghat was going to be on that night and I WAS familiar with their songs. I had no idea who KISS was. Though a picture can say a thousand things.

That night I stayed up late enough to see Foghat, but it was KISS who fascinated and thrilled me. My father, who shipped vinyl records for the local record pressing plant, often brought home freebies, and I requested the KISS album. Many rock acts would pass through the plant, like Paul Revere and the

Raiders, so my father was pretty open-minded about the music business and rock bands in general.

My record collection back then went from Deep Purple to Alice Cooper, Mott the Hoople, Slade, and other bands, but mainly English acts. I knew little about KISS, but I asked my dad for their first and only record, and he obliged, along with a pullout poster that came with it—perfect for taking to your school locker and scaring people.

Pop, as we called him, asked if I wanted to go to my first rock concert—except he'd have to go, too. My younger brother and I agreed, and we were to see Deep Purple play at Market Square Arena. Pop's major label was Warner Brothers, and their people would often give out free tickets. It was a way of thanking factory workers like my father for their hard work and dedication. Pop always tried to convince me of what I should be listening to based on what he was shipping the most of. That did not interest me . . . it probably turned me off at that age.

Deep Purple sold out fast, so as a consolation my father asked if I'd want to see KISS instead. I agreed, and we piled into a pickup truck on a cold December night to see KISS share the stage with ZZ Top at Evansville's Roberts Stadium. The free tickets at the will-call window did not arrive, so the lady at the window felt bad for my father and let us in after the show had already started. Another band, Point Blank, I think, was already performing.

Roberts Stadium has been the host of many great Indiana High School basketball games. It seats around 10,000 in a small, intimate circular shape surrounded by wooden bleachers. It was a Sunday night, and it was cold outside, so what else was there to do in Evansville, Indiana? Sure I saw KISS on TV that night, but this was a visual and audible assault on one's senses. The concert volume was so loud that you could feel it thumping against your chest and through the wooden bleachers.

You had this sense of fear, or at least fear of the unknown, because you did not know what to expect. I enjoyed the songs on the first and only KISS album I owned, but they sounded much, much different tonight—almost like they were being played way too quickly. I did not have time to catch my breath before something else happened. Sirens, flash pots, fire breathing, and blood puking —my first rock concert had it all. My father, who had a spirit of adventure in him, enjoyed the camaraderie that KISS had with their fans. To him it was like a group of athletes performing at full tilt while egging their fans on to show their support.

When it was all over, we agreed to sit through the first two songs of ZZ Top's set, just to say we were there. My father, who usually listened to Sinatra and Mario Lanza, after experiencing the KISS assault, decided that nothing else that night was going to excite like KISS. Father knows best. While he was not likely to listen to hard rock, I think he saw a degree of professionalism, work ethic, and rapport that KISS had that he valued. He dared my mother to take us to see KISS three weeks later in Indy, and she did, and KISS conquered once more.

Now, going back to Terre Haute and telling your friends how great your first rock concert was impresses no one." "Let's face it," they'd say. "It was your first rock concert, that is all." Fortunately, I had a good friend who shared similar music tastes, Jay Evans. Jay was not one to go along with whatever everyone else was doing. He knew what he liked and what he didn't, and he always loved to be on the cutting edge of new and obscure musical acts. He, too, owned the KISS album, and I shared with him every detail I could remember from both shows.

Our usual gathering point was in my parents' basement. There, they could better monitor what we did and who we ran around with. We probably could've performed animal sacrifices down there, but as long as we were in the basement, it was presumed that we were not causing any trouble. It was from my basement that Jay bravely called the radio station WVTS-FM for the first time to request some "KISS music." He was told that they were not allowed to play new acts and especially not KISS. However, we would continue to spread the good news about KISS. Jay would make copies of their albums with an 8-track recorder and give them out to anyone who believed us.

The radio station requests would not stop until one night one of the radio personalities felt sorry for us and spilled the beans. He said it was the program director, Rich Dickerson, who decided against playing the band. Someone at the station said they had witnessed him throwing the KISS records out and calling them "another New York fag band."

We too were subjected to the usual school bullies who would verbally harass us since we weren't the jocks, the rich kids, or the most popular like the class clowns. One of the ways you could be "branded" was by the bands you listened to. Jay and I would often hear, "KISS? KISS my ass," or "If they're so great, Starkey, why aren't they on the radio?" I couldn't answer that, and by now Jay and I felt we had a mission to accomplish. Eventually we were able to contact Rich over the phone and he laughed at us, telling Jay that "KISS is just a mediocre Bachman-Turner Overdrive." So calling the radio station had resulted in nothing. Jay was always joking about military stuff, yet neither of us was exactly military material. We decided to start a writing campaign calling ourselves the KISS Army. Headquarters? My basement. I was the president, he was Field Marshal Evans. Sitting in the basement laughing as we wrote insults to Rich Dickerson telling him how great KISS was and how the music and bands he played sucked! We would cut out a picture from *Circus* magazine of a flash pot going off or a flamethrower and warn the radio station that "something terrible would happen if they didn't give in to our demands." Other times we were blunter about our demands. Either way we were rock-'n'-roll terrorists with a pen and a phone line.

We convinced the younger kids in the neighborhood to paint up like the four members. We would parade them around the mall and at drive-thru restaurants. We called them "The Unknown Soldiers of the KISS Army." We were having a blast and recruiting new people to our cause. In April, I took Jay and two carloads of our classmates to their first, my third KISS show. That was the beginning of the real KISS Army.

One of the guys who went with us, Rob Smith, used the school's printing press to mass produce KISS T-shirts. We'd pick days when we'd all wear T-shirts to school, eventually posing in the restroom. Now others were calling the radio station on behalf of the KISS Army. However, this did not come without some backlash. Wearing a shirt of a band that couldn't get radio airplay was not popular, and we weren't the most popular kids in school to begin with.

By graduation, many of our army was planning for their first year of college, including my field marshal. A start-up radio station, WPFR-FM, had taken shape and gave in to our KISS demands because they were new and had fewer listeners. By September, *KISS Alive* was released, and everything I said about a live KISS concert was available to the masses. . . . WVTS too had surrendered to the KISS Army and even requested to borrow my own KISS albums to tape since theirs were "lost."

KISS had announced in September that they were coming to Terre Haute in November. Though by now other KISS fans may have called requesting KISS music to be played, only Jay and I ever signed our names to any letters to request KISS. So Rich Dickerson contacted me with a truce. He asked if I would write "The KISS Army Letter of the Day" to him, and he would read it every evening at 5 p.m. during the peak listening hours. This would go on for about two weeks until the concert. Nothing was off-limits. I could insult him, his music, other bands, other radio DJs at the station, and anyone else we considered the enemy. Unfortunately, for me Rich would always have the final say. He was brutal and clever, doing a good job of being a rock-'n'-roll "shock jock" well before the great Howard Stern. We stretched the limits of the FCC and bad taste. Even comments about Terre Haute's reputation as Sin City, due to its history of prostitution, were bandied about over the airwaves. Eventually Jay asked that I remove his name from the letters as he was getting teased about them by the upperclassmen at his campus hangout, The Grill. Sadly, I obliged him.

One evening when we were parading our Unknown Soldiers through the city, we decided to visit the radio station. We had done this before, and the DJ described us by saying, "The KISS Army have arrived like a hoard of painted devils." We were greeted that evening by Rich Dickerson's wife, Trisha Phillips. She was talking a mile a minute, and we couldn't understand what she was all excited about. She told us that the KISS show had sold out and that KISS's management had heard about it. They wanted to meet me and discuss the formation of a national KISS Army run out of Terre Haute.

You cannot imagine how stone-cold silent we were—stunned. I was going to meet KISS!!!?? That was not on our agenda. What was I going to do next? What was I going to say? Here I was without a job, let alone a car, and I was going to meet my rock-'n'-roll heroes! On November 10, 1975, my nineteenth birthday, I got a call from Mr. Alan Miller. Mr. Miller had once worked for Alice Cooper.

He told me that ANY publicity was good publicity. He was a shrewd negotiator and very good at getting his way. This was the start of daily long-distance calls between us in planning for KISS's arrival for the Terre Haute show. Welcome to the business of music, Mr. Starkey.

The calls were nonstop to the point where it began to annoy my mother. Miller wanted to pattern this after the KISS Cadillac promotion. I failed to do many of the things he asked for. No mayor or city council members to greet the band upon their arrival. No high school marching band either. But he had me convinced that I could do just about anything just by saying to me, "Do it for the band!" I started taking this way too seriously. To the point where it would backfire on me years later.

The rest of the story has been repeated many times. KISS came to Terre Haute to a sellout crowd that placed them only with Elvis in terms of sold-out concerts in Terre Haute at the time. I was called backstage unexpectedly right before Rush took the stage. I would watch the show from the side of the stage while sitting on an anvil case with Mr. Bill Aucoin, who I would meet for the very first time. I would come onstage to receive a plaque from the band with my name on it. But the real satisfaction came from seeing the faces of my high school classmates. The ones who loved to bully all of us about KISS and their lack of radio play. Now they were at the altar of KISS ready to enlist in the KISS Army themselves.

As years went by and KISS became even more popular than they were in 1975, the story of the formation of the KISS Army had gotten lost in the shuffle. I was having a hard time following the new additions to the band, and I was discovering new rock-'n'-roll artists who were emerging during the '80s. Always keeping an ear out for the band, I never completely lost interest in what they were doing, though I was going to fewer and fewer concerts.

Imagine my surprise when *KISStory I* was released and I quickly preordered my copy. I did it as a KISS fan not even realizing that I would be included in this awesome literary monument to KISS. However, I was a little bowled over by the description of how the KISS Army was formed—according to the band. "The KISS Army surrounded the radio station and threatened the DJ if he did not play KISS by 5 o clock." If he refused, then by such time, the KISS Army would surround the radio station not allowing him to leave. Wow! Incredible! I was flattered, to say the least. How I wished it had happened that way. I was made out to be a real badass who practically risked jail time for his favorite rock group.

I attended one of the KISS Conventions in 1995 and reunited with my rock-'n'-roll heroes. Gene came up to me and asked me about getting him a picture of the "kids surrounding the radio station" for him. I was totally confused. I explained that I did not know what he was talking about. Now *he* was confused. Incredibly, he asked me to join the band onstage and sit in HIS chair, marked "Monster" on the back. Paul introduced me to my fellow Hoosier KISS fans, and he told me half of the story about the kids "surrounding the radio station."

I was sweating bullets. What was I to say? Instead of finishing Paul's story, I danced around it trying to keep it as realistic as possible but not wanting to upset anyone—especially KISS, who were nice enough to let me share the stage with them.

Regardless, the KISS fans cheered widely and could've cared less what story we told. One of their own was onstage with their rock Gods! A mere mortal—me. Backstage I was introduced to the very talented and creative Susan McEowen. Susan once lived in Terre Haute, so I felt very comfortable approaching her about the book. I questioned her about the story behind the KISS Army and told her that that is not what really happened. She listened to me and after I was done said, "Well, I like Gene's story better," as she put it. Boy, did I feel two inches tall. I was not going to be the one to spoil the party, even though I know there were too many people around at that time who KNEW better. I owed it to them, but I hated to upset anyone, especially Gene and Paul.

Years later, the story behind the KISS Army was being retold and resurrected during KISS's *Farewell* tour with Peter and Ace. I would do a few interviews telling my side of the formation of the KISS Army, trying hard not to step on anyone's toes. I just felt that the story itself was "cool" enough and sensationalistic on its own merits. A kid in a small Midwestern city, who idolizes his favorite band, is told no by the one and only radio station. He enrolls others in his cause and is eventually rewarded by his heroes. The name they chose becomes an international symbol for KISS fans in all languages and cultures. It has all the making of a Hollywood story.

Years later, I would run into people from that era who remember even more details from that marvelous time than I did. We'd reminisce about our exploits and talk about the "Legend of the KISS Army." Of course, we're humbled by the many versions, realizing that our quest to get KISS on the radio station was more like Chinese water torture than a one-day military coup. And what about those kids surrounding the radio station and the picture?

Well, KISS did surround the radio station, and KISS was there to witness the phenomenon. The day of the Terre Haute concert, the band would make an appearance at the very same radio station I petitioned. Here they would play DJ for a while in the same studio that refused them just nine months earlier. The event was advertised, and kids from all over the Terre Haute area actually surrounded the radio station while KISS was inside. There were no police and little security to ward anyone away. The picture? Well, it was the one often seen with Jay and me holding the original KISS Army banner at Terre Haute's Hulman Field. It was taken at the airport waiting for the band's arrival. I have seen two versions of it, one even colorized.

So far I haven't disappointed anyone that I know of with my revised version of *KISStory*. Of course, I am honored and would gladly trade my story for the other more legendary accounts. But in my eyes the original tale, though less spectacular and less brazen to some, still hits its mark. For anyone who has ever been told that "it cannot happen, your band sucks, don't waste your time, or dream on," there is always hope. You can get your way sometimes if you persevere.

You can go from listening to your rock-'n'-roll heroes in a basement in Indiana to flying to New York City to hang with them at a rock-'n'-roll pool party on New Year's Eve. And the good thing about legends and tall tales is that they must be good enough to be continually told and retold decades later. I am living proof that it can happen.

Twenty years after the KISS Army was created, Bill Starkey met up with Gene and Paul at a stop on the 1995 KISS Convention tour.   *Courtesy of Bill Starkey*

Preface

Once you're in, you're in for life. It is an old line from the movies, commonly used to warn people off from getting involved in something they do not really understand, but also hinting at such dangers with defiance and pride. In a broad sense, the same holds true for people who admit to being KISS fans. Even those of us who tend to think their days as part of KISS fandom are behind them find themselves sucked right back in when KISS appears on television or one of the songs pops up on the radio. Suddenly, for three to four minutes, you are back to the same level of sheer joy you had years before when watching the band working their particular magic. Alternatively, as in another old mobster cliché, "Just when I thought I was out, they pull me back in."

Meanwhile, there are two things people who are not fans know about KISS. The first is that it is a hard-rock band with four musicians (some would put quotation marks around the word musicians, namely because such cynics are not very creative) who wear bizarre costumes, makeup, and use special effects in concert. Yet that is a simplistic review of a band that has managed to survive for nearly forty years of musical changes (both external and internal), label disputes, solo and group projects that have nearly jackknifed the band, waning and reemerging interest over the years, arguments, death, and even a merry-go-round of members being hired, leaving, and being rehired.

Why is there such a simplistic idea of KISS? It cannot be from lack of press coverage. There have been numerous biographies about the group since the mid-1970s, including one I wrote back in 1997 that gained enough interest to be updated in 2009 for a "tenth anniversary" edition (*Black Diamond: The Unauthorized Biography of KISS*). There have also been several reference guides to the band's touring, their merchandise, and even recording history to show the vast amount of material out there about the band. Autobiographical studies haven't been missed either, with a few from original band members (two by way of Gene Simmons, one from Ace Frehley, and a forthcoming one from Peter Criss), and a handful from people who have connections to—and in some cases even vendettas against—the band members. There has also been a cottage industry of official books from the band in recent years, from self-glorifying puff pieces like *KISStory I* and *KISStory II* to more serious works such as David Leaf's and Ken Sharp's *Behind the Mask*, the *KISS Army Worldwide!* book (also by Sharp), and photo books from Waring Abbott and Barry Levine. And more to come as the fortieth anniversary draws near.

Years of newspaper articles and magazine essays—sometimes as vast as one-off specials exclusively about KISS—have compounded the coverage. Then there are the many television appearances and interviews over that time, as well as an official three-volume set of DVDs covering the history of the band. There have been years of merchandise (the thing that seems to irritate the critics the most), albums, awards, jokes, homages, tours, movies, comics, and on and on. KISS has been noted for advancing stage concepts in rock performance, pushing hard-rock music at a time when most bands were giving up on it (albeit KISS has struggled with that as well), and showing that it was okay for musicians to actually be involved with the business side of the industry.

Yet KISS is dismissed as these four guys wearing makeup. Forget the history, forget the influences, forget even the twelve years where KISS found success without makeup. Forget all that has been written, filmed, and said about these men—to the naysayers it is all about the makeup. Perhaps one of the reasons we need so many books and videos about the band is to try to get people to see the band's rich history beyond the clown white.

Of course, the other thing many people remember about KISS is that they have a loyal fan base commonly referred to as the KISS Army. The KISS Army (created . . . well, details about that can be found elsewhere in this book) allowed fans of the band a mecca of tolerance and understanding in a sea of harsh critics—professional, friends, and family members—who looked down their noses at KISS. This came not only from the parents and conservative religious types who frowned upon what they saw as evil incarnate when the band appeared on camera or onstage, but from the very rock 'n' rollers who should have been defending the band. As for the rock critics, it seems they get a bit stuffy about the band because KISS managed to "expose the game" in a sense. The critics want to prove that the music they are focusing their careers on is important in shaping world events and documenting cultural changes, and yet here was KISS reminding everyone that the number-one objective of rock and roll was to have a good time. Oh, maybe throw in a point or two once in a while, but otherwise it shouldn't take itself so seriously.

Therefore, the critics beat up the band in defense, and the fans find themselves alone against what seems at times the masses. But, hey, that's alright, as Paul Stanley would tell the fans in "Crazy Crazy Nights," "we're a million strong."

This is why the KISS conventions (aka KISS expos once KISS decided to trademark the KISS convention naming) continue to go strong since they started back in the 1980s. Fans want to get together to see people who have worked with the band and try to find oddball merchandise for their collections, but they mainly want to get together with other members of the KISS Army and discuss the band. Better yet, discuss the foursome without worries of someone knocking them for their dedication. In such a relaxed atmosphere, fans can also mention KISS albums they love or even dislike with a passion they can't express with those who are not fans. Or what caused KISS to go in a certain direction with the band's material and when. Or possibly find "six degrees of separation" between KISS and someone not knowingly connected to the band.

This is the focus of *The KISS FAQ*. The various topics that fans discuss late in the night at the hotel bar after a KISS expo when feeling free enough to bring up topics they know would sometimes run them into ridicule otherwise. With that also comes the ability to admit that sometimes, yes, there have been some very silly things KISS has involved itself with over the years. That is no harsh statement—in every fandom, from baseball to *Star Trek* to NASCAR to music, even the hardcore fans need to have the release of laughing at themselves and their treasured hobby. No doubt, some topics listed within are more serious than others, but all are things that ultimately get very little coverage in the various bios and reference guides released about the band because they are exactly the types of topics that only fans bother to discuss. Thus, this book truly is a chance to learn everything left to know about KISS.

Not to say that it is the final word, of course. Many of the topics to be found here will be argued for years to come by the fans and maybe even some of the critics, but that is just the point. We're here as fans sitting around in a hotel bar booth, having a few drinks and discussing the many ups, downs, and sideways of KISS, with various guests and detours along the way.

There were plenty of individuals who helped with the making of this book, and a brief "shout it out loud" to them is necessary: Daniel Siwek for allowing me to use an excerpt of his interview with Gene Simmons in the Drug Reference chapter, as well as other comments that helped me focus some thoughts for the book; Tony Kazerrick for his collection of stills from the *KISS Meets the Phantom* movie; Bill Starkey for his foreword; Darren Rappa, Gilda Caserta, GG-Aaron Philpott, Jaan Uhelszki, Jeff Jatras, Jelle Jansen, Jim Arrington, Julian James, Julian Gill, Ken Sharp, Michael Brandvold, Mike DeGeorge, Nell Penridge, Rick Reese, Richie Ranno, Reuben Siwek, Ross Berg, Scott Phillips, Scotty Hagen, Steve Stierwalt Jr. , Brian Schnau, Sagafoo Foo, John Waggener at the University of Wisconsin, Bruce Kulick, Neil Zlozower, Tokyo Five, Darren Wirth, Danny Best, Jeff Guera (former publisher of *Oh Yeah!*), Dan Fisher, everyone at the Mego Museum for allowing me to reprint some material they have at their website, and anyone else I am sure I am forgetting at the moment.

Thanks to everyone at Backbeat for their help in getting this all together. Lastly, thanks to Jill and Maddie for being there and being tolerant of all this madness.

KISS FAQ

What a Way to Make a Living

Ten Lives Before KISS

Old hands at KISS history will no doubt wonder if there is any reason to go over the early histories of the band members once again. KISS officially covered the material many times over the years, even twice in their *Behind the Mask* book (although this was because the first half of the text was written in the late 1970s for the band and the rest was an oral history); and all the biographies certainly have. Even the reference guides have had some type of profile of the band members, and certainly a number of fans can rattle off the information in their sleep. Supposedly everyone knows that Gene Simmons's real name is Chaim Witz, that Peter Criss appeared on an album before KISS called *Chelsea*, and there was a band called Wicked Lester that nearly became the "hottest band in the land." Is there really a need to bring it all back up again?

Yet some casual fans tend to look at KISS as suddenly springing up in 1974, fully formed with the makeup, costumes, and an album. If that is the case, possibly a few reading the previous paragraph found one of the facts listed as new to them. The official outlets for material also tend to be a tad light about the careers of the players in the band from before they joined KISS outside of the original four. Fans have read numerous times about Simmons's love for comic books, but how often have Vinnie Vincent's years as a songwriter and studio musician before joining KISS been reviewed in those same books? Or Eric Carr's status as an accomplished and steadily employed musician who had worked in a variety of styles before joining KISS?

Naturally, as with most musical groups, no one arrived as an overnight sensation. Each member paid dues and gained experience over time while taking odd jobs and struggling to make it before they became successful. Perhaps some had to work harder than others, but not one of the men mentioned here decided one night to become a rock star and breeze into the job the next morning. Everything that happened to KISS is due to what these men were beforehand, and to wave it off—as sometimes the band itself has done over the years, by dismissing their earlier bands and ignoring the work of the subsequent band members from the 1980s onward—is to diminish the history of KISS itself.

Gene Simmons

Born: August 25, 1949. Sources in the 1970s frequently listed the year of birth as 1947. Born in Haifa, Israel, but early official biographies rarely if ever mentioned this. Even in 1980, when the band ran into accusations of using "Nazi symbols" in West Germany (see Chapter 5 for details) and Simmons's birthplace and heritage could have been used to defend the band, it would not become part of the company line until sometime later.

Birth Name: Chaim Witz. Some recent sources have recently been listing the name as Weitz, but Witz has been the spelling used since it was first mentioned decades ago in interviews and articles as well as how it is listed in his autobiography, *KISS and Make-Up.* When his mother moved to America after divorcing his father, Simmons and his mother reverted to her maiden name of Klein, and he took the first name of Gene. This became his legal name, and he still signs legal documents as Gene Klein.

Only very close family members reportedly call him Chaim, although some musical and business acquaintances have done so in interviews. Unfortunately, these have been cases where the person being interviewed was trying to act superior, possibly even anti-Semitic, or perhaps both. In other words, fans know his original name and that of Gene Klein, but refer to him as Gene Simmons out of respect. Those fans trying to be clever by calling him Chaim simply aren't.

History of Stage Name: By the early 1970s, Simmons was beginning to get work doing background vocals on songs for other artists (Lyn Christopher and Tommy James to name a couple of verified examples). His name appears in the credits of the 1972 Lyn Christopher album as Gene Simmons, so he had been using it for a time by that point.

Simmons has told variations of how he came up with the name and actually dismisses it as simply one he thought would look good for rock 'n' roll in his autobiography. One of the most common versions was that he thought it would throw people a bit in that it sounded like famed actress Jean Simmons, and perhaps turn a few heads that way, just as Alice Cooper would get people thinking they were going to see a folksinger and instead got five greasy-looking guys playing demented rock music. (Jean Simmons's reaction to the hoped-for confusion was to find it amusing when she got fan letters from boys who wanted to know more about her tongue.) However, there is more evidence that he based the name on that of early rockabilly singer "Jumpin'" Gene Simmons, who had an early rock-'n'-roll hit with "Haunted House" in 1964. Simmons has sometimes even referred to himself as "Jumpin'" Gene Simmons, and an interview with the rockabilly star from 1998 (*Rocktober*, issue #22) stated that the two had talked and the KISS frontman admitted he picked the name after reading about "Jumpin'" in an issue of *Rolling Stone* magazine.

Early Career: Started playing guitar after his mom bought him a Kent Guitar with a Premier Amp in 1965. Like most kids his age, he was attracted to rock music after seeing the Beatles on *The Ed Sullivan Show* and began playing in bands soon after getting the guitar. His early bands started with the Missing Links (also known as Lynx), and moved on to the Love Bag, Rising Sun, the Long Island Sounds (later to be known as simply the Sounds), and Bull Frog Bheer, typically with his close friend Stephen Coronel somewhere in the mix. His later college years saw attempts at bands known as Coffee (playing off the name of the band Cream) and Cathedral, while also attempting a more folk-oriented look (overalls and all) and sound as a solo artist for a time. In 1970, he formed a new band with Stephen Coronel called Rainbow, of which more about in Chapter 2.

Early Recordings: Simmons recorded a number of demos over those years, notably with or for Bull Frog Bheer." "Leeta" is best-known due to it popping up on the KISS five-disc box set collection from 2001, while fans commonly have heard of songs such as "Stanley the Parrot" (which transformed into "Strutter" for KISS) and "Eskimo Sun" (which morphed into "Only You" on the *Music from "The Elder"* album). In 1972, with Wicked Lester pretty much dead in the water, Simmons and Stanley recorded backup vocals and were credited on an album by an artist named Lyn Christopher. In reimbursement for working on the album, Electric Lady Studios offered the two free studio time, which led to KISS in early 1973 recording a five-track demo with Eddie Kramer producing.

Career Outside of Music: Simmons has stated numerous times that he learned his English speaking and writing skills from reading comics and watching old horror movies, with Marvel Comics a favorite and Lon Chaney Sr. movies being some of the first he saw on television. With this came his entry into science fiction and fantasy fandom by publishing "fanzines" (self-made, fan-created and written magazines) about these topics, including *Cosmos-Stiletto*, *Faun*, and *Tinderbox*, as well as writing to other fanzines about various movie and comic-book related topics. Simmons also supplied text as well as artwork for the fanzines, along with getting contributions from other fans. One reason why he has always been so dedicated to fandom and especially to the KISS fanzines over the years is due to his own history with the phenomenon.

Simmons had a variety of odd jobs to help make ends meet while growing up and had a keen eye for business opportunities. By 1970, he had saved up enough money to buy a sound system that he used and could rent out to other performers. He also worked as a "Kelly Girl" for businesses as well as an editorial assistant at *Vogue* and *Cosmopolitan* magazine for a time in the late 1960s and early 1970s. An associate degree in education eventually started him teaching the sixth grade at Public School 75 in Brooklyn, but the job only lasted a few months after he failed to nurture a relationship with his students. When an attempt to get the kids to do book reports based on issues of *The Amazing Spider-Man* led to complaints by parents, he quit and dove back into music full-time.

Simmons has been the most vocal in discussing his private life with . . . pretty much anyone willing to listen. Details about his mother being a Nazi concentration camp survivor were some of the most private he held, even when it could have been publicly beneficial for him to proclaim them (see Chapter 5 for more on this). He has also had little to say about his father, but even that has changed in very recent times when episodes of his reality series *Gene Simmons Family Jewels* followed him to Israel to visit his extended family. He has had two books written about his life, and one has been written by his then-girlfriend/now-wife Shannon Tweed; articles on Simmons have appeared in his short-lived magazine *Tongue*, and of course there is the aforementioned reality series, which has been on for years. Hence his private life has become his public career as much as KISS.

Paul Stanley

Born: January 20, 1952. Some early sources pushed back Stanley's year of birth two years just as with Gene Simmons, giving a year of 1950.

Birth Name: Stanley Harvey Eisen

History of Stage Name: As with Simmons, Stanley had begun getting regular recording gigs and had started using the stage name of Paul Stanley by 1972. He would continue to sign legal documents as Stanley Eisen for years, and some legal documents still use the name, but he has legally changed his name to Paul Stanley.

Early Career: Born with microtia, which left one ear deformed and incapable of hearing, Stanley was drawn to bombastic classical and opera music as a child. Eddie Cochran was a first love when it came to rock music, and Stanley spent his teenage years avoiding most of the pop and rocker-style songs coming out in order to focus on the Mod movement of the mid-1960s (groups like the Who, the Kinks, and—a personal favorite of his—the Small Faces). Picking up the electric guitar as a young teenager, he began playing in bands by the age of fifteen.

Stanley had a smoother transition between early bands than Simmons. His first, a trio called Incubus, evolved into Uncle Joe, a band that he would sporadically return to over the next few years. His next band was Post War Baby Boom, and then in 1969 he formed a band with Stephen Coronel called Tree that only lasted a short time before he went back to Uncle Joe. It was while back with Uncle Joe in 1970 that the band rented Simmons's sound system for a gig. Although Simmons and Stanley had met before—by way of mutual bandmate and friend Stephen Coronel—they had gotten off on the wrong foot and did not think much of each other until Simmons heard and saw Stanley during the Uncle Joe performance that used his sound system. This would lead to the two deciding to work together in the band Rainbow.

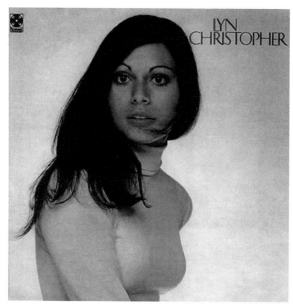

The album where Gene Simmons and Paul Stanley made
their first official credited appearance on vinyl.

Author's Collection

Early Recordings: Stanley recorded a song called "Never Loving, Never Living"
with Post War Baby Boom in 1967 at the CBS Columbia Studios in New York City.
He also recorded with Uncle Joe at the Mayfair Recording Studios in 1969. At
least one track was discovered years later, "Stop, Look to Listen," which appeared
on the five-disc KISS box set from 2001. The song is listed on the box set as being
from 1966, but this is at odds with Stanley's performance history (he has stated
a couple of times that he was fifteen when he first went into a studio to record,
which would put the year as 1967—when he was with Post War Baby Boom).
It has also been stated that the recordings were done in 1970 after one of the
band members (Neal Teeman) began working as an engineer for Jay and the
Americans and Uncle Joe was given time in the studio as a bonus for his hard
work. Stanley is also known to have worked on demos of "Firehouse" (which
he based on a song by the Move, "Fire Brigade") and "Sunday Driver" (which
became "Let Me Know" for KISS). Teeman, incidentally, will come back into the
picture when Rainbow starts looking into doing some recording.

Early Career Outside of Music: Stanley went to the Manhattan High School
of Music and Art and continued to study art at the Bronx Community College
in hopes of becoming a commercial artist. However, the need to create "on
schedule" burned him out on such a career, and he moved toward music instead.
He worked at a number of odd jobs and was working as a cabbie for a time while
KISS was evolving in the early 1970s.

Of all four original members, Stanley has been the least likely to talk about his private life, nearly in direct opposition to Simmons's intent on getting everything about his life in the open. Although fans knew of his deformed ear, many were unaware of his hearing problem until 2011 when he started campaigning on national television with tips for teenagers to save their hearing. Because of his inclination to remain private about his life, Stanley is the one mystery man of the group even though he is the lead singer and, in many ways, the focal point of the band in-concert. While Simmons, Frehley, and Criss have all written books about their lives, Stanley will probably remain the only KISS member autobiography free when all is said and done.

Peter Criss

Born: December 20, 1945, making him the oldest member of KISS.

Birth Name: George Peter John Criscuola. Sometimes listed in resources as Peter George John Criscuola. Sometimes listed—even in legal documents for KISS—with last name spelled Criscoula (with the o and u reversed).

History of Stage Name: In his book *Kiss and Make-Up*, Simmons makes the rather odd statement that he convinced Criscuola to shorten his name to Criss for KISS, but this doesn't match evidence from the Chelsea album released in 1970 that shows his name in that same shortened form (actually as "Peter Cris"

Album released featuring a pre-KISS Peter Criss.

Author's Collection

with only one s instead of two). Although done for commercial purposes, it did help people remember his name more than some of the others since it now rhymed with KISS. Even so, he was never one to deny using his real last name in interviews, even back in the 1970s when the band's history was supposed to be more "mysterious."

Early Career: Although just a few years older than both Simmons and Stanley, Criss's first influences in music came from another era, namely that of jazz, and drummers such as Gene Krupa who would break out as stars themselves during that era. Criss was also influenced by a performance on *The Ed Sullivan Show*, but it was Elvis's appearance back in 1956 rather than the Beatles' eight years later. By the time the Beatles were motivating younger guys still in their early teens like Simmons, Stanley, and Frehley, Criss had already worked professionally at the Metropole Jazz Club for Joey Greco and the In Crowd and had gotten advice from Krupa himself, who was playing the same club. He also was far enough ahead of the movement that if he wanted to play professionally, it meant being able to play anything that came at him, leading to his joining a Latin Beat-style band called the Barracudas in 1966 and on to a soul band called Sounds of Soul in 1967. Sounds of Soul transformed into the Brotherhood and then the Vintage during 1968. Then in 1969 Criss moved on to the band Nautilus until the mid-1970s, when he joined Chelsea through a "free musician ad" in the back of *Rolling Stone* magazine.

Chelsea soon got a two-record deal with Decca Records, with a self-named album released in 1970—making Criss the first member of KISS with an album released. MCA, Decca's parent company, tried to push the band, but the album did not do well, and guitarist Chris Aridas left in 1971, with Stan Penridge replacing him. Chelsea began working on material for a new album when Decca dropped them. There were also growing internal problems in Chelsea, as the two main writers for the group wanted to go in a folk direction while the other members were leaning toward a straight rock-'n'-roll sound. A gig at a bar called the Yellow Front Saloon found Criss, Penridge, and bassist Michael Benvenga playing a harder rock-'n'-roll show without the other two members due to them being late. This caused the band to split and Criss deciding to carry on with Penridge and Benvenga in a new band called Lips.

Lips continued for a time with the three, but Benvenga quit the music business in 1972, leaving Criss and Penridge to work as a duo. The two worked as such off and on over the next few months, while Criss made a little money with a cover band called Infinity between 1972 and 1973 and from going into the studio to work on ad jingles. At one of the duo's gigs in a working-class bar in Queens, two guys dressed as pretty boys from the glam days of rock came in to check out Criss, worrying Penridge that a fight would break out. Instead, the two men asked Criss if he wanted to join a band they had called Wicked Lester.

Early Recordings: With the Barracudas, Criss recorded a couple of singles released in 1967. The first was "It's Been So Long," backed with "Affection," with Big Band and R&B producer/promoter Morty Craft producing. The second, "Chicken," backed with "No Use," also came by way of Morty Craft and the Barracudas, and probably had Peter playing drums as well. Sounds of Soul did some demos of classic soul material in 1967 ("Since I Fell for You," "My Girl," and "Respect"), and the Vintage did a demo in 1969 for the song "What Is a Man," but nothing official was ever released for Criss's other bands until the 1970 Decca album for Chelsea. Chelsea continued with some demos for their second album, and Lips demoed a few songs, but nothing came of these. At least, not in their original forms. (Many turned up later on Criss's 1978 solo album.) One of these songs recorded in demo form for Lips was "Beck," which was later renamed "Beth" and would become one of KISS's biggest hits.

Early Career Outside of Music: Criss not only had worked professionally in music longer than Simmons and Stanley but also made a fair living at it. Working in cover bands and doing solo gigs helped pay the bills, although there was the added frustration that he was still doing two-bit gigs after years in the business. That would quickly change, of course.

Criss kept a lot of his private life low-key for years—most fans only knew of his wife vaguely and that she was the subject of the song "Beth" (which was not really the case, but was stated in promotion to better tie the song with the band). Criss opened up a bit more once he went solo in 1980 but then fell enough off the media radar that a homeless man in 1991 attempted to present himself as Criss to the public with much press supporting him, leading to Criss having to address the issue to the press and on *The Phil Donahue Show* later that year. Since then, he has been more active in public, leading to touring with Ace Frehley in the 1990s and the eventual reunion with KISS in 1995. In 2009, Criss announced that he had undergone surgery in 2008 for breast cancer and became an activist in promoting breast cancer awareness for men.

Ace Frehley

Born: April 27, 1951. Once again, early sources listed a different year of birth, commonly 1950, although 1955 has turned up as well.

Birth Name: Paul Daniel Frehley

History of Stage Name: Many stories are told about how Ace got his name, but he usually went by the nickname of Punky during the early years of his career. The most common version of the Ace nickname story is that he received it due to his "spaced-out attitude" or his love of science and science fiction. But the origin is perhaps a bit earthier: while in his band King Kong in 1968, Frehley had helped a bandmate hook up with a girl Frehley knew and was called a real

"Ace" for doing so. Although Frehley continued using Punky as a nickname for a couple of years after that, he liked the new nickname and began using it by 1970.

When it came to KISS, the band was hesitant about having two Pauls, especially since they wanted to make sure people saw each member as equally important. As both Stanley and Frehley were already accustomed to using their new respective stage names of Paul and Ace, it was an easily resolved situation, and Ace would remain his name from that point on. He still signs legal documents as Paul Frehley, however.

Early Career: Criss was known by some thanks to his years of having been in the business by the early 1970s. A few people knew Simmons and Stanley during the early years when struggling to get things going. Everyone, however, seemed to know Frehley, with acquaintances of KISS from those early days commonly saying they knew him from seeing him around long before he joined the band, as he was known as a party machine and always looking for a good time.

Frehley came from a musical family that encouraged his talent, leading to him getting a guitar when he was thirteen and never looking back. Self-taught, he usually performed in a flamboyant style on the guitar and in his stage antics— which would surprise KISS fans who are used to his slow, staggering stance in concert since the mid-1970s—jumping off the stage and dressing in ruffled shirts in a homage to Hendrix. While he would calm down a bit during those years in order to concentrate on his guitar work, this does explain to an extent why the knowledge that KISS would be in makeup and wearing costumes gave him no hesitation.

Frehley was in the most bands before KISS of any of the original foursome, but that is mainly due to him going through a number of short-lived bands as a teenager, which was typical for many musicians starting out at such an age. The years 1965 through 1967 saw him in bands that may have been little more than sketchy ideas rather than a group of musicians who actually performed, such as the Micro Organism, the Exterminators, and (most unlikely of all) the Muff Divers. An early band called the Four Roses did well enough to get gigs in various places, and Frehley continued on through bands that would get occasional gigs, such as Cathedral, King Kong, and Honey and the Magic People—all three of which he commonly referred to in interviews when pressed on what bands he had been in before KISS. The downside was that he began to get a swelled head, thinking anything he played was brilliant and slacking off on practicing.

After a bar fight in 1970 over not being paid for a gig, Frehley found himself sitting in a hospital with a fractured cheekbone (the repair of which Ace was never satisfied with and which was one reason why he has been particular about photos taken of him over the years). He was also broke. It was then that he decided he needed to get serious about being a musician if he was going to make a career of it.

From there he moved on to a band called Molimo, which managed to get a record deal with RCA in 1971. The band never quite jelled, however, even as they began recording demos for an album and promoting themselves through concerts and radio interviews. Instead, Frehley left the band in 1972 after RCA backed out of the deal and he had heard about another band that supposedly had a record deal all set to go was looking for a lead guitarist.

Early Recordings: Little has been heard of Frehley's early bands, although fans for years had heard that Molimo had recorded part of an album for RCA in 1971. In recent years, a copy of a syndicated radio show called *Rock Stars* surfaced (with rock author Richard Robinson as host) that featured the band for a short interview and most of a song from the proposed album called "East of Yesterday." Although there is no further background on the song, with Frehley being one of the band members interviewed about the track, it is safe to assume that he played on it. This is the only material before KISS known to have made its way to fandom for Frehley.

Early Career Outside of Music: Frehley concentrated a lot of his early career on music, but did take odd jobs here and there, including working as a postal worker and as a cabbie.

He seems to be the one man of KISS that people want to know more about; or, at least, to have made the choice of picking friends who would later want to write about him. Three books have come out since 1997 about him, all from the same publisher, with two from former associates and one from a former girlfriend. None of the books could be described as flattering. Frehley has been no stranger to talking about his alcohol problems since the mid-1980s when he returned to a solo career after disappearing from the music scene between 1982 and 1985. This has included both highs and lows in controlling his addictions, which is not that unusual for any addict, but worse for having to be so public.

Eric Carr

Born: July 12, 1950. Early reports listed Carr's year of birth as 1953, which was intentional misdirection by the band to keep people from guessing his real identity after he joined.

Birth Name: Paul Charles Caravello

History of Stage Name: As with Paul Frehley, the band wanted to avoid having two Pauls in the band (although, with him joining, one could say that they had three Pauls at the time). The band also knew that the new drummer they had hired in 1980 had performed with other bands and even appeared on some recordings under his real name. At a time when KISS still had the distinction of never having been photographed without their makeup, it would not have set well to have the "new guy" be the one to break the tradition (the same would hold true for the subsequent "new guy" in 1982, but more on that in the next entry). Thus, a complete name change was in order.

Along with giving Caravello the freedom to come up with a makeup design for himself, the band decided to give him the chance to come up with a new stage name. Seeing how all the other band members' names had a rhythm of 1-2 when spoken (Gene Sim-mons, Paul Stan-ley, Ace Freh-ley) and the drummer's was the only one the opposite with 2-1 (Pe-ter Criss), he decided to keep the same pattern for his new name. Shortening his last name to Carr, he decided on Eric Carr.

He would still sign legal documents using his birth name as well as having old friends call him Paul when they met.

Early Career: People tend to envision Carr as much younger than the other guys in KISS, thanks partly to his entry into the band years after they had become successful and partly because of physically looking ten years younger than everyone around him (officially making his birthdate three years later actually worked in his favor as well). Even so, he was not only of the same age group as the other guys, he was older than Paul Stanley. Like both Stanley and Frehley, Carr became interested in performing music thanks to family members while still a kid, and by the age of fourteen or fifteen, he was playing in a band called the Cellarmen that held enough promise that it would record demos as well as appear on a couple of singles—a bit heady for a group of young guys who had not even graduated from high school (even if one of the singles was more of a demo put to disc and only a handful pressed).

After a short skip and jump in bands such as Things That Go Bump in the Night and Smack, Carr joined Salt 'N Pepper in early 1970 and remained with variations of that band until 1979. Called Salt 'N Pepper because it was a mix of races, the band used the name Creation in the early 1970s and then moved to a name that Carr hated, Mother Nature/Father Time, from 1975 until he left in 1979. The band also worked in concert under the name of Bionic Boogie for writer/producer Gregg Diamond, and some of the members (including Carr) appeared on an album for Casablanca Records under the name of Lightning in late 1979 (where Carr was listed in the credits as Paul Caravello).

The group played many gigs over the year, opening for a variety of famous artists, but the show that many remembered the most had little to do with the band itself. On June 30, 1974, Salt 'N Pepper was playing at a place called Gulliver's in Port Chester, New York, when a fire—staged to cover up a robbery—broke out at a bowling alley next door. The fire spread quickly to the club, which had a dance floor built into the lower level of the building, and with electricity soon out and one exit locked shut, panic spread through the crowd. Carr had managed to pull the female lead singer along with him and battle his way out of the place, but many others were not so lucky. Twenty-four people died from smoke inhalation, including two members of the band. The incident made national news, and both Carr and another member of the band appeared on *CBS News* the following Sunday to discuss what had happened.

Although the band regrouped and continued to try to break through in a big way, they could never get past the point of being reduced to the opener or the stage band for someone else. Finally, in 1979, both Carr and the leader of the band decided that they either had to move on or else never get anywhere. Carr joined a rock band called Flasher in late 1979 and almost immediately regretted the decision as it slowly devolved into being a cover band. By June 1980, he realized that he was making less money as a musician at the age of thirty than he had when he was fifteen. He was ready to take a break from the music world and try to find a "real" job when a former bandmate of Flasher mentioned to him that KISS was doing auditions to replace Peter Criss. Carr decided to give the music world one last chance before hanging it up, at least for a while.

Early Recordings: Carr did a lot of recording in his career before KISS, including demos with the Cellarmen: "I Cry at Night" and "Your Turn To Cry" in 1967 and "I Found You (the One I Adore)" and "Then I Made a Wish" in 1968 (all four of which have appeared on various Carr-related tribute projects since 2000). The band also backed up a singer named Crystal Collins for a single released through Jody Records in 1969 called "No Matter How You Try," backed with "When You Grow Tired."

Demos from Creation appeared in the early 1970s, with two tracks making their way to the *Inside the Tales of the Fox* DVD released as a tribute to Eric Carr in 2000: "Stranger" and "I'm So Lonely." The band also released a single of "I'm So Lonely" in 1975 on the Prolific label, backed with "Something Tellin' Me."

Finally there was the self-titled *Lightning* album in late 1979 that featured five tracks, with Carr on drums and backing vocals. Ironically, the album was produced by Lewis Merenstein, who also produced the Chelsea album in 1971 on which Peter Criss appeared.

A number of Carr's demos for KISS and for his animated project *The Rockheads* were collected in 1999 and released on CD under the title *Rockology*.

Early Career Outside of Music: While working as a musician at night, Carr supported himself by working a variety of jobs including installing steel cellar and toilet partitions, working in the New York Criminal Justice system as a file clerk, and working as a courier for the Royal Tobacco Company at Kennedy Airport. The job fans know him best for was that of a gas-range repairman—a job he took in the late 1970s and was still doing at the time he tried out for KISS in 1980.

Carr had grown up drawing and had entered the High School of Music and Art (the same school Stanley had attended) to study drawing, but found his interest floating to music. He soon transferred to photography, a move he came to regret. He would continue to flirt with artwork for the rest of his life, drawing doodles for and of the band as well as working on the project the Rockheads.

The Rockheads were a group of small musicians mostly made out of hair that Carr envisioned as being part of an animated series, with original music being used in each episode. He worked on some material for the series with Bruce Kulick in the late 1980s, and while the project came close to reality in that time, things never quite worked out.

Carr seldom did professional interviews, mainly because the press was more interested in talking with Simmons and Stanley than the "other guys," but he commonly would talk to fans and did several quick interviews for KISS fanzines in his later years with the band. In 2011, an official biography of Carr was released, written by Greg Prato.

Vinnie Vincent

Born: August 6, 1952. As with Eric Carr, some early reports listed his year of birth three years later, to 1955 in Vinnie Vincent's case, in order to try to throw people off of who he was before KISS.

Birth Name: Vincent John Cusano

History of Stage Name: As mentioned above with Carr, the band did not want people being able instantly to link a new member with an image of them without the makeup and costumes. Hence, the need to give Vincent a new name, although it appears that Vinnie did not give as much thought to his new name as Eric gave to his. To help smooth the move over from the spacey Ace Frehley, the band tried to incorporate an out-of-this-world element for Vincent by calling him Vinnie "the Wiz" Vincent, but fans never got into the nickname, and beyond being a "wizard" at playing guitar, there really was not much of a Wiz there was when it came to his persona in the makeup and costumes.

He continued to use the name after leaving KISS, although he uses his birth name for legal documents.

Early Career: Vincent in a way represent a forerunner of what was to come with future members of KISS—that of being known as a professional studio musician. That may sound as if it implies such individuals are hacks, which is far from reality. In truth, many such musicians are the backbone of the recording industry; writing, playing, producing, and in many other ways creating music done for a number of artists and yet rarely getting credit for their hard work that the famous names get to plaster their names over.

Once again, another band member grew up in a musical family, although in Vincent's case he began taking lessons to play properly, leading to him teaching guitar to others during the late 1960s in Bridgeport, Connecticut. He also put in time in various bands in the 1960s, starting with the Younger Generation in 1965 and then Hunter in 1970. A variety of session work in the next few years ultimately led to him joining a former member of the Rascals, Felix Cavaliere,

An autographed inner sleeve from Dan Hartman's *Instant Replay* album, featuring a pre-KISS Vinnie Vincent smiling in the background.   *Author's Collection*

in the band Treasure, which released one album in 1977 along with touring for some time before splitting up in 1978. (Vincent's relationship with Cavaliere did give him the chance to play guitar on one of Laura Nyro's albums in 1978 as well as on Cavaliere's 1979 solo album.)

Vincent toured for a time with Dan Hartman after recording material for the latter's *Instant Replay* album, and then moved on to providing guitar for Edgar Winter when he toured in 1979. Vincent also did some work with former Vanilla Fudge drummer Carmine Appice, with one song finding its way to Appice's self-titled 1981 album.

In 1981, Vincent teamed up with some former members of the band New England (of which Paul Stanley produced their 1979 album; see Chapter 28 for more details) to start a band called Warrior. This band recorded a number of demos, many of which would appear on Vincent's solo albums of the 1980s along with a handful that would appear elsewhere. The band eventually split up, with Vincent joining KISS and some of the others going on to start the band Alcatrazz in 1983.

During the early 1980s, Vincent also contributed a song to the comedy series and *Happy Days* spin-off *Joanie Loves Chachi*. Music was not unusual in the show itself—the series tended to work as a type of mini-musical in most episodes, but fans of Vincent no doubt find it a tad odd in retrospect. The song was "Our

Love Was Meant to Be" and was sung by Scott Baio as Chachi in the October 21, 1982, episode.

Early Recordings: Vincent demoed three songs with the Younger Generation in 1965, and in 1970 cowrote and recorded a four-song demo with his band Hunter. Later, he found work at Connecticut Record Studio, playing on sessions for self-titled albums such as Black Satin and the Hitchhikers, both in 1976 (the Hitchhikers album featuring a song he wrote called "This Song's for You Mama"). The year 1976 also saw a rather odd single by him released under the name of Vinnie LeCoux called "Happy Birthday U.S.A" by Phantom Records. The song, cowritten by David Wolff under the pseudonym of Kid Cashmir, was a parody about the country's Bicentennial. Wolff would become famous in the early 1980s as the manager/boyfriend/video costar of Cyndi Lauper.

Vincent wrote two songs on the Treasure album released in 1977, "Turn Yourself Around" and "Innocent Eyes." He followed up by playing guitar on Laura Nyro's *Nested* and Dan Hartman's *Instant Replay* (on which he appears in a group photo on the inner sleeve) in 1978 and Felix Cavaliere's *Castles in the Air* in 1979. That year also saw Vincent work on three songs with Tommy Rock that were released as a 12-inch EP and produced by Kim Fowley for Line Records in Germany. He went on to play some guitar on the Heat album *Still Waiting* in 1981 and followed that up with writing a song on Carmine Appice's self-titled album the same year (which also features a song cowritten by Appice and former Wicked Lester guitarist Ron Leejack).

From 1981 through 1982, Vincent recorded a number of demos, both with Warrior and with other musicians, many of which would eventually pop up on a variety of other albums. "Tears" is one of the best known of the songs, as it appeared on Peter Criss's 1982 album *Let Me Rock You* as well as being a hit for singer John Waite in 1984. "Back on the Streets" was recorded in 1984 by a band called 3 Speed, while also being demoed by Ace Frehley for his first Frehley's Comet album in 1985. A number of other demos would be used in part or full for Vincent's solo albums after he left KISS. Finally, Vincent played some lead guitar on the track "Smile," which appears on the 1983 Was (Not Was) album *Born to Laugh at Tornadoes*.

Early Career Outside of Music: Many of the band members who have played with KISS had to take on various jobs outside of music while trying to make it. Vincent was one of the few who found all his work inside the music industry, which just goes to show not only his dedication to his musical career but also how sought after he was before he found himself part of KISS.

Vincent has kept details of his private life to a minimum, leading to all types of rumors about him, both good and bad. Unfortunately, many of the details the fans do know have come by way of incidents that made the news, and not in a happy manner. However, things were only looking brighter for Vincent as he began working with the band.

Mark St. John

Born: February 6, 1956, making St. John the youngest member of the band until Eric Singer joined in 1991.

Birth Name: Mark Leslie Norton

History of Stage Name: Although the band had taken the makeup and superhero costumes off, they still seemed to be stuck on creating new identities for new members as they had with Vinnie Vincent and Eric Carr. Obviously, those in power were a bit iffy about the last name of Norton really sounding as rock 'n' roll as they wanted. St. John took the name change in stride, although there would be other things down the line that would end up causing friction between him and his new bandmates when he joined in 1984. He continued to use his birth name for legal documents.

Early Career: Mark St. John mainly worked as a guitar instructor in California, a job he would go back to for a spell after leaving KISS. He also played in a cover band called the Front Page. Grover Jackson of Jackson Guitars had recommended St. John to KISS when they began looking for a replacement for Vinnie Vincent.

Early Recordings: No professional recordings appear to have been done with St. John before he joined KISS, at least none that have been made public.

Early Career Outside of Music: Mark St. John's career before KISS seems rather limited, but this was no doubt a plus to Simmons and Stanley, who were looking for someone who would "toe the line" a bit more after all the frustrations and arguments with Vinnie Vincent (who never had a worry about finding work beyond KISS). Thus, St. John's career really started with KISS, and his work after that would be due in part to his association with the band for the *Animalize* album, even if things did not go well due to conflict with the band members over aspects of the album and the tour that followed. His physical condition at the start of the *Animalize* tour also led to problems as he was diagnosed with Reiter's Syndrome, which caused his hands and various body joints to swell.

His concerns about this condition were under control soon afterward, but the band was already moving on to a new lead guitarist when St. John began to feel better, and he was out before much of the American tour for the album had started. Still, he was able to use his position in KISS to promote later projects, even working with Peter Criss for a time, and was never shy in talking to people about his brief days with the band.

Bruce Kulick

Born: December 12, 1953

Birth Name: Bruce Howard Kulick

History of Stage Name: Bruce Kulick is the first member of KISS not to use a stage name. If one discounts Thomas Thayer using the nickname Tommy, Kulick is also the only member to use his full first and last birth name in the band.

Early Career: With his older brother Bob Kulick involved in the music scene as a guitarist, it was no surprise that Bruce would take up a guitar as well, starting at the age of eleven. He rapidly began working in bands while in high school and college, most with a Cream influence. With connections already established in the business thanks to his brother, Kulick began playing guitar on tours for such artists as George McCrae, Andrea True, and Meat Loaf between 1975 and 1978 (with brother Bob appearing with him on the McCrae and Meat Loaf tours).

This type of exposure led to Bruce joining forces with a vocalist named Michael Bolotin in 1978 to form Blackjack. The band would release two albums between 1979 and 1980 before finally breaking up. Bolotin would soon change his last name in the process of becoming a superstar, but more about that in Chapter 30. While continuing to score session work for various albums (including Billy Squier), Kulick worked for a couple of years in a band called the Good Rats, who released one album while Bruce was with them.

Back cover photo of Bruce Kulick's pre-KISS band Blackjack from their self-titled first album. More about the guy on the far left in Chapter 30.   *Author's Collection*

Meanwhile, Bob Kulick—who had remained friendly with KISS after trying out for the band in 1972—had been after them to consider Bruce for lead guitarist since he became aware that Frehley was leaving. With Mark St. John having problems that prevented him from doing the first leg of the *Animalize* tour, and with the band not wanting to go through more auditions after have made such a big announcement over getting St. John, it made sense to hire someone already known to the band members. There was also the perception that Bruce looked enough like Mark that many fans would never notice the difference anyway (a point that would come back to play when Criss and Frehley left the band for a second time years later). Although thrown into KISS without much notice, Kulick would remain with them until 1996 and still works with the band members on related projects.

Early Recordings: Besides some demos with an early band, commonly referred to in KISS fandom as KKB, Kulick's first professional release was a promotional live album from Meat Loaf that came out in 1978 (*Meat Loaf Live*) featuring the concert band from the tour he appeared in. Bruce also worked with brother Bob on an album for Wendroff in 1978 called *Kiss the World Goodbye*, before moving on to the two Blackjack albums: the self-titled 1979 album and the 1980 follow-up, *Worlds Apart*. Bruce then played guitar on two 1980 albums, *Where's My Hero* for Rozetta (featuring one track he cowrote) and *Tale of the Tape* for Billy Squier. Kulick went from there to the Good Rats, appearing on their *Great American Music* album, among other things.

After appearing on Michel Bolton's first solo album in 1983, Kulick played guitar on an album for a singer named Stevie called *Gypsy!* in 1984. Although he would sign up with KISS after this, Kulick continued to do a lot of outside work for various other artists during his KISS years, making him probably the most prolific of the band members when it came to guest appearances on others' albums. Besides continuing to work for Bolton, Bruce appeared on albums for Maria Vidal, Ronnie Spector, Don Johnson, Bob's band Skull in 1991, and Blackthorne.

Early Career Outside of Music: Kulick worked for the New York Public Library while in high school and college. Like Vincent, however, he managed to devote much of his time to music without taking other external jobs.

Eric Singer

Born: May 12, 1958

Birth Name: Eric Doyle Mensinger

History of Stage Name: Eric Doyle Mensinger used the stage name of Eric Singer for years before joining KISS. As he was already well known in the industry by that name, and the band was no longer worrying about hiding names of band members under other personas, there was no concern about him continuing as Singer when he joined. He still uses his birth name on some legal documents.

After he took over the Cat makeup and costume in KISS, the name of the character slightly changed to pull away from being locked in to Peter Criss's interpretation. Therefore, instead of "The Catman" as for Criss, Singer became "Catman" or sometimes even "Beast King" (as in the Image and Dark Horse comics of the time). However, many casual fans still refer to the character as "Peter," while snarky fans tend to go with "Guy wearing Peter's Makeup."

Early Career: Singer began playing drums when he was eleven, typically helping with performances done by his father, a jazz musician who had worked with Perry Como, among others. In 1983, Singer moved from Ohio to Los Angeles in hopes of getting work as a professional drummer. After working with a band called Icebreaker and doing some video work as a drummer for a Playboy special, he signed up to tour with Lita Ford. After the tour, he began working with Black Sabbath leader Tony Iommi (who had been dating Ford at the time) and stayed with Black Sabbath for two and a half years and two albums (the 1986 *Seventh Star* and 1987 *Eternal Idol*).

After touring with Gary Moore in 1987 and doing some session work for the bands Drive and the Cult, Singer became involved with Badland. He stuck with this band until 1990 when he split over personal differences. While with Badland, he ran into Dennis St. James, who was about to go on a short solo tour with Paul Stanley in 1989. As Stanley was looking for a drummer on the tour, Singer was brought in following the suggestion of St. James. The break from Badland found Singer immediately back on his feet when he signed to take over on drums for Alice Cooper in 1990—a gig he would repeat for Alice many times over the following years.

When KISS decided they needed to start recording the 1991 album *Revenge*, Eric Carr was dealing with health issues related to his cancer that made it a bad idea for him to play drums. Remembering Eric Singer, Paul Stanley invited him to help out for a time while they began work on the album, with Simmons telling him that he would only be needed until Eric Carr recovered. As it happened, Singer played on nearly the entire album and found himself becoming an official member of the band that year as well. He would continue with them until 1996, and then bounce back for a bit before rejoining them on a permanent basis again (see Chapter 29 for more details).

Early Recordings: Before leaving for L.A. in 1983, Singer played drums with the band Pop Opera (aka Beau Coup), which recorded some demos that led to a deal with A&M Records after Singer had already moved on. He recorded some material with a mock band performing in the video "Playboy's Women in Rock" in 1984—a gig that got him connected to Lita Ford and appearing in Olivia Newton-John's music video for "Culture Shock" off her 1985 album *Soul*

Kiss (although he is not playing the drums on the recording, he appears in the video as the drummer). While he did not do any official recordings with Lita Ford or Garry Moore when touring with them, he was very much involved in their demos and the finished recordings done for the two Black Sabbath albums from 1986 and 1987. Some demo work for Drive and the Cult came next and then the Badland album of 1989. After playing drums on Bill Ward's *Ward One* album (released in 1990), Singer popped up next on a live album for Alice Cooper before working on the *Revenge* album for KISS and then becoming an official member of the band.

Early Career Outside of Music: Singer was another band member who found longtime work in the music industry, with even a move across the country in the early 1980s leading to him finding work quickly in the highly competitive L.A. music landscape.

Singer is easily approachable by fans and professionals alike and willing to go on record about things related to his professional work—sometimes to the point of being outspoken where other musicians who have worked with KISS have hedged. He is more close-to-the-cuff about private matters, however, and usually sidesteps questions of a more personal nature.

Tommy Thayer

Born: November 7, 1960, making him the youngest member ever of KISS. This does also mean that "young" refers to someone already in his fifties, but he still has ten years on many of the other members of the band.

Birth Name: Thomas Cunningham Thayer

History of Stage Name: Has gone by Tommy Thayer on all professional releases and was already known to KISS fandom as Tommy Thayer, so no need for a stage name when introduced into KISS. If one allows for grade-school nicknames, Thayer would be the second member of KISS not to have a stage name other than his birth name.

After taking over for Frehley in the makeup and costumes, the character changed slightly in name. Unable to get away with "Space Ace" for Thayer, the character became "the Spaceman" and was sometimes listed as "the Celestial" as in the Image and Dark Horse comic books of the time. As with Eric Singer wearing the cat makeup, casual fans still tend to go with "Ace" when seeing the character, and some hardcore fans smirkingly call the character "Guy with Ace's Makeup."

Early Career: Thayer began playing the guitar at the age of thirteen and started a band in 1979 with high school friend Jamie St. James (then known as James Pond) that would eventually become Black N' Blue. Black N' Blue signed with

In Heat album cover for Black N' Blue, featuring a pre-KISS Tommy Thayer.   *Author's Collection*

Geffen Records in 1983 and recorded a number of albums and tour extensively for a number of years but never quite took off the way other metal bands did in the 1980s. With the metal movement rapidly declining, the band broke up in 1989, but being in the band had given Thayer a chance to get to know Gene Simmons after they opened for KISS during the *Asylum* tour. Simmons produced two albums for Black N' Blue and invited Thayer to work on some material for the 1989 KISS release *Hot in the Shade* (in which two songs cowritten by Thayer were used: "Betrayed" and "The Street Giveth and the Street Taketh Away"). Thayer also popped up on other Simmons-related albums, such as King Kobra's *King Kobra III*, which Simmons was at one time to produce, and the album *Doro*, which he did produce.

Thayer wrote material and performed on albums for other artists, but his own career was in danger of stalling, with his bands All American Man, Harlow (which produced one album in 1990), and the Marx Brothers fizzling out. Looking to make some quick cash, the members of the Marx Brothers (including Jamie St. James) decided to do an all-KISS show in July 1991. From there, they began doing more shows under the name of Cold Gin and slowly began wearing makeup and costumes and putting on a full KISS show for clubs around the country. The band was good enough that after Simmons and Stanley had taken in a show, Simmons had them perform at one of Stanley's birthday parties.

Soon, Simmons hired both Thayer and Spiro Papadatos (who played Simmons in Cold Gin) to work for the band. Although Thayer continued to work on jump-starting his career outside of KISS—doing an album with a band called Shake the Faith in 1994—he worked for KISS up through the 1996–2001 reunion tours, where he eventually found himself taking over for Frehley in 2002.

Early Recordings: Four albums and some demos with Black N' Blue, along with various collections over the years that include new material. There is also an album from his band Shake the Faith (*America the Violent* from 1994) and Harlow (*Harlow*, 1990). Thayer also did backing vocals or played guitar on a number of albums, usually with Jamie St. James: Loverboy's *Loving Every Minute of It,* Jimmy Barnes's self-titled album of 1985, Malice's *License to Kill,* Ted Nugent's *Little Miss Dangerous,* Doro's self-titled album of 1990, and Medicine Wheel's *First Things First,* among others. He has written songs for many artists, including King Kobra, Cold Sweat, Ron Keel, Marc Ferrari (which Thayer also played on), and Iron Horse. He has produced a few albums as well, usually with Erik Turner, such as the self-titled albums from the Things (1998) and Shake City (2009). Thus, although snarky fans may think of Thayer as the "guy who delivers coffee for Gene," he had a pretty vast recording career before being asked to join the band.

Early Career Outside of Music: As with many of the other later members of KISS, Thayer found enough early success in the music industry to make it his career without much interference from outside jobs. That said, his work with KISS was not only connected with writing songs and helping with demos, but also doing odd jobs ranging from cleaning gutters to helping to edit the *KISStory* book of 1994. He worked with the band during their 1995 convention tour as well as being there for much of the reunion tour (where, on a few occasions, he was close to appearing onstage in Frehley's makeup and costume when the latter was late for shows). With Frehley's second departure from the band, Thayer became a full-time member. Since 2002, the band has been Simmons, Stanley, Singer, and Thayer—making 2012 ten years with the band having this lineup.

But that was long in the future in 1970, with Simmons and Stanley still wondering how they were ever going to crack the music business.

2

The Hottest Band in the Land . . . Wicked Lester!

Deciphering the Rainbow Connection

A s seen in Chapter 1, everyone has to start somewhere, and even a band like KISS has to go through some type of growing pains. Fans know this occurred for KISS during a period when they became a band called Wicked Lester, although the band for many years tried to keep that period a secret, down to even buying the album recorded and hiding it so that no one would ever release it. At least that is how the story goes.

The common story passed around for years is that Simmons and Stanley put together a band named Wicked Lester back in 1972, recorded an album with some nameless guys, hated the results, fired everyone, and started from scratch with KISS.

That is not quite what happened. The problem is that no one quite remembers the whole chain of events anymore. Everyone has their own story and timeline as to when and what occurred during the Wicked Lester years. Here is what can be sketched out, however:

The Lineup

One thing everyone agrees on is that Simmons would eventually start working with Paul Stanley one way or another. Both had Stephen Coronel as an ex-bandmate (with Stanley in the band Tree and with Gene in practically everything Gene was in since high school), and he had a feeling that the two would hit it off. However, like in a buddy movie, both initially could not stand each other. A meeting between them, where Stanley played a few songs for Simmons, found Simmons thinking of Stanley as a kid who had a long way to go and Stanley believing Simmons to be a conceited jerk.

In early 1970, Simmons was talking to Coronel about starting a new band together with Simmons's bandmate from his then-recent band Coffee, keyboard-ist Brooke Ostrander. Stanley, meanwhile, had left Tree and was back with Uncle Joe and regretting it—they were becoming more of a cover band, which may have gotten them gigs but was not a direction Stanley wanted to go with his career. Coronel suggested to Simmons that perhaps he should think about adding Stanley to their new band, but Simmons was reluctant. Yet, after seeing Stanley perform onstage with Uncle Joe for a gig where they had rented his sound system, Simmons changed his mind and asked Stanley to join him and Coronel in the new band. Brook Ostrander brought in a friend, Joe Davidson, as the drummer, but Davidson soon left and Tony Zarrella auditioned to replace him. The others liked Zarrella because of his double-bass drum setup, his adapting to their style easily, and because anyone who looked like Geezer Butler from Black Sabbath had to be good. With the lineup in place, the band was ready to start rehearsing material and play live gigs as Rainbow.

The major change in the band occurred after they had done a demo and got Epic Records interested enough to see them do a showcase. After the showcase, which Coronel would later state he could have done better, Epic offered a deal but only if they replaced their lead guitarist. Simmons eventually broke the news to Coronel that they would be replacing him, and Coronel went off in his own direction. His replacement was studio musician Ron Leejack, who would stay with the band for the recordings to follow.

The stories change a bit at this point, depending on who is doing the talking. One version is that Simmons and Stanley fired the three other members of the band in order to go in their own direction with the group. Leejack's version is that the two asked him to fire Ostrander and Zarrella and that he quit rather than do their "dirty work." Ostrander's version is that he got fed up and quit after the band's equipment was stolen from their loft and Epic kept pushing back the record's release date. No matter how it went down, the result was the same—by the fall of 1972, Leejack, Ostrander, and Zarrella were out of the band, and Simmons and Stanley decided to start from scratch.

They did auditions for a replacement and came up with Peter Criss. Soon after Criss joined, it was clear that Wicked Lester was dead, so they needed a new name and came up with KISS. The rest, as everyone would say, was history. (No, not KISStory. That is just silly.)

Name Change

The legend goes that the band started as Rainbow in 1970, played one gig under that name, then switched to Wicked Lester until after Peter Criss joined the band in 1972. However, Brook Ostrander states in *Behind the Mask* that the band did not change their name until they went into the studio, which would have been sometime in 1971, while Tony Zarrella on the very next page states that their first managerial contract was signed on July 1, 1972, with the band still going by the name Rainbow.

There is also the little matter of what made them change their name. Many have assumed over the years that this was due to the existence of Ritchie Blackmore's Rainbow—the band Blackmore started after leaving Deep Purple with most of the musicians, including Ronnie James Dio, from a group called Elf—but that band did not get started until 1975. However, there were definitely other bands using Rainbow as part of their name at the time, so there was still a determination to change the name of the band. Yet doing so because the name was too familiar seems like a more mundane reason than if it had been due to a bigger name like Blackmore (much like how Alice Cooper became Alice Cooper back in the late 1960s because Todd Rundgren already had a band called Nazz releasing albums), which is probably why the Blackmore rumor got such circulation over the years.

With a name needed, the legend goes that either Paul Stanley or Stephen Coronel came up with the name of Wicked Lester (no one appears to want to take the blame there, even at this late date). The story told for years within fandom was that the name came from the wicker furniture store called Wicker Lester below the loft where the band played, but it has been noted in recent years that the band was playing in a fifth-floor loft over the Norman Watch Company, thus torpedoing that version of the story. Instead, all now seem to agree that it was just a weird name that would hopefully attract attention to them, no matter who came up with it.

Still, the timeline seems fuzzy—when did Rainbow become Wicked Lester? Supposedly they only played one gig as Rainbow, but the number of gigs supposedly played doesn't jibe with the stories of them not changing it to Wicked Lester until months later when they went into the studio and as late as the summer of 1972 in one version. It does not help that the band members use both names when describing events during the time the band was together—sometimes both while describing the same event. Perhaps in some ways, it does make more sense to use the Wicked Lester name when discussing Rainbow, as that is how people commonly refer to the band as a whole anyway, but it gives the impression when researching the period that the band got rid of the Rainbow name much earlier than they did in reality.

Perhaps Ostrander's and Zarrella's stories aren't really in conflict anyway. The band went into the studio to record some demos, which were then used to try to cut a deal to record an entire album. It was probably at that time that they checked into the name situation, saw that there was someone else using Rainbow as part of their name, and then continued as Rainbow for a time anyway just because they had been using it to try to get work up to that point, while also thinking of other names they could use. Then again, most of the stories seem to center on the band's entrance into the studio to record the album and not just some demos. In that case, the recording sessions for Wicked Lester would make it starting in November 1971, with Epic hearing some of it, requesting Ron Leejack take over, and Leejack joining in December 1971. Yet the July 1 contract led to Lew Linet becoming their manager and helping to persuade Epic to take the band on. If so, that means that Linet would have become their manager back in 1971, not 1972, and thus, things fall a bit more into place. The band was Rainbow up to at least July 1971, and then getting the deal with Epic made them realize they had a similar name to someone else and change it to Wicked Lester probably just before going into the studios in November 1971. But if that is the case, it also means they definitely did more than one show as Rainbow. Speaking of which . . . .

Tour Dates

Common wisdom for fandom is that Rainbow/Wicked Lester played one show and then disappeared. This is easy to imagine in hindsight, as the band did take to a rather sporadic schedule once they started. The reason behind this was the same one they would use when putting together KISS in 1973: the band did not want to be another act that people would see "grow" into being good; or, as Stanley would later state in interviews, they did not want to have to try to win back people who thought they were terrible and had gradually gotten better. Even with the correction in mind, however, Rainbow had at least a year to be playing shows and are known to have played their first show at Richmond College in May 1971. Then came a B'nai Brith in Atlantic City, the McManus Junior High prom, a youth convention in Atlantic City (where the band decided to have at least one set with cover songs to please audience members that wanted to hear at least a handful of songs that they knew already), and a club in Manasquan, New Jersey. Simmons states that their third gig was at the Rivoli Theater in South Fallsburg, New York, which would make it during the Rainbow days as well.

That said, this takes into account pretty much all the dates known for them to have played as a live band. Could some gigs have happened after the name change in 1971? Possibly, although it appears the band was mainly concentrating on working on the album by that time. Which leads to another nail in the coffin for playing gigs as Wicked Lester—the band went into the studio in November 1971. If they did change their name around that time, and Ron Leejack became part of the band in December 1971, they would have only had a limited window to play as Wicked Lester. Why? Because everyone, from Leejack down the line, states that they never played live with Leejack except for a showcase for Epic to see if the band could continue recording the album. Thus, the stories of the band playing one gig as Rainbow and a handful of others as Wicked Lester appears to be in reality the reverse—a handful of shows as Rainbow and then one gig as Wicked Lester, and that was merely a showcase for Epic.

Either way, this leads to our next topic of concern . . . .

Recording

To many fans, there seem to be sixteen different versions of the Wicked Lester material that have circulated since the late 1980s (at a time when most fans really discovered for the first time that there was a band before KISS, much less an album of material floating out there). A lot of the differences have to do with the mix of the album they heard and what version of the tapes they heard. The first bootleg with the material came out in 1987 from a "company" called Rockwell & Good with the title *Wicked Lester and Progeny Demo Sessions.* It included nine of the eleven known tracks recorded by the band, along with the five-track KISS demo Eddie Kramer did with the band in 1973 and two demos from 1985 by Ace Frehley. It also had a lot of tape leakage from the reel-to-reel tape used for the master, which did not help songs that already sounded like an odd mixture of pretty much anything under the sun that could be used (banjos, flutes, country-flavored and psychedelic vibes, etc.). Nevertheless, this version quickly made the rounds on other bootleg albums and tapes swapped among fans over the next few years.

Then another version appeared about early to mid-1990s, this one not only with additional songs, but with different mixes of the songs heard before and without the tape leakage. Suddenly the mystery of the group got even deeper— not only were there official recordings of this band that fans knew little about, but there also seemed to be at least two different recordings done. As it turns out, a lot of this had to do with what Epic wanted out of the band and the fallout that occurred when Stephen Coronel was let go. It appears that the following did happen:

In 1971, the band was working on material to try to interest people. Paul Stanley contacted his old bandmate Neal Teeman at Electric Lady Studios to see if he could help, and Teeman got them in touch with Ron Johnsen, an engineer and producer at Electric Lady who—in a coincidence—had been

Bootleg album of the Wicked Lester material with a mock-up cover of what was intended to be used for the official cover.
Author's Collection

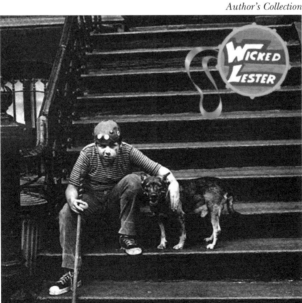

involved with Peter Criss's Chelsea album of 1970. Johnsen was intrigued by the band and helped them work on a three-song demo tape ("Keep Me Waiting," "She," and "Simple Type") to pass around while working as a manager for them. That summer the group got a chance to perform a showcase for Elektra Records with another prospect, Harry Chapin. Chapin got picked over them. The band attempted a couple of other showcases that summer and finally got a deal with Metromedia. This appears to be when they went into the studio in November 1971 to start recording their album. As they were progressing, however, the Metromedia deal died, and the band was let go.

Johnsen had already recorded a chunk of the album—including songs brought in from outside writers—when the deal fell through. With help from the band's manager Lew Linet (mentioned above as signing up the band in 1971) and some polish on the tracks along with some new material recorded, Epic Records was curious enough to see a showcase. The band performed for Epic, with Coronel feeling he had not gotten the hang of "Love Her All I Can." Whether it was for this reason, or because of other reasons mentioned over time (such as not "looking the role"), Epic stated that they would sign the band but only if they got a new lead guitarist. Stephen Coronel was then let go.

On December 15, 1971, the band hired studio musician Ron Leejack to play lead. Leejack then performed with them at a showcase where he sat for the duration, focusing on his guitar work rather than on the stage performance the others attempted to do. Whether this worked or not for the other musicians did not matter, as Epic liked what they heard and agreed to let the recording continue with Leejack.

From reports, it appears that Ron Johnsen then tried at first to remix the completed tracks with Ron Leejack's guitar work on top, but decided that the results were not working the way he wanted. He felt the band needed to return to the studio and start from scratch. This led to a long process between January and July 1972 where the band would assemble in the studio whenever there was free time available and work on material. By all reports, the album was finished in July 1972 and mixed for presentation to Epic that August.

Except Epic did not care for the mix, so they requested another one. The company received a revised mix in October 1972, but kept dragging their feet on a release date for the album. As everyone waited, there were problems brewing with the band—suggestions from Simmons that they begin wearing costumes, maybe makeup, and play roles onstage were meeting with resistance from Leejack and Zarrella—and Leejack, Ostrander, and Zarrella were all looking to split, while Simmons and Stanley were looking to see if they could get away from the others as well.

By this time, Simmons had seen Criss's ad looking for work as a drummer and contacted him about meeting. They would meet up at Electric Lady Studios, where Simmons and Stanley were working on backing vocals for the Lyn Christopher album (and supposedly Criss joined in by supplying clapping for one of the tracks). Simmons and Stanley would have Criss come up to the loft and do an audition on Zarrella's drum kit and then try again on his own drum kit at another audition, which got everyone excited about working together. After that date, the loft was broken into and everyone's equipment stolen. This was pretty much the last straw for most of the members, and the band broke up by November of that year just as Epic announced that they had decided to pass on the album.

As a side note, this also explains the ad put out in the *Village Voice* in December 1971 with the trio looking for a lead guitarist and promising that an album would be "out shortly." At that point, that probably was a fact instead of a stretch of the truth, as Epic was hemming and hawing over what to do with the completed Wicked Lester album when the ad was put together in November. It does, however, put to doubt Criss's long-held claim that the three played as a trio "for nearly a year" as he could only have joined Simmons and Stanley by mid-September at the earliest and Frehley was a member by January 1973. Thus, the most time they would have had together is three to four months, and that is with the odd situation of the Wicked Lester band slowly disintegrating while Criss was practicing with Simmons and Stanley.

The band members in reflection tend to look at the recordings made as flat-out odd and more the product of the time, as well as indicative of a band that was second-guessing itself over what would work for them. It would lead to the group taking on any and all ideas thrown their way and with the results being a mess when it came to musical directions. Even so, fans have come to love the recordings, even the ugly-sounding original recordings that turned up in the 1980s. The album cover picked by the band was from a group of generic covers Epic had sitting around for possible use on one of their artist's albums and featured a tough "Dead End Street" kid on the cover holding pool balls and a pool stick in one hand and draping an arm over an ugly dog sitting next to him on the steps of an old inner-city apartment house. The back cover was to have shown the band lounging around in rather expensive splendor—a photo commonly shown of the band in various official bios from KISS. The cover would be used years later for the self-titled first album by a band called the Laughing Dogs in 1979, leading to that band being forever remembered by KISS fans who probably have never even heard their album.

To deflate another myth about the recordings, the master tapes of the album sat in the vaults at Epic until 1977 when someone remembered that Simmons and Stanley had played on the album. With the explosive success of KISS ongoing at the time, Epic prepared the album for release. Simmons, Stanley, manager Bill Aucoin, and Casablanca Records owner Neil Bogart all decided that it would not help KISS to have the material appear and managed to work out a deal with Epic to buy back the recordings. The story goes with Simmons and Stanley paying out of their own pockets for the recordings, but it appears that Casablanca was the one doing the buying at the time.

The eleven songs known to have been recorded by Wicked Lester for the album are as follows:

"Sweet Ophelia"—Written by Barry Mann and Gerry Goffin and appears on Barry Mann's 1971 album *Lay It All Out*, which was engineered by Ron Johnsen. Johnsen remained on good terms with Mann and was able to work out a deal to get this song and "Too Many Mondays" for the Wicked Lester album.

"Keep Me Waiting"—Written by Paul Stanley and one of the songs the band would perform live. The 1971 Stephen Coronel version appears on the KISS box set from 2001.

"Love Her All I Can"—Written by Stanley and performed by the band live; this was sometimes listed on bootlegs as "Ladies in Waiting." The 1972 Ron Leejack version appears on the KISS box set from 2001. Stanley would in a sense disown the Wicked Lester attempt, saying that the version recorded by KISS for *Dressed to Kill* would be how he intended the song to sound. Stephen Coronel would state in interviews that it was his poor playing on this song in the Epic showcase that got him fired from the band.

"She"—Written by Stephen Coronel and Gene Simmons. The 1971 Stephen Coronel version appears on the KISS box set from 2001. Like Stanley with "Love Her All I Can," Coronel would later state that the version KISS recorded for *Dressed to Kill* was what he had in mind for the song. Brook Ostrander played flute. (Yes, this is the "flute song" fans always talk about when discussing how the Wicked Lester songs don't really seem like the KISS they would get to know.)

"Too Many Mondays"—Another Barry Mann song, this time written with Cynthia Weil. It too appears on Mann's 1971 album listed above.

"(What Happens) In the Darkness"—Written by Tamy Lester Smith, although the band with Coronel reworked parts of it in the studio. Also recorded by a soul band called Infinity and released as a single by UNI Records in 1972. Commonly listed on early bootlegs as simply "In the Darkness."

"When the Bells Ring"—Written by Austin Roberts and Christopher Welch. Also recorded by a group called Newport News and released as a single by RCA Records in 1972. This, "(What Happens) In the Darkness," "We Wanna Shout It Out Loud," "Long Road," and the Barry Mann songs were brought in through Ron Johnsen as Epic wanted a more diverse feel to the album, leading to the album sounding very chaotic as a result.

"Molly"—Written by Stanley. Commonly listed on bootlegs as "Some Other Guy" and "Going 'Round the Bend." It has been stated that Stanley wrote this as a challenge to Simmons, who was having trouble writing something in a "McCartney" vein.

"We Want to Shout It Out Loud"—Written by Allan Clarke and Terry Sylvester. The song would appear as "I Wanna Shout" on the Hollies' 1970 album *Confessions of the Mind* (released in the U.S. as *Moving Finger* without the "I Wanna Shout" track). Fans picking up the bootleg of the album for the first time would expect to hear an early version of the later KISS song "Shout It Out Loud," so it was shocking to hear this rather mellow song that made it on to the album.

"Simple Types"—Written by Simmons. This track did not appear on the early bootlegs.

"Long Road"—Written by an English team of writers, although no one seems to remember who. This, as with "Simple Types," turned up on later bootlegs.

3

From a Wizard to a True Star

The Early Influences of KISS

As already discussed, KISS did not just pop up unexpectedly and become successful based on ideas created for them alone. Members of the band have been more than open about their influences, some more readily apparent than others. The trick was to take them and present them in a unique combination that made the band stand out; perhaps not stand above their influences, but at least stand away from them in order to be seen in a unique light. Many of the inspirations were of course musical, but other elements played into the makeup of the band as well. There were certainly other influences beyond those listed below, but these were some of the most direct of that group.

Beatles

No surprise to anyone is that the Beatles were an influence on the band, as three of the four original members found themselves watching the group on *The Ed Sullivan Show* back in 1964 just like many kids who became the rock stars of the late 1960s and early 1970s (only Peter Criss would stand slightly outside of that group, due to being a tad older and focusing more on jazz and pop music at the time while working to be a full-time professional drummer). Both Gene Simmons and Paul Stanley have been vocal about their interest in the Beatles, as evidenced by the aforementioned "Molly" during the Wicked Lester days mentioned in Chapter 2. Simmons was also very vocal in his attempt to get several if not all of the Beatles to appear on his solo album in 1978. (He managed to get Mitch Weissman and Joe Pecorino of *Beatlemania* instead. Weissman would go on to cowrite and perform bass and guitar on three songs on the *Animalize* album as well as perform on "Thief in the Night" for the Simmons-produced Wendy O. Williams album *W. O. W.* He also turned up on one of Paul Stanley's Guest-VJ hours on MTV as a character named "not Paul McCartney.")

But it was the look and sound of the Beatles that drove KISS as well. The Beatles had a uniform look that still emphasized each member in a unique way (albeit this may have more to do with the group refusing to follow the rules and putting in little touches that made each one different onstage). This carried over to KISS with a uniform look of black and white makeup combined with outfits that looked similar but not the same—as if they were all shopping in the same store from outer space. KISS was also big on harmonies, another early trait of the Beatles to carry over to them (although Peter Criss's work with doo-wop and other close harmony groups no doubt played a part as well).

The biggest parallel between the two is, of course, the merchandising. Manager Brian Epstein was not shy about getting the band's faces on a number of items back in the 1960s, and Bill Aucoin was no different about KISS in the 1970s. The only difference appears to be that Aucoin got the band a bigger piece of the respective pies. That said, he and the band were also particular about what merchandise did appear, striving to make sure fans who spent their money got something for it and being directly involved with the production of items (this changed in the 1990s when the quality control became a bit looser for items fans were not that interested in buying). A review of some of the things released over the years appears in Chapter 24, but it is clear that KISS and its management looked to how the Beatles were marketed in the 1970s.

Alice Cooper Group

There had been other performers before Alice Cooper who added theater to rock music, but none reached the level of stardom they did in the early 1970s. Further, the Cooper group staged their performances as mini-plays, using props to convey elements of the songs—even early on, with Alice looking out a prop bedroom window as he sang "Nobody Likes Me"—as well as for shock value—the infamous chicken incident of 1969, for example, where a chicken thrown into the crowd soon turned into a bloody mess. Sometimes things were tossed around onstage for little reason, but eventually the band got to the point where they had a number of set-pieces to help convey a larger story of the Killer Alice, his escapades, his execution (in a variety of manners), and his reemergence for the encore.

The members of KISS and Bill Aucoin always said two things about Alice: That they saw KISS as a chance to have four Alice Coopers on stage, and that the best thing that ever happened to them was the Alice Cooper group breaking up in 1974. Cooper was considered a premier American band, with a string of hit songs and sold-out shows, but the band had been playing and recording consistently for years by that time, and everyone needed a break from each other. Cooper would quickly rebound on his own with the smash *Welcome to My Nightmare* album in 1975, but the breakup took a band that was reaching the level of superstardom of the Rolling Stones and the Beatles and cooled their momentum while the audience was still hot for more. Cooper as a solo artist was still huge, but there was a magic with the original band that could never be recaptured.

KISS took that energy built up by the Cooper band and went in their own direction, with stage pieces involving the band members (namely Simmons, but all four had pieces that were done in concert that became standards, like

Frehley's smoking guitar, Criss's levitating drum kit, and Paul smashing his guitar). Although there were other acts that were using theatrical presentations in their concerts at the time (notably David Bowie, Funkadelic, and Genesis, to name a few) that the band members would have seen, the Cooper group's emphasis on comic-book violence would reverberate within KISS when they began putting their shows together.

KISS pushed theatrics to a new level that would affect how rock bands would perform ever after, but without the earlier efforts of the Alice Cooper group to show that the audience would eat it up, it would have been much harder for KISS to prove their case. To have Alice turn up for their first huge Casablanca showcase to the press in 1974 stood out as a passing of the baton in a way and another reason why KISS has always been quick to point to Alice Cooper when discussing what influenced them as a band.

Coincidentally, just as the Alice Cooper band would break up roughly six years after recording their first album due to constant touring and recording, so too would the original lineup of KISS break up six years after recording their first album due to bickering aggravated by constant touring and recording.

Slade

As Simmons pointed out in his book *Kiss and Make-Up*, KISS looked to Slade as one to emulate when developing their own group. That may seem as a stretch in some ways, at least in broad visual terms, as although Slade are considered a cornerstone band of the glam rock period of the early 1970s, they certainly did not project the image of many from that period, at least from this side of history. For many, glam tended to be the flamboyant style of people like Elton John, David Bowie, and others, with long hair and androgynous features, while Slade, who never seemed that concerned about the whole hair thing (they were even skinheaded for a time), wore work boots and jeans. Glam seemed to try to capitalize off the hippie movement, while Slade looked like the type of guys who would beat up on hippies on a Saturday night. They were one of the few bands of the era—Alice Cooper being another—that looked more like something out of *Clockwork Orange* who would likely beat up anything that even looked the wrong way at them. They were somewhat frightening, which made the music behind the image that much more powerful.

Mainly, however, it was the music that Simmons was drawn to—a band that had created hard-rocking songs that worked as anthems, such as "Mama Weer All Crazee Now" and "Cum On Feel the Noize." KISS would do the same with a number of attempts at such anthems over the years, some more successful than others. On the other hand, in the book *Behind the Mask*, Simmons claims that Aucoin was the one who suggested the band write a song that could be seen as an anthem and that both Simmons and Stanley had to look up the word to understand what Aucoin was getting at. But this may have been Simmons in one of his "storyteller" moments.

Slade hit it big with "Cum On Feel the Noize"—a song that supposedly led to KISS writing "Rock and Roll All Nite."   *Author's Collection*

Black Sabbath

The band loved Led Zeppelin—several of them had gone to see the same
concert by Led Zeppelin before KISS started and made no bones about playing
Zep covers in sound checks—yet perhaps the biggest influence that band had
on KISS was in a mocking gesture that came by way of Black Sabbath. Simmons
once mentioned that the first ad he ever saw for Black Sabbath was one from
1969 that read simply "Louder Than Led Zeppelin." He thought it was a perfect
snot-face attitude for a band to have—not that Black Sabbath was "better" than
Led Zeppelin or had more fans or was more musically inclined, just louder. It
was a linchpin to the direction KISS was to go from there—not worrying about
trying to achieve art, but rather to entertain.

Roy Wood

Paul Stanley has made no bones about his love for the Move and Roy Wood,
pointing out that "Firehouse" was him riffing on the Move's "Fire Brigade"
among other songs with such references. (Several songs in the KISS catalog play
off riffs from other songs by Mountain, Deep Purple, etc. "Love Her All I Can"
uses a riff from the Nazz's "Open My Eyes," for example.) More importantly,

The band Gene Simmons loved because they were "louder than Led Zeppelin." *Author's Collection*

Wood—along with stars like the Nazz's own Todd Rundgren, the Hello People, Arthur Brown, Funkadelic (again), Alice Cooper (again), and others were all experimenting with makeup as part of their album and stage work. One look at Wood's *Wizzard's Brew* album from 1973 and one cannot help but wonder if it, along with other factors, helped formulate ideas for the band wearing makeup on stage.

The New York Band Scene in the Early 1970s

People tend to look at KISS as basing their act on bigger acts they had seen. That is partially correct, as mentioned above; for without people like Alice Cooper, David Bowie, Elton John, Marc Bolan, and many others, KISS would have had a harder time coming together and being even as awkwardly accepted by the public as they were by 1974, when their first album came out.

The thing is, KISS was not a sole experiment in the world of music at the time—there were plenty of other bands in the U.S. and elsewhere trying anything and everything to make it. In particular, New York was heavy with bands that were attempting various concepts in concert to attract audiences. This was helped in part by the remnants of the hippie scene from the 1960s, which saw an openness for music to be more than x-number of guys standing on stage and playing instruments. The Pretty Things' *S.F. Sorrow* and the Who's *Tommy* had already blasted open the doors for rock bands to consider the idea of full conceptual musical drama, while Broadway was eyeing the success of rock musicals such as *Jesus Christ Superstar, Hair,* and *Godspell,* as well as a number of others that never quite made it or off-Broadway productions such as Smokerise's *The Survival of St. Joan* (a full rock opera that was released as an album and performed a number of times in the New York area just as KISS was looking to get off the ground). The timing was right in the music scene, and people in the New York area felt comfortable enough with it that a number of bands at least experimented with theatrical concepts without feeling like the "odd man out."

Naturally, the New York Dolls are one of the first bands think of as coming out of this period of experimentation. The band started in 1971, with Johnny Thunders and David Johansen playing at American versions of Keith Richards and Mick Jagger, and became known for their early-punk style of music. They also got stymied after an attempt at cross-dressing in order to give the audience a shock. It was a look that lasted as long as photographing their first album cover—they had already moved on to another look by the time the album was out—but one that would be an iconic symbol for the band through the years and one that even KISS copied for a brief time when trying to get their own band off the ground (explaining an early picture of the guys looking more in drag than makeup, which the band discarded due to them not looking effeminate enough to pull off the look). Later in the 1970s, Johansen would state that KISS did the right thing by finding a look and sticking with it, as the Dolls jumped around too much with their look for fans not able to attend their shows to really identify with them.

Other performers were trying things as well, such as the notorious trans-sexual singer Wayne/Jayne County, who would sometimes play on the same bill with KISS in their early club days and was known for being an act that was set to repulse the audience as much as get people to see him (Paul recalled County performing a song while eating dog food out of a toilet onstage). There were plenty of others as well, such as the Harlots of 42nd Street, who cross-dressed like the Dolls and were big enough to put together their own fan club and offer fans attending their shows special "Harlots of 42nd Street" bubble gum—showing that riffing on the childhood concepts of joining fan clubs and getting special merchandise was not unique to KISS. Nor was the fire-breathing, which was a staple of the Magic Tramps (at one time featuring Warhol Superstar Eric Emerson and at times a pre-Blondie Chris Stein), who had a member called Satan who would come on stage and eat and spit fire during the shows.

With clubs like Max's Kansas City and CBGB pumping out bands—and in some ways creating their own roster of bands that would perform at the clubs on a regular basis—a number of other clubs were spitting out bands struggling to make it as well. As much as KISS fans wish to imagine Coventry, where KISS had their first gig at the end of January 1973, as a hole-in-the-wall, it was actually a well-established bar with an active music scene that saw the roots of acts like the

Cover of first New York Dolls album—a band image that KISS tried to
adopt early on.   *Author's Collection*

Ramones and others start there. Plus, there were acts that played everywhere,
such as the Brats and Isis (an all-female band that had three albums in the
1970s), Teenage Lust, and the Dictators—all remembered for trying to shake
up the music scene in the early 1970s.

In some ways this scene helped KISS—they were among the many trying
to find a way to express themselves in an experimental and open time in rock
music. On the other hand, they were one of many willing to "try anything" in
order to make it. There may have been elements of some of the other acts that
worked their way into what KISS would become, but the biggest thing was that
the four members of KISS had to rise above the already considerable talent
available in the New York music scene to be noticed; making them that much
better in the end by forcing them to be that much more over-the-top.

Art School

People tend to forget that three of the four original members of KISS, as well
as Eric Carr, had studied art in some capacity. Paul Stanley had studied at the
High School of Art and Design to become a commercial designer. Peter Criss
went to art school for three years as a teenager. Ace Frehley studied graphic art
in high school after a counselor suggested it as a possible outlet for his creativity.

Eric Carr also went to the High School of Art and Design. The only exception is Gene Simmons, and he was drawing artwork for and creating the editorial design of his own fanzines while in school (several of the KISS documentaries have shown sketches he has done over the years about various KISS projects as well as his fanzine work).

This is not uncommon for rock musicians, who tend to knock aside the "norms" of being a rock 'n' roller and risk ridicule from the critics. Bands such as Queen and the Tubes (both emerging a couple of years from either side of KISS) came out of art school backgrounds, had big visual ideas for shows and albums, and were widely criticized for not taking it "seriously." As with these other bands, having dealt with art—drawing and design in particular—allowed KISS more freedom to deal with their presentation of their look. Other musicians would balk at the suggestion of costumes and makeup (the other members of Wicked Lester certainly did, with the exception of Brook Ostrander, who as a schoolteacher saw it as a way to stay in the band and still work as a teacher without conflict), but the four KISS members could see the potential. They also knew enough about the development and procedure of creating artwork to realize that it was not going to be an overnight change; it would take effort and time to get it to pay off.

Many have pointed out over the years how much people like Bill Aucoin, Neil Bogart, and Sean Delaney helped form certain aspects of the band's look. Yet, without the band members having the foreknowledge to appreciate what was being done for them and take it to another level (besides coming up with ideas of their own that were incorporated into their look), all the outside preparation would have done nothing to help them achieve their goal. The art training they received as teenagers (either in school or through practice) helped prepare them to let their imagination run wild when it came to the band and allowed them to bring their outrageous ideas to fruition.

Comic Books and Fantasy Movies

While other bands were trying various aspects of theater in their shows, KISS went in a slightly different direction. No doubt based on a cue from Alice Cooper's act of violence and retribution, Simmons and Stanley began looking at the band as a group of characters together instead of at a number of stunts performed within a show. The concept went back to the days of Wicked Lester, where Simmons was envisioning himself as a caveman while another member would be a card shark out of an old Western.

Within the new framework of KISS, the members began to see their characters as unworldly, as if from out of a comic book or fantasy movie. Ace Frehley quickly adapted to being a "spaceman," even an alien from another world (his character's backstory was that he was from another planet and unused to the gravity on Earth in order to explain his clumsy footing at times in concert); and Simmons slowly morphed into some type of monster-like creature who could spit up blood like a deranged vampire and spit fire to dazzle the crowd. By the time the band was ready to release their first album in February 1974, they had established a relationship with horror and science fiction movies. Album covers like *Destroyer* (see Chapter 10 for more details on how closely related this artwork was to the fantasy genre) made the band look like something out of a sword and sorcery fantasy novel. Once they got their own superpowers in the first Marvel comic (see Chapter 23 for more details on that and other comic book outings), there was no way to deny that KISS had become the first superhero rock band. Using songs on the album to compound the concept snowballed the image—"Goin' Blind" sounds like a song an undead demon of the night would sing to a girl; "Rocket Ride" could be taken to be Frehley suggesting an outer-space journey . . . even if we know it is not what he is really talking about.

KISS took theatrics and played by their own rules—even Alice Cooper would eventually get tired of being "Killer Alice" and try variations on the theme with onstage characters like Maurice Escargot (*Lace & Whiskey*) or Apocalypse Alice from *Flush the Fashion*—but KISS was always these four characters, and the personas became what the band was about. In some ways, it led to problems for KISS redefining themselves in the 1980s, when the kids listening in 1976 felt they had outgrown the comic books and horror stories of the band by 1980. But for a time in the 1970s, those elements would influence the band and help make them a household name, more so than if they had just been four guys in makeup with no personas behind those images.

4

Looking for Flash and Ability

The Tryouts in 1972

G ene Simmons and Paul Stanley were looking at a band falling apart in the summer and fall of 1972 and, in some ways, not overly concerned about it. The year spent working on the Wicked Lester album had burned out everyone, and Simmons's idea to put on costumes and makeup had been met with a bit of anger from his bandmates. Further, it was increasingly clear that the band's relationship with their studio-bound lead guitarist, Ron Leejack, was not working out, even if Leejack had a hand in keeping their Epic Records deal back in December 1971. Wicked Lester was soon to die a natural death, but Simmons and Stanley were already starting to eye another life after that one in the summer of 1972.

Most stories give the idea that the two began their search for a new member of their band in late August, possibly even early September 1972, when they found Peter Criss's free musician ad in the back of an August issue of *Rolling Stone* (the magazine used to allow musicians to solicit work free of charge through a small cluster of classified ads in the back of each issue). But it is possible they had started looking even sooner than that. The much-rumored tale of Twisted Sister guitarist Jay Jay French once being a member of Rainbow pops up in conjunction with this story, and French in 2006 would attempt to clear up the many rumors about him being in the band by stating he never was. Instead, he had auditioned with Simmons and Stanley over a period of a couple of weeks, and had remained friendly with them, but things never gelled and French would go on to join Twisted Sister in December 1972 while KISS was auditioning other guitarists for the band (he went on to state that he came over to watch the group practice with Frehley and thought they had a lot of potential).

Yet the thing about French's clearing up of the fable is that he mentioned he had auditioned for the band back in July 1972. This would put it just as Wicked Lester was finishing up their recording of their album and waiting to see what would happen next. French could have been thinking of the tryouts where Frehley was first heard, but one would think that the change in climate and such would be enough to keep French from suggesting a midsummer date for something that occurred in winter. There is also a possibility that Simmons and Stanley were looking to see who they could hire to take the place of Leejack, who was pretty much heading out the door by then anyway. This would explain why French remembers it as "not KISS" but something else.

So if Simmons and Stanley were already looking at other band members by July, then having come across Criss's ad was probably not a fluke in August of that year—the two were probably actively looking for replacement players, if not a whole new band. Over time, there has rarely been a mention of anyone other than Criss trying out for the new band. Further, his first audition with them was with Tony Zarrella's drum kit, so the audition may have been more discreet than other biographies of the band would suggest.

Criss's ad would lead to Simmons calling him during a party at Criss and his wife Lydia's place to ask him a few questions. Some biographical sketches of the band say this was immediately after Criss and Lydia had gotten married, but their marriage happened in 1970, so if a party was going on in August/September 1972, it was for other reasons. Criss was amazed that Simmons was asking more questions about what he looked like and how he dressed than about his musical ability, but from Simmons's point of view, after being in a band where no one looked quite right next to each other, he wanted to be sure that the visual appearance of the band was there from the start.

A meeting at Electric Lady Studio led to Simmons and Stanley seeing Criss perform at the King's Lounge in Queens with Stan Penridge (the gig where Penridge thought there would be a riot because it was a traditional working-class bar in Queens and Simmons and Stanley were glammed up). The gig went over well enough with Simmons and Stanley that Criss went to their loft to audition on Zarrella's drums and then later on his own kit. At first, he was unsure of the

The ad that would lead to Ace Frehley joining the band. Contrary to multiple interviews over the years, the ad makes no mention of the guitarist needing "balls."

Author's Collection

other two, as he could not see what was so good about the Wicked Lester material. Then they played a new song called "Strutter," and Criss immediately snapped into place with Simmons and Stanley, and they decided to give things a shot as a trio.

In that form, the band would put on a showcase for Epic near the end of November 1972 in hopes of keeping their Wicked Lester contract alive. By this time, the trio had decided to name the band KISS, thanks to Stanley brainstorming off Criss's old band Lips and no one objecting to the new name (much to the relief of Stanley, who figured the others would call him out on picking such an obvious—and possibly silly—name for the band). Don Ellis and two other higher-ups at Epic Records went to hear them perform at the showcase, with the band ready to negotiate the contract to be this new band KISS with the white face makeup, costumes, and what props they could bring—including a fire bell and a bucket of confetti.

The presentation was new to the men from Epic—they had known Wicked Lester as a five-piece band who looked pretty much like everyone else in rock at the time. Now suddenly it was a trio, with a drummer they had never seen and with all these gimmicks flying around in front of their eyes. Plus, performing songs that were not part of the hippie/folksie mishmash that made up the Wicked Lester album. When the group wrapped up with "Firehouse," Stanley grabbed the bucket of confetti and threw it at Don Ellis as bells went off. This was supposed to send Ellis out on a high about the band. Instead, he exclaimed that they were crazy to think of changing the band so drastically.

Whereupon, Criss's brother, who came to watch the show, threw up. The story changes about whether he did this on Don Ellis or just in full view of him, but either way it confirmed Ellis's belief that nothing would ever come of the band he had just watched.

With the Epic deal no longer possible, the band had to start from scratch (and with one major label scratched off the list; three if one includes the failed Metromedia deal and a rumored deal from Buddah Records that Simmons had turned down for Wicked Lester because he thought they could find better). Still, they were told that Epic was still considering what to do with the Wicked Lester album, and so the trio decided to start auditioning lead guitarists for KISS, leading to a *Village Voice* ad (another free one) in December 1972, with the band stating that they would have an "album out soon" and were looking for a guitarist with "flash and ability." Those who called (including Ace Frehley, who talked to Stanley on the phone) about the ad got an invitation to an audition on January 3, 1973, although the word got out and several others arrived on top of those who called.

The auditions themselves were a bit strange to many of the guitarists who showed up. Outside the loft, each person auditioning was given a form to fill out, detailing experience and such while waiting to go in front of the guys inside. If it seemed frustrating to the men auditioning, there was frustration inside as well: for every decent guitarist the band saw, they saw several that had no business being there. Kids bringing in family members to watch, a guy who claimed to be an expert at the guitar after only two months of lessons (and being told afterward that he sounded like he had been playing for two months), and an Italian fresh off the boat who needed his wife to interpret for him were just a few of the delusional ones wasting their time. There were serious contenders as well, fortunately, with the trio surprised at how many known names were calling for an audition, including members of Long John Baldry's band and that of Hookfoot. Bob Kulick, who had played with Hookfoot, impressed the trio enough in the audition to have Simmons explain the makeup/costume concepts of the band. Kulick hesitantly agreed to the setup, which concerned Simmons and Stanley, as had Kulick's beard and his not physically looking like the person they were hoping to find.

While Kulick was auditioning, Ace Frehley arrived. Looking as cocky as possible, he blew off the application and the line and walked into the loft while the band was talking with Kulick. This threw the band a bit, and they were tempted to toss him on his ear for sabotaging the auditioning process, but they finally agreed to see him next after Kulick. Inadvertently, this would kick-start one of the most famous rumors about KISS that has continued to crop up over the years, but more about that in Chapter 31.

The trio was shocked to find that the "Chinese-looking guy" with mismatched sneakers clicked with them when they began playing the first song of the audition, "Deuce." After all the auditions were over, Simmons, Stanley, and Criss decided it came down to either Kulick or Frehley. The group went to see Frehley perform with his band at a club and liked what they saw enough to invite him back for a second audition. This went well, and an offer was made. Frehley stated later that he had to think about it, as he was not sure about the other guys, but he readily saw potential there and finally accepted the offer.

January 1973 would see the original four members of KISS agree to work together. Nobody knew then what was coming, but by the end of the month they would do their very first live show. The costumes and makeup would still need a lot of work before they settled into the styles everyone knows today, but one thing was settled before the end of the month—the KISS logo. Even that took some work before finally becoming what it looks like today, and little did they realize how much controversy it would cause years down the line.

5

The KISS Logo

Charges and Changes

With the four members setting out to create a band that would be a package of costumes, makeup, and effects, it was only natural to want to come up with a logo design for their name. The style would need to convey their uniqueness, while suggesting something powerful or even startling at the same time.

Ace Frehley, having studied graphic design in school, suggested a logo idea that Paul Stanley embellished into the form used to the present date: a boxlike K that flares out for its legs, the solid I, and the SS in a lightning-bolt fashion. Over time, a font series would be created for the entire alphabet based on these three letters—commonly referred to as the KISS font, although programs online have typically listed it as the pun-ish "Dienasty" font—but for the moment just having the three letters was enough to get them going.

The first version was made up of solid black lines, but before the year was out the band added a border to each letter for emphasis, and this would become the most common version of the logo used by the band over the years. The borders would sometimes disappear for certain pieces of advertising and such, and there have been circumstances where the font has been vertically stretched, but otherwise the logo remained untouched. It usually came with a solid color within the letters and a different color for the space between the letters and the borders

KISS concert ad from 1973, with an early version of the KISS logo. *Author's Collection*

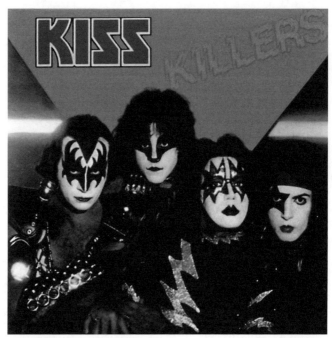

Compilation album featuring the German version of the KISS logo.
It was the first time for many American fans to discover that the band
had to change their logo.   *Author's Collection*

and sometimes for the borders themselves (*Lick It Up* is one of the few times
the band has showed the logo bearing no colors at all). It also did not appear
in the ad for their first appearance at Coventry at the end of January 1973, but
quickly was in use for other appearances. By the end of 1973, Bill Aucoin had
paid for a 164-bulbs lit sign showing the logo (albeit with two extra columns of
lights in each of the S's that threw off the balance of the design a tad).

Once the logo was there, it was natural for people to wonder about the
"lightning bolts" at the end of the name. It was not hard to imagine it looking
like the symbol worn by the Nazi Schutzstaffel, otherwise known as the SS. To
be fair, there were some differences between the two—the Nazi symbol, using
a variation of Sig Runes, has two slanted lines of equal length to form the S,
while KISS shortened the top line and lengthened the bottom for theirs; the
Nazi symbol also lands each letter at a point, giving the "SS" a lean to the left in
order to effectively create the jagged lightning-bolt urgency of the symbol, while
KISS flattened out the top and bottom in order to match up with the boxlike
nature of the rest of the font. Even so, it was very unlikely that the similarities
between the two would not be spotted by someone early on, and certainly not
when the band got signed to Casablanca and had their album distributed by
Warner Brothers in early 1974.

But one must remember the times. The Nazi symbol had been used by bikers and street gangs since the 1950s as a mark of defiance, violence, and outsider status. Later in the 1970s, the punk movement would use it and the swastika as a means to shock the general public, many times without even understanding the history behind the symbols. By the late 1960s, it was not uncommon to see rough characters in movies wearing the symbol as an easy way to mark their violent nature. Of course, by the 1970s, everyone was used to seeing the symbol ridiculed weekly in repeated episodes of *Hogan's Heroes* as well. It was popping up in music just as frequently; Black Sabbath would play with the symbols, using a variation for the font used on the cover of their December 1973 release, *Sabbath Bloody Sabbath,* and their follow-up *Sabotage,* while other bands who needed some type of break in their names would use a lightning-bolt symbol within their name (such as AC/DC would do in the 1970s). It was there and everyone could see it was there, but by the 1970s, it provoked mild anger and disgust more than hatred and shock. To Americans it nearly became a kind of cartoon violence—a symbol to laugh at rather than fear—and KISS used something that was one step further back from even that. In other words, varying the lettering made its point about the band being this question mark of possible frightening violence, while pulling back just enough to be able to say, "Oh, these are just lightning bolts! Who would think of the SS when they see this? Besides, if you come after us, what about all those bikers and others who use the real things?"

For years, the band used the symbols without incident beyond the few protestors who were sure that they were "Knights in Satan's Service" and had evil intentions. Even in West Germany—where laws forbad public display of Nazi symbols—there were no problems from 1976 through 1979 when the band's label there, Bellaphon, had released KISS material or in 1980 when Phonogram released *Unmasked* and the "Shandi" single with the standard KISS logo (EMI had been a bit skittish about it between 1975 and 1976, admittedly). However, 1980 also saw a political confrontation in an election for chancellor that led to a huge court battle over an opponent painting another as a Nazi by using the SS symbol on campaign buttons. The lawyers defended the usage by pointing out

The classic version of the KISS logo.   *Author's Collection*

that KISS was able to do so without any conflict. This led to confiscation of KISS albums and possible charges against the band right when they needed to prove their popularity in Europe as their star was falling in America.

In other words, the easiest thing to do was to cave, and Phonogram and Aucoin Management quickly came up with a variation of the logo that dropped the lightning bolts for what fans commonly refer to as, "backwards Z's." There was also press from Phonogram pointing out that the band's management was Jewish, although nothing on the same being the case for Simmons and Stanley. Nor any mention of Simmons's mother being a concentration camp survivor, which shows that he preferred to still keep some things of his past private at the time (although it easily could have been that he did not want to upset the apple cart any further with an additional reminder of Nazi atrocities). This was enough to placate everyone and allow the band to tour West Germany in 1980 without any difficulties (although they did face problems that year in Italy, where some members of the public considered the band to be a group of fascists, leading to rocks being thrown at them during shows and at least one riot).

It is common for KISS fans to find European albums and merchandise from over the years that looks the same in many ways as the American versions, with the exception of the altered logo. For some, this just makes it one more item to pick up when trying to complete collections—thereby creating sales for the band. One would almost think that the band had intended so from the start.

6

Why Would You Want to Hide This Face?

Makeup, Costume, and Stage Changes Through the Years

R apid change was bound to happen with the look of KISS, especially in the early days when the band members were experimenting with different concepts. Things calmed down once the first album came out, and the makeup was pretty much set in stone beyond some minor tweaks; but even so the band would usually make some type of major change to costumes and the stage shows with each new album released. Not always, but often enough to give the various styles the band went through a look.

Makeup

Makeup and costumes were one of the first things they worked on, with Simmons, Stanley, and Criss showcasing for Epic in 1973 in whiteface and rather generic rock-'n'-roll outfits (if one can call the rented sailor suit Simmons is wearing "rock-'n'-roll"). By the time Ace Frehley joined, the four rejected the whiteface and went for a look that was more derived from the New York Dolls (whose look came from other bands like the Rolling Stones for their "Have You Seen Your Mother, Baby, Standing in the Shadows?" picture sleeve single). This was the look—a bit of eye shadow and feminine clothing, although Criss looks like he stepped straight out of a Hello People gig—that was seen in the early photo of the four many fans finally saw of the band when it popped up in the 1980s, as well as one that proves Simmons's assertion that they couldn't carry off the look the way the Dolls did. Realizing that they had to go in another direction, they took their cue from bands like the Hello People and attempts by artists like the Stones, Roy Wood, and Todd Rundgren to use makeup to make their appearances unique instead of just covering up the face. There were some stumbles along the way, with Stanley being the most indecisive of the four on what worked best for him, but by the time the first album was released, the characters' makeup was set in stone. Only minor adjustments would occur after that.

Gene Simmons seemed to get the general idea of his makeup the quickest, moving from black around his eyes to give a skull-like texture to his face, on

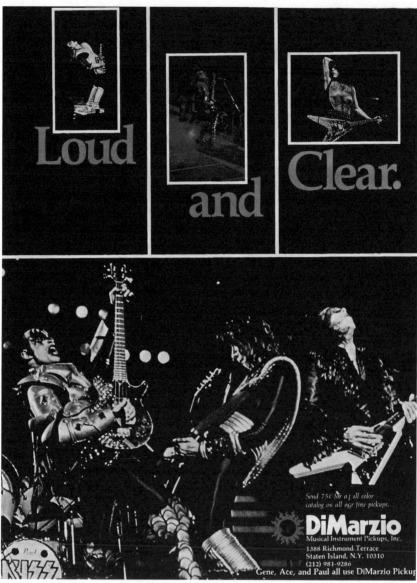

An ad for guitar pickups also gives an evolutionary look at the band's costumes in the mid-1970s.   *Author's Collection*

to the widow's peak and the flaming black mask around his eyes that gave the appearance of batwings. From there, the makeup would firm up, with black lines up and down the nose to define the "wings" a bit more. Although he would vary the thickness lines every so often in the years since, by 1974 he was set on the makeup for his persona.

Ace Frehley was the second member to get a handle on his makeup; already settling into the blast-out starlight silver look that made him resemble an alien before midyear in 1973; yet for many months he went without whiteface underneath the silver and only later added black lipstick, thus taking a bit more time to fall in line with the others who had begun using whiteface as a base by then. He would begin soon enough, however, and by the time they were signed with Casablanca that fall, there was a uniform look to the four with the whiteface makeup. Eventually he found that he had an allergic reaction to the silver around his eyes and switched to a pale blue eye shadow to complete the look. From there, Frehley had his character for the duration of his stay in KISS.

Peter Criss was next in line in getting his makeup settled, although he fiddled with it a bit more over 1973–1974 due to the complexity of various colors and styling necessary to get the cat look the way he wanted. By midsummer 1973, he had the general look down, with a cat nose (changing from silver to black and then back to silver again), a pair of whiskers across the each cheek, and elevated makeup around his eyes that would reach a point like cat ears (although he would round these off and have points off toward his temples for a time as well). In 1976, he added green makeup around his eyes, a final touch that would cement his look for the rest of his makeup days in the band.

Paul Stanley first attempted something that looked similar to Alice Cooper's spider eyes from the early Cooper period before attempting a star over the right eye. He then moved on to a circle over one eye that everyone teased him about as making him look like Pete the Dog from the old Little Rascals shorts. From there he attempted a look that fans typically call the "Lone Ranger mask," which covered both eyes as the Lone Ranger's mask did. He would flirt with this style straight into 1974 and even be photographed in staged color photos in the early part of 1974 while also going back and wearing his star makeup. It was then that he decided to stick with the star from that point on.

When Eric Carr joined, he found himself in the unique position of having to create his own makeup for the band, after others had decided that his new character would be based on an animal to show a lineage with Criss's cat. It was decided to make Carr a hawk, and although he had skill in drawing, the makeup would never quite come into sync—Carr's contention was that if it looked like a bird from the front, it would not from the side and vice-versa. When a costume arrived with yellow-orange feathers that he felt made him look like a giant chicken, the hawk concept was trash-canned. Instead, at a very late point in time, he hit upon a fox concept that he felt fit him personally, more than the hawk makeup anyway (seeing himself as small and cunning like a fox). Because the process was rushed—the Australian tour book for 1980 when he joined showed a badly airbrushed picture of the band with someone who looked more like a drunk attempting to imitate a French Charlie Chaplin from outer space than a fox—Carr worked on it more after they played their first show with him in makeup. The silver outline soon disappeared, leaving red makeup around the eyes with black around it that went up in points like fox's ears (although one could rarely see this through his hair) along with silver on the tip of his nose. He would finalize the makeup so that the silver was gone, and instead a line of whiteface went down his nose until the tip, whereupon black was added to give the makeup an even greater fox look.

Vinnie Vincent was the last performer in KISS to need a makeup persona, and his was one that, as Carr's riffed off of Criss's, so too would Vincent's be a cousin to Frehley's. This was accomplished by keeping the design simplistic yet otherworldly, with a golden Ankh on his face—the arms and head of which were stationed above his eyes and the staff going down to the tip of his nose. Vincent would wear the makeup for a period lasting from the *Creatures of the Night* tour until the makeup came off for all of the members of KISS by the time of *Lick It Up*. Interestingly, fans have for years speculated what Mark St. John and Bruce Kulick would have worn if the band had continued with the makeup, showing that the fans never quite gave up on the idea even if the band did. As for Eric Singer and Tommy Thayer, they too would eventually wear makeup with the band, but their story is one for another chapter.

Surprisingly, for a band that had just washed off the greasepaint, there sure did seem to be a lot of makeup going on the faces of the four when it was time to go "naked" for the cameras and the stage shows. Actually, the band was a bit more restrained on television, but onstage, the harsh lighting of flash photography during shows brought out the heavy, caked makeup of the three men upfront. It was as if they had been dealing with clown white for so long that they had no concept of how to appear onstage without something covering their faces. Simmons and Stanley began to tone that down over the tour and into the next, although Simmons then had the misfortune to have to wear a wig to offset his short hair, which had been cut for the *Runaway* film he was making before the *Animalize* tour. This was held on by a headband, which may have kept it good and snug, but also was like a neon halo around his head saying, "Look at this wig!" On the positive side, it did give the band a head start (no pun intended) in looking into proper hairpieces for subsequent tours (although Simmons went overboard when it came to the *Asylum* tour, with enough frizzy hair on his head to give Eric Carr a run for "biggest hair" on that tour).

Makeup and hair stayed pretty tame for the next few years, but for the 1992 *Revenge* tour Simmons decided to go with a Van Dyke beard that would stay with him up until the 1996 Reunion tour announcement (and which he sometimes reverts to during periods where he is not needed in makeup). Simmons was not alone there, however, as all of the other members tried a little of the same during those years, but only he really stuck with the look for the entire period.

In 1996, the band returned to the stage in full makeup as they had from 1974 to 1980. Since then, there have been minor variations made to the makeup, especially when Eric Singer took over for Peter Criss and Tommy Thayer for Ace Frehley and needed to redesign the makeup for their faces. Nevertheless, after nearly four decades, the makeup personas have remained recognizably the same since they were cemented in place back in late 1973.

Costumes

After the Dolls look of early 1973, the band would jump around in a variety of flashy outfits before starting to settle into a unified look for all four members in the summer of 1973. Gene Simmons and Ace Frehley once again led the pack by finding black tops that fit their personas: Simmons with skull and crossbones on a T-shirt, and Frehley with a phoenixlike emblem on the front of a button-down shirt. Eventually this would change to T-shirts for all four that had their names or the band's logo sewed in sparkles on the front, but the band members would still shift back and forth with other outfits until signing up with Casablanca (and Frehley would still pull out the phoenix shirt on occasion for quite a while after that). Studs, black leather, and platform shoes were the motif of the outfits from the end of 1973 until 1979 and the *Dynasty* album.

The year 1974 was a time of continuous touring for two albums—the debut album and the follow-up, *Hotter Than Hell*, both released that same year—and thus costumes (as well as the staging) stayed the same through both albums. The main attention-grabber of Simmons's outfit was that of the batwings that connected between his arms and his torso so that they would flare out if he raised his arms (which he did often in order to show the wings off). While batlike in nature, it actually looked a bit like how Steve Ditko would drawl Spider-Man for Marvel Comics back in the 1960s with webbing under the arms (a comparison Simmons probably did not mind at all). He began wearing the batwings in late 1973 and would continue with variations throughout most of his time in costume over the years.

During this period, the wings were connected to a pair of leather horns on the back that rose up above his shoulders. He would fall back to the skull and crossbones for a time either on his chest or on the back of his outfit, but he also went with a laced-up leather shirt or one that had a studded opening in the front to show off his chest. The pants had openings on the side as well, while the boots went from standard platforms to ones that had a silver top in front above the knees.

Stanley's outfit also varied a tad during this period but stayed very much in the same mode through the year: a leather jacket draped over a shirtless chest, a studded collar, pants with a top that was studded in various designs and went up to the ribcage, and platform boots that would eventually have a star on the front of the shin area. Peter Criss's outfit was even simpler, with a black, studded, string vest over black studded pants with holes on the thighs—much like Simmons's—and a very low set of platform shoes that he would soon trade in for sneakers when on tour. Frehley had two unique outfits for the year—the only one of the four to really change costumes between the tours for the albums. One outfit had a series of lightning bolts that went around the torso and down the legs of his platform shoes, and another, seen on the *Hotter Than Hell* cover, was a diamond-shape shaped chest-piece that went over the shoulders and had a series of clock faces along the trim.

Blockbuster Music single for the *You Wanted the Best* live collection, which was titled after the famous phrase used to introduce the band in concert. *Author's Collection*

Frehley went back to the lightning bolts for 1975, which saw the band doing the *Dressed to Kill* and *Alive!* albums. In his case, the new outfit had a bolt that reached around the torso and then down the legs of his one-piece outfit. Two silver discs were on the shoulders of his costume, looking a bit silly, while he wore platform shoes that looked more like moon-issued sneakers. Criss's outfit for the tour was also a one-piece, with silver trim and holes on the side of the suit by the ribcage. A large cross around his neck would also become much more prominent—probably in reaction to the "KISS is satanic" movement that was gaining steam at the time (which hit him the hardest of the four members, but convinced the protestors that he was wearing it in mockery of the Christian faith—such is their way). Although his outfit had platforms with it, Criss continued to wear more traditional footwear in concert in order to play the drums. Stanley kept the studded collar he wore before (and made collars a traditional piece for many of his outfits before and after the makeup era), but now had a one-piece that bared his chest and had a series of stars all over. A pair of platform shoes with multiple stars completed the look. Simmons continued with the batwings, but now had a series of "spikes" (made of cloth) along the arms of the costume. The open-chest top met with a huge studded codpiece-belt combination and black studded pants. The platforms were black and had fangs painted on them. Both Frehley's and Simmons's outfits would return for the *World Domination* tour of 2003, although on that tour Stanley and Eric Singer would resort to the *Destroyer* outfits. Stanley and Singer would join them for the 2004 tour, *Rock the Nation*, although Singer's outfit was a more streamlined version of Criss's from that period. They would continue with these outfits until 2008 when the *Alive 35* tour would see them once again head back to the *Destroyer* outfits.

This brings us to *Destroyer*, with the new album artwork dictating what the costumes for the tour would look like. In Simmons's case, it was an advance on what came before, keeping the studded codpiece and batwings but adding armor on the chest, shoulders, and arms. He also added one of the most famous pieces of KISS costumes through the years—the dragon boots (platforms built up with silver scales and demonlike dragons on the tips of the boots, with red eyes). Stanley would wear a one-piece that again showed off his chest, with a series of small studs that covered the crotch and branched out over the rest of the costume. There was a long-sleeve variation of the outfit, as well as a black jacket with feathers for the lapel. Criss had an open-chest one-piece with rows of studs that arrowed down to the crotch on the front and came in a long-sleeve version as well. Finally, Frehley wore an outfit that seemed like a mishmash of his 1974 and 1975 costumes, with the shoulder pads now smashed down and folded over the shoulders, while the timepiece diamond had been slimmed down and the clocks removed when added to the shoulder pads. This was also the start of him wearing what fans refer to as "moonboots"—padded silver platform boots. All of these outfits returned for the *Psycho Circus* tour with some modifications due to age and other factors (Stanley's outfit no longer had a top and instead came with a removable jacket, for example). They would remain this way through the 2000 "Farewell" tour. As listed above, the outfits would then return for all four on the *Alive 35* tour of 2008 (which, as one could immediately see, were the wrong outfits for a tour celebrating the thirty-fifth anniversary of the *Alive!* album, but this is the point where even some fans feel complaining about it gets a bit too picky). The band continued with this for the *Sonic Boom* and *Hottest Band in the Land* tours in 2010, although Tommy Thayer was given a slightly revised outfit that had additional lightning bolts added to the chest-guard of his outfit.

Love Gun saw new costumes for a 1977 tour, with Frehley wearing a leotard, a silver padded vest over it, and a variation of his earlier moonboots. Criss still kept it simple with a string of silver and black padding, made to look like a couple of ammo belts, over the chest and black leotards with studs. It should be mentioned that he rarely wore the ammo belts other than for some photo sessions. He also had a couple of different vests with this and sometimes wore a black laced shirt underneath. Stanley had a stripped-studded vest with leotards showing stars down the thighs and two jackets—one with studs and the other with feathers on the label and wrists, and very similar to one used in the previous tour. Simmons seemed to go a step backwards with his outfit for the tour—no more armor and instead black leather with a series of studs that went from the shoulders down to the codpiece. The batwings stayed, along with the dragon platform shoes, although the "scales" of the previous costume were traded in for more silver studs and the heads modified a bit on the dragon faces. He also had a Dracula-style cape that he wore in some photo shoots as well as briefly in the *KISS Meets the Phantom of the Park* movie. The costumes for this tour would be used for the television movie in 1978 and would eventually pop back up for the 1996 Reunion tour.

After completion of the *Love Gun* tour, the band took a break from touring in order to concentrate on the television movie and the solo albums. When they came back for the *Dynasty* tour in 1979, the album cover did not show new costumes; nevertheless new ones were created—the most flamboyant of them all. Stanley's costume had elements from the past while also a lot of additions: a black, open-chest leotard with purple "feathers' in various places, as well as black platforms with more of the same. The really new piece was the stylized shirt that came with it in purple and silver with black gauntlets. The shirt had slits in the arms and was open at the chest as well, with a cape that featured large feathers like those on the pants and boots. Stanley usually abandoned the shirt and cape soon within the shows, although he wore them in the videos done for the album and its follow-up, *Unmasked.* In contrast, Criss kept to a black, open-chest, one-piece leotard with studs set in areas of swirls. The big addition to his outfit was the cape, which had green lion heads on the shoulders with puffs of green fur flowing down (green being Criss's color from the solo albums, just as Stanley's was purple). This too was used mainly in photo shoots and at the start of the shows and was quickly abandoned. Criss also wore green gauntlets, which he usually kept on for performances. The same was not true for Frehley, who typically ripped off his fractured-mirror gauntlets early on in shows along with the long silver cape he had with his new outfit. The blue gauntlets were part of a larger motif of the costume, with another chest-plate over his shoulder that featured even more of the mirrors all over (which is why fans commonly refer to it as the "fractured-mirror costume"). Armbands of the same material were included, and the chest-plate contained a center crystal that evidently could be lit up, although that was quickly abandoned in practice. The belt-codpiece was a series of puffy silver columns, giving the suit a superhero look as intended. Silver boots with more of the mirrors were the norm for the outfit as well. Just as Stanley's outfit was dramatic in appearance, so too was Simmons's, with a built-up outfit and boots (with crawls) that made him look like he was wearing dinosaur hide (hence the suit was commonly referred to as the "Godzilla costume"). A red cape usually went with this suit, although there are some pictures of Simmons wearing an alternate back-piece—that of a giant skeleton of a mutant spider, with a web draping off it. As it stands, it was the first costume to not feature the batwings as a standard.

Since the band only toured in North America for *Dynasty*, it was convenient for them to remain in those costumes for the 1980 *Unmasked* tour, as can be seen in the "Shandi" music video done for that album. However, Stanley would soon decide to go back to a variation of his *Love Gun* outfit with some purple added here and there. There was also the aspect of having Eric Carr join them in his new role as the Fox, and so a costume had to be created for him. With the failure of the Hawk costume for him, Carr had to pull together a costume himself, which was simply a variation of what Criss had before him—black leotards with studs around the edges, a studded belt with a fox head for the buckle and a red jacket draped with orange fox fur. It was not the perfect solution, but as a last-minute costume, people were satisfied with it.

Next came the 1981 album *Music from "The Elder,"* which all intended to be the launch of a new tour, but other events caused its cancellation. This was to be the new era of KISS—the serious KISS, the 1980s KISS. What we got in costumes looked like a group of waiters in an S&M bar. Carr had a black jumpsuit with multiple zippers for no practical reason other than to have zippers. Frehley had a black one-piece that had a silver lightning bolt going from the right shoulder down diagonally to the left leg and silver sneakers. Simmons had chain mail pants, a leather studded codpiece, a leather strap across his chest, shoulder pads, his hair in a ponytail and will be your waiter for this evening. Stanley wore a black two-piece pants and jacket with pirate boots and a purple bandana around his head, making him look like he wanted to conquer the seven seas after some aerobics. As can be guessed, many fans were not happy with the look, seeing it as just one more misstep along the way during *The Elder* period.

The following tour for *Creatures of the Night* in 1982–1983 saw the band heading back to styles that had worked before. Frehley appeared briefly for a

The Stanley-Simmons-Singer-Thayer version of KISS from 2005. *Author's Collection*

European promotional tour, wearing his Elder outfit, but after that it was some old and some new for the band members that made the tour. Stanley wore black studded pants and a short vest that was reminiscent of his *Love Gun* outfit; meanwhile, Simmons brought back his dragon boots from the earlier tours along with armor plating similar to that of the *Destroyer* day, while the rest was a slight variation of his *Elder* outfit. Carr's outfit was very much like his *Unmasked* one, with a few more studs, silver fur lining and without the jacket. New member Vinnie Vincent found himself doing with his costume just as he had with his makeup—playing off of it from the member he was replacing. In that regard, he wore a black long-sleeve, one-piece with a silver moon on it (at least it got him away from Frehley's lightning bolt) with a black studded vest on top. It was not flashy, but with Vincent coming in on the *Creatures* tour a tad incognito (at the beginning of the tour, KISS promised fans that Frehley might join the tour as well as remaining a full member of the band, so a big push for the "new guy" may have caused more problems than it helped at that point).

With the makeup coming off for *Lick It Up*, the costumes were discarded as well. No more "uniforms" for the guys in a traditional sense, although that did not stop them from sticking with certain outfits for each tour. Helping in the switchover was that black spandex would be a fashion rule for metal bands for most of the 1980s, so it was not like the band would suddenly switch to blue jeans and T-shirts after wearing leotards for so many years (even though Stanley is seen wearing blue jeans in the "Lick It Up" video, the first music video they did without makeup). Instead, the band could still keep black in their stagewear—especially Carr—with Carr and Stanley tending to go with the spandex (Carr did not completely leave the look behind until his final tour with the band), while Simmons flirted with the style for a time during the *Animalize* tour, but soon realized that outside of the Demon character it did not really work for him, especially when concert photos gave him the appearance of wearing a black saggy diaper that leaks, which along with the obvious wig made him a fashion nightmare onstage. Boots were common for Simmons and Vincent, while everyone else usually went with sneakers of one type or another. Stanley, Eric Carr, and Vincent also went with cut-off T-shirts (Stanley usually sticking with a KISS T-shirt from the tour). As mentioned in a later chapter, the *Animalize* tour also ushered in a brief period with a lot of bandanas, fur, and fringes that dates the period much more than when the band were wearing superhero outfits.

This changed a little for the *Asylum* tour in 1985–1986, with the costuming reflecting the neon, vaguely psychedelic colors of that album cover. Long jackets for the guys with heavy shoulder pads and sparkling, neonlike colors everywhere, along with a military styling to the jackets. The outfits underneath were similar in design and as much uniforms for the tour as costumes from the makeup years. Simmons's blousy outfit, along with huge hair and a bit too much makeup, led to his *Asylum* time being labeled his "Bea Arthur period" by fans, which he has acknowledged in more recent years as being an accurate description of what he looked like.

Crazy Nights found the guys getting a bit more relaxed. Simmons tended to stay with black leather and black T-shirts, but the look worked for him, and he would stop trying to fit in with the others and stick with what worked for him from this point on. Stanley began wearing blue jeans with multiple patches and tears in them, along with going back to T-shirts (again, sometimes those from the tour itself). Bruce Kulick would sometimes stay a little more traditional, but usually wore a T-shirt, with his BK shirt (actually shirts promoting the British Knights shoe company and not designed specifically for him) becoming even more of a standard around this time. Carr would also get a bit looser in look, wearing a T-shirt with an open button-down shirt on top of it at times, although he still went with spandex on several occasions.

Although Gene Simmons and Kulick continued to wear more traditional stagewear in the *Hot in the Shade* tour, both Eric Carr and Paul Stanley moved more toward typical streetwear in their outfits onstage. This would continue into the *Revenge* tour, with both Simmons and Bruce Kulick looking more casual but still sticking with a look to their clothing for the stage that Eric Singer and Stanley tended to not do as much. This would all wrap up with the 1995 KISS convention tour and *MTV Unplugged* taping, where the band was mainly down to jeans and shirts. Now they could simply step off the streets and head up onstage to perform after years of making so many costumes adjustments.

And then the following year they were back to being superheroes.

Staging

The early days of KISS could only be basic as the band members were struggling to eat, much less put together an impressive stage show. One of the first steps taken toward a bigger look was one Paul Stanley came up with of creating a series of fake Marshall cabinets to stack up on the stage to give the appearance of a lot of power behind the band even if the reality was that they were playing through cheap knockoffs of Marshall amps that, as Stanley put it later, "sounded like we were playing through cardboard boxes." There was also the problem that if the stage lighting was off, the audience could see right through the amps and realize they were fakes. Flashing lights for "Firehouse" were soon added to help move the show along, but otherwise it was not until Bill Aucoin signed the band in August and Casablanca signed them for an album that there was enough of a cash flow to allow for additional effects in the staging.

By the beginning of 1974, the band had their name in lights behind the stage, sometimes alternating between that and a spiderweb backdrop they had used since sometime in 1973. The empty Marshalls were slowly being replaced by the real things, while candelabras were added to the stage. (This would lead to a happy coincidence when a power failure occurred during the April 1974 appearance of KISS at the Columbus, Ohio, Agora, and the candles from the candelabra were passed out to audience members while waiting for power to return.) Simmons introduced his blood-spitting around this time, as

Paul Stanley making his way to the center of the arena via cable in July 2004.   *Courtesy of Ron Riddell*

well as his fire-spitting during "Firehouse" (setting his hair on fire during the first public attempt on New Year's Eve, 1973), while Stanley wore a fireman's helmet that he would sometimes toss into the crowd during the song (a standard bit that he would use for years). The first drum riser came in 1974 as well, which was chain driven and would sometimes skip a link while going up (not to mention causing problems for Peter Criss in clubs with lower ceilings). Criss also had a special pair of drumsticks that would shoot flares out over the audience, but two mishaps ended their use: Criss accidentally setting fire to Black Oak Arkansas' backdrop while on tour with them, and an incident in December 1974 where his roadie had to be rushed to the hospital after nearly blowing his hand off while working with the devices. As for Ace Frehley, he got the idea of a smoke bomb inside his guitar in February 1974 that ruined the guitar but led to a workable idea where smoke could be coming from the guitar without destroying the guitar in the process; this would be a big fan favorite through the years to come when Frehley did his solo (John Robison's best-selling autobiography *Look Me in the Eye* covers some aspects of his building the gimmick into the guitar and other work he did for KISS). Fireworks, flamethrowers, and flash pots were also added to the stage effects.

By 1975, the band was releasing their third album and working on new costumes for the *Dressed to Kill* tour, but could add little to their stage setup due to once again being short of funds. A confetti storm was a new thing for the shows, along with Stanley breaking guitars at the climax of each show (at first thanks to a deal with a guitar company for cheap guitars to destroy). Later, with a little more cash, the band was able to get a better drum riser system for Criss. Otherwise, the staging and effects stayed the same. The biggest addition was actually not visual but sonic, as the announcement, "You wanted the best and you got the best . . . the hottest band in the land, KISS!" was first uttered during the touring in 1975. It would be slightly modified from there, but otherwise would be the traditional opening for nearly every show since.

With the success of *Alive!* and the slowly rising power of *Destroyer* occurring in the spring of 1976, KISS was finally able to expand on their stage concepts with the tour called *The Spirit of '76*. Sean Delaney worked with designers to create the stage in five sections—the riser above and to the left and right of Peter Criss's drum riser with the "ancient cats statues" (the originals were stolen during the tour and had to be replaced), Ace Frehley's moonscape, Gene Simmons's ruined castle, and the front for microphones. The stage came with a pair of staircases, which were expanded on with the next stage as well as lead to near-disaster for Frehley during a show where faulty wiring gave him an electrical shock when grabbing the handrail of the stairs. The KISS logo had grown for the tour and was no longer a blanket of lights, but just the outline of the letters. A large tree appeared on Simmons's side of the stage, and large KISS Army banners hung around the stage to remind fans of the new official fan club for the band. At the beginning of the tour there was also a large Telsa coil that was created by Ken Strickfaden (who had done similar effects for movies such as the 1931 *Frankenstein*) and used to produce lightning-bolt effects in concert. However, the machinery was not only dangerous but weighed more than half a ton and was cost-prohibitive to use for any length of time. There was also some vague talk and even some storyboarding done of having a car crash into the stage during "Detroit Rock City," but again it was a logistical and financial nightmare to get beyond the drawing board. Most of the earlier effects and showstopping moments from the past remained or were expanded on—Frehley would not only make his guitar smoke but would then "blow it up" with another guitar during his solo, Simmons would stand within his castle as he spat blood, and Criss's drum riser would levitate, only this time with a banner unfolding underneath it to show symbolic cat figures with reflective eyes.

The *Destroyer* stage set continued to be used into the *Rock and Roll Over* tour, but slowly begin morphing into a new stage, losing all the showy bits and stage dressing—like the castle and the tree—to become a gleaming sea of metal, with the stairs set to light up (leading to Frehley's electrocution onstage in December 1976). The *Love Gun* stage, which was credited to Frehley at the time, finally replaced it in time for the 1977 North American summer tour with a longer and larger lit staircase, hydraulic scaffolding to the left and right of the stage for the members to use to travel down to the stage floor at the beginning of the show and two hydraulic platforms—commonly referred to as the cherry-pickers—at the front of the stage to lift Simmons, Stanley, and Frehley up and over the crowd for the finale of the shows. The drum riser still went up into the air, but this time it also moved forward toward the audience—something that would return in the 1980s and beyond, but in a more spectacular manner. One last touch was Sam the Serpent over on Simmons's side, a snakelike creature wrapped around a large pole that could blow out smoke (and can be seen being picked up as a weapon—well, kinda—during the final fight scene in *KISS Meets the Phantom,* also featuring the *Love Gun* stage).

KISS took a break after a Japanese tour in April 1978 and did not return until June 1979 for a tour to promote *Dynasty.* The main objective of the new stage for the tour was to allow fans in any seat to get a clear line of the stage; thus, there was no real "back" to the stage, with four ramps placed around the drum riser to allow the band to move around as much as possible. Frehley would add his neon-lit guitar, which fluctuated in a number of patterns as he played, along with another variation of his smoking guitar/shooting guitar bit from the previous tours (although this time the smoking guitar was usually taken up into the air for him to shoot flares at from his other guitar). Simmons also got into the air for the first time with this tour—flying up to a spot among the lighting to sing "God of Thunder." The drums once again came forward, but this time also swiveled to the left and right—getting closer to something that would be used in an upcoming tour. The riser rose as well, but this time with a single cat image on the banner instead of two. A few other things were suggested for the tour, but most were just too complicated to be functional; many dealt with lasers of one type or another, such as a laser curtain and a stunt where Stanley would shoot a laser from his eye like in the KISS movie (which no doubt the band was hoping fans would forget about by that point). The laser-eye was completed and tested, but Stanley declined to wear it even with pressure from Aucoin about the expense of the device.

A smaller version of the stage was used in 1980 for the *Unmasked* tour, with some minor changes to the show (the banner under the drums was now a series of painted flames instead of a cat, since Criss was no longer in the band). As the *Dynasty* tour had not gone to Europe anyway, it made sense to conserve and use a variation of the same stage for the next tour. Besides, plans for the one to come were going to be the most expansive since the *Destroyer* days.

Music from "The Elder" came out in November 1981, with a three-month tour planned to begin in December of that year. When estimates ran to a $200,000 loss for a successful tour—at a time where the band and its management knew they were dealing with a declining fan base—everyone went back to the drawing board to come up with something for a tour to start in July 1982. The revised estimate from February 1982 looked to be set to make a profit for the band, including a weekly salary for a possible Ace Frehley replacement (as they already had a good idea he was not going to be around after the event that occurred at Studio 54; see Chapter 20 for details). But it became clearer in early 1982 that the album had been both a commercial and critical flop (contrary to popular belief among fans, most critics did not take to the album and thought it was the worst thing KISS could do—try to be taken seriously). Logic showed that there was no reason to attempt a tour for an album that was dead in the water, and so plans were to head back to the studio for a new album instead.

The Elder tour ideas are sketchy, although a number of drawings made by Gene Simmons have circulated in fandom. So many ideas were tossed around—from a giant mock-up of the door from the album cover as a backdrop, to a pyramid on stage, to a lighthouse, a mock-up to make the stage look like a spaceship, a glowing orb for the band to see bits of a story for the production (making the show more of a musical than a rock concert), to even a rocket guitar for Frehley to hold on to and fly around the arena. It was all over the place, but two ideas stood out for possible future use—huge inflatable replicas of the band members to appear by the stage (an idea revived for the Reunion tour in 1996) and the drums being set on a riser that would resemble a tank.

The tank idea was incorporated into the next tour, for *Creatures of the Night*, and with songs like "I Love It Loud" and "War Machine" being performed, the tank motif (which was included on some of the official T-shirts sold on the tour) made perfect sense. In fact, the whole stage would be the tank, with the gun being set on the front of the drums, and when it advanced and swiveled during the show, it would eventually aim at the cabinets above the stage and "shoot" them out so that confetti would rain down on the audience below. Besides this addition, a sequence at the beginning of the show that allowed the band to rise up on the stage (a trick that was usually spoiled by the flashes of cameras, unfortunately), and the elimination of Frehley's tricks (as Vinnie Vincent was now in the band), the shows were similar to the tour before that. And the one before that. And the one before that. Ticket sales were staggered because, although there were few changes, they were not enough to drive the remaining fans back to see them again.

The removal of the makeup for 1983's *Lick It Up* album certainly did shake things up for the band and fans, but KISS was not in a position to pour money into a new stage. Instead—knowing that the *Creatures* tour had been limited in sales, they kept with the tank stage from the previous tour without many qualms from anyone coming to the shows. Most of the pyro and special effects for the tank stayed, as well as Simmons's spitting fire. One thing he did drop was the spitting up of blood, however. Rumors have abounded for years that he did attempt this in their very first show without makeup, but the effect was termed a failure without the Demon character being there—he just looked like he was deathly sick instead of sinister. Yet this has never been verified beyond hearsay, as there has never been any photographic proof of it, and it could be a case of people misremembering. If anything, Simmons probably tested the look in a dress rehearsal and decided to can it.

Animalize saw a redress of the stage, literally, with animal skin décor covering everything including the stage floor (which was a re-creation of the album cover). The drums stayed where they were for the first time in many years, neither rising nor moving around, and steel ramps were added around the stage for the rest to run around on if wanted (although Bruce Kulick seemed the only one to bother with it for the most part and usually just to say something to Eric Carr). The band would arrive on a rising platform behind the drums, and the finale of the show saw Simmons, Kulick, and Stanley run up to a catwalk among the lighting and onto a platform that would then lower them to the stage (hence, instead of the drums going up, the guitarist came down for the finale). A variation of this—with the drums being lowered as well—returned for the band's Farewell Tour of 1999–2000.

The stairs used had small balconies on stage left and right for the band members to use that hung over the audience and allowed fans in typically distant seating on the sides to getting a better look at the guys. This was the tour where Paul Stanley began doing a stunt where he would swing out over the stage near the end of the show from a trapeze, but this was not used at all of the shows (although it does pop up in the music video for "Rock Hard" from the *Smashes, Thrashes, and Hits* album).

Asylum featured a stage similar to the one before it, with the main advancement being that of a gigantic KISS logo behind the drums that was large enough for traditional stage lights to be used within the logo to light it up along with bulbs for the borders of each letter. Balconies on stage left and right remained, but the only way to get to them was by running up very steep yellow ramps—referred to by the band as bananas, although they were supposed to look like lightning bolts—at enough speed to get to the top or else not make it. Eric Carr once ran up one during an encore, tripped, and smashed his face into the ramp, much to the amusement of the rest of the band and fans nearby.

Simmons would bring back one of Ace Frehley's old tricks on the tour—the rocket-firing guitar for his solo, which was timed with fake speaker cabinets above the stage exploding (a gag that Frehley would revive in the Reunion tour). Another returning effect was that of Carr's drums moving forward during his solo.

Even though *Asylum* was a bit stripped down, it was nothing compared to the *Crazy Nights* stage, which had one huge ramp that circled the drums and was so steep that the band members rarely used it. It was built so that at the end of the show there would be a series of fireworks that would "blow up" the ramp in a couple of places, but they never worked right and were finally abandoned. The huge KISS logo returned from the previous tour, but that was all, and by the time KISS were to tour Japan, the decision was made to forego trying to bring such a blank stage to another country (hence the Japanese television special showing the band playing on a smaller stage lined with speakers).

The next stage, for *Hot in the Shade*, seemed to be in retaliation for such a dismal one from the tour before, with a forty-foot sphinx—nicknamed Leon— that would light up and open its mouth on cue to display a series of lasers inside. While this was impressive, a return to a smaller KISS logo was less successful. The logo was to rise above the stage near the end of the show, but a revised logo did not look right—the K was the wrong shape—and an earlier one brought back for use could not be raised properly and tended to appear lopsided when it did appear—hardly the look the band wanted there. Meanwhile, Leon was considered a big enough success to reappear in 1994 when the band did a small number of shows that year.

Tommy Thayer in his "Space Ace" costume on the 2004 touring stage.   *Courtesy of Ron Riddell*

Revenge was next and, working off the Sphinx, the new tour featured a stage showing a replica of the top quarter of the Statue of Liberty. The stage in front of this was metal and speakers, with some at odd angles and sections of the stage meant to look like a postapocalyptic New York. The show ended with the Statue of Liberty crumbling away to show a metal skull inside the face and the arm holding the torch now reduced to the hand giving "the finger." The objective was, no doubt, to be patriotic, by showing America can give others the finger . . . but in reality it offended a good number of fans who thought KISS was directing that message to the audience (especially when the band members directed the audience's attention to the hand at the end of the show by pointing at it proudly and then leaving the stage). Local strippers were brought up onstage for the song "Take It Off," the first time that anyone other than the band would be used onstage during a tour as part of the shows. Finally, a huge banner dropped down behind the "angry" Statue of Liberty with the KISS logo to close out the show.

The next few years were a jumble of one-off shows here and there, and then the 1995 KISS convention tour that found the band performing interactive "unplugged" shows with the audience, which required little staging beyond some amps, microphones, and instruments. Things would certainly pep up with the 1996 tour, however, as this was the Reunion tour with the original four and a chance to show off many of the old favorites in special effects and such for the audience attending. Surprisingly, the stage was rather flat and unengaging, with a wall of screens for live video footage of the band to appear above the drums and rows of speakers on both sides of the drums as well. The stage did featured cherry-pickers for the guitarist to ride at the end of the show, as Criss's drum riser went up like the old days. Meanwhile, Simmons began flying once again, while Frehley had the rockets go off on his guitar as well as the smoking guitar. Stanley started swinging out over the audience to a small stage in the center of the arenas during the last leg of the tour (given the name of the "Lost Cities" tour, as they were cities the band did not play the first time around for the 1996 tour). The tour featured giant inflatables of the band members, which were supposed to appear at the end of the shows by the stage but commonly were placed outside and only if the weather was good. Even so, it was not unusual to see these dominating balloons slowly being drained of air and hanging limp by the time the audience was leaving the arenas.

The stage was again minimal for the 1998 *Psycho Circus* tour, but additional effects were added. The biggest was the one the band promoted with their music video and the album cover as well—that the tour would be in 3-D, mean-

The look of the band from the time of the 2009 tour.
Author's Collection

ing that people could watch effects on the huge screen over the stage and see 3-D images leaping out at them. This meant that audience members got cardboard 3-D glasses as they came into the arenas (some latecomers missed out) and would put them on at the beginning of the shows, only to find that the 3-D effects were limited in variety (typically the same bits over and over again of computer animation and stuff from the "Psycho Circus" video), in how often they appeared, and in the vantage points where the effects even worked in the arenas. Peter Criss once commented that he would be watching the audience looking confused as they pulled the glasses off and on throughout the shows— but one has to give the band credit for even trying.

Initially, the tour was also to play off an old idea of

Gene Simmons's (just as the giant inflatables had been one he had in mind going back to *The Elder*)—that of "KISS World." The concept went back to the *Dynasty* days where he envisioned the band having huge festivals outside of the arenas and stadiums where they were to play; a place where families could come to play carnival games, take in rides, and see circus performers and bands play before the show; essentially turning a KISS concert into a whole-day event. This was looked into for the new tour, with the idea that the band would have circus performers do their act before the show while music was performed. This was attempted for the Halloween show done at Dodger Stadium in 1998—of which bits can be seen on the Fox Network when promoting the tour—but it was abandoned after this due to the cost involved to transport the performers, their equipment, the staging space needed for them, and the amount of insurance it would take to cover the risk of stunts done during their portion of the show. An attempt by the circus performers to become co-headliners was the final nail in the coffin on the idea, and it was abandoned.

The drums this time would rise up and out, going over the first couple of rows of the audience before returning while Criss did his solo. Simmons, Frehley, and Stanley did their usual things in the show, while an attempt to have risers that lifted the guitarists (like a variation of the cherry-pickers) was only used twice. A giant curtain like that on the cover of the *Psycho Circus* album would fall to open the show.

The platforms for the guitarists finally came into use during the Farewell tour of 1999–2000. Other elements stayed the same as before, while the afore-mentioned platforms from the ceiling brought the band down to the stage as it did for the guitarists during the *Animalize* tour. It was to be a sign of what was to come, as the band from this point on would continue with the same type of staging they had used since the beginning of the Reunion tour in 1996 and go back and forth on effects from previous tours to entertain the crowd. There would be a familiarity to the staging even after the band released a new album in 2009, but it seems it was what the audience wanted. In some ways, the shows had finally reached a level of that of famous magicians, where the audience demands to see certain tricks unique to the performer no matter how many times they have seen them before, thus not allowing the artist to try anything new. KISS, like those other performers, are giving the audience exactly what they want, but in the process have perhaps boxed themselves into a corner where they can no longer be the innovators of old and have to toe a "company line" dictated to them by the fans.

But as long as the audience keeps asking for it, who can blame KISS for giving it to them?

7

KISS Is Still KISS

Ten Commonly Perceived Turning Points for KISS

One easy conversation for fans to break into when meeting up is discussing where and when there have been career-changing moments for KISS. Some were moments that saw the band rise to superstardom; others where they slipped and fell; and then the events that helped KISS rise once again from the ashes and prove how hard it was to kill them off. Some seemed immediate, while others needed time to percolate before blowing.

The ten situations listed below are perceived by many as major turning points for KISS over the years. In some cases, perhaps the common notions of what occurred are not the reality; for others, the effects felt were in a variety of ways instead of just one. Yet all in some way did help steer the band in certain career directions, whether for good or bad.

"Beth" was the Moment When KISS Became Successful

This one is very popular among people who are not very familiar with the band's history in the 1970s. Then again, it was a popular view of the general public back in 1976 when "Beth" first became a hit as well. The perception of such commentators is that KISS was this goofy band playing so-so hard-rock music who stumbled upon a ballad that got them noted by people who would not normally listen to KISS and made them more popular than ever. There is some truth to that, but there is more to the picture than simply a case of one song turning the tide for KISS.

KISS had struggled to find an audience with their first three studio albums, but—contrary to what some may think—the band was definitely building an audience over the first two years of albums. KISS manager Bill Aucoin has often stated that the first album sold (with some shifting figures depending on his mood) 40,000 copies; the second twice that and the third nearly twice again. Sales were moving upward—Atlantic was offering the band a serious contract to leave Casablanca after *Hotter Than Hell* was released because sales were obviously getting larger. Then it was decided to do the live album in 1975 because a) it was cheaper than doing a new studio album, and b) it was recognized that more people were showing up to see the band live than buying their albums. When

Alive! hit three million in a short amount of time, it was obvious that KISS had broken through.

The problem was the "sophomore slump." This is where someone produces an album that everyone clamors for and then the performer has to go back into the studio and create a new album that shows the first was not a fluke. True, *Alive!* was not their first album, but it was their biggest, and it was also a collection of songs from the earlier albums. In a sense, to many at the time, *Alive!* was the band's first album. So the follow-up had to prove that there was something there to keep the listeners coming back for more.

The perception was that "Rock and Roll All Nite" had turned the trick for the band and that—as discussed in an earlier chapter—they needed to concentrate on anthems like that one in order to keep people coming back. This explains why *Destroyer* had three singles released in a row that were the anthems from the album: "Shout It Out Loud," "Flaming Youth," and "Detroit Rock City." Repeat an earlier success was the agenda, and it was not a bad idea—"Shout It Out Loud" reached #31 on the charts and helped get the album selling well. Yet "Flaming Youth" did not chart as radio stations were simply not that interested in playing it or "Detroit Rock City." But some stations were getting favorable response from the flip side of "Detroit Rock City," which was "Beth."

This brings up another misconception of the time. For some reason everyone who worked on the album has flipped back and forth from loving the song and demanding it be on the album to hating it and wanting it off the record. The only ones who seemed to favor the song being on the album and have never changed their opinion about it have been Gene Simmons and Peter Criss. Everyone else goes back and forth, saying it was their doing that made the song a success (Simmons is guilty of this as well, suggesting he convinced Criss to change the song from "Beck" to "Beth," while producer Bob Ezrin has claimed the same), or that they fought to keep it off the album.

It was, however, the band's first serious ballad, which is why there was concern about even including it." "Goin' Blind," from the earlier *Hotter Than Hell* album, has the heart of a ballad, but the lyrics pay off as a twisted fairy-tale for laughs more than an attempt to emotionally connect with the listener." "Beth" had a core topic that many could deal with because it was about work having to take priority over home life and love. Because of those lyrics—which were namely the work of Criss and Stan Penridge, as previous recordings prove out, no matter what anyone says—the song connected in a way that went beyond the anthems being hyped. The orchestration certainly moves the song along as well, but an electric version probably would have worked just as easily, perhaps even more so. Yet Ezrin was a master at taking an artist who was known for savage imagery (his work with Alice Cooper was already legendary at the time) and wringing out material that showed a softer side. Furthermore, he had shown he could do this, make them hits, and not affect the darker aspects of the character-driven performer he was working with (as proven by his success with "Only Women Bleed"—reaching #12 on the *Billboard* charts—for Alice

Japanese single from 1979 that turns back the clock to have "Detroit
Rock City" dominate as the A-side over "Beth."

Author's Collection

Cooper on *Welcome to My Nightmare* the year previous)." "Beth" was simply the
same for KISS.

Nor is it necessarily true that the record label wanted to bury it. True, it came
out as a B-side in the U.S., but "Beth" was already released as an A-side in the UK
three weeks before that, which hardly seems the way to "kill" the track in order
to prove it was not a good song.

But was it something that really broke the band? As already stated, KISS was
selling millions of copies of albums before *Destroyer*. The point had already been
made. What "Beth" did do is help push *Destroyer* into another league where they
were getting crossover play on other radio stations than the ones that played
them before then. It also got them media attention, from the *People's Choice
Award* to the *Paul Lynde Halloween Special*. It further got listeners thinking the
band could do more than a group of hard-rock songs for teenagers and perhaps
could do something "more serious." Most importantly, what it did was solidify
KISS as a player in rock music and not just a temporary success (even when
critics at the time were predicting that *Destroyer* would lead to the band being
exactly that) when it helped keep *Destroyer* on the charts for months after it was
starting to dwindle in sales in the summer of 1976.

But perhaps the most influential thing that "Beth" did was to convince the band to put ballads on their albums (as a side note, Alice Cooper would also follow this line of thinking after "Only Women Bleed" did well for him). Ironically, the word has always been that Paul Stanley was the most vocal about not putting "Beth" on the album, yet he has since done many of the ballads that have appeared on the albums after *Destroyer*—and some of their biggest hits besides "Beth" ("Hard Luck Woman," "Shandi," "Forever," and many others)— while Peter Criss concentrated more on rock 'n' rollers for his tracks. It also moved the band into allowing for more pop influences as well as an ability to experiment on their albums (although this perhaps had more to do with Ezrin's willingness to experiment through the *Destroyer* album). Thus, fans got disco on *Dynasty* ("I Was Made for Lovin' You"), ballads on the subsequent albums, right up to the conceptual album, *Music from "The Elder."* In other words, the very music that some fans objected to in the late 1970s and early 1980s from the band.

Thus, although "Beth" did not break the band open, one could say that it did lead to things that eventually would disturb the waters for fans' dedication to the band.

KISS Became a Kiddie Band

When KISS came on to the scene in 1974, there was really no reason to see the band as anything other than a hard-rock act that just happened to wear makeup. After all, as reported in a previous chapter, other bands were doing the same type of thing, so costumes and makeup was not an automatic sign of "we're happy clowns playing music for your children," as some people later in the decade and beyond would see them. In fact, the band was quick in trying to push the menace of their personas—for example, in the infamous Fin Costello photo session of them surrounding a woman with whips and other sadomasoch-istic devices in those early days, and the notorious "party" pictures taken for the *Hotter Than Hell* album cover (discussed more in Chapter 10). Nor were the lyrics tame in the early albums, with explicit sexual references made in a number of them—perhaps hidden but still there.

Yet things begin to change in 1975 with the Cadillac, Michigan, event. This was where the band got involved with a high school's homecoming and performed a show in the gymnasium after the football team used KISS music to motivate its players the previous season. Ironically, Fin Costello was there to take photos of the band parading around (literally) with the high school band and the football team, getting awards from the city council and happily blending in with a typical middle-class American town. It was a great photo-op for the band at a time when they needed it (*Alive!* had only recently been released, so they were still struggling for any publicity they could get), but it thrust them into the area of being "sweet" and wholesome, which had never been part of their identities before.

Destroyer with its superheroic album cover and the household popularity of "Beth," along with the emerging television appearances on stuff like *Paul Lynde*, which was directed at kids, helped with the image makeover as well. Tie in the merchandise over the next few years of Halloween costumes, lunch boxes, bubblegum cards, and action figures, and it was clear that the band was trying to attract a younger audience. By the time of *Dynasty*, there were even thoughts of things like "KISS World," which would be a "fun for the whole family" daylong activity. A look at the audience for *Creatures* showed that the trend continued, with families attending, even as Paul Stanley began to swear during the shows (something he kept to a bare minimum in the earlier days of the band, even when they were supposed to be hooligans).

Yet the music did not change. Even as kids were begging to stay up long enough to watch the KISS movie in 1978, the band was churning out material like "Love Gun," "Plaster Caster," and "Sweet Pain." Perhaps the parents were so taken in by the cartoon nature of some of the stuff being done that they never paid attention to the lyrics or the act in general. Admittedly, KISS did clean up their act to attract the kids, but in other ways the product being presented was still adult in nature (well, as adult as you can be when singing about women wanting "rocket rides").

The band never truly fell into becoming tagged as a kiddie band, but that was not for lack of trying at times. And while a bulk of that trade-off happened around 1978, the beginnings of the transformation could be seen as early as those days in Cadillac, Michigan, in October 1975. The most interesting aspect of the shift is that the band could never washed it away, even after the makeup came off and the songs supposedly got "harder."

The 1978 Solo Albums

The popular notions about the 1978 solo albums—where each band members recorded a full-length album of their own, and all four were released at the same time in September 1978—is that it was forced on certain members of the band and the record company as threats by other members. That is the polite way of putting it—the typical rumor was that everyone bent over backward to do the albums because Ace Frehley and Peter Criss threatened to quit unless they got to do them. With that type of talk common, it is easy to see why most fans see the solo albums as a signpost that the band was ready to split up long before Criss left in 1980.

While there may be some elements of truth to these statements, they stand as broad generalizations of what happened. An important thing most fans don't realize is that Casablanca was already thinking about solo albums from the band members back in 1976, as a contract signed by the band commencing January 1, 1977, made several specific references to solo albums: how each would be incorporated into the total number of albums required by the group contract, how royalties would work for such albums, and, most interesting of all, how

Casablanca could request individual members of KISS to record them. Not demand, but request, with the members being able to say no without repercussions. More importantly, nothing in the contract said the members could demand to record a solo album.

The assumption is that this all came about because the success of "Beth" drove Criss to want to go solo, but the song would not hit gold in the U.S. until January 1977, and Criss has reported in other sources that it was Christmas 1976 before he found out that the song had helped push *Destroyer* back up the charts. It should also be remembered that *Destroyer* was considered a failure by a good segment of fans at the time who thought the band was trying to be "too" experimental (one reason the band recorded the "almost-live" *Rock and Roll Over* in the summer of 1976 was as proof to the fans that they had not been deserted). Thus, there is no indication that any of the band members—especially Criss— were in a position to request solo albums at the time of the 1977 contract. Yet the contract clearly shows that someone had the idea of seeking solo albums from the members, and with Casablanca indicating they could "push the button" on such projects, it appears to be the label itself that was looking at doing it.

True, it was not completely unusual for some bands to have solo albums occur from members still with the band; for example, Todd Rundgren went back and forth with his band Utopia during the period and the members of the Who would do solo albums. Therefore, it is possible that Casablanca was just covering itself with the solo album provisions in case one member decided to do one outside of the company. But the same contract makes clear the band members were under restrictions if they did such a thing anyway (albeit mainly if they did so based on material recorded for Casablanca, but no doubt in any such situation the label would have looked upon it as a possible breach of contract). Thus, we still fall back to the idea that Casablanca was thinking ahead to solo albums.

While some of the people at Casablanca looked at the solo albums as a big mistake, there was a momentum to see the simultaneous release of the four solo albums as a major "first" for the band and the label, which could be capitalized upon. Nor was there any sense of either the band members or the label being forced into a corner to work on the albums. Although it was June 1978 when Casablanca officially announced the albums could be recorded, there had been rumblings of such a project in interviews with Aucoin, Casablanca, and KISS since 1977. In fact, both Neil Bogart and Bill Aucoin were telling the press and others in a joint conference about Casablanca Records in May 1977 that the band planned to do solo albums, so it was already in the works nearly a year before the band members would begin recording basic tracks for them. Further, for a project that supposedly demanded by Peter Criss and Ace Frehley, it was Gene Simmons and Paul Stanley who had already finished recording most of their basic tracks for their solo albums back in March and April that year, before they had gotten the official go-ahead in June. Frehley had a chunk done by then, so he was safe. Criss, however, was the furthest away from finishing, having only four basic tracks ready and still recovering too much from injuries received in a car accident to do a lot of work on his album (which led to his use of material written by Stan Penridge, as covered in Chapter 7). Some would say it was just the nature of Frehley and Criss to fall behind, but it does make clear that Simmons and Stanley were quick to jump on the bandwagon when it appeared the idea was going to come to fruition—especially for a project that, as per the contract, could have been ignored by any member who so wished. Further, Simmons saw his chance to make the project very personal, with a long checklist of "guests" appearing (or hoping would appear) on his album as well as going through the trouble of getting Disney's "When You Wish Upon a Star" for the record. In fact, it is probably one of two albums he has done that he has poured his emotions into—the other being *Music from "The Elder"*—so harsh reactions to it from fans and the critics no doubt burned a bit. As stated before, none of them had to do a solo album per the contract, but there was obviously the stigma of not having done so when the opportunity arose that kept them going (not to mention that if one were presented with such an opportunity anyway, it would be prudent to jump on it as soon as possible).

The other side of this coin is how it affected the band after the albums were released. To be fair, it was natural for all four to want vindication through better critical reaction and sales over the others. According to *Cash Box*, Frehley's album did the best, peaking at #25, with Simmons next at #30, Stanley third at #47, and Criss in last at #59. Frehley also stayed on their chart the longest of the four at 24 weeks. *Billboard* reported slightly differently, with Simmons reaching the highest at #22, Frehley at #26, Stanley at #40, and Criss at #43, although once again Frehley stayed on the chart the longest of the four at 23 weeks. He was helped with a strong single, "New York Groove" (written by Russ Ballard), which reached #13 on the charts and was the only single of the four released from the albums to do so (although Simmons's "Radioactive" got a lot of airplay and came close to charting, while Stanley's "Hold Me, Touch Me" nearly did so as well). Critical reception was also the most favorable about Frehley's work, while not being as strong on Criss's or Stanley's and typically looking unfavorably on Simmons's (although this may have been more due to critics wanting to find fault with the man many saw as the band's "spokesperson" than to what was actually on the album). Hence, if anyone were to come out of the project demanding more freedom on the albums, it would have been Frehley, while Criss would have been pushed back a step or two. (Fans could and have also fallen into the argument that if Simmons or Stanley had charted over Frehley, they may have a different attitude about the albums in hindsight these days, but that is strictly a fan argument over a "what if" scenario at best.)

Of course, there was the obvious problem of how Casablanca pushed the albums. It would have been logical to limit production and shipping of them based on the popularity of each members (Mego would do this with the KISS poseable action figures released in this time period, shipping fewer of Criss than Simmons because they knew they would sell more of the latter, so doing so was not some way-out idea, it was the norm for the entertainment business).

Instead, the thinking pretty much amounted to "if we can sell a million of a new KISS album, then we'll sell a million of each solo album by KISS!" Of course, this did not take into account either the popularity of certain members or even the financial burden on kids, teenagers, and even adults running out and buying four albums together at retail prices. In the end, all four sold well, but nothing like the "dream" Casablanca wanted. Further, when the returns finally moved on to the record stores' cut-out bins (so named as albums discontinued by the label would have a corner cut out of the record cover), it seemed that there were plenty of these cutouts gathering dust in the bins for years, so it was natural for the public to see the albums as a flop. Yet there was never the reaction from the public that because the solo albums did not "succeed" that it was the end of the band. Doing the albums in the first place left more of a lingering feeling among the fans and public that the band would break up, and their status as "failures" instead created more of a feeling that "these guys need each other" rather than "these guys are going to break up."

Internally, it did cause some friction. Although all four members were considered equal partners in doing things, Criss and Frehley usually left many decisions in the hands of Simmons and Stanley. Frehley's success with his solo album and Criss's newfound freedom in pursuing his own project caused problems upon returning with the others to work on the next album. Now all four had their own agendas with the next album, as well as finding more to say about the production. In some ways, the solo albums made them grow up a bit. Perhaps faster than if they had tanked the project and done another group album instead. But eventually those feelings were going to come to the fore one way or another. That said, the band was already in disharmony even before they got back together for *Dynasty* in 1979, so the solo albums merely added another ingredient to the arguments between them.

Simmons, Stanley, and others have pressed the idea that the solo albums were the linchpin to the band breaking up within the next two years. This is similar to how some say that the television movie broke up the band, or that *Dynasty* broke up the band. It simplifies a big issue by saying "this was the cause." In doing so, it denies the fact that all these factors and many others led to Criss and Frehley going, plus it tends to "punish" the solo albums as being wrong, which belittles some of the excellent music that all four did on them. The albums are also vivid signposts of the four's future and past: Criss's album comes from his earlier involvement in Chelsea and Lips and will represent things he'll be doing for a time in the 1980s with Stan Penridge. Stanley's is a straight commercial album that probably would have had more hits if it hadn't been from "that KISS guy." Simmons's is probably his most personal album out of anything done through the years. And Frehley's is an excellent starting point for what he would do on his own in the next decade and beyond. They may not have been the best albums the band ever did, but there is certainly no shame in what came out of this attempt to do something different, no matter who tries to color it that way.

The Original Band Breaking Up Was the Fall from Grace

Even Peter Criss has stated that he was the "complainer" of the group going back to 1973 when they had no choice but to play little rundown clubs. He was thought of lacking control in his singing voice, impulsive, ready to pick fights, and constantly threatening to quit the band for slights real and imagined. Members of bands before and after KISS have stated that they have seen a similar pattern from him. That said, he was an innovative drummer, dedicated to KISS through the years (maybe not to Simmons and Stanley, but certainly to what they did together as a band), and someone who could bring emotional depths to songs like no one else in KISS.

Things had been brewing for a while between Criss and the others. He had been happy to see "Beth" be the band's biggest hit at the time, but he respected the idea that they would work as a collaborative team when putting together albums and tours. Even so, he felt he would get more of a say as to what got on the albums after such a success for them. That did not happen. Instead, his songs were left at only one an album, no matter how many demos he brought in, and songs were being rejected for reasons that seemed questionable (a song called "Love Bites" was dropped from *Rock and Roll Over* because—according to cowriter Stan Penridge—Stanley and Simmons thought "it was too raunchy" for KISS fans). The solo album in 1978 had given him a chance to try something on his own, but due to other complications, it turned out different than he had hoped. Then he fought for his solo album producer, Vini Poncia, for *Dynasty*, only for Criss to feel that Poncia agreed too often with Stanley and Simmons, betraying him. The biggest threat to his role in the band, however, was that he found himself drifting from Frehley, who was being seen in a new light thanks to his solo album success and was given more of a say on some aspects of the band. Typically, the two had always been able to work as a block against Simmons and Stanley when voting on things, but now Criss found that he was on his own more often than not. He was also still recovering from injuries—at least this was the reported story—and the others decided to bring in drummer Anton Fig to record his parts, leaving him even further adrift from his own band.

The *Dynasty* tour was a sour experience—the band found that they had to cut back due to slowing ticket sales, and it was leaking over into their performances and attitudes. One show saw Simmons and Criss getting into a fight backstage, with Criss ready to attack Simmons with a broken bottle by the time they were separated. There was one show where Criss began slowing down his drums in what was seen as an intentional protest, creating more fighting backstage. By the time the tour was near its end, he had already told the others that he planned to quit. In response, everyone else was fine in seeing him go.

The band did want to keep the news of Criss's departure low-key, even if everyone was feeling better now that the shoe had dropped. The reasoning was simple—fans had been wondering if the band would be breaking up ever since the solo albums were first announced. Slowing ticket sales coincided with slowing album sales, and although "I Was Made for Lovin' You" did well on the charts and the album made the top ten, there were still concerns for the future. Concerns were legit: PolyGram was pushing hard on Neil Bogart and the running of Casablanca Records, finally buying Bogart out in February 1980 and looking to start cutting corners. The last thing KISS needed was to look like there was panic within the group and give the label a reason to start eyeing them as an expense no longer needed.

So, Criss agreed to play along with the idea that he was still with the group as *Unmasked* was recorded (with Anton Fig playing for him again) and a music video done for "Shandi," but after that he was out and happy to be so. His journey after that is covered in Chapter 29, but for KISS there were ramifications to consider as to how fans would feel about a replacement for him.

The band did an effective job in introducing Eric Carr as Criss's replacement in 1980: getting national television time to promote him, showing support from Criss in Carr replacing him, and getting publicity for a concert at the Palladium in July 1980 that introduced the revised band to the press and public. The problem was that the coverage was limited in the U.S. So, the band went on tour in Europe and Australia for the *Unmasked* album, leaving the U.S. behind. In an age before international news and the Internet, what this meant was that the band had disappeared after the release of the new album in the U.S. With weaker sales than expected, the assumption by the American public was that KISS was gone for good; for the fans in America that still cared, there was concern that the band was in deep trouble.

Then came *Music from "The Elder."* The objective was understandable—KISS needed to go in a bold new direction in order to entice listeners and get them back into the arenas to see the band perform. Perhaps even finally get that chance to branch out into the area of theatrical movies, which had been dead in the water after the television movie in 1978. Gene had a general outline for a movie, and from it came the idea that the band could write a series of songs based on the movie's plot. KISS got Bob Ezrin involved, which made sense— Ezrin had worked on previous "concept albums" for other artists and had just had a huge success working on *The Wall* for Pink Floyd. With Ezrin involved, the band began working on material with outside sources, including Lou Reed, who contributed to three songs on the album: "A World Without Heroes," "Dark Light," and "Mr. Blackwell." Plans were put into place for a huge stage show that would incorporate elements of the plot, while actors were brought in to record small segments of dialogue "from the script," and talk was that actor Christopher Makepeace (*Meatballs, My Bodyguard*) was set to play the "boy" of the saga in the movie. There was even talk of a sequel album, to be called *War of the Gods*, which would then be followed by a soundtrack album of the eventual movie made from all the songs.

Not everyone was onboard. Eric Carr, still new to the group, felt so unsure about the project that he confronted Simmons and Stanley about it, saying it was the wrong direction for a hard-rock band, especially in light of the fact that heavy metal was starting to gain headway on the charts. Carr was told not so much to mind his own business, but to let the two "who had been doing it longer" take care of it. He was not alone, however, as Frehley hated the project and was not happy to find that his choices for songs were being changed or dropped. As Carr would say years later, Frehley had stuck with the band up to that point because he felt that with Criss leaving he would have more say in things. Instead, he was finding himself looked upon as the hired help for Simmons and Stanley's project. Unhappy with the mix of the album, he was ready to walk and only reluctantly helped promoted the album (in most cases; one he intentionally missed is covered in Chapter 20). For Simmons and Stanley, Frehley was not acting as a member of the band; he was uncommunicative and even recording away from the others, so they were feeling less confident in his decisions anyway.

When the album died in the charts and a tour was impossible, Frehley felt that the others would listen to him, but the damage by all involved had already been done. After a car accident in April 1982 banged him up pretty good, Frehley decided that for his own health and future career he needed to leave the band. As with Criss, the band kept it quiet that they were looking for a replacement, later reporting Frehley as still being part of the band when Vinnie Vincent went on tour for the subsequent album *Creatures of the Night* in late 1982.

It was a lie, but an effective one. Fans privately may have questioned some of the details but admitted Vincent into the KISS Army easily, wishing him the best with the band as a guitarist who was stuck in a hard role through no fault of his own. Meanwhile, Frehley kept low, allowing the band to deflect questions about his departure for quite some time until they could finally announce that he was no longer with them. In doing so, KISS had managed to pull off an original member's departure without feeling the wrath of fans (although there had been stories for years that Simmons was holding out hope of convincing Frehley to return to the band, especially when conflict began developing between the band and Vincent. The real concern, however, was that by the time of *Creatures*, fewer and fewer fans were showing up to see KISS no matter who was in it. Which brings us to the next much-talked-about milestone in the band's career.

Lick It Up Saved the Band

Creatures of the Night had been a return to a harder sound for KISS after the misfire of *Music from "The Elder."* The tour had featured a new stage set and the first chance for most of America truly to see Eric Carr in action on the drums, and those attending were not disappointed. Nor, as mentioned above, was there much uproar about Vinnie Vincent replacing Ace Frehley (although some fans still kept their hopes up that he would return at some point).

Yet the album had sold even worse than *Music from "The Elder,"* and the tour had only been mildly successful and eventually cut short, losing nearly half the number of shows planned. PolyGram was still uncertain about the band as well. Something would have to change to shake up things and draw attention to the band soon, or else there were reasons to think that KISS was in trouble.

Talk of taking off the makeup may have seemed blasphemous to fans, but it was always on the table with the band over the years. In 1977, Bill Aucoin stated at a UCLA conference on music that KISS had discussed taking the makeup off when sales tanked on the first album in 1974, but decided to hold off when they began to attract media attention thanks to getting on *The Mike Douglas Show* and *In Concert* soon after. Eventually, the makeup became part of the mystique of the band, so it was hard to leave behind, but after nearly ten years and with the band's image trapping them with the "kiddie band" tag—it was still mostly families coming to see KISS in 1982, not the metal fans—it was time to consider other ideas.

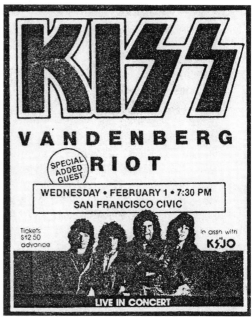

Ad for the first KISS tour without the trademark makeup.   *Author's Collection*

Paul Stanley has gone on record as saying that he began openly discussing the idea of the band taking off the makeup while they were recording *Music from "The Elder,"* but found the others and management reluctant to push the band that far into unknown territory. When the *Creatures* tour showed that the audience they used to attract was moving on, Stanley brought up the topic again, feeling that the makeup was locking them in the 1970s while everyone else was moving into the new decade. A further argument in favor was Gene Simmons's ambition to get into movies; taking the makeup off would allow him to do so with no further delay. By midway through the tour, he had agreed to the next step, just as the band parted ways with Bill Aucoin. With all band decisions now down to Stanley and Simmons—both Eric Carr and Vinnie Vincent were seen as hired hands at such times—if they agreed to something, it was the way the band was going to go.

There were other problems at play as well. The band needed new material, and while most of the songs on the *Creatures* album had been a step in the right direction for proclaiming their metal roots, it had attracted little attention. They needed to find a consistent hook on the next album to convince listeners that the band was not at loose ends, especially when making the jump from the makeup. The last thing they needed was to get more of the same from when *The Elder* came out and be lectured that they were grasping at straws.

Fortunately for them, Vinnie Vincent had a lot of material already sitting in the wings from his demos recorded with his band Warrior and even earlier. With the other band members working with him, eight of the ten songs for the new album were Vincent's creations (only "Fits Like a Glove" and "Dance All Over Your Face"—both by Gene—did not have input from Vincent). Although the single, "Lick It Up," did not do well in the charts (it reached #66 according to *Billboard*), the music video for the sound got a lot of airplay on MTV and other music video outlets at the time, exposing (no pun intended) KISS to a new audience. The album, *Lick It Up*, would reach #19 on the *Cash Box* charts and #24 on *Billboard's*, showing a definite increase in listeners for the band. The tour also began to pick up in sales as it went along.

Things were starting to look better, but there were still struggles ahead. Gene Simmons, for one, found that he was having some problems adjusting to being "Clark Kent" onstage after years of being "Superman." The music video for "Lick It Up" found him still trying to use body movements that worked great for a bat-demon, but looked like he had crippling gas pains without the makeup and costumes. He would soon discover that taking off the makeup meant also stopping some of the effects he had used for so long: gone was the blood-spitting and so too was the showstopping "God of Thunder" for concerts as it seemed so tied into the character he played that he did not feel it worked any longer without the makeup (he would still do the fire-spitting, however).

The other problem had to do with Vinnie Vincent's role in the band. The album had done well, and some critics were quick to point to his involvement as the reason the album was selling. Yet the other argument was that people were giving the band a second chance due to the makeup coming off and that Vincent's involvement was secondary to their newfound success. It was a "chicken-egg" argument that still goes around in fan circles today: were people drawn to the album because of Vincent's writing and then saw it was KISS unmasked, or were they drawn because it was KISS unmasked and then they liked songs cowritten by Vincent? Either answer points to one thing, however: that people liked what Vincent was writing with the others.

This caused a rift in the band, though. Simmons and Paul Stanley had been the decision makers for a good deal of time by this point and saw their decision to take the makeup off as being the reason for their rebound. Vincent, on the other hand, had good reasons to think his music was what was drawing people to KISS. Some later would state that Vincent saw himself as the guy who saved the band and therefore was the new leader, which did not sit well with Simmons and Stanley. There were also problems in that Vincent had never signed the contract making him a member of the band, as he felt it would put him in a position where he would have little say in matters dealing with his own career, much less those dealing with KISS. This created financial headaches for the band, who could not cover Vincent under their insurance as an employee as they would with the others and made them question if he was serious about being in the band.

After the European tour, Vincent was either fired or quit, depending on whose side of the story one hears. Because there was little time to find a replacement, KISS talked him into coming back for the American tour, but things rapidly soured again. Vincent's solos in the show were a major linchpin to trouble, as the band felt he was dragging them out much longer than the time allotted to them, while Vincent felt the band was deliberately cutting off the solos before his time was up in order to "keep him in his place." The difficulties would lead to a near fistfight between Stanley and Vincent backstage at one show, and fan-filmed video of a show in March 1984 shows the other band members fuming onstage as they wait for Vincent to finish his solo long after being introduced by Stanley (Vincent's cue to stop). When it was discovered that Vincent still had not signed his contract to become a member of KISS, the decision was made to go their separate ways. Vincent would play his last show with the band in Evansville, Indiana, in 1984, and then he was gone. His parting shot in *Kerrang!* magazine was that he gave KISS "musical credibility that they never had before" but was not recognized for it.

Lick It Up turned out to be a test for the band in gaining back fans after a dry spell that would have killed other bands. Stanley even once said that if the album had not done well, the band probably would have decided to split, with everyone moving on to other things. Yet the risk in taking off the makeup had helped draw attention to them with an album that included many solid songs from one songwriter and thus one linear train of thought for the album. The band would continue their rise from the ashes with *Animalize* later in 1984 and through the rest of the 1980s, proving that they were stronger than just one member. It would be the start of over a decade of performing without makeup, touring consistently for many of those years, and putting out several studio albums that sold well. The risk had paid off.

Further, it had shown Stanley and Simmons that they had to hold a tighter rein on anyone new added to the band. Vincent had been given what they believed was plenty of room to do what he wanted and still be a member of KISS, but the two felt they had been taken advantage of for being so slack and giving a new member so much power within the band. From this point on, Stanley and Simmons would make the decisions for KISS, including what the new employees hired to be in the band could do or say.

The Way Eric Carr's Passing Was Handled Splintered the KISS Army

Carr had not been feeling well during the *Hot in the Shade* tour in 1990, sometimes complaining of the flu and avoiding the meet-and-greets between the show (a true rarity for Carr, as he was the most anxious to talk to fans during tours). When the tour ended, he wrote the symptoms off to exhaustion and other things, while talks began in February 1991 of the band working on their next album, *Revenge*. Yet when the symptoms returned, Carr was persuaded to seek help and found out that he had a cancerous growth on his heart. He went into the hospital for an operation to remove the growth in April 1991, and seemed to be doing well after the surgery (footage of him in the hospital goofing around with the video camera can be found as an Easter egg on one of the *KISSology* DVD box sets). Yet no one thought he would be in shape for recording in May 1991 of the band's cover of the Argent song "God Gave Rock & Roll to You" for

Presskit folder cover advertising the release of the solo albums in 1978. For many fans, on reflection, it was a sign of the band members being on the outs with each other.

Author's Collection

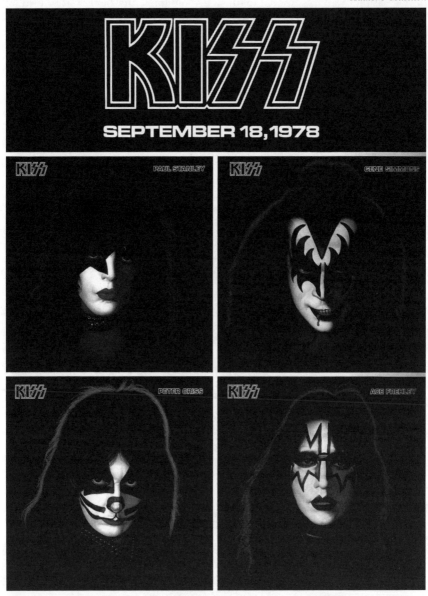

the soundtrack of the movie *Bill & Ted's Bogus Journey*. With Carr out, Paul Stanley remembered Eric Singer from a short solo club tour he did in 1989 and asked him to play while Carr was recovering.

Singer came in for the song, although Carr sang backing vocals as well as appeared in the music video for the song. Carr was set to return, but results of testing later in May showed that the cancer had spread to his lungs. He began chemotherapy in June while the band began recording the album with Singer on drums. In September, he was in good enough health to appear at the MTV Music Awards, but on the 16th he suffered a brain hemorrhage. He would begin to recover during October, but in November he suffered a second hemorrhage. He died on November 24, 1991.

It was a shakeup for the band and the fans. Eric Carr had connected well with fans over his time in the band, talking to them backstage and at the hotels while on tour and willing to be interviewed for the fanzines and fan clubs without any qualms. He was also a longtime member of the band, having played with them for over ten years at that point, and so was considered as much a part of the band as Simmons and Stanley were.

There were also issues inside the band as well. Carr was having difficulty in recovery, and although he was determined to be in the studio with KISS for the recording of the album, many agreed that he was not in the best of physical shape and should have been recuperating rather than risking his health by being there. The plan with Singer was that he would come in and record with them until Carr was ready and then head back to his normal gig with Alice Cooper at the time, with Simmons being firm in his thoughts that Singer was there only temporarily (Singer has stated that Simmons pulled him aside during the recordings to make clear that Carr was still coming back and to not see it as a full-time position). This jibes with Singer's tour dates with Alice Cooper, as Singer would tour with Cooper from July through most of October before he returned to work full time on the *Revenge* album.

But in trying to keep things "in the family," the band left fandom in a vacuum. As could be expected, all kinds of rumors began floating around about how Carr was being mistreated by the band. Carr himself did not help matters much when he would make statements in fanzine interviews that implied he was being forced out. Then again, when rumors began surfacing in September that Singer had already been made an official member of the band and that Carr was being dropped from medical coverage under the band's insurance, it no doubt added stress for Carr (and the others) whether there was any truth to it or not.

Simmons wrote to *Rolling Stone* after Carr's passing, infuriated that the magazine had glossed over Carr's death (only a portion of the letter saw print in the magazine). Yet when a fan-based tribute concert was being discussed for 1992, with money to go to cancer research, the band stated that their "hearts would not be in it." This upset some fans, who read the comment to mean that they did not care enough to do something in Carr's honor, instead of the intended feeling that it was not the direction they wanted to go in remembering him. Although they would add a tribute to Carr on the *Revenge* album ("Carr Jam '81"), some fans could not be pacified (or thought they were being patronized).

Eric Carr's death hurt the band. The album was promised to the label, and so recording had to begin while Eric was recovering; yet, after all the things that occurred after that, the album got pushed back and was not released until May 1992. *Revenge* sold well, but the singles did not, and MTV was at a stage where they had little use for showing KISS videos and did not give them as much airplay as in the past. The tour that followed was scrapped after dismal ticket sales. Meanwhile, Simmons and Stanley were becoming quite vocal in interviews downplaying the work of previous members no longer in the band. With that and the rumors about how supposedly indifferent the band was to Carr's struggle, there grew a split within the KISS Army. Back in the 1980s, most fans had agreed that whether you liked the masked or unmasked KISS, you were still a fan of everyone associated with the band. Now it was suddenly a case where you could only be a fan if you liked the current version and dismissed anything the others had done; or you could not like anything done after Carr, and only those that had left the band had talent.

In trying to keep private matters private, Stanley and Simmons unintentionally created an atmosphere where fans thought they were being secretive and "up to something." Yet, if they had made a big deal out of Carr's passing, they would have been roasted for exploiting his death. It was a no-win situation, and so all they could do was move on, which caused problems as well. As stated before, Carr had always been a glue between the band and the fans. With his passing, the fans began feeling a disconnect between themselves and the band. One that KISS never fully recovered from.

The Reunion Tour Splintered the KISS Army

What most fans don't realize is that reunions had been talked about for years before 1995 and the *MTV Unplugged* concert. The first movement toward such a thing happened in 1988 when Gene Simmons and Paul Stanley jumped up on stage to perform with Ace Frehley during a Frehley's Comets show at the Limelight in New York. The two were only there for one song, but it sparked a considerable amount of interest in fandom.

Then in October 1989, KISS was about to release *Hot in the Shade* just as Ace was about to release his *Trouble Walkin'* album the same month (both of which, coincidentally, contained the song "Hide Your Heart"). KISS went to Frehley with an idea of a tour that would feature him performing with Eric Carr, Stanley and Simmons in makeup, and with all the special affects (Peter Criss was never considered as part of the deal at the time). Frehley gave it some thought, then suggested two shows on each coast of the U.S. and filming them. Simmons and Stanley did not care much for the idea and came back with another—the two being about to tour for their new albums, why not have Frehley open for KISS on the tour and then have him come out for KISS's encore to do a couple of numbers with them. His label at the time, Megaforce, pushed for Frehley to accept the offer, but he finally turned it down. To his way of thinking, it would be as if he had to have KISS there in order to get gigs, and after years of fighting to get his solo career going, it seemed like a step backwards. Everyone finally agreed that it was a nice try, but it was not going to happen.

Finally in 1995, the original foursome got back together for the MTV special and then announced a tour for 1996. In general, for fans in the KISS Army, this was great news. Peter Criss had dismissed the ideas of a tour for years, saying it would never happen, and after the ruckus caused by Simmons and Stanley (and subsequently Frehley and Criss in retaliation) about the talents of each other, it was like a dream come true.

But there was a downside to this as well—once it became clear that Bruce Kulick and Eric Singer were no longer going to be members of the band and that the reunion of the original four was going to continue past one tour, some fans took offense. These fans, of course, were those who had become fans during the band's nonmakeup days. They had grown up with that era and had seen Kulick and Singer more as KISS members than Frehley and Criss (to be fair, Kulick had been a member for nearly twelve years at that point, a few more years than either Criss or Frehley). They were also the fans who had liked the band's music from *Revenge* and knew that they had recorded an album's worth of material (later released as *Carnival of Souls*) that was supposedly in the same style as the previous album. Now that was to be buried, forgotten for—in their eyes—a nostalgia act.

There was already a split among fans thanks to the public infighting among the original members—turning a portion of the KISS Army into "Makeup Only" and "Nonmakeup Only" fans who hated the opposite—losing Singer and Kulick only further drove a wedge between fans. The next step certainly did not help matters.

Psycho Circus Splintered the KISS Army

As is obvious by now, there is a pattern to how KISS fans perceive the events of the 1990s. So much splintering you'd think someone blew up a lumber factory.

The Reunion tour of 1996–1997 was over, and the band announced they were to go into the studio to record a new album in January 1998. What was seen as the "return of the gods" to fans turned into a rather unpleasant experience in the end for the band and fans. Rumors were soon flying that Bruce Kulick was recording lead guitar on the album instead of Ace Frehley. Then Peter Criss was vocal in his dissatisfaction that all four songs he had brought in were rejected, while Frehley had brought in even more and only got one, "Into the Void," accepted, and even that was rewritten by other members of the band. Simmons and Stanley countered that they had just as many songs rejected by their producer, Bruce Fairbairn, to show that it was a producer's decision and not an "us vs. them" situation. However, just as the album was being released in September of that year, Fairbairn went on record to state that Stanley and Simmons made such decisions for him. After all, he, Criss, and Frehley were employees and did what they were told.

The album was released on September 22, 1998, and although the band tried to present a front in favor of the album, it was clear that neither Frehley nor Criss was happy with the results. Fans who had been used to how the two played were also quick to jump on the album, feeling that the music heard was definitely not that of Frehley or Criss.

In defense of Simmons and Stanley, they had spent many years working in the studio on KISS albums and others under the guideline that if you need someone to come in to record a few licks here and there, that was the nature of the business. They had been doing so since Frehley first "had a poker game" back at the time of *Destroyer*, and both Simmons and Stanley were ready to admit through the years that at times both had disappeared and had a session player or other member of the band record in their place. So to do the same for their new album was status quo rather than looking to hurt someone's feelings.

Even so, it was not what fans were looking for when they got the new album. They wanted to hear the four original members locked in a room and cranking out songs like they had in 1974. Perhaps such a thing was impossible nearly twenty-five years later, but when the results look as if they did not even try—and then to compound the issue by pretending it was the four (even when Frehley and Criss were making clear it was not)—it helped to further splinter fandom into those who felt "Gene and Paul had to do it to get the album completed" and those who felt "Ace and Peter are obviously the only ones that cared enough to want to do the album the way fans wanted." Yet all was not lost; at least the band was still together and performing as the original foursome.

At least for a couple more years, as it turns out.

Spaceman and Catman After the Millennium . . . Well, You Can Guess

There had been all types of speculation as to how the 2000 tour would end. Fans knew that Frehley and Criss were contractually signed with KISS until the end of 2000, so many thought it would be a good place for the band to end. Thus a final blowout concert was just bound to happen, and when the tour was announced as a farewell, it was easy to dream of where the last show would be. Would it be at Shea Stadium? Madison Square Garden? Area 51? As it turns out, it was none of those. From Simmons and Stanley's thinking, the 2000 tour was just going to end, and then they would move on ahead to the next tour in Japan. That did not set well with Criss, who felt he had earned a spot into either getting more money to continue or just ending it. Because things could not be sorted out, his last show was October 7, 2000 (which is discussed in more detail in Chapter 17).

Then it gets a little funny. There was an old joke among KISS fans back in the 1980s that the band was going through so many lead guitarists it was as if there was a revolving door for them to come and go as they pleased. The next few years would find the band doing the same for both their drummer and lead guitarist.

With Peter gone and negotiations fallen through (Simmons would insist that Criss's lawyer never contacted them, while Criss would insist that his lawyer never heard from the band), KISS went to Japan in March 2001 with Eric Singer taking Criss's place. This was a shock to fans, as it was not like the previous one-off during the Reunion period where Criss's drum tech had to replace him for a night— this was a former member of the band doing a full tour in Criss's costume and makeup and being referred to as the Catman. Some fans tried to write it off as a one-time thing; "they had no choice as they were already

Dynasty tour ad, with Judas Priest opening. Just weeks later, Peter Criss will have left the band.
Author's Collection

booked and promised the four faces, so Eric had to wear the makeup," they proclaimed. Same for the short Australian tour that followed, which concluded the "Farewell tour." Besides, some would say, Ace Frehley was still with them, so if he was okay with it, what was the big deal? Frehley would then make a couple of appearances with this version of the band for televised events in February 2002, but after that he walked away from them, never to return.

With Frehley out, Tommy Thayer—who has been put into Frehley's outfit and makeup for a couple of shows during the previous tour when it appeared Frehley was going to be late—put on the makeup and outfit for good. Thus, fans got the Simmons-Stanley-Singer-Thayer version of KISS, but only for two oddball events: a private show in March 2002 and an appearance on an *American Bandstand* special. Again, some fans claimed that it had to be done and did not "really count" as they were both one-off situations.

It got weirder. A new tour started in 2003, but suddenly Eric Singer was out and Peter Criss was back, even after Criss had been vocal about his departure and his indignation that his makeup was being used on someone else. Criss would continue to tour with the band until December 20, 2003, with Thayer in Frehley's makeup. Fittingly, Singer would soon be making the rounds at KISS expos complaining about his dismissal for Criss in very much the same manner that Criss had before him.

Yet, after the tour was over, so was Criss's tenure in the band. He was gone once again, and Singer returned to the makeup without any complaints. After that, KISS would officially become Simmons-Stanley-Singer-Thayer and has remained that way ever since.

The replacement of two original members of the band would have not caused much of a ruckus if handled differently. If the band had decided to drop the makeup when bringing in Eric Singer and Tommy Thayer? Fans had been down that road before and had no problem with it; some probably would have even cheered it as a chance to return to the *Revenge* days. If the two had been brought in with new personas or at least slightly different makeup? Both Carr and Vincent's makeups were simply variations on the themes created by Criss and Frehley, so again the fans would have been fine with it. But this felt to some fans like having all the options laid in front of you and picking the worst one for the worst reason—not because fans demanded it, but because it would royally cheese off Criss and Frehley. In doing so, the band would manufacture the biggest split in the KISS Army ever.

Before this, when a new member had become part of the band, there had always been the objective of creating new personas, such as in the case of Eric Carr and Vinnie Vincent. The reason given then was that Peter Criss and Ace Frehley were so closely associated to their makeup and costumes that it would not make sense to put something else in them (of course, at the time there were also the problems with the respective musicians owning their makeup; by 2000 this was solely in the hands of KISS and not Frehley and Criss). Now they were doing exactly that with Eric Singer and Tommy Thayer. To their way of thinking, however, people were coming to the show to see the makeup and the costumes as much as they were to see the same effects and songs they had for years, and to change that would spoil the show for the ticket buyers. Gene Simmons in one interview equated it with going to see *The Phantom of the Opera* and saying that the makeup would have to change because it is a different actor in the lead role.

The band had gone through such assumptions in the past. Bruce Kulick was seen as being close enough in appearance to pass for Mark St. John, and there was no need to explain who he was and where St. John had disappeared to on the *Animalize* tour. Although they could clearly not pass off Eddie Kanon as Peter at the one show on the earlier tour, they saw that fans were not exactly walking out in droves either. Admittedly, many people going to the shows did not even know that Criss and Frehley were no longer in the band, as they saw the makeup and costumes and just assumed it was Singer as Criss and Thayer as Frehley anyway or just didn't care. Yet a certain segment of fans couldn't help but wonder, why be so lazy? If the band couldn't bother with something as simple as new makeup, knowing the potential marketing and profits to be made by it; if they were satisfied in just spinning their wheels in the past; why bother doing anything new in the future?

Either way, the rift widened for fans—those who did not care because as long as it was KISS it was fine, and those who felt it was admitting to defeat as a functioning band wanting to create new things. KISS tried to prove that was not the case. It took them nearly a decade to do it, however.

Sonic Boom, a Walmart Exclusive

When *Psycho Circus* and problems with working out record labels (see Chapter 9) turned out to be a major headache, KISS stepped away from the studio for the longest period of their career, with a return only occurring eleven years later. The album was called *Sonic Boom*, which featured Eric Singer and Tommy Thayer performing (and each getting a lead vocal as well as Thayer cowriting many of the songs), and it came out in October 2009. It was the first full studio album to be released under the band's own label, KISS Records, but the more intriguing element of it was that it was released in the U.S. as a Walmart exclusive.

This was not completely unheard of. AC/DC, Journey, and Foreigner are just some of the artists that went the route of Walmart exclusives and had some handy success in doing so. Guns N' Roses had done so with *Chinese Democracy* through Best Buy, and other bands have worked with Target and other department stores on such exclusives. KISS was just another act to try the method. In their case, they sweetened the deal a bit by making it a three disc set—the new studio album, a "best of" that featured new recordings of old songs (called *KISS Klassics*, but really a rewording of a Japanese album called *Jigoku-Retsuden* that was done mainly so the band could have their songs in a form they could sell to advertisers without payout to the label that owns their original recordings), and a DVD featuring six live songs from a show recorded in 2009 in Buenos Aires. Walmart pushed the album with some space in their super-department stores for a "KISS Corner" for additional KISS merchandise, although they did not bother going the whole nine yards and calling it a "KISS Korner." (Something to commend them for, actually.)

Yet to older fans it seemed a bit embarrassing—a band that once had a major label behind them now reduced to selling through stores like a K-Tel record of the 1970s. Other fans, who had various reasons for not shopping at Walmart, were frustrated that they had limited resources in getting copies. Independent record stores were even buying copies on sale at Walmart just so they could slap their own prices on the packaging and resell them through their stores because of the exclusive. However, the numbers don't lie—the album did well in sales and got #2 on the *Billboard* Top 200 charts, even though some reports would have it that it was a mild disappointment from Walmart's expectations. Better yet for the band, it proved that they could move out on their own with their own label and get noticed. It would be a little over three years, but 2012 will see the release of another studio album through their label, tentatively titled *Monster*, proving that there was still some mileage left in KISS after all. Although there has been no word if it will be a Walmart exclusive.

8

Professionals Only to Respond

The Tryouts in the 1980s

W hen the tryouts occurred for a lead guitarist back in 1972, it was a case of three nobodies putting out a free ad in a paper and looking for results for a band that "maybe" had a record deal, maybe not. There was no need to be secretive or take special precautions when trying to find a new member. When Peter Criss left the band in 1980, it was a different arena for them. KISS had requests swamping them to try out for the band from anyone who could play—both famous and unknown as well as those that could not play at all.

1980

KISS was still huge at the time of Peter Criss's announcement in May 1980 that he was leaving. Thus, looking for a new drummer was going to be a big task. Even so, they did have at least one, maybe two, internal candidates for the job. Anton Fig, who had played drums on both *Dynasty* and *Unmasked*, had been heavily considered for the job to the point that Aucoin Management was officially not denying the rumor even in the pages of the band's official KISS Army Newsletter. There had also been rumors for years that Allan Schwartzberg, a session drummer who had worked with Gene Simmons on his solo album and many times with producer Bob Ezrin, was under consideration. However, both were known in the industry, and Fig had been pictured often with his various bands, so the "mystic" issue came into play. KISS needed someone they could package as being not only new but also a mystery, so that the "nobody knows what we look like without the makeup" gimmick could stay in place. Thus, known drummers from other bands were pretty much out of the question and a newcomer the way to go.

KISS already had some ideas even in this area, but for the others, Aucoin Management had drummers not already known to the band put together the following and send it into the offices: A resume, photos of what they looked like, and a cassette tape featuring the drummer performing and singing. All applications had a cutoff date of June 17, 1980 (a Tuesday). Eric Carr had heard about KISS looking for a new drummer from an old bandmate just as he was getting ready to take a break from music and find a full-time job. Carr put together the required information over that weekend—his demo tape including two KISS songs, "Shandi" and "Torpedo Girl" along with two from Van Halen, "And the Cradle Will Rock" and their cover of "You Really Got Me"—but then procrastinated on sending it in until June 18, the day after the cutoff. It was an action he would reflect on for years in interviews as never quite making sense to him.

Even so, it did him no harm, nor did putting the information in a bright orange folder, as the color caught the eyes of people working at Aucoin Management, who passed it on to the manager. On June 19, he had an interview with Bill Aucoin to discuss the audition and was told that he would need to lose the mustache as "the guys won't be able to see past it." His audition was the following Monday, June 24, where he had to perform five songs—"Black Diamond," "Firehouse," "Detroit Rock City," "Strutter," and "Is That You?"—with the band and be interviewed by Gene Simmons, Paul Stanley, and Ace Frehley.

Carr would later recall a number of drummers being there to audition, many of whom he knew or knew of. The only name to have repeatedly come up as being there is that of Bobby Rondinelli, soon to be the drummer for Richie Blackmore's Rainbow and later for Black Sabbath in the 1990s. Often

After extensive auditions, the band decided to pick the session player helping to write the new album to replace Ace Frehley.

Author's Collection

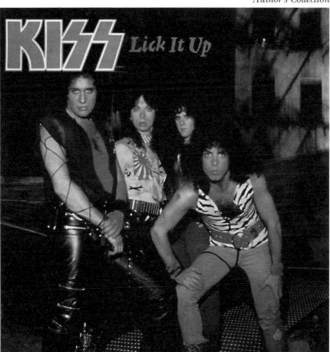

mentioned also was a "near-famous" drummer (never named in any telling of the story) who arrived with his own roadie, anvil case, and arrogant attitude; all of which Carr knew would work against the man when auditioning. Carr went in to find a double-bass drum kit setup with a video camera in front of it along with the three members of the band behind a table for the interview. Once the interview went well, the three went over to the drums and picked up instruments to play with him. He would later state that all three were a bit rusty after not playing for a while and that only Frehley remembered how to play the parts from the original recordings—which is what Carr had learned—instead of how they had come to play them live.

Carr was thanked for his time and told they would be in touch. Thinking he might as well take a chance, he asked the three to sign his letter from Aucoin that came about the audition and left. On July 1, 1980, he was left a message on his sister's answering machine that he had gotten the job. It had been down to him and Bobby Rondinelli, with Carr getting the edge because he could sing better. Rondinelli had already decided to go with Rainbow after the audition anyway, so even if the band had offered him the gig, Carr would have gotten it. As it was, a rejection letter was sent to Rondinelli instead, which worked out just fine for him.

1982

Since Peter Criss's leaving was a public affair, finding his replacement was just as public (although an attempt was made to keep it as low-key as possible under the circumstances). Replacing Ace Frehley was a different affair, however. KISS did not want to make waves with the public while looking for a replacement for him. Ads appeared in early 1982 in *Billboard* and *Rolling Stone* announcing that an "American Supergroup" was looking for a lead guitarist who "must be outstanding onstage performer, tall (6 ft. range), long hair and must sing and write." A tape, photo, and resume were to be included. While the name of the band was not mentioned, people in the industry very easily found out, and a good number of people sent in resumes or were asked to come out to audition. Eric Carr would state that the band itself was looking at the packages sent in, but that it was usually up to him to do the major sorting through the various folders received as Simmons and Stanley would take one look at a picture and discard some guitarist that Carr believed would have worked well.

The number of guitarists was reduced to forty as the band continued to prepare *Creatures of the Night* for release by having cowriter Vinnie Vincent play lead on the album. Other guitarists who played on the album were Bob Kulick ("Danger" and "Keep Me Comin'"), Steve Farris ("Creatures of the Night"), and Robben Ford ("Rock and Roll Hell" and "I Still Love You"). Rumors ran rampant for years that such guitarists as Jimmy Page, Eddie Van Halen, and Randy Rhoads had attempted to work on the album as well but were considered "not good enough" (a good indicator of how truthful such rumors probably were).

It is known that a number of popular guitarists tried out for the band, or were at least interviewed for possible auditions. Stories of guitarists from Chicago and Heart asking to audition have surfaced as well but have not been confirmed. Gene Simmons would state in the book *Kiss and Make-Up* that Eddie Van Halen had gone to him, wanting to join KISS in order to get out of working with David Lee Roth, but there has never been any official confirmation of this from Van Halen himself, and most other sources tend to treat this as Eddie making a joke at the time.

Some of the guitarists who auditioned or requested to come out for audition (and some of the bands they had or would in the future perform with) included:

Doug Aldrich—Whitesnake, Dio, Lion, House of Lords.

Yngwie Malmsteen—Major founder of the shredding guitar technique; mainly known as a solo artist, although he played with Alcatrazz in 1983 (joining two members of Warrior, the band Vinnie Vincent was in before KISS). Was also in a band called Steeler.

Adam Bomb—Then known as Adam Brenner. Replaced Yngwie Malmsteen in Steeler briefly and then established a solo career.

John Verner—Ambrosia, Skylark. He was picked by Paul Stanley to audition.

Spencer Sercombe—Shark Island (popular L.A. band of the early 1980s), Riverdogs, Bill Ward's band.

Steve Farris—Mr. Mister and a number of other artists including Howard Jones, Gary Wright, Celine Dion, Tori Amos, and Alice Cooper.

Richie Sambora—Bon Jovi, plus solo artist. Known for dating Cher in the late 1980s, who was a former girlfriend of Simmons.

Joe Shikany—Toured with Paul Rodgers. Was big in the Seattle Music Scene and had been in a band called Bighorn that opened for several major bands in the late 1970s. Killed in a freak accident in 2008.

Marq Torien—BulletBoys. Was with RATT for a spell. Played a bit at Motown.

Robbin Crosby—RATT. Died in 2002.

Tom Lafferty—Crown of Thorns, Jean Beauvoir's band. Beauvoir had convinced the band to let him try out.

1984

So—after all the tryouts, the band made their decision by hiring the session musician working on their album. Actually, it made sense, Vinnie Vincent had cowritten three songs on the album (including "I Love It Loud," the first and only single from *Creatures of the Night*) and had proven himself in the studio. Unfortunately, as discussed in a previous chapter, things did not work out. Now

B : 孤独のハンター LONELY IS THE HUNTER   ¥700

Mark St. John's heavily praised introduction to the band was soon
curtailed by illness, and he was replaced with Bruce Kulick.

Author's Collection

KISS was in a position where they needed to find another guitarist after less
than two years.

This time around, the band decided not to open auditions and instead
send out invitations to a few guitarists to audition for them one-on-one—mostly
through recommendations made to them. Bruce Kulick was one of the few to try
out with the band, after his brother, Bob Kulick, mentioned him, but the band
ultimately decided to go with Mark St. John. Evidently, Norton (St. John's birth
name) had sent in a resume and tape back during the auditions to replace Ace
Frehley, but it was only when the band began looking again that Paul Stanley
remembered the tape and asked Norton to try out for the band.

KISS made a major push for Mark St. John when the *Animalize* album came
out—making it sound like he was to be a huge asset to the band. Then things
went sour with both St. John's health and his relationship with the others. Soon,
there was talk of replacing him. This after all the hoopla of him joining. To make
the transition, Bruce Kulick was called back in—a man the members knew and
who could be depended on to watch what he said and who he said it to while still
being a great lead guitarist in his own right. From then on, Kulick would remain
a part of the KISS family for many years and is still known to work occasionally
with the various members of the band.

1991–2002

Eric Singer's audition for the band was his "pressure under fire" performance in working on the *Revenge* album while still part of Alice Cooper's live band and the emotional time of Eric Carr's last days. There was no need to bring in several drummers to look over, as Singer clearly knew his material and was already on good working terms with Paul Stanley as per live shows due to Singer having played on his 1989 solo tour.

When Peter Criss left in 2000, it was easy to ask Eric Singer if he wanted to come back and take over. Same with Tommy Thayer taking over for Ace Frehley in 2002, as Thayer had performed as Frehley in the tribute band Cold Gin and had been on the tours working with KISS for several years at that point, so he knew what to expect and when, just as the others knew what to expect of him.

After years of looking for unknowns outside of the group to spice things up, KISS found that looking closer to home was the easiest and safest way to deal with replacement members.

9

The Image Is Getting Clearer

Morphing Record Labels over the Years

When people think of KISS, they think of one record label (if they bother to think of any at all), and that is Casablanca Records. That is understandable, as the two were synonymous back in the 1970s. When Casablanca needed to show their track record, KISS was always dragged out front and center, even when disco was raging. Casablanca, however, only lasted for about a fifth of the band's recording career. The rest would be a journey that the band actually had little control over.

Casablanca Records

In 1973, Neil Bogart left Buddah Records—taking a number of people with him in the process—to form what he initially envisioned as a new label based on a place in his favorite movie, Emerald City Records. When he was informed that the name of the city in *The Wizard of Oz* was already in use, he decided to go with Casablanca Records instead, in homage to the classic Humphrey Bogart movie. He had set up a distribution deal with Warner Brothers for the label, but soon found himself in conflict with Warner, who were less than happy with the roster of talent Bogart was throwing together. As KISS was finishing their second album, *Hotter Than Hell*, the promotional department of Warner began telling their staff to not bother pushing the album as it was bound to fail. Bogart demanded to be released from his distribution deal with Warner, and in September 1974 got his wish granted.

It was a risk to be an independent label, but Casablanca found their niche even after a few stumbles along the way (such as the *Here's Johnny* album discussed in Chapter 30). The pattern was to find acts that stood out from the pack, and when KISS finally exploded in 1975, along with the success of Donna Summers, Parliament, and the whole disco takeover of America with groups like the Village People and others, it looked like Bogart and his crew knew what they were doing.

Because of that success, the European label PolyGram decided to buy 50 percent of Casablanca in 1977 (they also bought 50 percent of RSO, the other big label in disco at the time). It was an attempt to build up their business, but it would later be seen as a mistake. Casablanca's knack for finding new talent had fallen off quickly as the 1970s progressed and desperation began to set in, with the label pouring more and more money into obtaining new talent only to do little with them and then letting them go. There were also over-expenditures on partying and lifestyle choices that were bleeding the company dry. PolyGram at first tried to stop the hemorrhaging by bringing in employees from their Polydor offices, but this ended with those employees being swayed to Casablanca's view as if they had joined a cult and nothing was resolved. Finally, in February 1980, PolyGram bought out Casablanca completely, forcing Neil Bogart out and taking over the functions of the company.

PolyGram

PolyGram was created in 1962 out of the merger of two other companies, officially becoming PolyGram in 1972. To establish themselves in the U.S. and elsewhere, they had acquired a number of existing labels, including MGM, Decca, and Mercury (so their acquisition of Casablanca was not that unusual for them).

Polygram would continue to support the Casablanca Records label on their albums for a time, mainly in hopes of fixing the problems within the company and keeping the brand name going. Meanwhile, they began cutting out the driftwood, leading to the precarious situation KISS found themselves in when dealing with Peter Criss and later Ace Frehley leaving. *Creatures of the Night* would be the last album released in the U.S. under the Casablanca Records label for KISS. After that, PolyGram moved the band to their Mercury label.

Mercury

Started in 1945 as a jazz and classical label, Mercury was bought out by what would become PolyGram in 1963. When Polygram obtained Casablanca, most of its artists were moved to Mercury, which is why the 1983 KISS album *Lick It Up* was the first to be released under Mercury. Mercury would stay with KISS as it developed to include a lot of other hard-rock and heavy-metal bands such as Def Leppard, Bon Jovi, the Scorpions, and others.

The parent company, PolyGram, were bought by the distillery company Seagram on July 17, 1998. Seagram would merge PolyGram with MCA (which was bought as part of a deal with Universal Studios) and create a new umbrella company called Universal Music Group. In January 1999, Seagram laid off 500 employees and 250 artists in their L.A. and New York offices, while combining Mercury with the Island Def Jam label.

Magazine ad from the time of *Revenge* showing all the albums up to then—the name of the label may have changed multiple times, but the band remained loyal for decades.

Author's Collection

Universal Music Group

KISS was one of the lucky ones for the moment and remained under Mercury through Universal Music Group, but they would only release the 1998 album *Psycho Circus* before trouble started. When the band came back with what was supposed to be *Alive IV*—the Millennium Concert recorded with the original foursome on December 31, 1999—Universal at first promoted the release (on their Island Def Jam label, which threw fans a tad) with magazine ads but then pulled it, although still keeping the rights to the material. Soon enough, it was announced that Universal would no longer be producing newly recorded albums with the band.

KISS and Universal split at this point, although the two worked together to release the five-disc box set in 2001, among other projects. KISS would have to seek a new label if they wanted to see new material come out. They would find it with Sanctuary Records.

Sanctuary Records

Sanctuary Records is a small label in London that was started with the metal band Iron Maiden. Eventually they built up a reputation as a label for acts that wanted to put out new material but were considered out of step with the times and/or uncommercial. Many metal acts of the 1980s would eventually move to the label in the 1990s as the market for such offerings was dying out (or at least viewed as such by the bigger companies). KISS turned to Sanctuary in 2003 when they decided to release a live album taken from a February 28, 2003, concert done in Australia with the Melbourne Symphony Orchestra. This became the album released as *KISS Symphony: Alive IV*.

The company would fall into financial problems a few years later and eventually be bought out by Universal Music Group, meaning that KISS had left one company only to find the one recording they had done outside of it now once again a part of it.

Live Nation/Concert Live/Concert Online/Simfy Life

On the 2004 *Rock the Nation* tour, fans could purchase made-on-demand discs of the shows they just saw. Live Nation was a spin-off of Clear Communications. The discs were done for a number of the venues along the tour.

Such discs were done for the *Alive 35* tour from 2008 to 2009, with the company Concert Live doing them and then Concert Online eventually taking over. The *Sonic Boom* tour would be documented in a similar fashion through a company called Simfy Live, which was another name for Concert Online.

KISS Records

KISS decided to do *Sonic Boom* under their own label, which was then distributed through Walmart department stores in the U.S. In what may seem like a weird twist of fate, Roadrunner would distribute the album in Europe. The label had a deal through Universal Music Group and was mostly owned by Warner Brothers (and eventually swallowed up by Warner in 2010). Thirty-five years after their first release, KISS was running into Warner Brothers once again.

10

Got My KISS Records Out

Ten Greatest KISS Album Covers . . . and Ten Questionable Ones

T here is an argument made by people who hate KISS that the only reason they became and remain popular was due to the makeup and the costumes. Of course, one could point out the many, mostly success-ful, years of the band's history where they went without makeup, but since their career began with, and today still uses, the characters, costumes, and makeup, it is how the public sees them. Yet, even if one ignores those nonmakeup years, this is still a band that has produced many studio albums of new material, with many of those albums reaching gold and even platinum status. No one produces so much without people buying them, and those sales are not just because "they wear makeup and costumes." There has to be something to the albums and the music on them that makes listeners become and remain fans. If the spectacle was all that mattered, other performers who have attempted costumes and makeup after KISS would still be churning out material at the same rate.

Still, there is no denying that KISS has always been a visual as well as a musi-cal experience. This extends to the various KISS album covers, which show the band in images that have long been associated with them to the point of parody by other performers over the years. In contrast, some covers have been icono-clastic through the use of the band members' images in otherwise "normal" surroundings (or at least their makeup, as with the *KISS My Ass* tribute album showing a 1950s domestic traditional family dinner, but with the family in KISS makeup). Many have worked, but as can be seen below, there are a few that make fans wonder what everyone working at the record company was thinking after seeing the results.

While researching this book, I asked fans to give me their opinions as to the top ten best and "most questionable" KISS album covers. The responses presented few surprises—fans always enjoy poking fun at the missteps of their favorite bands as much as celebrating their triumphs—although the number of "disagreeable" album covers came more readily than the successes. But in some cases, it appears fans' reaction to an album's music, or to circumstances loosely connected to the release of an album, may have influenced their favoritism/

dislike of some of the covers as well. This will be discussed in the lists below, starting with the top ten best covers in order of least to most favorite.

Alive II

Number ten on the best list and already there has to be a disclaimer; for while many fans remember this album cover well, it is not the front or back of the album that they like, but rather the inside gatefold of the double-LP set. The front cover, designed by Dennis Woloch (who did work through Howard Marks Advertising on several covers in this chapter), is obviously intended as a direct visual assault to the buyer: Boom! KISS logo. Boom! Album title. Boom! Four pictures of the band members in action (with Gene Simmons looking particularly vicious thanks to being drenched with water and having airbrushed blood on his face). It is intended to be in-your-face and defiant; yet in execution it comes off as oddly stagnant and dull. In pushing the envelope by making the logo and title the focus, the images shove the visual excitement of the band in concert into the lower right-hand corner of the frame. This after the vibrancy of the first live album cover (*Alive!*). Furthermore, the back cover does nothing more than inflate the photos of the band members from the front—it is all very nice, but where is the excitement?

A so-so cover with a memorable gatefold photo of the band in action.
Author's Collection

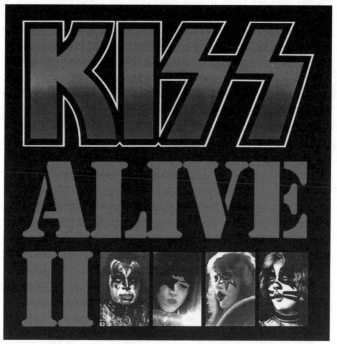

Then one opens the gatefold cover to see the photo of the band on the *Love Gun* stage: The drumset riser is up and displaying the cat scenery well remembered from that tour; Simmons, Frehley, and Stanley rise above the stage on their platforms; meanwhile, fire and fireworks explode from and around the stage. The photo by Barry Levine is a quintessential moment of the band's live performance, even if it was staged without an audience and airbrushed to make it bigger and better than ever seen in concert. Oddly enough, the gatefold photo complements the cover and vice-versa—the front cover easily sells the concept of who is on the album and what it is but is merely a rumble to the visual explosion found in the inner gatefold.

Which is why reactions from fans on voting for this album cover were almost unanimous in stating, "*Alive II*! Uh . . . but only for the gatefold cover." Yet without that front cover, the photo within does not quite have the same effect, nor would the gatefold cover have worked on the front, especially if reduced in size to fit. Still, although the front cover has never completely won over fans, the inner gatefold photo is enough to push *Alive II* to the number ten spot of favorite album covers.

Unmasked

Number nine of favorite albums covers is the last album to feature the original foursome, with Peter Criss leaving soon after completion (albeit, as was later discovered by fans, with Criss actually not participating much in the recording of the album). It would also see the beginning of the end for the "Super-KISS" era, with the mania for the band that had swept the nation (and world) quickly fading away. The album would see no tour and little in the way of promotion in North America beyond an early conceptual music video for the single "Shandi." Further, it came with a title that played with the concept of the band members revealing their bare faces after years of keeping them secret for publicity reasons, as if disposing of the myth behind KISS once and for all (which leads into reasons that . . . well, see the Ten Questionable Album Covers listed below for more on that front).

The cover, illustrated by Victor Stabin—who would go on to do a variety of artwork over the years, including that of U.S. postage stamps—and from a concept by Mark Samuels and Jose Rivero, plays with the well-worn idea of the band being glorified comic book (or even cartoon) characters by presenting them in a comic strip. The storyline for the comic strip cover is that of a photographer's attempts to take a photo of the band members without their trademarked makeup (including an illustration of Gene Simmons in his well-known kerchief that he seemingly wore day and night to hide his appearance from the press when stepping out with some famous women in the 1970s). The comic strip ends with the band agreeing to reveal their true selves to the photographer, only to pull away their masks (i.e., their makeup) to reveal that their real faces are the same as the masks they were wearing.

Magazine ad for *Animalize* and various other albums in the KISS discography.
Author's Collection

To some fans, the cover shows the band as defiant and refusing to back away from the images that some felt pegged the band as nothing more than a children's performance. Hence the members' superhero look in the strip and even the final panel gag of the photographer not getting the underlining message being revealed. To those fans, the band's message was that they knew certain people would always see KISS as a joke, but so what? KISS was not about to change for the sake of the naysayers or the press, who were clueless anyway.

Of course, as fans know, the band truly would go unmasked within three years of this album's "line in the sand" cover, which in hindsight dims the stance made.

KISS

As told by Paul Stanley and Gene Simmons in a number of sources (including their own oral biography, *Behind the Mask* by David Leaf and Ken Sharp), when the band arrived to have their picture taken for the cover of their first album with their makeup on, photographer Joel Brodsky thought they wanted to do something in a humorous vein. Yet after supposedly getting ready to hand out helium balloons for at least one of the band members in order to convey a circus atmosphere, the foursome explained that they had no intention for the album cover to come off as if they were clowns and instead had a rather serious pose in mind.

It is an amusing story but seems a tad embellished. After all, Brodsky—who was nearing the end of a long period of photographing rock musicians for album covers and other types of publicity, including some of the most famous shows of Jim Morrison and the Doors—no doubt was used to the peculiar attitudes and demands of those he was photographing. Four guys in weird getups at this point would have not been that unusual and certainly would not have automatically suggested the circus, so it seems odd that he would go for a gag shot without at least asking what the four wanted to do for the cover. Furthermore, with a makeup artist there to help with putting the makeup on the four (more on this in a moment), it is clear that Brodsky had been informed of the band's intentions and was hardly in a position to clap his hands and expect the band to "play it like Bozo." Further, longtime fans should be able to recognize that the band's version of the situation as a standard from the "us versus the world/ nobody understood us" catalog of anecdotes that Stanley and Simmons tend to use to coat many of the events they ran into in the early part of their career. Thus, it is perhaps best to take this story with a grain of salt.

Nevertheless, if Brodsky did get the wrong idea, he quickly recovered, creating a cover that easily made a lasting impression on fans and certainly to first-time buyers who picked up the album of the new band and wondered what these four guys in makeup were all about. With a diamond-studded KISS logo at the top of the front cover, the photo shows the four members draped in black so that only their faces appear—as in homage to the *Meet the Beatles* album cover, which featured the faces of the four Beatles emerging from a sea of black. Yet there was also something ominous about the cover beyond that of a tribute, with a deep fiery red background edging into the blackness from above the foursome's heads as if a conflagration glowed behind them. There was a story at work within the photo, and it sold a menace that was atypical at the time.

KISS certainly was not the first to wear whiteface or outlandish makeup on their album covers—as discussed in a previous chapter—but beyond Alice Cooper, there was not much of a sense that someone wearing clown white could look threatening. KISS managed to do that with this cover, simply by reinforcing the makeup on their faces in their own individual ways and giving an individuality to the members of the band: Stanley giving us a kiss; Criss attentive and

The back cover for *Hotter Than Hell* with Peter Criss and Paul Stanley
at "the party."   *Author's Collection*

bemused at the same time; Frehley looking heavenward, as if he were some type
of priest from outer space; and, lastly, Simmons's wide-eyed stare and gaping
mouth that is obviously supposed to elicit fear from the viewer (although, to be
totally honest, with the gold kerchief around his neck—used to balance with the
other three members wearing necklaces or collars—he looks more like a Phyllis
Diller impersonator than a monster). But even if one picks it apart, the answer is
still the same: the cover sums up that KISS was never going to be modest about
the theatrics and certainly was not about to treat it with self-parody humor.

Much has been said over the years about Peter Criss's makeup on the cover
looking unnatural compared to his usual look. This is, of course, thanks to a
professional makeup artist doing it for him, while the others did their own
(admittedly, his "whiskers" nearly reach a Groucho Marx level in thickness and
angle). Yet a closer view in hindsight reveals that only Paul Stanley looks as many
remember him; both Simmons and Frehley have enough variations in their early
days of their makeup personas that they don't look quite "normal." However, this
actually adds to the oddity of the cover, as the fans know who these four are, but
the unusual early interpretation of the makeup makes the four members look
unique here among their album covers featuring them in makeup. They stand
out—both at the time as four young men serious to take on the world and in
reflection as four men about to take a big ride in the music business.

This cover is one of the best known of Brodsky's work (it was typically mentioned alongside the Morrison photo in articles that appeared after Brodsky's death in 2007), and it is clear why—as a visual introduction to the band, it effectively displays to the viewer that there was something deeper going on than just a bunch of goofy guys in clown makeup. No wonder fans have such affection for it, placing it at number eight on the list.

Dressed to Kill

If the cover for *KISS* shows a formidable group of musicians ready to take on the world, the cover of the third album, *Dressed to Kill* shows just how unnerving they can look in certain situations. Ironically, number seven in the list of best album covers does so by having the band appear on a street corner in business suits.

Taken by famous photographer Bob Gruen (as seen throughout this chapter, KISS has had a knack for obtaining the services of well-respected photographers), the stark black-and-white photo has the four up against a lamppost and looking like a cross between a bad family photo and a street gang from *The Warriors*. The awkward poses and ill-fitting suits of Simmons and Stanley merely accentuate the wrongness of the picture. (Criss evidently had a suit, while Frehley appears quite comfortable in his, even if borrowed. Rumor has it that manager Bill Aucoin loaned Simmons, Frehley, and Stanley suits from his wardrobe, although Gruen has stated that two of the suits were from *his* own wardrobe [Tokyo Five 2009], or at least some of the ties used were, while the clogs Simmons wore were those of his ex-wife [Sharp and Leaf 2003]). Although Criss is looking upward—and it should be noted that there is always at least one member of the band looking elsewhere instead of "at the camera" in all their photographed album covers up to *Dynasty*—the others appear to be asking for trouble, with Simmons's smile demonstrating that a fight would be happily appreciated. Photographed while Gruen was shooting pictures of the band for a "photo comic" in the April 1975 issue of *Creem* magazine, it is a picture postcard from hell and continues the promotional agenda of the band at the time of four guys who may be wearing makeup but could likely do you some serious physical damage if you messed with them.

Creatures of the Night (Original Blue Cover)

Photographed by Bernard Vidal (who gained notoriety with some fans for covers listed in the subsequent section of this chapter), the number six best album cover was for the band's 1982 return to a stronger hard-rock beat after the weak response to their concept album, *Music from "The Elder."* Before its release, fans worried that KISS was troubled (and, as it turns out with Ace Frehley's subsequent departure and little interest in the recording of the album, those concerns were more on the mark than they realized at the time), not to mention the public notion of the band being a relic of the 1970s with the makeup and effects. Thus, the album had to send a strong message, both musically and visually.

Vidal's photo elegantly does just that. A simple portrait of the foursome (the first official all-new material album release with Eric Carr, Peter Criss's replacement, on the cover) bathed in blue light and with the eyes of each musician glowing white-hot (as if a cue from the film *Village of the Damned*), the image is one of solidarity and defiance, with a dash of mysticism for good measure. Oddly, it would be the last posed photo cover to show such a close unity within the group, not to mention that later statements from the band members show that such unanimity was far from the truth at the time.

Admittedly, even with such a message in the cover and a solid musical album to boot, the album struggled to find an audience and sold even less than *Music from "The Elder"* at the time of their initial releases Eventually the album would be reissued in 1985 with a revised cover that . . . well, we'll get to that in a bit.

Love Gun

Number five is the first nonphotographic cover in the best covers list and the second created by fantasy artist Ken Kelly for KISS (*Destroyer* being the first). Due to his success with the *Destroyer* artwork—a defining image of the band that has been used repeatedly through the years to the point where parodies of it are instantly recognized—it was no surprise to see him come back for another soon after. The focus is a tad different this time around: in contrast to the action movements of the foursome in earlier covers, *Love Gun* shows them merely standing on a small platform. Even so, the surroundings are what really make the cover memorable for most fans (and certainly the younger male fans)—the numerous "fantasy females" draped at their feet. With that image and the album title, there really is no need to say anything else. Which, unfortunately, may explain why the back cover is just a drab look at the stairs and columns after everyone has packed up (or maybe paired off) and left the room.

As a side note, this cover is referenced in Jeff Godwin's antirock book *The Devil's Disciples* as being "too perverse to print" even as an example of the evils of rock music for his text. Ironically, this makes it seem much more enticing than what Kelly painted.

Hotter Than Hell

KISS was still struggling to break through as this album, number four on the best covers list, came out in October 1974. With it being their second album, and with the first causing only a slight ripple in sales, there was no need to worry about sticking with an "image" other than that of how the band wanted to see itself. Well-known photographer Norman Seeff took photos of the band members while they were in Los Angeles for the recording of their second album, and the front cover is from a photo session of them goofing around for the camera instead of expressing any serious conceptual objective. That came later, to be returned to in a couple of paragraphs.

Of course, more notorious in fan circles and perhaps why some fans remember the cover so well are the photos on the back cover, which shows the band members having a bit of fun at what appears to be a party. Not a "happy birthday, gee you are swell" kind of party, but one ready to get down to some serious areas of craziness. For those not familiar with Seeff's work, he is known for drawing out different reactions from the people he is photographing in a variety of ways—such as bringing in audiences to watch or even participate in the photo sessions with the artists in front of the camera—and this was the case with these photos. Rumors, perpetuated by the band as well, had it that it was a wild party atmosphere and that the band members (with the exception of Gene Simmons) were liquored up in order to get them "in the mood," but other reports state that the party was not quite as wild as suggested. Even so, there were rumors for years that Paul Stanley got so trashed he had to be escorted out to a car by Simmons and "locked in" to keep him safe (and a mild pondering of that story means that Stanley was so drunk he couldn't figure out that the car doors were locked on the inside with him and he could have easily escaped if he has been sober).

No matter if one wishes to believe the party was wild or merely photographed to appear that way, it was certainly a brief glimpse at the reckless and sexually dangerous side of the band that they would abandon by the following year and especially after 1976 and the adjustment to be family oriented. Which may explain why several of the photos from the "party" would turn up for a time in rock magazines (especially *Creem*), only to disappear as the '70s wore on and the "safe" image of KISS came more into play.

Another rumor to address about this album cover: Ace Frehley's makeup. Fans discovered that he had been involved in a car accident and could only cover part of his face in makeup for the photo-shoot. This would suggest that his makeup had to be airbrushed in for the cover and on the back in order to make it complete. However, Seeff himself has posted the contact sheets of the photos sessions on his official website, and it is clear that, while Frehley did only use a half-face makeup for one of the sessions (showcasing a nasty scar at the bridge of his nose), he would eventually put on the full makeup for other sessions, including the one used for the front cover and at the party; therefore, no airbrushing was required.

The hoopla and rumors behind the cover's photos are not the full reason this album has made the top five of favorite KISS album covers. Instead, the entire package really sells it to fans. Seeff, working with John Van Hamersveld, would fashion the cover to look like an import album from Japan. Seeff has stated this was to play off the Kabuki-style makeup of the band, but with the Japanese writing and feel to the album cover, it gives the buyer the idea that they are from another country or that the album was a rare import. Either way, it made both the band and album feel exotic and unique from everything else out there, even their first album. The first album cover looks like an introduction; the second looks like photos taken at the scene of a crime in a foreign brothel.

Finally, for those interested in such trivia, it is the band's first usage of the Chikara symbol (Japanese for power or strength). After its front-and-center appearance on the front cover, the band would repeatedly return to it in their career, including on a "best of" album under the same name, as well as using the symbol for Eric Carr's drums in the latter part of the 1980s.

Rock and Roll Over

Number three on the list of best album covers continues with the Japanese theme that first appeared with the *Hotter Than Hell* cover, although this was out of coincidence rather than any intention to bounce off the earlier design. Graphic designer Michael Dorat arrived by way of Dennis Woloch and Howard Marks Advertising with a design that Dorat had springboarded from an earlier design he had done for a Japanese graphics magazine. Looking at the album title, Dorat wanted to present an image that could be "rolled over" without defining a top or bottom; in essence, there would be no right-side-up to the artwork. What he created was another classic image of the band that expands (although probably not his intention) upon the "superhero" personas of KISS, giving each member their own background representing something about them, as well as having lasers shooting from Ace Frehley's eyes. KISS would develop the idea of unique backgrounds for the members with the solo album covers soon after this, thus making the *Rock and Roll Over* cover an important first development in the way the band was presented to the public.

Having the album cover on a small-size sticker included within the album itself as an "extra" helped get it seen pretty much anywhere kids could stick them as well, keeping *Rock and Roll Over* fresh in people's minds for years to come. Even if it meant scraping stickers off walls and items around the house and at school.

Destroyer

Already referenced above for his work on the *Love Gun* cover, Ken Kelly first worked with the band on a cover that would become one of the most iconic images of the band ever created. A fantasy artist who had gotten some early training with Frank Frazetta (as well as being related by marriage), Kelly had already done fantasy magazine and paperback covers for years when the offer came to do the cover for *Destroyer*. The band—namely Gene Simmons—had decided to have their next album cover present them in a fantasy setting and more like superheroes; an image that could not be convincingly conveyed in the style of photographic covers done on the previous albums. When a brief attempt to get Frazetta himself to do the artwork fell through during negotiations, the record company approached Kelly. His initial concept was considered "too violent," but once the flaming rubble of the destroyed city was toned down and moved to the back cover (as well as the proper costumes being added for the band members), everyone was in agreement that it was a startling image of KISS that pushed them to an otherworldly level.

The cover has been parodied many times over the years and used intensively by the band on a multitude of merchandise. Even so, the image of the four members bursting toward the viewer after causing rampant destructive never gets old and places it at the number-two spot I the best album covers.

Alive!

The definitive album cover for the band, highlighting them in what they have always done best—performing in concert. The photo, shot by Fin Costello (another early photographer of the band) at a rehearsal area in the Michigan Palace, shows them in action onstage as smoke rises in the background. Sure, it is easy to tell that it is posed and even somewhat static in the positioning of the band members—Ace Frehley holding his guitar the wrong way around so that the instrument's face is toward the camera is a clear indication of being posed for visual and not musical reasons—but there is an energy present that suggests a live show by these four men would be at least visually exciting.

Further, the back cover helps sell the album and band as strongly as the front. Featuring two young fans—Bruce Redoute and Lee Neaves—holding up a handmade KISS sign in front of many fans waiting for the KISS concert to begin (or are they? See the rumors chapter for more details on this supposed legend), the photo shows the early stages of what would soon become known as the KISS Army. This was not some staged, squeaky-clean attempt to show that there were fans out there (which could have been done by showing everyone in makeup, holding huge professional banners, or even the number of waving arms that appear in the inner sleeve of *Alive II*); this was obviously a fan-made sign by two guys who wanted to show their devotion to KISS. It showed that there was a growing fan base out there, ready to do anything to show their support, even if for the moment it was just two young guys with a cardboard sign. Furthermore, the photo demonstrated that KISS was recognizing the fans on a more personal level than other groups had at the time. True, the names of these two young men do not appear on the cover, so it was not as if the band was getting tremendously personal about the fans; nevertheless, it verified the importance of those who were supporting the band by coming to the shows. After all, this was a major two-disc release that goes for the hard sell on the front cover, only to avoid any pictures of the band members on the back and instead focus on a couple of teen-age fans. This was even extended to the advertising for the album, which heavily featured the back cover photo of the two, thus proving that the photograph was deemed important to the atmosphere the record company and band wanted to present to the public for *Alive!*

Ken Kelly's iconic portrait of KISS, created for the *Destroyer* album.
From here on out, they would never be less than superheroes.
Author's Collection

This was also KISS's first album to include "extras": an eight-page album-sized booklet with the band's history told in photos as well as "personal notes" by the band members in the gatefold cover. Such items became standard from this point on for the band during the rest of their original makeup period. Thus, the album is the perfect combination of everything the fans wanted from KISS—good music, over-the-top packaging, and an album cover that sold their frantic madness. The first three studio albums were a start, but *Alive!* has always been seen as the point of no return for KISS into something more than being "just another band."

And the Top Ten Questionable Ones

KISS fans are a determined bunch. Having faced the ridicule of friends and family over their love of the music and theatrics of the band, the KISS Army will sometimes dig in their heels and refuse to admit that there are times when the foursome have done some rather ridiculous things. Or, if refusing to see the band as humans who sometimes make mistakes, even admit that there have been times they could have done better. Still, late in the evening, when everyone has had a couple of drinks and can relax with fellow fans, there are faint echoes of criticism and admissions that some of the album covers were not the best ideas in the world is one of the few arguments that will not typically end in a fistfight.

Make no mistake—KISS has gone through the years with some tremendous album covers, as seen above. But even so, there are some that usually raise a few snickers and shaking of heads, and these are presented below, going from ten as the least problematic to a number one that still leaves fans scratching their heads at the point of it all.

One interesting aspect of the entries listed below is that in many cases the photo and art created are actually quite good, but it is how and even when they were used where the problems come into play. For examples, the revised *Creatures of the Night* photo and the one used for *Carnival of Souls* are solid pictures of the band members at those points in time, but they bothered some fans for other reasons. Thus, one cannot simply look at an album's cover artist and say, "here is the problem": in the finest term of what a business association is all about, it took a whole team of people to mess these up.

In putting together the results from a poll on the Top Ten Questionable Covers, it should be mentioned that fans requested the many compilation albums—typically cut-and-paste jobs or, at the most, dull—not be included in the list or they would be the only ones appearing, Even so, many fans pointed to *Smashes, Thrashes, and Hits* as their least favorite of the compilation covers, which displays the band proudly standing in what appears to be a field of arms, ready for harvesting

On a personal note, I was surprised to discover that *Music from "The Elder"* did not make the list of the ten least favorites. Although I am a fan of this album and have always put it in my top five of their releases, I have to admit that the cover does not visually "sell" it to purchasers. A concept album full of superheroic derring-do that was to be a soundtrack to an exciting action-fantasy film is ultimate represented in all its might on the front cover by . . . a door knocker. Oh, and Paul Stanley's hand.

Sonic Boom

Michael Dorat made the Top Ten Best Album Covers above with his work on the cover for *Rock and Roll Over*. Thirty-three years later, he would return to do the cover for this album, the first studio album by the band with Tommy Thayer and the first since the release of the 1998 album *Psycho Circus*. It was also an exclusive Walmart release, which created its own controversy for the album, but that is not perhaps the reason this album cover made it to number ten in the Top Ten Questionable Album Covers.

Dorat described the design as "*Rock and Roll Over* turned inside out" (Tokyo Five), and it is an apt description as it does appear to be an inverted revisitation to the earlier theme. In fact, the fault fans have with it does not necessarily come from Dorat's design, but rather what he was given to present to buyers: namely four band member in the corners of the cover that appear . . . as if they're not really quite the people we expect to see on the cover of a new KISS album. This is partially due to age and a plastic surgery or two having unavoidably caught up with both Gene Simmons and Paul Stanley, so that even in the makeup they look like imposters doing good imitations of the Starchild and the Demon instead of the two men people knew from earlier albums. (*Psycho Circus* at least avoided any concerns about age by using caricatures of the foursome on its front cover, and that was eleven years before *Sonic Boom*.) Meanwhile, infrequent fans were vocal in thinking both Peter Criss and Ace Frehley did not look anything like themselves. Of course, this actually is the case, as Criss and Frehley were long-gone from the band by this point, and the two on the cover are Eric Singer and Tommy Thayer respectively wearing the Cat and Spaceman makeup. Pushing aside the whole "Should Singer and Thayer have continued with the others' makeup" argument within fandom (as it is covered in another chapter), it is impossible to deny that there seems something odd about how they look in the makeup, because obviously it is two other men and not Frehley and Criss. Thus, the four corner figures combined to create a portrait of some kind of alternate universe version of the band, or of a local KISS cover band: individuals who looked somewhat like our heroes but not quite. It felt wrong.

It is with this oddness that the emphasis behind the cover does not succeed. The aim is obviously to convey a jolt to the viewer, the feeling of a visual explosion in sound; in other words, the sonic boom of the album's title. Instead, with four odd and rather bored-looking men on the cover (even with his tongue out, Simmons appears to be more going through the motions of what is expected—compare his look here with that used on *Dressed to Kill* or even *Dynasty*, where there is a sense this man could do someone physical damage), the message appears to be "Here is an album by these guys, thank you for shopping Walmart." Also, the album's logo, while interesting, seems reminiscent of the early 1980s, and with a generic title for the album to boot, the cover has all the feel of a K-Tel "Greatest Hits" album from 1983. (A front sticker on the cover that heavily promoted a bonus disc of "re-recorded KISS Klassics" [*sic*] no doubt helped confuse matters even more for some potential buyers.) In all, the album appears to be a lost entry from the past instead of what it is supposed to showcase: the band's future.

Dynasty

This is the first posed photo cover for a studio album since the 1975 release of *Dressed to Kill* and the first studio album from KISS in nearly two years (after the release of *Love Gun* and the solo albums). With the band still riding high on their superhero personas and with an audience that was all-ages—not to mention that the album and tour were based around the concept of "The RETURN of KISS!"—the cover should convey a new high in visual excitement, especially with a name like *Dynasty* as the title.

Instead, as number nine in the questionable covers list, we get a washed-out gray cover with the four band members' faces staring out. No doubt, it was meant to show a rock-solid intensity to a viewer—here is KISS, you cannot look away from them even if you say you hate them. Yet the cover of the *Alive II* album had attempted this same concept, and, as discussed above, it did not work well there and certainly did not get any better the second time around.

That is not to say that the photo is bad. Famed photographer Francesco Scavullo did a fine job photographing the foursome, and, while Frehley and Criss may look as if they just spotted their bus, at least Stanley and Simmons bring some emotion to the moment. While much discussion has been made about pasteups done to fix minor concerns, namely due to Stanley not being happy with how he appeared in the chosen photo (Sharp and Leaf 2003), the pasteups are not noticeable and do nothing to hurt the composition of the photo (unlike what was to come with the *Animalize* album a few years later). On all fronts, Scavullo's work is great as a promotional photo of the four. As an album cover, however, it seems more of a placeholder than one that would display the intensity of what "the RETURN of KISS" to the world stage was all about and thus comes off as a disappointment when finally released.

Unmasked

The only album to make it to both lists is here at number eight. This may say more about the ages of fans at the time of release than anything else.

An older, more experienced fan would see the cover in much the spirit that would earn it a place in the Top Ten Greatest Album Covers by the band—it is meant to be a joke on the critics who would never understand the band. Ultimately, KISS is going to remain KISS, no matter what outsiders think or want.

Now imagine you are a young teenage fan in 1980. You have to deal not only with parents who may not approve of your interest in the band, but also with the ridicule of your peers, who see KISS as a "kiddie band." Nevertheless, you have stuck with KISS and its army because there was a unity to the ranks—everyone else may be against you, but the spirit of the band and the fans were one and the same. KISS may do a bad television movie, write a disco song, or appear on merchandise geared toward kids younger than you (no matter how much you wanted your own set of KISS dolls . . . er, action figures), but the shows and 99.9 percent of the music stood strong. You could depend on KISS to stay the course no matter what.

Then *Unmasked* arrives. An album not only full of pop songs instead of the hard-rock music you expected, but with a cover that says to you, "Yeah, this is all pretty much a joke, is it not?" The generals in charge of the KISS Army not only have gone to the other side but have publicly stated their contempt for their soldiers. No wonder some fans found the cover demoralizing.

That, or they just did not like the artwork.

Psycho Circus

While the graphic design of the CD has left some fans with distaste, this album may be more of a case where the memories of its production have more to do with why fans put it into this category of "questionable album cover" than the artwork itself. Even so, it is here at number seven.

More details about this album are elsewhere, but to put it bluntly, *Psycho Circus* was to have shown the band having learned from previous mistakes and putting aside all differences in order to give fans a new exciting album featuring all four original members performing their jointly agreed-upon material. As it turns out, no matter which side one wants to believe, that did not occur. Instead, fans got an album that was blatantly slanted toward Gene Simmons and Paul Stanley, and no amount of publicity claiming that Ace Frehley and Peter Criss were happy with it could convince fans after a couple of listens that they had much input on it.

The finger-pointing and arguments by band members and among fans tainted the album in many ways, including its cover. Illustrated by fantasy artist Peter Scanian, the cover is rather a strong representation for the concept behind the album and subsequent tour—that of the circus atmosphere—with stylized portraits of the foursome in the banner on the circus wagon. The main problem appears to be with the art direction and design by Louis Marino; or rather, the determination of all involved to give the cover a 3-D effect to tie in with the 3-D concert-experience planned for the tour (and, yes, the obvious crack by a lot of people at the time was, "is not every live concert a 3-D experience?" But let us disregard that for now). Although there were attempts made to come up with a new method to display a 3-D effect for the cover, the record company ultimately went back to a long-serving standard called Lenticular printing in order to get the effect needed. The downside of this was that the artwork became somewhat muddied in the process, making the four characters look blurred and distorted. Admittedly, the huge gaping-mouth clown at the center of the artwork no doubt turned off some fans as well who saw the focus diverted from the band itself. In combination with an album deemed by many fans as a missed opportunity, the cover never had a chance to receive much appreciation from the fans. A shame, as standing alone without the 3-D effect, it is a nice piece of art.

Crazy Nights

This is the high point of the band's party period in the nonmakeup era, with song after song about having a good time and living your destiny to the fullest. This is represented on the cover by the grim faces of the band members reflected in the shattered remains of a mirror. Some party, right?

This was the last album cover with involvement from Dennis Woloch, who had worked with the band since the early days, although the concept for the cover came from Paul Stanley. Woloch brought in game creator and trick photographer

CD-Video single featuring the album artwork from *Crazy Nights.*
Author's Collection

Walter Wick to rev up the idea into one that worked like some of Wick's picture puzzles, but when the results were vetoed due to the images of the band members not being clear enough, another attempt was made that satisfied the band but lessened the potential impact of the idea (Sharp and Leaf 2003).

Perhaps the biggest reason for the lack of excitement about the cover, however, is that by this time the cliché of a broken mirror relaying the images of an artist or band had been done to death in movies, television, and even in rock videos. At a time when some fans were questioning the band's reliance on following the leads of others (remember, this is the era some refer to as KISS being Bon Jovi clones), such a cover did not help dispute that argument, and thus it ends up at number six.

Creatures of the Night (Rerelease Nonmakeup Cover)

By 1985, KISS was rebounding thanks to the success of both *Lick It Up* and *Animalize.* To capitalize on this, Mercury decided to reissue the band's final album in makeup, the 1982 *Creatures of the Night*, in hopes of drawing in those who may not have been fans at the time of its original release. To further confuse the issue, Mercury not only remixed some material but slapped on a new cover. This would not have been a major issue if Mercury had gone with a picture of the band from 1982, or least one with Vinnie Vincent standing with the other three members of the band—as he certainly had played more on the album than Ace Frehley, who nevertheless appears on the cover of the original 1982 release.

Instead, July 1985 saw the reissue of the album with a picture of the band with (at the time) new lead guitarist Bruce Kulick. This ironically meant the album was twice released with neither cover showing the proper lead guitarist on the album. Compounding the problem for fans was the fact that the new cover— a rather good portrait of the band by famed photographer Neil Zlozower—did not convey the emotional power of the original. Fans fondly remembered the original cover because the photo cover goes back to the old premise of the band being something otherworldly. The new one appeared to be part of a promotional shoot for them, with the band members politely standing outside at dusk while Paul Stanley looks a little chilly. As it turns out, a promotional photo is exactly what it was (see Neil Zlozower's interview in the next chapter).

Hot in the Shade

The three-legged dog of KISS albums. This was the point where Gene Simmons had gone on record in various interviews to state that he was back 100 percent to work with KISS after a time of working in the movies and producing and managing others. Simmons would fall back into old habits soon enough, but for the moment, *Hot in the Shade* was to be his triumphant return to the fold. It is also considered a musical mess by most fans (although credit has to be given for experimentation on the album, with a variety of musical approaches thrown into a heap of tracks), but that is not why the cover falls into the "questionable" category and is number four on the list.

The cover, designed by Michael Kanner and Scott Townsend, shows the Sphinx wearing sunglasses, with the album title appearing as a postal stamp off in the upper right-hand corner. As such, it is a one-joke idea and nothing else. Further, it was a gag that in one form or another had already been done (such as for the single of ZZ Top's "Sleeping Bag" back in 1985 with a sarcophagus wearing shades). Worse still, the album actually had a rather interesting photo concept for the cover when it was to be *Crimes of Passion*, which was shot but not used. The photo, showing the four members in blindfolds as if in front of a firing squad, appeared as the bottom image on the cover of the limited-release compilation album, *First KISS . . . Last Licks*. To lose the one for the other puts *Hot in the Shade* this far down on the list.

Carnival of Souls: The Final Sessions

Released in 1997 after the original foursome had gotten back together, the album was recorded in 1995 as a safety measure for the band in case things fell through with getting the 1973–1980 lineup in sync for an album and tour.

The bootleg-ish cover for *Carnival of Souls*.   *Author's Collection*

Because things did work out—at least for a time—the completed album sat in
the vaults, with little concern about doing anything with it,

Then the music was leaked to the public—with radio stations playing some
songs and fans openly trading murky copies of the album on tape. Finally, the
interest led the record company to release the album in the U.S. nearly a year
and a half after completion. Although a single was released, "Jungle," there was
not much push behind the album, which was logical for both the band and the
record company—no point in confusing fans with this "old" version of the band
when the "once and future KISS" was now back together.

This thinking obviously led to the album cover, which shows a manipulated
photo of the band, evidently squeezed in order to make everyone look thinner.
The back cover is a simple photo of the foursome looking bored, a song list, and
some minor credits. The problem was not so much the picture itself—shot by
William Hames, who managed to get some better pictures of the reunited KISS
soon after this shoot—but the design work, which makes the album look like
a bootleg. Perhaps that was the intention, but considering how many pirated
copies of the album were already available to fans, a legit one given that same
appearance hardly says, "Buy me." Liner notes for the CD detailing what the
album was about, why it was done, and why it was now being released would have
been a good idea as well. Instead, it appears no one wanted to bother working

on it, and they rushed it out merely to shut up fans clamoring for it. Of course, with the renewed interest in KISS focused around the four original members in makeup anyway, it no doubt was a hard sell to the record company to put much time and effort into the release.

The album itself is not that bad, but the packaging does nothing to interest buyers, which is the ultimate mistake packaging can have for an album. Thus, number three on the list.

Asylum

There is no way around it—heavy-metal was immensely popular in 1985 and would continue to grow for a few more years. Nevertheless, popularity tends to take those things that are unique enough to attract attention in the first place and homogenize them into safe products for public consumption. Thus, an element of "fun" and harmless psychedelia began to bleed through in at least the costumes and performances of the more popular heavy-metal artists at the time, with a retread into the glam movement of the early 1970s peeking through but without its sexual menace. With this came a dependence by bands on top and those struggling to fit in to go with bright, nearly obnoxious-looking colors, sequins on everything, and heavy eyeliner and makeup.

CD-Video single featuring the infamous *Asylum* cover artwork.

Author's Collection

Of course, as it turned out, all this "innocent fun" led directly to the death of the movement by 1990, but for the moment, everyone was living in a sparkly, colorful world indeed, and KISS made no apologies for following the trend along with everyone else. This was never more obvious than with the *Asylum* tour and music videos and especially the album cover. As some KISS fans smirked, the band in 1985 seemed to be wearing more makeup than when they were wearing clown white in the 1970s.

This explains to some extent why the *Asylum* album cover, number two on the list of questionable covers, looks like an Andy Warhol rip-off, with neon paint coloring rough photocopied-style photos (taken by Bernard Vidal) of the band members' faces. Attempting to be "hip" to the times, it does not even come off as so much an imitation of a style but just a ghastly-looking mistake in judgment. Fans at least gave the band credit for making sure that the colors used on the lips of each member corresponded with those used on the 1978 solo albums. Strangely enough, most fans saw this as a look back at the legacy of the band that allowed the two replacement players, Eric Carr and Bruce Kulick, to pay homage to their predecessors. The year 2000 was a long way off at this point.

Animalize

Considered the worst album cover by a number of KISS fans, it is one of their few albums where the back cover inspired as much as or even more ridicule than the front.

Animalize was released in 1984, before the glam retread had kicked in (as witnessed above for *Asylum*). While the twinkly shininess of that era was still to come, the dress code of the well-dressed heavy-metal person at the time was not much better: spikes, leather, bandannas tied over every square inch of the body, and animal fur hanging somewhere off the body—as if to give the appearance of just coming fresh from a kill, but unfortunately usually looking as if moth-bitten weasels had jumped out of a hamper and attacked an unfortunate soul. Thus, you end up with an album called *Animalize* in the first place, but to symbolize the concept by haphazardly throwing a bunch of animal skins on the cover like fur rug samples at Sears does not really convey the "dangerous/wicked" atmosphere that was probably expected by those who put it together. Further, for the band's second album without makeup—still a strong motivator for people to check them out at the time—to relegate their faces to the back seems to be missing the point.

This is where deeper criticisms come into play for *Animalize*. Photographed by Bernard Vidal, the image plays off of the at-the-time already heavily clichéd idea of band members standing among the twisted metal and fires of a posta-pocalyptic world (a promotional poster for *Creatures of the Night*, also shot by Vidal, of the band standing on a fog-drenched rocky mountain top is very similar in nature and pose to the *Animalize* back cover, so it was not even a unique image of the band by this point). If that had been the end of the story, the photo would

Mark St. John's autograph on the *Animalize* album, stating, "This is not my real head!"   *Courtesy of Jeff C*

probably not be remembered as well as it is by fans today; after all, KISS had been down this dead-end alley before with their videos for "Lick It Up" and "All Hell's Breakin' Loose" from the previous album, so it was "more of the same" to many in the KISS Army. What bugged fans had more to do with the awkwardness of the four band members in the photo itself: Paul Stanley with an impossible cotton-candy mass of hair on his head and an abnormal-looking left arm, Eric Carr with one leg that appears to be shorter than the other, Mark St. John looking as if they had put his head on Helen Reddy's body and his legs at a weird angle from each other; all of these elements readily told the knowledgeable fans that a lot of pasteup work had been done on the photo.

This was exactly what had occurred, as St. John readily pointed out in interviews after leaving the band. When some members declared the photos unsuitable, it was decided to manipulate the image so that the background looked more dangerous (with brighter, heavier fires and more smoke) and—more importantly—the guys looked their "best." This led to much time and expense put into getting the results found on the back of the album—one that St. John saw as looking much worse than the original photos. As he told the website KISS Asylum a few years later, "Why did we even do a photo session, ten hours of pictures, if you are chopping it all up anyway?"

In hindsight, it is a good statement about how the 1980s were running away from KISS, even as they were beginning a second rise in popularity. The band that at one time could pull over to the side of a street and quickly take a picture that becomes an iconic moment for them (*Dressed to Kill*) within just a few years needed hours of pasteup work in order to create a back cover that is remembered by fans as being a big mistake.

The 1985 Creatures Cover

Interview with Photographer Neil Zlozower

A nyone with an interest in hard rock and heavy metal is bound to have seen plenty of Neil Zlozower's work. Known for his photos of Van Halen and Mötley Crüe, among others too numerous to list, Zlozower has taken several quintessential photos of musicians over the years. In that list of names are those of KISS and the individual members of the band, including the covers for Bruce Kulick's *BK3* and Paul Stanley's *Live to Win* and a well-known Ludwig Drums ad featuring Eric Carr. Zlozower has shot photos of KISS since 1974 and continuing up to the current lineup with photos of the band that have appeared on the cover of *Rolling Stone* and *Classic Rock*.

Zlozower also has the distinction of being involved with the photo used for the cover of the rerelease of *Creatures of the Night* in 1985. As mentioned in the previous chapter, this cover is well remembered by fans due to how the photo was used—a nonmakeup photo of the band with Bruce Kulick for an album that 1) was recorded during the makeup period of the band and 2) that did not feature Bruce Kulick performing on it. Of course, the objective was to sell the album anew to fans who were becoming interested in the band now that the makeup was off; in other words, to a new generation of fans. Still, because of this, the cover has gained some notoriety. Ironically, with the reissued album featuring some remixing that was not used for the subsequent CD reissue in 1997 (which also reverted back to the original Bernard Vidal cover), the 1985 reissue with Zlozower's cover is now considered the rarer version of the album and is sought after by collectors.

DS: On your website, http://www.zloz.com, I noticed a photo you took of KISS from 1974. I then saw that the next photos you have of them there seem to come about during their 1980s nonmakeup era.

NZ: I shot them backstage once in 1974, back when no one even knew who they were. But the first studio shoot I did with them was when Mark St. John got into the band. Then, since he did not last too long, the next one I did with KISS was when Bruce Kulick joined them in 1984.

DS: Was this for the cover of *Creatures?*

NZ: What happened was that they came to my studio to do a normal, regular photo shoot for press and magazines. They did not come to me and say, "Neil, we need a new cover for a new version of *Creatures of the Night.*" I do not believe they did that. They came in, like, "Hey, we have a new member in the band so we need new photos with the new member." Because Bruce was new and Eric Carr was fairly new at the time and they thought it would be a good idea.

One thing I am sort of well known for at my studio is that I have stairs where you can walk right upstairs to my roof and do photo shoots. We never did that before with KISS, and they liked the idea, so we did individual shots. I do not remember if we ever did do group shots actually, but I do remember individual shots of Eric, Bruce, and Paul up there. I honestly cannot remember shooting Gene by himself up on the roof.

A few weeks later the band called me up and said, "We are going to re-release *Creatures of the Night* and we thought the shots that you did, Neil, with the sun setting behind them were perfect." So, to be honest with you, you could say it was an afterthought because we did not shoot them for the album cover, but once they saw the photos, they really liked them and said, "Okay, let's use them."

DS: Having photographed the band over the years, with and without the makeup, do you find there is a difference between how they work through a photo shoot when in makeup and "in character" than when not in the makeup? For example, there was a period in the 1980s where the members at times seemed a bit unsure of themselves without the characters they used to have to portray on stage and in videos and such.

NZ: Well, with the makeup, you have a mask to hide behind, or you have an outfit or whatever. When I shoot photos of them without makeup or when I shot photos of them with makeup, do they seem a little bit more untouchable, more confident? I don't know, you know? That is hard to say, because being a photographer, my job is to make everybody look as good as possible. And Gene and Paul, I honestly think are the two stars of KISS. Don't get me wrong—I love Eric Singer and Tommy Thayer more than anyone on the planet, but I never had a problem shooting Gene and Paul without makeup. Listen, when you have sold as many albums as they have and you have done as many concerts and have played all over the world, masked and unmasked, in their minds they know what they have accomplished and I don't really think that they need clothes or makeup to hide behind to bring out the confidence in their persona when they are doing photos. So even when they did not have the makeup on, I never got the feeling they were uncomfortable or insecure.

The 1985 reissue of *Creatures of the Night* replacing the original cover artwork with Neil Zlozower's photo of the band.   *Author's Collection*

DS: When working with a band like KISS, how closely do you work with them on what to shoot?

NZ: With some photographers, a band will come in and the photographer will say, "Okay, I want to do this with you and this is my vision and this is my concept," and the band may not go along with it, and the photographer sort of pushes his ideas on whoever he is shooting. But with me, I am a paid professional. A lot of times I like to have a little chat with the band before they ever even get to my studio and ask what they want to do and what kind of vibe they are looking for.

I continue to work for KISS and do a lot of their current photos for their books, albums, and tours. When you deal with someone like Paul, he is very artistic and very creative, and for the last few photo shoots we did, Paul has come up with very specific concepts/ideas that he wanted me to execute. I come up with some ideas as well, and they have liked some of them, but in reality Paul really seems to be the shot-layer and says, "Here is my idea, Neil. Let's make it work."

I try to treat everybody the same and not get starstruck. I can deal people like David Lee Roth and KISS, and I have dealt with people like Axl Rose and Slash, and I treat them the same as I would treat you or my family. If something is great, I will complement them; if something is not right, I will be the first to say so. I do not hold back. I am not shy, and I have a big mouth.

KISS is one of the biggest rock bands that ever graced this planet, and they have in their mind the right to be a little egotistical and arrogant, but they do not pull that on me. I think they consider me part of the KISS family. I have worked with them long enough, and I have paid my dues with them. I think they appreciate the detail that I put into the photos, and I think that they know if their hair or makeup is not right, or if they are posing in an unflattering way that I will open my mouth and give them advice on what to do to make them look better. So when they come to my studio, they do not seem any different to me with the makeup or without the makeup. I treat them the same and they treat me with respect and courtesy that I think they feel I deserve to be treated with, because I have proven myself time and time again with them.

The Record Is Cool, but Where Are the Extras?

Trivial Album Notes

I t is not unusual—most performers run into situations where what was to be released on albums is altered in ways that make the albums much different than was originally intended. KISS has been no different, going back to their very first album. There have also been times where what fans perceived to be the case with an album turned out to be slightly different—such as the number of times guest musicians have played on albums instead of the band members. Below are some minor notes about some of the KISS albums over the years that are of interest but don't quite fit into any of the other chapter categories.

KISS

When first released in February 1974 (catalog number NB9001), the album featured nine tracks, all written by the band members. "Nothin' to Lose" was released as the first single in March 1974 to utter indifference, and the band was unsure what could be done. Neil Bogart, however, had what he thought was a great idea—the band would go back to the studios with producers Kenny Kerner and Richie Wise and do a cover version of the old Bobby Rydell hit "Kissin' Time," and it would be their next single.

KISS and the producers hated the idea and only reluctantly went into the studio knowing beforehand that they would have to change the lyrics to make it tolerable for them to record. As a group shouting out anything that came into their heads, the band finally recorded the song, and it was released as the second single in May 1974. It pretty much stiffed on the *Billboard* chart, reaching #83 before sinking. However, Bogart was able to use the song as momentum for a kissing contest to draw attention to the band. To the grumbling acknowledgment of the band, the contest helped get KISS noticed, leading to appearances on both *The Mike Douglas Show* and ABC's *In Concert*, so it did pay off.

Still, KISS was not thrilled when Casablanca decided to add "Kissin' Time" to the album. This was done at first with copies of it not including the track on the back credits, so a sticker was added to the front cover to make fans aware the song was there (further pushing the idea that "Kissin' Time" was the type of material the band wanted fans to hear over everything else). The album was later reissued as NB7001 with the song added to the back credits as well, and it has remained so on all reissues since then.

Hotter Than Hell

Originally planned as *The Harder They Come.* The original CD reissue from the 1980s was considered a very poor mix of an album that some fans do not believe ever had a good mix. The 1997 remaster fixed this somewhat.

Dressed to Kill

Listed in one source with a possible alternate title of *KISS at Midnight*, this

album was produced by Neil Bogart. He took over the production from Kerner and Wise (who had produced the first two KISS albums) after the two had joined KISS and Aucoin in a revolt against Casablanca in order to get some funds or find another label. Some felt Bogart used the production job as a way to become friendly with the band in hopes of getting them to fire Aucoin and sign him as their manager. As the band was not entirely happy with Bogart's work on the album, and were quite happy with Aucoin's services, they had no intention of doing that.

Alive!

The original inner sleeves that came with the vinyl album showed the cast of the movie *Casablanca* on one side, their faces blurred in a fog, with the

Japanese ad for the *Dressed to Kill* album with the band in their suits. *Author's Collection* slogan, "The Image is Getting Clearer." On the other side of the sleeve showed pictures of many Casablanca releases, including the first three KISS studio albums.

Destroyer

The first album to feature an outside musician replacing one of the four (*KISS* featured Bruce Foster on piano but did not replace a member). Whether one wishes to believe Ace Frehley couldn't be bothered to perform on the song "Sweet Pain" or that his guitar work was dismissed for that of Bob Ezrin regular Dick Wagner is up to the fans to decide at this point. Most fans missed the hidden final track on Side Two (which was only available on the first pressing of the vinyl but has since been added back with the remastered CD). The track featured Paul Stanley singing with the choir in a warped minute and a half bit of frenzy. Ezrin, Wagner, cowriters Kim Fowley and Marc Anthony, and engineer Corky Stasiak had all worked on Alice Cooper's 1975 album, *Welcome to My Nightmare*.

Rock and Roll Over

The first studio album to come with a true "extra," in this case an 8 ½" by 8 ½" square sticker of the front album cover. Produced with as live a feel as possible, the album was rumored at the time to be KISS's apology to fans who felt that *Destroyer* was an example of the band trying too hard to please critics. Paul Stanley had written "Hard Luck Woman" for Rod Stewart, but it was given to Peter Criss to sing on the album." "Queen for a Day" was long rumored to have been recorded for the album for Ace Frehley, but for many years KISS denied the song even existed. Eventually talk turned to a musical track being done but no vocals (which was to be Frehley's singing debut). However, a

I WANT YOU	LOVE 'EM AND LEAVE 'EM
TAKE ME	MR. SPEED
CALLING DR. LOVE	SEE YOU IN YOUR DREAMS
LADIES ROOM	HARD LUCK WOMAN
BABY DRIVER	MAKIN' LOVE

A songbook for *Rock and Roll Over*, which featured another iconic album cover of the band. *Author's Collection*

list of tapes sent to England for mixing of the *Double Platinum* album has the song listed on two reels (along with three other songs from *Rock and Roll Over*).

Love Gun

Second album to feature a goodie, this time a popgun that could be assembled. The *KISS Army Newsletter* from Spring 1977 listed three songs that did not make the final version of the album: "Have Love Will Travel," "Sincerely," and "Tunnel of Love" (the last turning up on Simmons's 1978 solo album). There is a demo of "Christine Sixteen" that features Alex and Eddie Van Halen playing on it at a time when Simmons had some interest in trying to get Van Halen a record deal (also done was "Tunnel of Love" and "Got Love for Sale").

It was the second album to have a cover by the band: "Then She Kissed Me", which had been a hit for the Crystals as "Then He Kissed Me."

Alive II

There is some consensus that the final "studio" side of this album was done to satisfy part of the band's 1976 contract with Casablanca, as an "album unit" in the contract could be one made up of "a playing time not less than 25 minutes." Of course, that side is actually less than 25 minutes, but since certain portions of the other three sides were studio recorded, there is still a chance that this was the case (as it does fit with the number of albums KISS was to record according to the contract).

Bob Kulick was brought in for the first time to play three of the five songs off the final side: "Rockin' in the U.S.A.," "Larger Than Life," and "All American Man." Rumors for years have said that Rick Derringer played lead on "All American Man," and he is even listed on the 2001 five-disc as having done so, but Derringer has never stated this was the case, and Kulick has adamantly stated over the years that it was himself. Paul Stanley played lead on "Anyway You Want It," while Ace Frehley played on his own "Rocket Ride," which he would claim later also featured Anton Fig on drums, as they were working on the song for the proposed solo album (although that would be an example of the solo albums being planned long before what was commonly thought to be the case).

This was the album the band was supposed to have recorded "Jailhouse Rock" but had abandoned after the death of Elvis Presley.

Some misprinted covers added "Do You Love Me?" and "Hooligan" to the songs. These are considered collectible by some fans.

Double Platinum

The band's first official greatest hits package has some drastic remixes of songs and includes a disco-ish update of "Strutter" called "Strutter '78." The mix is considered quite dismal by fans. The original vinyl album lists "Rock Bottom" on the wrong place for Side Three, and then not at all on the CD reissue.

Dynasty

With the solo albums covered elsewhere in this book, the next album is that of this 1979 release and marks the first major absence of a band member, with Anton Fig playing drums on all but the one Peter Criss written song, "Dirty Livin'." "I Was Made for Lovin' You" was written by Paul Stanley on the premise that he could quickly write a disco-flavored song that would be a hit. Producer Vini Poncia also produced a Lynda Carter album the same year (see Chapter 30 for why this is worth a mention).

The album would feature the first song cowritten by Desmond Child, who would go on to write many tunes with the band over the years (usually with Stanley).

Unmasked

Anton Fig played all drums on this album. His Spider bandmate Holly Knight played Keyboards on "Shandi" and would write with the band in the 1980s. Tom Harper played bass on "Shandi." Peter Criss would appear in the music video done for the album ("Shandi"), even though he was already on his way out the door in 1980. Eric Carr would perform songs from this album on the subsequent European tour. KISS would not tour America for this album, which probably did not help its sales.

Poster included with *Unmasked*; this was a replication of the final panel of the album cover comic strip, only with Peter Criss winking—a possible acknowledgment that he would soon be leaving?   *Author's Collection*

Music from "*The Elder*"—an album that still causes strong arguments
in the KISS Army.   *Author's Collection*

Music from "The Elder"

Allan Schwartzberg played drums on "I" and would return to record with the
band on several other albums during the 1980s. Tony Powers played keyboards
on "Odyssey" and would make a music video of the song for his *Don't Nobody
Move, This is a Heist* album.

"Escape from the Island," the instrumental of the album, was dropped for
the Japanese release, and when the CD was issued in the late 1980s, the song was
missing as well. The later remaster added the song back in. The original mockup
of the back cover of the album had the songs in a different order.

Supposedly the band was starting on a heavier album that got scrapped when
they decided to go with the *Elder* concept. Songs at least demoed during this
period included "Deadly Weapon," "Feels Like Heaven" (which Peter Criss did
on his *Let Me Rock You* album), "Reputation, "Fractured Too," and "Breakout."
"Breakout" would be altered and added to the 1991 release *Revenge* as "Carr
Jam '81."

And everyone associated with it seems to really have a pissy attitude about
the album. Unless they think otherwise.

Creatures of the Night

Eric Carr played bass on "I Still Love You." *Kerrang* magazine stated that three songs from the compilation album *Killers* were to have been on *Creatures*: "Down on Your Knees," "Nowhere to Run," and "Partners in Crime, with the last two featuring beefed-up drums. The new mixes were not used until the rare promotional compilation album *First KISS . . . Last Licks.*

Eric Carr was chiefly behind a 1985 remix of the album with Bruce Kulick on the cover. People tend to prefer the original mix.

Lick It Up

First album without makeup, although rumors went around for years that the band had all their costumes and makeup ready for the album shoot if they decided to chicken out. This was just a story to make the changeover to non-makeup more dramatic than something planned since the middle of the last tour. Rick Derringer played the guitar solo in "Exciter."

Animalize

First and only time Mark St. John played with the band on an album. Jean Beauvoir played bass on many of the songs since Gene Simmons was not around to record them. Bruce Kulick played guitar on "Lonely Is the Hunter" and "Murder in High Heels." Mitch Weissman has stated that he played and sang on all three tracks he cowrote for the album. Allan Schwartzberg returned to add some drum fills.

Asylum

Originally to be called *Out of the Asylum.* Jean Beauvoir played bass on "Uh! All Night." Allan Schwartzberg once again did some additional drums.

Crazy Nights

Original to be called *Who Dares . . . Wins. Condomnation* was also tossed out to the press although supposedly never seriously considered. The last album associated with Glickman/Marks, who had been with the band since 1973.

Smashes, Thrashes, and Hits

The band's second "greatest hits" package has several remixes and included two new songs (for which music videos were done): "Let's Put the X in Sex" and

"Rock Hard." The band had asked Peter Criss permission to put "Beth" on the album, without mentioning that they were going to have Eric Carr sing to the original musical track instead of using Criss's vocals. A picture-disc version of the album was also released.

Hot in the Shade

Another title tossed around was *Crimes of Passion*. Tommy Thayer supposedly played some guitar on "Betrayed" and "The Street Giveth and the Street Taketh away" (both cowritten by Thayer). Phil Ashley played keyboards on the album. Pat Regan played brass on "Cadillac Dreams." Kevin Valentine supposedly played drums on "You Love Me to Hate You." This album featured the first lead vocals from Eric Carr on an original song.

Revenge

Vinnie Vincent was brought back in to write songs for the album, only for the relationship to become strained once again. First album with Eric Singer, although there were rumors that he played drums on "Read My Body" off the *Hot in the Shade* album. Dick Wagner returned to play guitar on "Every Time I Look at You." Kevin Valentine played drums on "Take It Off."

Alive III

A rumor that the album would be called *World War III* circulated before the album was released. Other rumors were that the album would come with guitar picks from Simmons, Stanley, and Kulick along with miniature drumsticks from Eric Singer. Came with a "family tree" that was as accurate as possible for the time and from another country (it was created by the Japanese fan club).

Japanese ad for *Revenge*.   *Author's Collection*

KISS title:REVENGE
CD限定盤:¥2,800 通常盤:¥2,500   (PH)
ニュー・アルバムは新戦力として加入したエリック・シンガー（元バッ
ドランズ）のパワフルなドラミングが聞ける。またエリック・カーが8
1年に残した幻のドラムソロ「カージャム」も収録！
●写真集付き限定盤、通常盤同時発売！

Carnival of Souls: The Final Sessions

Bruce Kulick sang his first lead vocals on this album as well as played bass on several songs." "Outromental," an instrumental, only appeared on some advance tape copies of the album, but it did appear with "Childhood's End" on the 2001 five-disc box set. This album was recorded in 1995 as a "Plan B" if the Reunion tour did not work out, with bad copies of the tracks leaking out to fandom to the point that the record company finally released it officially. It would be the first studio album released in six years and only the second and last to feature the Simmons-Stanley-Singer-Kulick lineup.

Psycho Circus

Bruce Kulick played some guitar on "Within." Most of the lead guitar work was by Tommy Thayer, with Kevin Valentine on drums. It would be the last studio album released for eleven years until *Sonic Boom* in 2009.

13

How Much Is a Deuce Worth?

Tackling an Age-Old Argument over a Title

T here have been a few cases of KISS song lyrics over the years that have stood the test of time. Not really because they're profound, although it is hard to not give in to the simplicity of "Rock and Roll All Nite," but because they have left people scratching their heads in bafflement.

Sometimes it is a turn of a phrase that is not as common anymore. A while back on a popular KISS forum, people debated the lyric "Two-fisted to the very end" in the song "I Love It Loud." Some assumed it was actually "True-fisted," which made even less sense, but most knew the proper phrase yet had no clue as to what it meant. Because it is KISS, and because it is Gene Simmons talking, the assumption was that it was something sexual. This was completely off-base, unfortunately, and would take the song in a completely wrong direction for one single line. A song about standing strong against the naysayers who were ready to tear down the band is hardly a time to just toss in a line dealing with an odd sexual practice. Instead, the fans who remembered that Simmons is/was a big comic book reader would have immediately jumped to a reference to the old EC comic *Two-Fisted Tales*, which featured a series of action stories. Nothing more. Still, people took it in a new direction.

But the biggest one is "Deuce." The story—this year Old Jim is working hard (evidently unlike in other years when he is hardly working; you see, it's a twist on the saying . . . never mind), so the "little woman" at home is advised to get her grandmother out of the house (or room, or porch, just out of the immediate area, basically) and to do what he tells her to do. Why? Because he is worth a deuce.

Okay, the lyrics tell us that "he's worth a deuce," and good for him, but what in the heck does that mean? The definition seems to fall into one of two lines—sexual or emotional. Sexual in that supposedly (as it seems to be a "friend of a friend" definition) it means either having sex two times (or in two different positions) or it's a '70s slang term for a twenty-dollar blow job. Emotional in that it means to give the man twice the attention, which goes back to something Simmons himself has referenced in one of his books—a man is working hard, so when he comes home to the "little woman" she should shut up and give him the attention he deserves (admittedly, even Simmons has stated that such thinking is pretty sexist on reflection, and if he thinks so, it must be pretty bad in hindsight).

Then again, both he and other members of the band have also been on record as stating it did not mean anything at all. It just sounded cool.

The other link some fans see is by way of Bruce Springsteen's "Blinded by the Light" and the line "Cut loose like a deuce, another runner in the night." (Or, as in the Manfred Mann's Earth Band's version—which is a little clearer in meaning—"Revved up like a Deuce . . . .") The Deuce referred to there is the 1932 Force Deuce Coupe, which is commonly seen as a hot-rod type of automobile. In the Springsteen song, the line can be taken to mean to cut out like a shot, to speed away. So while it probably doesn't mean, "You know your man is working hard, he's worth a 1932 Ford Deuce Coupe," it probably could be seen as meaning, "He's worth cutting some slack," which gets back to Simmons's earlier mention.

Even if one chooses to go with the interpretation that deuce is meant to be feces, as in the phrase, "drop a deuce," it leads straight back to the same results— in other words, "he's worth a shit." Thus, a number of interpretations end up at the same results, that a tired man needs loving attention from a woman when he gets home, and not so much the whole sex angle (although, no doubt, if people wanted to see it that way, it was not going to hurt Simmons's feelings). Of course, this all goes out the window once someone mentions that a deuce is the name of the No. 2 playing card.

Maybe he just likes lots and lots of gin rummy.

14

I Was There!

The Real Locations of the Live Albums

A *live!* has been listed in many sources as a quintessential album of the 1970s and certainly one of the better live albums ever produced in rock music. With that type of reputation, the album has always been a proud one to point to when people ask which of the KISS albums to have if they wanted to hear what the band sounds like.

Then there came a bit of a backlash. In the mid-1980s, producer Eddie Kramer made the error of mentioning that the band had gone back into the studio in August 1975 in order to correct some mistakes for the live album. Suddenly rumors flew off the charts—some suggesting the whole album was recorded in the studio, while most trying to play it down to just a few areas where it was impossible to get a good mix from the live recording of all the instruments. Mixed in was the fact that the album was not all recorded at one single show but several, and its reputation took a nosedive because it was not "real" anymore.

Kramer and the band have come out in defense, pointing out that such overdubs in the studio were common for live albums by all artists. Nor was it necessarily true that most of it was done in the studio, as there was not the time or money to do such a thing before its release. Even with that, however, no one seems quite sure how much was from the shows themselves and how much was "sweetener" from the studio.

The same thing would occur with *Alive II* and *Alive III* as well (and by *Alive III*, many fans were joking about how much was probably redone in the studio). One thing for sure was that neither of these albums would be from a single concert but from a handful each time. Several of the original live performances have turned up in fandom over the years, making it easier to figure out when and where certain tracks were recorded. This also pointed out how little sweetening was needed for many of the tracks, proving Kramer's and the band's story that it was never a case of orchestrating entire "live" albums in the studio.

After *Alive III*, other producers took over work on the live albums, and most have, due to the situations in which they were recorded (*MTV Unplugged* being a studio recording with multiple takes done, for example), overdubbing grew less. Also, with the amount of information fans were able to obtain, it no longer made sense to try to "hide" additional recordings as being all from one show. Thus, only the first three *Alive* albums were affected by the practices of the time.

The album that proved the band could be successful. Although pushed as being recorded at one show, it was actually recorded over several different dates. *Author's Collection*

Alive!

The assumption for years was that the album was recorded exclusively at Cobo Hall, May 16, 1975, in Detroit, Michigan (some sources say two shows at Cobo Hall). The actual locations were:

May 16, 1975, Cobo Hall Arena, Detroit, Michigan

June 21, 1975, Cleveland Music Hall, Cleveland, Ohio

July 20, 1975, Orpheum Theatre, Davenport, Iowa—Two shows recorded the same night for use on the album. "Let Me Go, Rock 'N' Roll" on *Alive!* has Simmons mentioning Quad Cities, a group of five cities along the Mississippi River that includes Davenport, Iowa.

July 23, 1975, Wildwood Convention Center, Wildwood, New Jersey

August 1975—Overdubbing at Electric Lady Studios.

Alive II

Listed as being recorded between August 26 and August 28, 1977, at the Los Angeles Forum (buttons were even handed out to let those attending proudly proclaim "I Was There" for the recordings, so it was much ballyhooed as being recorded for a live album at the time). Unlike *Alive!*, this was truer to being correct, although there were still some extras added.

August 26–28, 1977, L.A. Forum, Los Angeles—The concerts as well as sound checks done on August 26 and 27. "Tomorrow and Tonight" appears to have been from one of the sound check shows.

April 2, 1977, Budokan Hall, Tokyo—Two shows recorded the same day. When KISS hit Japan for the first time, it was decided to record some of the shows for a potential second live album. To that end, Eddie Kramer recorded the two shows performed on April 2 at Budokan Hall. However, his edited version of the effort, rumored to be called *Rock and Roll Party in Japan*, was boxed away after being turned into the label either due to sound quality, because it was too soon for another live album, or both. Nevertheless, both "Beth" and "I Want You" were taken from these recordings for the *Alive II* album.

September 1977, Capital Theatre, Passaic, New Jersey, as well as Electric Lady Studios, New York City—When the band went into the studio to record the final "studio" side of *Alive II*, the band used that time to finish up the overdubbing of the album as well. Peter Criss has stated they had tried "Hard Luck Woman" onstage but no one was happy with the results, and it was recorded in the studio instead.

The second live album, featuring a doctored gatefold cover, along with some doctored recordings.

Author's C

Alive III

The first live album in sixteen years would see Eddie Kramer returning as well as the editing of a variety of shows, sound checks, and in-studio sweetening to make up the album's tracks. Strangely enough, for an album that is probably closest to being a true live album, it is usually considered the weakest of the *Alive* albums.

November 27, 1992, The Palace, Auburn Hills, Michigan—Both the show and sound check recorded for the album.

November 28, 1992, Market Square Arena, Indianapolis, Indiana—Both the show and sound check recorded for the album.

November 29, 1992, Richfield Coliseum, Cleveland, Ohio—Both the show and sound check recorded for the album.

15

Gimme the Last Original Solo Killers

Ten Unique Compilation Albums

*D*ouble Platinum was the first "best of" collection done for the band and in some ways set the standard of what was to come in the sense that fans were never quite happy with the results. It was deemed a chance to spice things up a bit by having Sean Delaney (working with Mick Stone) twiddle with the mixes in order to bring out the drums and other musical-compression tricks that were popular at the time that are seen now as disruptive to the music as it was original intended.

Since then there have been many compilations over the years, especially after Universal saw how they could repackage the old hits in the past ten to twenty years into multiple compilations. Some are better than others—the five-disc box set release that contained outtakes and early demos, for example—but many were just the same old things in new packaging. There were a few standouts over the years, however, that fans usually hunt down for their collections even if they have all the material already.

The Originals—Released July 21, 1976, by Casablanca Records

After the success of *Alive!* and the emerging success of *Destroyer*, Casablanca decided to get the first three studio albums back out in the marketplace. This was done by simply reissuing the albums, but there was also an attempt to do something special by putting the three albums together in one big package called *The Originals*.

The album cover, which shows the band from the first album superimposed over an atomic blast, opened up to reveal pockets on both sides for the three albums and a sixteen-page album-size booklet with pictures and text by Richard Robinson. It also included a KISS Army sticker and six perforated bubblegum cards of the band members.

Each of the first three studio albums came in its own paper sleeve that reproduced the cover of the album. The set was limited to 250,000 copies, and when that sold out, a second pressing was released in May 1977 (and states "Second Pressing" in the top right-hand corner of the front cover). An edition was also released in Canada, while the Japanese edition released in March 1977 came with an additional booklet of lyrics.

Because of the limited pressings of the album, and how easy it was to lose pieces of the collection over time, complete copies of the first, second, and Japanese pressings are sought after in fandom.

Originals II—Released March 25, 1978, by Victor, Japan

A Japanese-only release, this was done to coincide with the band's second tour of Japan as well as to push the next three studio albums in the catalog (*Destroyer*, *Rock and Roll Over*, and *Love Gun*). If fans think *The Originals* is hard to find, *The Originals II* is next to impossible, especially in complete form. The cover shows artwork of the four members, superimposed over the atomic blast this time. As with the previous release, it contained the three albums in paper sleeves that matched the covers of the albums. It also came with two booklets—one with pictures and text and the other with lyrics and a biography.

Over the years when copies of this album have popped up, all kinds of additional premiums were supposedly to be had with the vinyls. However, the only other extra that has been determined to have been included were four full-sized cardboard masks of the band members. There have plenty of pirated copies of this and the first collection over the years, but they have never been officially reissued and certainly not on CD (even though some nicely put-together pirates have turned up).

The Best of Solo Albums—Released in Australia, France, and Germany, and Elsewhere Between 1979 and 1981 through Casablanca

Some have speculated what a true KISS album would have sounded like if the "best of" each 1978 solo album were put together in one package. Then in 1979, when KISS was still drawing major attention in Europe and Australia with rumors of a tour in 1980, such compilations were released there to appease fans.

The best known of these is the red cover *Best of Solo Albums* package that came out in Germany, as it readily turned up in many record stores in the U.S. during the early to mid-1980s as an import. As mentioned in another chapter, the German release in 1980 came out with the original logo, but after that was reissued with the "backward Z's" logo better known in Germany. What is interesting to note is that the original German version also mixed up the songs, while subsequent issues and reissues would group the album's tracks by each of the four members. It also appears that each foreign country had its own selection of songs for the album—some of which do not appear on some of the other versions of the album—which has made each edition of interest to collectors.

The Singles—Released March 1985 by Concept, Australia

This collection was only available through a mail-order commercial that ran almost exclusively during late-night television in Australia. Because of this, sales were limited at the time, although eventually more copies were found through distribution channels, and the album has been a bit easier for collectors to find.

The album is mainly of interest to fans for the variety of material, as it collected songs that were released as singles in the country, some of which sold very well and would be considered hits in Australia when they weren't in other countries. Thus, this "best of" collection includes material like "I," "Shandi" (a strong hit in Australia), "Then She Kissed Me," and "Talk to Me"—all songs that normally would not have been considered for such a package elsewhere.

Killers—Released 1982 in Australia, Europe and Japan, with Multiple Reissues After That

This one popped up in the U.S. around the same time as the *Best of Solo Albums* collection, usually as the German release with the "backward Z's" KISS logo. The album was never released in the U.S. other than as an import, even though it contains four songs that were not included on any album until compilations that came much later.

With a wait between *Music from "The Elder"* and *Creatures of the Night*, Phonogram requested that KISS give them some songs for a new release. The four songs were "Nowhere to Run" (developed for the hoped-for second *Elder* album), "Partners in Crime," "Down on Your Knees" (cowritten by Bryan Adams), and "I'm a Legend Tonight." The first two were considered album-worthy by the band and would repeatedly turn up as extras on a variety of singles through the rest of the decade as well as on the rare promotional collection *First KISS . . . Last Licks* (see details below). Although Ace Frehley appears on the cover of the album—a photo-session shot of the band from the time of *The Elder*—it was Bob Kulick who went into the studio with the band to record the lead guitar, as Frehley was already effectively out by this point.

Each territory went their own way on certain tracks for the album, although most are the same. "Talk to Me" appears on the Australian edition, "Sure Know Something" on the European one, and "Escape From the Island" on the Japanese edition as the last song on Side One, while "Shandi" was added as an additional track for the Japanese edition as well.

Because of the four unique tracks added to the compilation and the changes to the track listings, each variation of *Killers* is sought after by collectors.

Chikara—Released May 28, 1988, by Nippon Phonogram, Japan

Released just as the band was about to tour Japan for the first time in ten years. The album was limited to a 100,000 pressing and came with a patch of the

Rare Japanese compilation album.   *Author's Collection*

Chikara symbol, so nearly immediately became hard to find. The CD itself is of interest to fans for including a seven-minute version of "I Was Made for Lovin' You" (which had never been released on CD) and the songs from *Creatures of the Night* being from the 1985 remix of the album. It has been difficult enough to find that pirated versions of the album have popped up in recent years.

First KISS . . . Last Licks—Released November 1989 by Mercury Records, USA

This was a bit of a sneak attack for fans. Just as they had gotten used to the idea of the band releasing things in a very standard way without much care for the past, suddenly this little item snuck out. Limited to a pressing of 800, the vinyl album (never released in any other format) was a compilation with a difference. The two tracks from *Killers* had been remixed for the new release, and this marked the first-ever official appearance of two songs from the original 1973 demo that Eddie Kramer recorded with the band ("Deuce" and "Strutter"). These four tracks were on the second side of the album, while the first side contained four tracks from the then-recently released *Hot in the Shade* album. The front cover was a collage of two photos—one of the band in makeup on motorcycles, shot back in the 1970s, and the other of the band in blindfolds against a wall as in front of a firing squad. The back cover contained a number of handwritten notes from Gene Simmons and Paul Stanley about the creation of each song on the album. Truly a very nice collection and a sign of changes to come in the 1990s as the band begins to do more with their extended catalog from the past.

Universal Presents Gimme KISS—Released January 1990 by Mercury Records, USA

Just as the *First KISS . . . Last Licks* package popped up, another very offbeat compilation hit the market, this one even harder to find than the first, although rumored to have had the same number of copies pressed. A cassette tape release, the collection has two songs from *Alive!* ("Deuce" and "Strutter"), two songs from *Alive II* ("Detroit Rock City" and "Shout It Out Loud"), a collection of other songs from the makeup period ("Christine Sixteen," "Calling Dr. Love," "Love Gun," and "Beth"), "Lick It Up," and three songs from *Hot in the Shade* ("Forever," "Rise To It" and "Hide Your Heart"). Interesting to note that although the release was to promote the new album, only one other song besides the three new ones was from the nonmakeup era of the band.

There was also a tape going around at the time called *DCC Remasters*, which was rumored to be a first attempt by PolyGram at remastering the KISS catalog for CD. While the quality was rather good, the selection of songs to be remastered was a bit odd from a sales point of view: the theme song from *Shocker*, "The Oath," "Hard Times." As copies of this circulated only on a "friend to friend" basis and it has never been seen in an official form, it is most probably some type of bootleg.

The extremely rare cassette-only compilation *Universal Presents Gimme KISS.*   *Author's Collection*

First KISS—Released 1990 by Mercury Records, USA, 846-766-2

Rumors began floating around in 1989 that Mercury Records planned to release a new box set for KISS, a massive repackaging of the first few albums in a new vibrant form with all kinds of extras. Some had hoped for something like a CD equivalent of *The Originals*, possibly with better-quality mastering of the material than had appeared on the first CDs of the older albums released in the States. Instead, what came out was a clear plastic shell, roughly the size of a vinyl record album, holding the standard (at the time) CD releases of *KISS, Hotter Than Hell, Dressed to Kill*, and *Destroyer*. A red sticker was slapped on the front of the box stating "First KISS." Supposedly this was a limited edition of 1,000, and it did seem hard to find in stores when released. However, considering the set had nothing that most fans would not have already owned (except if one really wanted a clear plastic case with a red sticker on it), the box set did not sell well and was considered a massive disappointment by fans who went out of their way to search for it or who confused it with the much superior promotional album *First KISS . . . Last Licks*.

Limited-edition promotional compilation album that featured many rarities.   *Author's Collection*

The much sought-after collection that reissued the first three studio albums together.   *Author's Collection*

KISS Alive! 1975–2000—Released November 21, 2006, by Universal Music Group, USA

In 1997, it was announced that the KISS catalog would go through a remastering process for rerelease on CD. This was exciting news for fans who had been disappointed with the slapdash nature of the CDs released of the older albums up to that time (unfortunately, with record companies rushing out CD reissues of earlier vinyl albums when the CD market began to boom in the mid-1980s, such mediocre to poor reproduction on CD of an artist's album catalog—in sound as well as packaging—was pretty much the norm for everyone, not just KISS).

It was an appreciative work, with an attempt to add some of the original extras from the vinyl editions to the remasters as well as commentary from

Robert Conte—an associate of the band who was working on the remasters—included with each album. However, response to the remasters, with *Alive!* being among the first four released in July 1997, was mixed among fans, who could not agree if the mix was better, worse, or equal to what had come before. Also, while the remastered *Alive!* came with a nice reproduction of the booklet included with the 1975 vinyl album, some fans were puzzled as to why the album had to still be released as a two-disc—and thus more expensive—set when all the material could have fit on one CD. The same was true for *Alive II* when its remaster was released in August 1997. Meanwhile, the May 1993 released of *Alive III* had come and gone with some disappointed with the mix, as well as the lack of the track "Take It Off," which appeared on foreign versions of the CD as well as the vinyl edition released in the U.S.

Finally, there was some fan interest in *Alive IV*, a proposed 2001 release of the "Millennium Concert" recorded by the band in Vancouver, Canada, on December 31, 1999. Due to varying issues—some say label issues, but rumors circulated that the band and/or the label was not completely happy with the recording—it was shelved, and instead the *KISS*

The rare Japanese reissue of the second trio of studio albums by KISS. *Author's Collection*

Australian compilation album that was available through a television advert. *Author's Collection*

A solid compilation of live tracks from the various *Alive* collections,
which usually gets glossed over by fans.   *Author's Collection*

Symphony: Alive IV album was released in 2003 of the Australian symphony presentation from earlier that year. This, after the album cover for the "Millennium Concert" version of *Alive IV* had been featured in ads and one of the tracks presented on the 2000 five-disc KISS box set, which just made the recording even more of a mystery.

Thus, the 2006 box set of another remastering of the first two *Alive* albums, a remastering of the third (including the missing track), and the official release of the scrapped *Alive IV* were of much interest to fans. The four-disc set—finally putting the first two albums on single discs instead of the two-discs spread of the past—lost some of the physical extras of the remasters but included a booklet with text from KISS biographer Ken Sharp, as well as photos, interviews, and additional track information that had not been seen before in the earlier releases. The Japanese version came with an additional booklet of lyrics and the traditional obi. Best Buy released a version with two additional tracks for the "Millennium Concert" set—"2000 Man" and "God of Thunder," while iTunes added "Detroit Rock City" to the mix. Amazon began selling an MP3 download of the "Millennium Concert" separately, including the two Best Buy tracks, in 2008.

Although still available in shops, its release came after there had been two previous issues of *Alive!* and *Alive II* on CD, the still-quite-available 1993 *Alive III* album, the 1996 live compilation album *You Wanted the Best*, and live material collected on the five-disc KISS box set of 2000. Because of this, and the fact that some fans may have mistaken the Symphony disc as being the fourth one in the box set, this particular box set is not so much obscure as it is ignored by fans when there are other compilations of equal or greater interest. This just goes to show that by the mid-2000s, the KISS Army had been saturated with special KISS collections to the point where fans began to pick and choose what to get instead of getting "everything that came out." Not that that has stopped the marketing machine from releasing even more of the same since then, even as the fans began to clamor more for fresh material.

16

Are You High?

Drug References in KISS

P eter Criss told Tom Snyder in a 1980 interview that "KISS was never about drugs." Of course, fans know through interviews and biographies in recent years that, drugs certainly did have some sway in the band, but what Criss said was not far from the truth—the band avoided drug references that would have been clearer in other bands. After all, Gene Simmons has been very prominent, nearly defiant in some cases, in his antidrug beliefs, as well as his dislike for alcohol and cigarette smoking. Paul Stanley has participated in antidrug public service announcements. Yet with KISS, there has always been an uneasy alliance with drug imagery and endorsement mixed in with the message. After all, if one is rock 'n' rolling every night and partying every day, there has to be something to keep one going beyond music; at least that would be the easy assumption to make. And if one of the most popular songs from the band deals with "Cold Gin," and is introduced from the stage by Stanley asking if everyone is high or if "some of you like the taste of alcohol!" to the cheers of the crowd, one wonders if the line is just as blurred at times in KISS as in many other bands.

It is not that the band is unaware of this, or that they happily play into it without concern. In 2002, writer Daniel Siwek interviewed Gene Simmons and got him to touch on this very topic. With his permission, he has allowed me to reprint his question and Simmons's response:

> Daniel Siwek: You've always been against drugs, yet Paul would shout out "Are you high?" Was that a compromise you made somewhere, saying, "OK, it's good for the band's reckless, rock and roll image, so I'll let that slide." How did you deal with that stuff?

> Gene Simmons: It's interesting. It's a very good comment. I haven't really come to terms with that notion yet, because. . . I said one thing, and yet I was in a band with two alcoholics and drug users, and uh. I don't know, it's a good valid point. I'd have to think about that for a while, because there is no question Paul would get up with everyone's OK and say, "Hey, how you doin'? Is everybody high tonight" Yup. It's true.

> Daniel: Because that was the day, it's what the audience wanted to hear at the time. For a lot of kids/fans it was all about the rock and roll and

getting fucked up, you know, the 70s excess thing. I was just assuming that you guys, as craftsmen of rock and roll, knew what a rock and roll audience wanted to hear and were OK with it.

Gene: I'm OK with everyone deciding for themselves what to do, I'm not sure if we were OK in getting up there saying, [impersonating Paul] "Hey, is everybody high? Let's get cold gin!"

Daniel: But you did.

Gene: Yes. Oh yeah.

Of course, it is easy to see skeletons in every closet at times. When Paul sings about "wheeling and dealing," it would be simple to say that since "dealing" is sometimes a drug reference, the lyrics must be about drugs. Other times, however, such imagery—even if not the focus of the songs—was obviously put there to help push the song along. Such examples are presented below, as well as some less obvious ones.

"Cold Gin"

Although the song is pretty much a *Lost Weekend* scenario, with the protagonist knowing that alcohol is giving him problems and his temptations will always win, in the end it seems to also celebrate that level of despair. Considering the song usually (as mentioned above) opens with Paul Stanley asking if people like the "taste of alcohol," it is obviously one that makes those who do drink feel proud, in a way.

"Cold Gin" was written by Ace Frehley, a recovering alcoholic, and there has been some pressure on whether to continue to perform it even though it is considered one of his biggest hits. Back in 1994 when touring, Frehley would for a time introduce the song in concert by pointing out how alcohol nearly ruined his life. The reaction? He was being "a downer" and would find himself getting booed onstage. Since then, he has performed it without commentary, although in interviews he has admitted that he still feels awkward in singing the happy-go-lucky, down-and-out drunk song considering that alcohol nearly killed him.

"Detroit Rock City"

There is a moment in the *Paul Lynde Halloween Special* for ABC where Paul Stanley sings the line "First I drink and then I smoke," and holds his hand up to this mouth to pantomime the smoking. Either he had suddenly decided to smoke like a Gestapo agent, or he is looking like he is smoking a particular brand not on the common market. One could also press on the line itself, as we're talking about a guy speeding through traffic to get to a KISS show, drinking and smoking as well.

The B-side to Ace Frehley's hit single "New York Groove," a term already being used as a drug reference at the time of release.

Author's Collection

"2000 Man"

A bit of a cheat here, as it is a cover song. Still, when Ace Frehley sings about having "funny flowers" on his windowsill, the reference is pretty obvious. The band probably could have changed some of the lyrics of this Mick Jagger/Keith Richards song if they wanted, but did not.

"100,000 Years"

Paul Stanley would shout out "Are you high?" during the "100,000 Years" drum solo at least for a time during the 1976 tour.

"Hard Times"

The lyrics mention cutting class in order to go to the park and "space our heads out."

"Snow Blind"

Although the lyrics appear to be about missing a girl far away, the connotation of snow-blind as being tanked up on cocaine was very familiar to even a casual audience by the time the song appeared on Frehley's 1978 solo album. Being so snow-blind that one is "lost in space" helps to seal the deal there.

"Strange Ways"

A drug argument could be made for this song as it seems to imply drugs while delivering a sexual message with a slowed tempo and lyrics like "It's a strange line you've been deliverin'" and "don't want to fight it, just wanna feel some more."

"Mainline"

Although the lyrics do not imply anything to do with drugs, the title was such a standard drug term that one can readily see it there. After all . . . .

"Dirty Livin'"

Features the lyric "Mainline out of China is due in tonight," an obvious drug reference and centered in a song about a guy who cannot get enough of what he needs while making a "livin' out on the streets."

This maxi-single features not one but two KISS tracks that include drug references in the lyrics. *Author's Collection*

"I"

For as many instances where drug references appear to be present in KISS songs, a few focus on the downside of drugs. In "I" from *Music from "The Elder,"* the protagonist realizes that in order to win he has to believe in himself even if others won't. During the song, Gene Simmons throws in that he doesn't "need to get wasted, it only holds me down . . . ."

Surprisingly, or rather sadly, this actually drove some KISS fans away from the band for daring to suggest that taking drugs was not A-OK. On an album that was already causing problems with some fans, it was just one more nail in the coffin to some.

"Rock Soldiers"

Although not a KISS song (it is from Ace Frehley's Comets days), it references Frehley's descent into addiction and his car-wreck of the 1980s (okay, one of many, but still) leading him to realize that he needed to clean up his act. This song would become a standard of his tour at the time and made into a music video. Thus, while there was a tendency to let slide the drug references, the reverse sometimes took hold as well.

17

Where the Band Really Came *Alive!*

The Most Influential Concerts in KISS History

O ne defense against critics all KISS fans have used without hesitation over the years is that the band knows how to put on an entertaining live show. Argue about the makeup, the costumes, the merchandise, or the music, and even the strongest KISS supporter may concede on at least a weakness in those areas at one point or another. Yet the band's least energetic concerts (and fans would no doubt debate such a category) have been so finely shaped to entertain that even the harshest criticisms of their performances over the years have yielded the game to KISS in response to the crowd's reactions. Call the performances calculated (as if artists never predetermined to get a set response from the audience), but no one can deny that the audiences left those shows happy with what they saw and heard.

Thus, it may be hard for some fans to narrow the focus of what concerts are the most relevant in the band's career when there is a uniform determination to always give the audience 100 percent in performance. Of course, fans would also tend to want to focus on firsts (and every fan's first show would find a spot on such a list), but in a few cases listed below, it is actually the second or as far as the thirty-fourth concert—as in the case of the 1980 tour listed below—that, in hindsight, proved influential in directing the goals and career of the band.

Which is the definition of the concerts listed here: live performances in front of audiences where—sometimes intentionally, sometimes by accident—KISS found themselves being pulled into a new direction that would affect the band, the band members' careers, and sometimes more, whether for better or worse. Some could argue that a few television performances done under audience conditions should be included, but those are discussed in another chapter of this book.

Coventry/Popcorn Pub, Long Island City, New York, January 30–February 1, 1973

It was a small ad in the back pages of the *Village Voice* for a club in Queens, with an announcement that the "discotesque" (*sic*) was changing its name to Coventry being of more importance than the acts performing there. Of those acts listed, KISS appeared in the smallest font, almost as an afterthought, and only listing two of the dates played there. The first show has always been remembered as having an audience total that could be counted on one hand; the remainders not many more. The show consisted of a few Wicked Lester leftovers and some assorted songs that would, with refinements, make their way onto the first three KISS albums. And it would take several months of bouncing between Coventry and the Daisy, a club in Long Island City, before the recognizable costumes and makeup were refined, but no matter. Something about these dismal shows clicked for the foursome, inspiring them to keep soldiering onward. By the end of the year, the band had a new manager, a record deal, and had begun stealing the thunder of other bands better known than them in the press. Yet it all started that first night, playing to four people in a club where the club changing names was much more important than the birth of a phenomenon.

Cadillac High School, Cadillac, Michigan, October 9, 1975

The year 1975 was a pivotal one for KISS, thanks to their diligent touring through America that began in 1974 (and subsequently would continue with only a few short breaks until 1977) and lead to a strong following through Middle America. Many fans look back on this year as one in which Detroit was important to the band as well, especially in light of the "common knowledge" that *Alive!* was recorded at Cobo Hall in Detroit that year. However, only a portion of the live album was actually recorded in Detroit (see Chapter 14 for more details on that story), and while the city has a special place in the band's history, a more relevant concert to their career took place elsewhere.

When the Cadillac High School football team needed some inspiration in the fall of 1974, the assistant coach, Jim Neff, suggested letting the boys play some rock music in the locker room, including KISS. The team would go on a winning streak, which they credited to their defense unit nicknamed the "KISS Defense." In honor of this, fall 1975 would see the student body decide to make KISS the theme of their Homecoming, and Neff got in touch with the band's management about the festivities.

Alive! would soon become a game-changer for KISS, but its success was still to come when Neff contacted KISS's management. To the band, the offer was a publicity bonanza that would lead to them getting a key to the city, a parade, many photo-ops with people in KISS makeup, and a chance to perform for everyone at the high school—which is where this concert comes into play. It was a clear sign that KISS was becoming more than just another rock band and was moving into an area where the fans would motivate the public and the press to cover the band.

More importantly, it was a turning point for KISS's image. Before this, the band had typically tried to demonstrate "tough and dangerous" personas that would allow them to win over teenage fans and simply scare parents and older people. There would be the "party" photos on the back of the *Hotter Than Hell* album and comments made in interviews that were grittier than would be common after 1975 and the band's thrust toward becoming a household name. There is even a whole set of staged photos of them surrounding a young woman in various states of undress that suggest they planned to do more than simply pose with her. Then comes the concert in Cadillac, where Gene Simmons was persuaded not to spit blood because it would offend parents in the audience (albeit, as *Rolling Stone* reported at the time, it was Simmons's suggestion that he not spit blood and he only did so once there was some mild hesitation on the part of the Head Coach) and they were marching with the high school band and posing with city officials in KISS makeup. A year before, none of that would have fit into the image the band wanted to present—see their reaction to suggestions that they make a joke of the makeup on the first album cover in Chapter 10 for an example of what they thought of such attempts. Now, with a chance to get attention, everything was up for grabs when it came to how KISS would appear to the general public. From here, it will be comic books, superhero movies, and appearances on kids' shows as they steadily slip into becoming a band for the whole family. Even if they were still offering songs like "Sweet Pain" and "Rocket Ride" in the albums to come in the 1970s.

Anaheim Stadium, Anaheim, California, August 20, 1976— Ted Nugent, Montrose, Bob Seger Opening

The *Destroyer* tour was ongoing at the time of this concert; a tour that saw the band steadily raising their profile after the success of *Alive!* in 1975 and what would soon be the triumph of the next studio album, *Destroyer*, and the main single from that album, "Beth." With Ted Nugent, Bob Seger, and Montrose (replacing Uriah Heep at the last minute) opening for KISS, this was more or less just another festival in a series for the stadium—renowned for the number of "big event" rock concerts and festivals done there in the latter part of the 1970s—but to the band and fans, an attendance of over 40,000 people was a sure sign that KISS was on its way to superstardom.

With the success of *Alive!* still fresh at the time, producer Eddie Kramer was enlisted to record the show for possible use on a follow-up live album (just as he would be when the band would go to Japan in 1977). Although those plans fell through, it led to the recordings making it to the fans with the release of *Destroys Anaheim* (released as two separate vinyl albums, *Vol. I* and *Vol. II*) by Idle Minds Records. Although subsequently reissued under various other titles and through various other bootleggers over the years, *Destroys Anaheim* is one of the best-remembered bootlegs for the band over the years (along with such faves as *Fried Alive* and *Sneak Attack*). Eventually, video footage of the concert turned up in fan circles as well, continuing to make the concert a favorite for KISS fans in the underground markets.

Lakeland Civic Center, Lakeland, Florida, December 12, 1976

The band was touring for their new album *Rock and Roll Over* in a year that saw them constantly going from touring to recording and back again (the following year would see them doing much the same with *Love Gun* and *Alive II* being released). Due to problems setting up the stage for the show—not helped by an impatient audience that began throwing fireworks at the roadies—the lighting fitted around a staircase railing onstage was not properly grounded. With Ace Frehley having some problems walking (some would joke with or without platform shoes), he grabbed the handrail only to send electricity through his body. Tumbling to the bottom of the stairs, he was unconscious for a time but later returned to the stage to complete the show, even though his arms were numb from the shock.

Fans commonly remember the event as the genesis for a Frehley-penned song, "Shock Me," that made it onto the *Love Gun* album the following year. More importantly, the incident would lead directly to the band switching to cordless microphones and guitars and becoming one of the first (if not the first) popular bands to switch to the radio-transmitter system for their equipment (Paul Stanley would occasionally go back to a corded microphone in concert, but mainly as a prop for some last-minute stage tricks at the end of a concert). Such equipment is common today for many bands, and although it denied Gene Simmons the ability to sadistically use his guitar cord like a whip in keeping with his Demon character (see him doing such during the *Paul Lynde Show* clip of "Detroit Rock City"), it allowed the band much freer movement on stage. This would come more into play in the 1980s as the band lost the further restrictions of the platform shoes and the costumes and could run around the stage, but it would also allow Simmons to do his soon-traditional flight up into the air and on to a platform above the stage for part of his bass solo/"God of Thunder" segment of the show.

Budokan Hall, Japan (Osaka, Kyoto, Nagoya, Fukuoka, and Tokyo), March 24–April 4, 1977

It was the band's first tour of Japan in the hall made most famous to rock fans by having the Beatles appear there back in 1966. At the time, no rock act had ever appeared there, and doing so was considered in bad taste; however, by 1977, the furor had died down after several other acts had played there in the years between. Still, for most American fans, the prospect of KISS playing the hall was one of prestige—as if it meant they had reached a pinnacle in their fame.

The band would make the most of it, with the two shows from April 2 recorded for use in a television special (see Chapter 20 for more details) that became a popular video in circulation among fans in the 1980s and 1990s; while Eddie Kramer recorded some of the proceedings for a possible live album. These recordings eventually led to multiple bootleg albums released in the years since, usually as some type of "Lost *Alive II* Album," although some of the material would eventually sneak its way onto the official *Alive II* album that came out in 1977.

Toledo Sports Arena, Toledo, Ohio, December 16, 1979

Fans did not know at the time that this would be the last concert with the original four performing together until 1995. Yes, there were vague rumors flying around that something was up, but based more on tabloid speculation that no band as popular as KISS at the time could continue to remain without changes or avoid completely burning out. Nor was the word to hit for several months to come, with the band recording an album, the 1980 release *Unmasked*, with Peter Criss's proclaimed participation in order to show that solidarity of KISS. It was only in May 1990—six months after their final show together—that KISS announced his departure. Later still did fans find out that the split had been in the works for some time, with Criss determined to leave the band after the *Dynasty* tour and the others settled with the idea of finding a replacement. Even *Unmasked* was eventually uncovered as not even featuring his drumming beyond his own cowritten track "Dirty Livin'" as well as some additional vocals.

But the details of *Unmasked* and Criss's departure were still in the future at the time of that final *Dynasty* concert on December 16, 1979. To those attending, there was an excitement due to it being the end of the tour, but nothing to tell those on hand that it was also the end of an era. Even so, it was a conclusion to one chapter in the band's history that would radically change their structure, leading to a period of revolving replacements (albeit more for the lead guitarist than the drummer, thanks to the steady work of Eric Carr for the following ten years); changes in the visual look of the band; and the focus moving from four equal members to that of two leaders—Gene Simmons and Paul Stanley. Although Criss would return to the band in 1996 for a few years, it would never be the same again, no matter how much the band and the fans tried to imagine otherwise.

The Palladium, New York City, July 25, 1980

Do-or-die time for the band. Peter Criss had long left the band by this point, yet the others spent months struggling to come up not only with a replacement but with a way to demonstrate to the public that they could soldier on without one of the original four. To some critics, KISS's success rest solely on Criss's "Beth" becoming a hit (there was certainly more to it than that, as detailed elsewhere in this book, but lazy critics like the notion of pulling away one element in order to topple the success of someone). Now their "hit-maker" was gone, and having already jumped into the dying disco trend with "I Was Made for Lovin' You" for a quick (and, some would say, safe) hit, the band was looked upon as gasping for air.

Simply finding a drummer who could play their catalog was not the end-all to the situation, either. KISS had always prided itself on being, as evidenced with their early concept of "four Alice Coopers on stage," four unique individuals working as a unit. A replacement had to be photogenic, personable in interviews, and able to draw buzz from fans on his own without the other three members propping him up. Thus, a drummer who would play circles around everyone but couldn't mumble more than two words or couldn't sync with the others in front of the press would never work (such personality conflicts would eventually create friction that led to the early demise of Vinnie Vincent and Mark St. John in the band years later). There was also the agreement by all involved that a new member of the band would automatically have to have his own distinct makeup, costume, and character—this assumption would change a couple of decades on, but the argument could be made that the reasons for not doing so with Eric Singer and Tommy Thayer were vastly different. The band needed people to forget about Peter Criss, so a new persona was needed as well.

Which leads to Paul Caravello joining just a few weeks before this show. In that time, he had to not only rehearse with the band to put on a show that would impress those in attendance but also come up with a new name for himself and what would be his character and makeup (with others working to throw together a costume). When attempts at Hawk makeup went sour—Eric Carr would later refer to it as making him look like "Chicken Man"—he jumped back to the idea of a fox. This led not only to an identifiable and easy makeup design but also to one that had a lineage to that of the Catman that made sense (such as Vinnie Vincent's later Wizard character, who would have a spacey type of ancestry with the Space-Ace).

Still, the main goal was to demonstrate to people at the Palladium that KISS was still KISS, even with the departure of Peter Criss. With the show going off without any problems, and Eric Carr falling in step with the others for the show, as well as personal appearances afterwards, the stage was set for the band to go on their first long European tour. Ironically, things did not go quite as planned.

Australia/New Zealand, November 9–December 3, 1980

KISS had come back with Eric Carr replacing Peter Criss and planned to kick things off in a big way by touring Europe starting in August 1980. But things had changed radically in Europe in the four years since the band had played there. The era of glam that they had seen when touring there in 1976 was gone, replaced with the by then smoldering ashes of the punk movement and its glowing, fractured remains that would branch out into the new wave, goth, and

New Romantics movements of the 1980s. Political unrest was high in Europe as well, with KISS seen as a reminder of the "rich, fascist American state" that was doomed to destroy the world. Ticket sales were moderate, and the band began to find themselves facing physical abuse at the hands of what a few years before would have been the age range of their fan base, including rocks being hurled at them mid-show. The tour of Italy even found the band forced to hide out in their dressing room while a full-scale riot went on in the stadium they were to play. To all involved, it appeared that there may have been something to the critics' taunts that the band's best days were behind them.

Then came Australia and New Zealand. *Unmasked* had done incredibly well in these countries after its release in June 1980, with "Shandi" reaching #5 on the charts (common myth is that "Shandi" reached number one, but this was due to someone in marketing pulling numbers out of the air instead of anything like the truth) and "Is That You?" hitting the Top 40. With the announcement that the band would finally tour Down Under, the reaction could only be described as a revival of Beatlemania, with fans taking to the streets to see them in public appearances, a variety of products released with their name and images slapped on them, and multiple television appearances to promote the tour.

Being able to bring the *Dynasty/Unmasked* stage set was a plus as well, as it allowed the band to perform for the fans in their best venue (later tours before the reunion would find them simply foregoing their American stage sets overseas due to transportation costs). After the dismal returns of the earlier part of the tour, the Australian trip helped them rebound. Unfortunately, it also showed the band that they could continue to go in their own direction and the fans would follow, leading to the production of *Music from "The Elder"* in 1981—an album that caused damage within the band and within the KISS Army as well. But for the moment, the glory days of the 1970s were hanging on strong in Australia and New Zealand, giving new drummer Eric Carr a glimpse of what the band's superstardom days were like.

The December 3, 1980, show in Auckland, New Zealand, would also be the very last full show Ace Frehley would play with the band until the Reunion tour. After this, he would continue to make television and radio appearances with them until after the release of *Creatures of the Night* in 1982 before finally leaving the band and being replaced by Vinnie Vincent.

Bismarck Civic Center, Bismarck, North Dakota, December 29, 1982

Creatures of the Night was released in October 1982 with mild fanfare from the record company, leading to mediocre sales. This transferred over to problems with the tour as well, which was not helped by a two-month delay between the release of the album and the tour to help promote it (oddly enough, KISS would do this several times in the future with their touring in the 1980s). Even the attempt to make the tour important by advertising it as the Tenth Anniversary tour for KISS in merchandise and in ads seemed to only bring out slight interest from ticket buyers.

That is not to say that the tour was a complete failure, however. Some shows may not have done well in sales, but others were sold out, and it was clear that people definitely were coming out to see the band perform. The only problem was that many buying tickets assumed the shows would still be in the mold of the *Dynasty* era and one for the entire family and kiddies, which made Paul Stanley's decision in this tour to become a "pottymouth" when rapping between songs (as he would throughout the nonmakeup years) a bit perplexing. Further, things worked well when Vandenburg and Night Ranger were opening for KISS early in the tour, but things got more unsettling for some audience members when later spots on the tour had bands like Mötley Crüe and the Plasmatics opening instead. Suddenly it seemed that the opening acts were more shocking than the headliner, which did not fit into the image of KISS. Thus, the seed to change the look and direction of the band was planted in this tour thanks to sales on the weak side and the rapidly changing look of the bands performing with them.

Sports Palais, Lisbon, Portugal, October 11, 1983

There was no turning back for KISS by October 1983—the *Lick It Up* album had been released nearly a month before with a photo cover of the band sans makeup and the "Lick It Up" music video had begun airing, showing them awkwardly playing with their newfound freedom from their stage characters. News reports had surfaced on television and in print with photos of the band "unmasked" as well, while Gene Simmons and Paul Stanley—who did the majority of interviews about the shift in the band's direction (and who would do the majority of interviews for KISS from this point forward instead of making them group efforts)—were determined to present to the press that everything was going smoothly and that the fans would be happy with the new look. More importantly, that the move to go without the characters was not a desperate grasp for attention.

But the real test would be when they tried out their new personas—that of themselves instead of characters in costumes—on paying concertgoers, and the performance at the Sports Palais in Lisbon was the first time KISS played a full show to the public in this fashion. There were some missteps along the way— as mentioned in a previous chapter, a reported attempt by Simmons to continue his blood-spitting in "God of Thunder" went poorly without the costume and makeup and was quickly abandoned, for example (fans still contest if he actually performed the stunt at the show or not, as no photographic evidence of the incident has ever been produced)—but all in all the newfound freedom of movement outside of the platform shoes and sometimes awkward costuming gave the band a new energy to explore the stage and interact even more with the audience than before (certainly true with Paul Stanley's intros between songs, which would soon become epic in proportion to his quick pronouncements back in the 1970s).

Playing for an appreciative crowd who were hungry to see them in action certainly helped, but without the band's dedication to make the switchover work in this show and the tour that was to follow, KISS could have easily found themselves laughingstocks and old history, seen only as a once-famous band that has desperately tried to make themselves over for a new era and failing (as many bands and performers have had to deal with over time and the changing sands of fashion). Instead, they proved an old argument of theirs and the KISS Army: take away the makeup and the costumes, and KISS was still KISS when it came to playing music.

Cobo Hall, Detroit, Michigan, December 8, 1984

The *Lick It Up* album and tour had shown a groundswell of old fans returning to the fold as well as new fans. Still, there were many who felt this was due solely to those curious to see what the band looked like and how they performed without the makeup and costumes. Such critics were positive that the interest would die quickly with the follow-up album and tour. Fortunately for the band, the interest by fans continued to climb with the release of the new album just as the band began demonstrating that they could still be solid fare to watch live in concert with the superhero trappings (although it could be argued that they still wore costumes of a sort, but more in the style of what was popular for the time in heavy metal; see Chapter 6 for more details).

The band's newfound success in their nonmakeup format was defined by this concert on two fronts: a live radio broadcast of the show and the filming of the show for airing on MTV and eventually release on VHS/Beta/laserdisc in the home-video market as *Animalize Live! Uncensored* (see details in Chapter 20 on this video). With these releases and the proof that fans were happy to see their band even without the more theatrical hardware of the past, critics had to beg off from calling for their demise.

Yet there were also concerns as to how the public would react to a new lead guitarist being brought in after all the hoopla of Vinnie Vincent's role in the band being publicly burnt to the ground in recriminations and omissions. Even at that early stage there were fans who thought it was his writing on the *Lick It Up* album and his guitar work that saved KISS, even more than the dropping of the makeup. Now Gene Simmons and Paul Stanley were having to prove that they could move beyond Vincent and still keep the fans with a new lead guitarist. In fact, the band would have to deal with the situation twice and in rapid succession during the early days of promoting the album and tour. Interviews and promotional material for the new album and tour heavily pushed the replacement of Vinnie Vincent by Mark St. John as being a vital part of the band's new direction. This would have been all well and good except that, with the tour about to start, St. John found himself suffering from a form of arthritis that kept him from playing guitar. This led to the band quickly bringing in Bruce Kulick, the brother of old KISS associate Bob Kulick, to replace the ailing St. John for what was hoped to be a few shows at the beginning of the tour. Instead, St. John would play only two full shows (and part of another), while Kulick performed at all other shows. By the time of this concert, it was clear that St. John was on his way out for good.

St. John would later go on record to say that one of the main reasons Kulick replaced him was due to him looking enough like St. John to fool the audience into thinking it was him and therefore would not cause any kind of disruption in the show by people upset that the new guitarist was not there. On a personal note, I witnessed several incidents on the *Animalize* tour where fans shouted out Mark's name as Bruce performed onstage, including a show in Evansville, Indiana, where Mark was standing behind fans in the seats, sipping a drink and shaking his head at how easily fooled the audience could be, so Simmons's and Stanley's position did have some merit. It is an interesting aside in the band's career—an unavoidable situation that that could very well have been the genesis of the idea that band members could be easily replaced without fans' objections as long as they looked the role.

Limelight, New York City, June 26, 1988

Ace Frehley had been out of the band for essentially six years by this point (he would be still an official member until the end of 1982, when it was clear that Vinnie Vincent had replaced him), but it had taken time to get his solo career going thanks to contractual obligations (he was not released from his KISS contract until 1984) and label problems (a signing with Bronze Records in 1985 ended with the label folding before Frehley could record an album, leading to him not signing with a label until Megaforce in 1987). He had done some shows once he emerged from his time away from the spotlight, but it was not until he had created his band Frehley's Comet that he began touring on a regular basis.

It was at such a show at the Limelight in New York that the fans who attended got a treat. There had been a buzz in the audience in the first place when it was evident that Gene Simmons and Paul Stanley had come to see their former bandmate perform, but the excitement was intense when the two came onstage at one point to perform "Deuce" with Frehley's band.

The moment went by quickly, with Stanley not even picking up an instrument to play, merely singing; but it sent a big wave through fandom at the time. Before this, a lot of bad blood had erupted in print between the former members, with Simmons and Stanley presenting one front as to the inability of Peter Criss and Frehley to perform and thus "being fired," followed by rather bewildered responses from the other pair as to why airing such dirty laundry was even necessary. While Criss took such comments closer to heart and responded in an intense manner in some cases, Frehley tended to brush aside many of them with humor. He was also not shy in promoting the band's earlier work

Japanese flyer mentioning the 1995 KISS Convention tour, which would lead directly to the reuniting of the original foursome.

Author's Collection

and continuing to perform a good number of KISS songs in his concerts as well. In essence, while there were still problems between them, there were still some warm feelings. Thus, while fans were surprised to see Simmons and Stanley perform with Frehley that night (to KISS fans it was the equivalent of George Harrison and John Lennon joining Paul McCartney in concert during the 1970s), to the musicians it was just a one-off situation that was fun for the moment and nothing to warrant excitement.

Or was it? Frehley would later report that KISS contacted him in 1989 about doing a tour—perhaps even one in the old makeup and costumes, but with Eric Carr back in his old Fox makeup instead of Peter Criss. For the time, Frehley passed on the idea, as he was still working to establish his solo career (then technically only two years old, thanks to the first Frehley's Comet album not being released until 1987). Ironically, that same year would see the demise of Frehley's Comet thanks to record company interference (they believed the band concept and name were keeping them from profiting from pushing Frehley's albums as pure solo efforts) and internal problems in the band. Frehley would lay low for a time before touring again in the 1990s, eventually joining Peter Criss on a joint tour in the mid-1990s; a tour that would lead him back to KISS and the Reunion tour of 1996. Just when he thought he was out, they pulled him back in.

The Ritz, New York City, August 12–13, 1988

After playing arenas and stadiums for most of their career—and right before embarking on a monthlong tour of the same, including the Monsters of Rock festival on August 20—KISS decided to return to the clubs for a two-night stand at the Ritz in New York, followed by a show at the Marquee in London on August 16. Paul Stanley would comment to *Melody Maker* that the shows were "a nightmare" thanks to the heat generated in the club during their performances (leading to the band members nearly passing out from heat exhaustion), but obviously something about the shows must have gone over with him well: within six months he commenced a solo tour of such clubs in order to play more intimate versions of KISS hits and songs from his 1978 solo album. His band would include both former KISS associates, such as Bob Kulick and Gary Corbett (who played keyboard on part of the *Crazy Nights* tour, besides some studio recordings for the band in the 1980s), and a future KISS member, Eric Singer. Stanley's association with Singer in this tour would lead to Singer taking over for Eric Carr in 1991 on the *Revenge* album and becoming a permanent member after that.

KISS would flirt with clubs in the future, including a short tour of such venues in 1992 in preparation for their *Revenge* tour (featuring a return to the Ritz), while doing small acoustic shows for fans during the 1995 convention tour (albeit in vastly different staging conditions than would be normal for clubs), proving that the band could adjust well to more intimate settings. Meanwhile, 2006–2007 saw Paul Stanley doing his second solo tour, this one in support of his album *Live to Win*, showing perhaps even more than the band that he enjoys the chance to perform up close in a club atmosphere.

Madison Square Garden, New York City, November 9, 1990

Eric Carr was anxiously waiting to start a new tour by the beginning of 1990, perturbed it would take place in the U.S. months after the release of their latest album (*Hot in the Shade* in October 1989). Further, he was vocal in his comments to interviewers at the time that the band had gotten sidetracked after 1988 by outside projects, typically emphasizing Paul Stanley's solo tour of 1989 as a main culprit for the delay. Then again, having spent years performing on a nightly basis in live bands through the 1960s and 1970s, Carr saw a band's main purpose as performing for audiences rather than sitting in studios tinkering with knobs and tapes or doing interviews talking about themselves.

So when the tour finally began, Carr was in high spirit and went through his common practice of spending time with fans in the various meet-and-greets before the shows as well as back at the hotels and elsewhere. Yet, as the tour continued, he began to beg off from such encounters, commenting that he was not feeling well. A persistent cough led him to believe he had some type of infection, but it emerged after the tour was over that he had cancer of the heart. In November 1991, he passed away from complications of the disease.

But just a little more than a year before that, Eric Carr was onstage at one of the biggest, most remembered arenas of the world, playing to thousands on the final night of his latest tour. One last time to a cheering crowd, before the future would take him away.

Burbank Airport Hilton and Convention Center, Los Angeles, June 17, 1995

There is no doubt that by the mid-1990s KISS was profiting from a look back at their history—thanks to their own tribute album, multiple video releases, and their own book, *KISStory*, detailing their past—while at the same time struggling to see where they could go after the so-so returns of their past two studio albums (*Hot in the Shade* and *Revenge*). Meanwhile, a number of gatherings had popped up since the late 1980s for fans to get together, buy old and new KISS collectibles, listen to live bands perform old KISS hits, and occasionally get autographs and partake of some interviews with past band associates. These KISS conventions drew the attention of the band immediately, with Eric Carr appearing at an early one, while the entire *Revenge*-era band appeared at a fan-created convention in London on May 21, 1992. Eventually, it would lead to the band taking action against some people associated with the conventions, the biggest being that of a large collection of KISS props and costumes that were being displayed at several such shows. In 1994, the band confiscated some of these items at a convention in Detroit and copyrighted several variations of the term "KISS Convention" in hopes of stopping such gatherings from occurring without their okay (which is why such events are now commonly referred to as "KISS expos," as it was one of the few terms that was not copyrighted by the band in the 1990s).

Another big reason for such actions was that they had decided to do their own convention tour in 1995, traveling to a series of hotels and convention centers to essentially do a variation of what all the other fan-created conventions before had done, only with the added benefit of the band appearing to sign autographs and perform an acoustic set at the end of the day. It was at an early one of these in Los Angeles that Peter Criss appeared, pressed by his young daughter to attend. Upon checking into the convention, he was approached about coming onstage with the band and performing a couple of songs during the acoustic set, "Hard Luck Woman" and "Nothin' to Lose." The response from fans and excitement from fandom in general after the news broke—along with a reconnection between Gene Simmons and Paul Stanley with Ace Frehley and Peter—would lead to the *MTV Unplugged* recording on August 9, 1995, and ultimately to the Reunion tour of 1996.

Weenie Roast, Irvine Meadows, Irvine, California, June 15, 1996, and Tiger Stadium, Detroit, Michigan, June 28, 1996

A tie here, as some would argue as to which appearance is more important to the legacy of the band: the Tiger Stadium show, featuring the first full concert of the reunited original foursome, or the Weenie Roast, the first appearance of the original members playing together in front of an audience? The KROQ Weenie Roast, an annual music festival for the California radio station, occurred nearly two weeks before the Detroit show, making it the first time the band performed in full makeup and costumes for an audience in nearly seventeen years. However, the appearance was only as part of a larger festival, leading to the band performing a smaller set list than would be the norm, while also working its way through various missteps that are always common with first live performances in a tour (including a fire that broke out on the rigging above the stage at one point of the show). In many regards, it was a practice run for what was to come.

On the other hand, the Detroit show would be the official start of the tour, selling out Tiger Stadium within an hour and featuring the band's full show and set list. True, there were still misfires (literally—the fireworks from Frehley's guitar refused to go off at one point, leading to him apologizing to the audience for the mistake), but over 38,000 fans saw the band perform its first full show since 1979 with the original lineup. Because of the size of the show, to many outsiders the Tiger Stadium show was the premier event of the reunited band, forcing the Weenie Roast to be unfortunately a footnote in preparation for bigger things to come, although the fans are always sure to remember them both well.

Columbus Civic Center, Columbus, Georgia, April 5, 1997

Everyone involved in KISS was aware that Peter Criss had come back to perform with the group in 1996 with concerns. He was older, as they all were, but still fit for his age and mentally ready for the challenge; the problem was more physical. As with other longtime musicians, he had begun to have trouble with his arms due to a physical ailment (although, while many names such as tendonitis and bursitis were thrown around, no official reason was ever given), and a series of exercises had been created to help him work through his issues for the tour. For much of the tour, things had gone well, and even the show the night before Columbus had gone smoothly. Yet the morning of the Columbus show, he had woken to find he was having trouble lifting his arms.

Determined to make the best of it, Criss did physical therapy throughout the day in order to get into shape for the show that night, managing to work himself up into a state where he felt he could perform. However, the band's management, as well as the other members, was concerned if playing the show was for the best—not only for Criss but also for the band. The next night would see them perform in Nashville, Tennessee, for a group of possible merchandising investors, and if Peter was in worse shape the next day and could not play, it could cost them financially as well as with publicity.

Fans were already in the arena when all agreed that Criss should rest for the night in order to be in better shape for the concert. With no wish to cancel the show at such a late point, the band decided instead that Ed Kanon, Criss's drum tech for the tour, would put on the Cat makeup and a costume and perform the show while Criss stayed at the hotel to rest. As Kanon told Sakis Nikas, Ace Frehley was upset with the decision to perform without Criss, and Gene Simmons was nervous as to how the crowd would react, but both agreed to go ahead with the show anyway.

The band was quick to make sure that fans knew the situation, with Paul Stanley introducing Ed Kanon clearly and early into the concert that night. Of course, many fans attending were disappointed that Criss was not playing. However, the other side of that coin was that they were witnessing what—to them at the time—was a unique event: a KISS concert with a sudden replacement. Rumors had flown around for years that there had been at least one show back on the *Dynasty* tour that—ironically enough—Criss had to be replaced by another drummer for a show, but there had been no physical evidence of this occurring and certainly no announcement by the band at the show that a member had been replaced out of the blue (which at the time would have been a damaging thing for them to admit—right when fans were starting to lose patience with them and wonder if a member would be leaving soon). Now fans were seeing the real thing for the first time, and it was a big event. Of the fans, who would not have wanted to be there to see it for themselves?

Thus, they stayed and were happy with the concert. For the time, that seemed to be the end of it—Criss came back the next night, and the band played the rest of the tour and more with him having no problems (at least none that the fans knew about from the front of the stage). Just a side note to the tour and nothing more.

Yet history has a way of turning what seem to be trivial events into something bigger, whether accurately or not. Both Gene Simmons and Paul Stanley commented later about the fans not demanding their money back when they saw that the guy in the Cat makeup onstage was not who they thought he was. This leads into the whole situation in 2000 where Eric Singer was brought in to replace Peter Criss after Criss's last contractually obligated concert and put on the Cat makeup for a tour of Japan. To those who felt it was an insult to the original creator of said makeup and character to shove someone else into the same gear, there was always the argument by some in the band that no one seemed to be that upset back in 1997 when it happened, so why now? To some, it now looks like the event was almost a test run of what was to come (and in hindsight Mark St. John's comment about Bruce Kulick replacing him by being told "he looks enough like you that no one will notice" seems to fall into the same category).

A few fans have also pointed out that there were at least two other concerts since KISS put their makeup back on where the band had a member unable to perform for one reason or another, and yet no one was rushed out to replace him wearing their makeup and gear. However, both cases involved circumstances very different from the one that faced Peter Criss that night in 1997. In the case of the Osaka Castle Hall concert in Osaka, Japan, on January 22, 1997, Gene Simmons lost his voice and could not sing. Yet that did not mean he could not play the bass, and so the show went on with him performing as Ace Frehley and Paul Stanley replaced him on vocals when needed (and hence another KISS concert that was truly unique for the fans attending). The second situation occurred on July 27, 2007, at the Soboba Casino Arena in San Jacinto, California. After a sound check, Stanley went to a hospital due to a "cardiac event" (first reported as throat problems, it was explained later by Stanley on his official website as an accelerated heartbeat). He recovered but was in no shape to do the show that night. In that situation and with his okay, Simmons came out with the other members of the band (by this time Tommy Thayer and Eric Singer) and asked the audience if they wanted to hear the three perform. As with the previous two events discussed here, the fans were enthusiastic to see such a unique show, and in this case KISS performed as a trio.

Thus, three situations where the band went on even though one member was unable to perform. Yet it is Peter Criss's incident that gets remembered the most of the three, due to what was coming down the line in October 2000.

North Charleston Coliseum, North Charleston, South Carolina, October 7, 2000

Peter Criss had rejoined the band for a five-year contract in 1995, as did Ace Frehley, with the intention of seeing where things led in the Reunion Years before deciding if anything would happen after that. For a time, especially after the dismal financial and emotional returns on the *Psycho Circus* tour and album for everyone involved, it appears that the band would be wrapping up things for good. Hence, what was literally called a "Farewell Tour" started in March 2000 and would continue until possibly the end of the year. This seemed a perfect way for the band to go out, with all sorts of "final concert" plans in motion that would see KISS bowing out for good in a huge show at perhaps someplace like Shea Stadium or Madison Square Garden or even a whole slew of shows at the latter venue.

And then . . . nothing happened. The tour was extended into October, with a final show set at the North Charleston Coliseum in South Carolina before what was referred to by Ace Frehley and Peter Criss as "the band's final show," and referred to by Gene Simmons and Paul Stanley as the "last show before taking a few weeks off." As the weeks grew closer, and everyone's lawyers grew richer negotiating what was or was not to be, Criss began adding a teardrop to his makeup. Many fans took it to mean that the band really did plan to end things for good and this was his way to show it, while others wondered if perhaps he was just vying to get fans on his side for any possible contract negotiations.

Finally, October 7 came for the end of the tour. For the most part, the band would go on to perform their standard set with little indication that anything was unusual. That is until the final moments of the show. As the reunited foursome played the final notes of "Rock and Roll All Nite," Criss began tearing apart his drum kit, smashing it to pieces.

For the moment, it was his last gesture as a KISS member before leaving—a statement of finality about his place in the band. For a while at least, he would be back for a time in 2003, but by then Ace Frehley was no longer in the band.

Since that night in October 2000, KISS has continued to perform, but never again with the original four members of the band that kicked things off back in a little club in January 1973.

18

Surprising Openers

Ten Bands That Opened for KISS

W hen KISS first started, rock concerts were a smorgasbord of varying musical styles. The early 1970s had reached a point where there was a certain amount of freedom on the radio (no matter how commercial it got), mainly because the older men in charge had pretty much given up on trying to figure out what the audience wanted. Eric Carr once told me that it was easy for a white guy to be in a soul band in 1974 because the market was free enough to let people of different races listen to any kind of music on the radio and in the clubs, and it was only as the 1970s progressed that the men in charge grabbed hold of things and pigeonholed music to be for certain formats and such. With that in mind, it was simply a way of life for KISS to go out on tour opening for bands as diverse as Renaissance, Manfred Mann, Iggy Pop, and 10CC just as often as opening for bands like Blue Oyster Cult and Black Sabbath.

Plus, as a band trying to push their first and second albums, the objective was just to be seen by as many people as possible, so it did not matter who they opened for, as long as people talked about them. Of course, becoming known as scene-stealers who were frequently blowing the headliners out of the water when it came to their live shows did not help the band much. Nor did incidents where they were getting banned from opening for certain bands after incidents (like one with Argent's manager that involved stuffing him in an anvil case while KISS went out to do an encore; or one where the band ignored requests to not do pyro and accidently set fire to the backdrop for Black Oak Arkansas). Yet gradually that changed when KISS started becoming the band that people were heading out to see as the headliner instead of the opening act.

KISS became headliners just as the concert scene was becoming more structured around packaged touring, with a headliner having the same opening act for most if not all of a tour. Soon enough, KISS would be doing shows with an opening act for many weeks in a row, usually with some type of agreement to having such-and-such band opening because the band members wanted those performers to open for them.

It would be easy to fill the list below with names such as Sweet and others who played once or twice with KISS; in most of those cases, the bands rarely mingled, and they were not presented in the sense of "KISS presents" as a common tour headliner does when having an opening act these days. Instead, the names that follow are situations where people performed with KISS over several nights, sometimes ending things on not the best of terms but other times finding that getting a chance to open for KISS helped them move on to bigger and better things.

Blue Öyster Cult

Blue Öyster Cult was the headliner at the New Year's Eve show in 1973 that has typically been seen as KISS's first huge show. Also performing that night was Iggy Pop and a band called Teenage Lust, and KISS did not even get a mention in advertising for the show, but they did get heavily reviewed afterwards, sometimes taking up more type-space than the review of the headliner (having Gene Simmons accidentally set his hair on fire when spitting fire might have helped).

Over the next year, KISS would find themselves opening for Blue Öyster Cult. During that time, some of the management of Blue Öyster Cult was very vocal to the press about how KISS was insignificant compared to Blue Öyster Cult and would soon die out. In 1975, KISS would be using BOC as their opening act, while BOC would be doing special effects in their show that the KISS members noted looked somewhat similar to someone else's act.

Rush

Rush was looking to get things going around the same time as KISS in the early days, and both found themselves working together very often during 1974 and 1975. Because they were struggling for acceptance and stuck together so often, the two bands got along well, and both have had members talking about the good times they had during those years. Rush would, of course, soon take off on their own in 1975 and 1976 with albums such as *Fly by Night* and *2112*.

Cheap Trick

Cheap Trick had released their first album in February 1977 and were touring as they waited out the release of their second, *In Color*, in September of that year. In

KISS opened for Blue Öyster Cult at this show in 1973 without even a mention in the ad. Within two years, Blue Öyster Cult would be opening for KISS.   *Author's Collection*

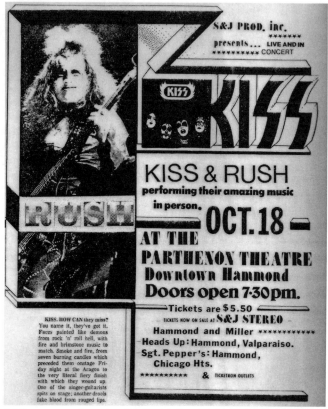

KISS. HOW CAN they miss? You name it, they've got it. Faces painted like demons from rock 'n' roll hell, with fire and brimstone music to match. Smoke and fire, from seven burning candles which preceded them onstage Friday night at the Aragon to the very literal fiery finish with which they wound up. One of the singer-guitarists spits on stage; another drools fake blood from rouged lips.

Ad for concert featuring KISS with Rush. The two bands both saw their fame rising as they toured together. *Author's Collection*

between, they toured for two months with KISS in July and August 1977. The experience went so well that Cheap Trick would go on to make KISS part of their lyrics to their popular hit "Surrender" (which would lead to a bit in concert where Rick Nielsen would throw KISS records out into the audience during live shows).

AC/DC

AC/DC was establishing itself in the States in 1977 with material like "Dirty Deeds Done Dirt Cheap" getting airplay. The band would only do a handful of shows with KISS before moving on, but they has always been one named by Gene that KISS helped support in their early days.

Plasmatics

Wendy O. Williams's band the Plasmatics opened for KISS on the *Creatures of the Night* tour for a number of shows. Gene Simmons liked what he saw with Williams and decided to help her with her career by producing an album for her in 1984 called *W. O. W.* after the Plasmatics came to an end. He wrote half of the tracks for the album, as well as played bass under the name of Reginald Van Helsing. He also pulled in a track called "When the Legend Dies" that had been recorded by KISS during the *Creatures* recordings and gave it to Williams as "Legends Never Die" (which is why Eric Carr—who also cowrote a track with Simmons and Vinnie Vincent—appears as a special guest on the album). Ace Frehley was brought in to help on the track "Bump 'N' Grind," while Paul Stanley appeared on the track "Ready to Rock." In other words, the *Elder*-era lineup of KISS all appeared on Williams's album, although only KISS fans seemed to show any interest in the fact. The song "It's My Life," by Simmons and Stanley, was written at the time of *Creatures*, and the KISS original would eventually turn up on the 2001 KISS five-disc box set. "Thief in the Night," written by Simmons and Mitch Weissman, would turn up on *Crazy Nights* in 1987.

WLRS & Sunshine Promotions Welcomes

THE SHOW OF SHOWS!

Special Guest AC/DC
Monday, Dec. 12—8:00 p.m.—FREEDOM HALL
All seats $7.50. On Sale now at:
Freedom Hall Box Office, Vine Records,
Karma, Subway, Leatherhead, Beethovens
and Ticketron, Lexington.

Ad for show featuring AC/DC as the opening act.   *Author's Collection*

Judas Priest

Opened for KISS for the month of September 1979. This was near the end of touring for the band and during a very emotional period where Peter Criss would soon be walking out the door. Nevertheless, Judas Priest's Rob Halford reported at the time that it was a trying tour as KISS ignored them for the month when they had commonly had a good line of communication in the past with other bands they performed with. Priest would release *British Steel* in 1980 and help reignite metal for the 1980s with Iron Maiden (who opened for KISS in 1980) and a handful of other bands as the decade began.

Sammy Hagar

Hagar began a tour with KISS in February 1977 on good terms. However, he found himself at the mercy of a common situation at KISS shows—the impatient KISS Army waiting to see KISS. During his opening performance at Madison Square Garden on February 18, 1977, Hagar got so frustrated with the constant heckling and booing that he smashed his 1961 Stratocaster on the stage, pulled down his pants and made an obscene gesture with his genitals. As could be expected, Hagar was soon off the tour, although it did not seem to hurt his career in the long run.

Mötley Crüe

Would open for KISS for the last four shows on the *Creatures of the Night* tour. Rumors had been circulating for years that the group had been kicked off the tour by Gene Simmons for inappropriate behavior (what that was has changed many times over the years), but as the tour itself was cancelled after the band's last-night opening for KISS, it seems that if there were reasons, it really did not matter in the end. Beyond that of making for a good rock-'n'-roll story to tell for Mötley Crüe, of course. With KISS touring with the band in the summer of 2012, it is clear that even if there were problems nearly thirty years ago for a handful of shows, they do not remain today.

Aerosmith

Actually, this was not a case of Aerosmith opening for KISS, but rather a co-headliners tour that had KISS and Aerosmith touring together in 2003. Each band called the tour something different, however (*Rocksimus Maximus* for Aerosmith and *World Domination* for KISS). Saliva and/or Ted Nugent opened the shows. One element that caused some infighting in KISS fan circles was the way the show were set up. Unlike other co-headlining tours where the two head acts would flip places in the lineup each show, KISS always went on first before Aerosmith. To some fans that suggested that KISS was essentially opening the show for Aerosmith no matter how many songs KISS did (the two acts commonly did sixteen songs each to keep a balance). The situation has not been repeated since, but for a moment there it was looking as if KISS was starting to head back down the ladder.

19

KISS Will Be My Instrument

The Making of *KISS Meets the Phantom of the Park*

KISS Meets the Phantom of the Park, **NBC Network, Airdate October 28, 1978 (released theatrically 1979–1980 in various parts of the world in several alternate titles)**

For those unfamiliar with the movie's plot: Abner Devereux, an inventor of rides and animatronic creatures at an amusement park, has been fired due to cost-cutting and malfunctioning rides. Convinced that the park's planned KISS concert led to his sacking, the mentally unstable Devereux plans to destroy the park and KISS through the means of robot duplicates of the band. Devereux puts his assistant, Sam, in a resistor-induced trance to help in his revenge, but this leads to Sam's girlfriend Melissa seeking help from the band in finding him. With superhuman powers given to them by a box of talismans in their possession, KISS fight their mechanical twins in a climactic battle onstage, saving the park and Sam, while (possibly) driving Devereux into a catatonic state. Oh, and a trio of goofballs eat up a few minutes of film time by hassling people and robots in the park before getting theirs in the Chamber of Thrills.

Chapter 7 was a review of major turning-points for the band, some of which were seen by fans as decisive moments where the original foursome would decide to split up. To some of those in the KISS Army, this made-for-television movie is one such moment. Of course, such thinking tends to be that of fans wishing to find one cause for the breakup that occurred in 1979, as it makes life a bit easier to understand. However, the disintegration of the union between Simmons, Stanley, Criss, and Frehley had many causes, with the frustrations felt by all about this film to be more of a footnote to other, bigger issues within the band.

Rather, *KISS Meets the Phantom of the Park* is the moment where the band's Achilles' Heel became evident to the public. Before the movie aired on NBC in 1978, people looked to KISS, either with amusement or disgust, as pulling off every "stunt" they did. From albums to television appearances to comic books to concert gigs, they seemed to have a golden touch for any venture they attempted. Even the solo albums released that September and considered a risk looked a triumph at the time (see Chapter 7 for more details on when and why that attitude changed). Before it aired on television, *KISS Meets the Phantom of the Park* looked to be just one more step on the way to bigger things, and there was no reason to assume otherwise. Gene Simmons told one reporter in the summer before it aired that the band were close to signing a deal to do a series of movies for a major studio between 1979 and 1982, while other sources were reporting that a studio was offering KISS a movie with a $10 million budget—a huge amount at the time. From all appearances, KISS could do no wrong, they knew it, and it was really starting to bug the critics of the band.

Then came *The Phantom*. Promoted as a decisive entry into the movie world for the band, fans and critics saw the movie then and see it now as a laughable mess; perhaps a lovable one to some, but still a mess. Attempting to play off of the superhero personas of the Marvel comics (partially created by longtime KISS associate Sean Delaney and covered in more detail in Chapter 23), the movie was already on unsteady ground by attempting to conjure a fantasy world on a television budget—even one that cost more than was typical for a television project. Hanna-Barbara's involvement probably did little to help excite fans from the get-go, as many knew of the company for their work on cartoon programs such as *The Flintstones* and *Scooby-Doo* and assumed the movie would be a cartoon (which confused some music historians who had not seen it but wrote about it as if it were an animated feature). In hindsight, although it took more than just Hanna-Barbera being involved to do it, fans were not far off in their concerns. Suddenly, after years of being untouchable, the band had a huge public mess for everyone to tear apart, from 8 to 10, Eastern Standard Time on NBC, and soon to come to a theater near you.

Which gets into a rumor circulated for years that *KISS Meets the Phantom* was planned as a theatrical release in the U.S.—which simply was not the case. In May 1977, Bill Aucoin told a group of reporters at a Casablanca event that the band planned to do a television movie the following year, and publicity for the movie that was put together around the time it was completed clearly states it was intended to be aired on NBC in October. Director Gordon Hessler and others have also stated in interview that it was always to be a movie-of-the-week; in fact, Hessler would comment later that he was surprised the film was eventually released to theaters as he figured the idea would have been abandoned after people saw it. He was not alone in that feeling, although things did not quite start that way

Besides, making a television movie to air on a network to be later released to theaters in foreign markets was perfectly logical, so talk of a "theatrical film" in a sense was not completely out of perspective. This may seem odd or even cheap in today's climate, where everyone in the world knows what everyone else in the world is watching and can get access to it within minutes via the Internet, but it was not so at the time. A common practice was to release certain television

Ad from *Variety* at time of film showing in Cannes. Note that a long explanation of the band's superpowers had to be given for attendees.   *Author's Collection*

movies in foreign counties as theatrical films, sometimes with additional footage or inserts to make it look more "theatrical" in nature. For example, the miniseries version of Stephen King's *Salem's Lot* was edited down to a two-hour movie with additional gore for such a release, while several episodes of *Man from U.N.C.L.E.* were eventually turned into eight semi-coherent films for the same reason. To do this with KISS when it was a known and accepted practice just made financial sense. Even so, thanks to initial excitable press about the movie going to theaters, but only released that way in foreign markets, and some minor airings in scattered theaters in the U.S. a few years later, the impression was that it was "dumped" on television after review.

What is incredible in retrospect is how so many people dismiss *KISS Meets the Phantom* these days as a "what were they thinking" endeavor without seeing why the project seemed such a moneymaker in the first place. Gordon Hessler came onboard having been a director on a variety of suspense television programs (such as *Alfred Hitchcock Presents*, where he was also a producer, and *The Night Stalker*). He had also directed horror films such as the Vincent Price vehicles *Cry of the Banshee* and *Scream and Scream Again* (which had movie poster art done by Ken Kelly; see the albums *Destroyer* and *Love Gun* in Chapter 10 for reasons why this makes Hollywood a rather small world), as well as one of the best in the Ray Harryhausen special-effects extravaganza Sinbad series, *The Golden Voyage of Sinbad*.

Meanwhile, scriptwriters Jan Michael Sherman and Don Buday were not known for their work in horror, fantasy, or even scriptwriting at that point; they had only done one film before the KISS movie, a thriller with exploitation star Cheri Caffaro called *Too Hot To Handle* in 1977. However, as they told *Variety* in the October 25, 1978, issue, they had worked in music publicity before branching out into film, which—combined with their work on the earlier film—gave them enough of a resume to get the job. Although the two really did not get a chance to use any of their musical background in the movie, they at least attempted to write a script based on the personas of the band members, while also working in bits of the Marvel comic book storyline, such as the box of talismans that give the band members their powers. (It should be mentioned that a 1977 treatment from scriptwriter Michael Winder for the movie, under the title *KISS at the Park*, has popped up in recent years among fandom. The twenty-plus-page treatment is not much like the film itself, but it is intriguing to think what a writer like Winder—who has worked on fantasy, SF, and action series such as *The Avengers, The Saint, Ace of Wands, Space: 1999,* and the film *The Beast Must Die*—could have done with such a script.)

As for a musical score beyond that of the few KISS songs peppered in "live performances" throughout, one would think that Fred Karlin was an excellent choice. A well-respected composer who had scored films such as *Up the Down Staircase* and *Lovers and Other Strangers* (a movie that earned him an Oscar for the song "For All We Know," later a hit for the Carpenters), he had also done action and fantasy films like *Westworld* as well as musical genre movies like *Leadbelly* and the Jan and Dean biopic, *Deadman's Curve*. He may have been concentrating more on television work than on films, but he certainly knew how to compose for movies and would go on to write well-regarded books on composition and recording.

Of the cast, Anthony Zerbe as Abner Devereux—the Phantom of the title—is known for his work in movies and television, appearing in a number of fantasy/horror films (*The Omega Man, The Matrix* series, and others), and demonstrates that he could bring some emotional depths to even minor roles in outlandish pictures, even when chewing the scenery. Carmine Cardi, who built a career on playing either mobsters or police officers in movies and television (including roles in all three *Godfather* movies), is quite solid in his limited role as the park's owner. Other actors would move on to bigger things after the film as well, such as Lisa Jane Persky (Dirty Dee), who also appeared in the cult-classic drama *The Great Santini* and several other films over the years as well as in an episode of the

1980s version of *The Twilight Zone* that found her in another rock-'n'-roll fantasy film, this time in a story about Elvis ("The Once and Future King"). Of course, Ramones fans would spot Don Steele, famous L.A. radio DJ, from his role in the film *Rock and Roll High School* as "Screamin' Steve," as well as appearances in *Death Race 2000* and *Gremlins*, among others. Even Chopper himself, John Dennis Johnston, appeared in a brief role as a police officer in Woody Allen's *Annie Hall* before making the KISS movie and would have a solid television career on various detective series over the years. Of course, one of the best known of the secondary cast would be Brion James, who would do a lot more television work before getting a huge theatrical break by appearing as one of the replicants in the movie *Blade Runner* as well as a small role in a big hit of 1982, *48 Hours*, and its sequel. After that, he would alternate between television and the movies, but commonly in bigger roles and typically as the villain. Thus, the cast for the film is actually quite solid, with actors already on their way to bigger things when production began.

All of this—a director known for his work in television and movies in the fantasy genre, an Oscar-winning composer, a script built on an established mythology from the comics, a cast full of actors on their way up and four men who knew theatrics and music—and yet . . . well, we ended up with *KISS Meets the Phantom of the Park*. For all the factors that would suggest people went into the making of the movie with high hopes, the results showed more signs of things not turning out as expected. The thing is, one cannot point to one element of the movie not working; it seems as if nothing really clicks into place anywhere in the film.

As always, the problems started at the script stage. While Sherman and Buday threw in elements of the Marvel comics, there is no explanation for the band having superpowers, as if it was expected that viewers had read the comics and did not need any details. (An origin story showing how a musical act becomes superheroes would have been more fitting for the first movie, one would think.) Further, the plot is an updated "evil scientist and his robots" movie from the 1950s with some music thrown into the mix, but lacking in character development or even comedy beyond a few quips from Ace Frehley that were later edited out (the *Dr. Goldfoot* movies of the 1960s—which share some remarkable similarities as to the main plot—at least had comedy going for them). There is also a disconnect between the band and the story, with KISS there to perform music and romp in some fight scenes, but doing little else to move the story forward (with only mild rewrites, any band could have worked in their place).

Most importantly, nothing about Devereux's scheme makes much sense. Devereux creates lifelike replicas of people controlled by the villain from his lair, but then he also has the ability to turn people into zombies that he can control. (So what is the point of creating robots when a resistor in the neck of a live person will do the same trick?) His goal is to destroy the park, but his plan is to do this by having KISS sing a song that tells the audience to "Rip and Destroy"? It is as if "Detroit Rock City" makes kids crash their cars after hearing it. Why not just hold the band in their cage until the time of the show and have the concert canceled? That certainly would have caused a riot, as anyone who has seen shows canceled could tell you. (And speaking of an angry crowd, how did the guy giving the band the finger make it into both the NBC and theatrical versions of the film? Don't believe it? Take a look at 1:13:57 in *Attack of the Phantom* on the *KISSology* Volume Two DVD box set. The guy is not only proud to be flipping the bird, but seemingly afraid his bird will fly away from the way he glances up at his hand gesture.) In addition, why not just have the electronics blown up at the show, which would have ruined the reputation of the band and destroyed the park? Seems all this work on robots is a bit unnecessary for the end goal. (Then again, Devereux is not thinking straight by the time the band turns up in the park anyway, so a loopy plan such as his may seem logical to him.) And what happened to him at the end? Did he die? Did madness shut down his mind? Did he replace himself with one of his own robots? Was he thinking about where he left Chopper and his bunch? Or did he ever wonder how escapees from a *Beach Party* movie turned up in the park anyway? No wonder he lost his mind.

But fun speculation aside about the plot, the dialogue is a field of land mines for the actors, with characters given little to do beyond provide info dumps to advance the story and a lot of staring into space waiting for cues. In addition, there was the added grievance by Ace Frehley before filming that he was really given nothing to do or say in the movie, although this appears to have been more his own fault than that of the scriptwriters. He had pretty much ignored

Promotional flyer for *Attack of the Phantoms*.   *Courtesy of Tony Kazerrick*

the writers when they had come to talk to him about the script, and so they decided it would be best not to give him any dialogue beyond an occasional "Awk!" (A phrase Frehley would use at times when he did not want to bother saying anything at all). In an ironic twist, once he complained, he received all the comedy-relief dialogue in the movie. In another twist, all that material was edited out of the 1979 theatrical version of the film, leaving him with little more to say than "Awk!"

Yet, although there were concerns about the script from cast and crew, they could do little about it. Gordon Hessler told Anthony Petkovich in *Shock Cinema* #38 (page 39) that those in control at the studio were "looking at this script as if it was a work of God." So production began on in early May 1978 at Magic Mountain in Valencia, California (although, according to the April 5, 1978, edition of *Variety*, the movie was originally scheduled to be filmed at King Dominion in Richmond, Virginia) with a script that was pretty much untouchable by the cast and Hessler.

Speaking of Hessler, a comment from Bill Aucoin in the book *KISS: Behind the Mask* suggests that the original director was fired because he was doing too many takes with the band members. It is an odd, out-of-the-blue statement, as the suggestion that there was someone directing before Hessler has never cropped up in interviews or articles about the filming. Further, there is documented evidence of Hessler discussing the movie with producer Terry Morse back in March of that year, nearly two months before filming would even begin, making the idea of someone shooting twenty-five takes of the band for several days before being replaced by Hessler impossible. Instead, it appears that Hessler got the project early on through Louis "Deke" Heyward (who had worked with Hessler on previous films and was executive producer at Hanna-Barbera at the time), and he accepted because, as he mentioned in the same interview, "television work was very steady money."

As stated before, the director was familiar with special effects, fantasy/horror, and television production and would seem a perfect match for the movie. On the other hand, he had a script that was heavy with special effects and was working with a television crew who, while creative, were either inexperienced or felt there was no need to risk their careers doing elaborate stunts and effects on a low-budget television movie starring a gimmicky rock band. Although the director and the cast would sometimes wonder if effects were going to look good based on the rapid pace of filming, there was always the assurance that they were in good hands and the effects would look tremendous (to the point Gene Simmons would wildly boast in interviews about the effects that fans would see). Ultimately the effects were clearly guys on wires in front of a black background with twinkling lights, with rays coming out of the general vicinity of Paul Stanley's eye and fire coming somewhere about eight inches away from Simmons's mouth. (And just how does Stanley shoot a laser from his eye that he then can walk down like a ramp without being there to keep the laser-ramp going at the top? But that is the fan again asking questions.)

Hessler's concerns were immediate during filming. He knew that restrictions on him to do the script as written and as quickly as possible (less than a month, as filming was completed before the end of May) meant that he had to concentrate on simply getting the film finished with whatever resources were available. With this in mind, he worked with the band on the weekend before production began to get them familiar and comfortable with the dialogue, which was not easy to do with the four starting to splinter in their working relationship—both for logistical and emotional reasons.

By the time filming had begun in May 1978, the band members would arrive for rehearsals and shooting in their own private, chauffeured cars and have little to do with each other when not in front of the cameras. While some of this was due to just wanting a break after nearly five years of nonstop touring and recording together, there was also the task of the solo albums due for release in September of that year that was necessitating time away from each other. Although Simmons had pretty much finished his album before the filming, and Stanley was in good shape with his, Frehley was still working on his, while Peter Criss would not begin to record until after filming. Thus, everyone had their own agendas to worry about on top of the television movie.

Further, it was clear early on that there were also differences in how each member saw making a movie. Both Simmons and Stanley were keen to show their ability to act—Simmons was already seriously looking at a movie career even back in '78 (and started auditioning for movies by the early 1980s) and would begin acting lessons to help him toward that goal, as would Stanley—but Frehley and Criss had two strikes against them. First, both were musicians who were impatient with the drawn-out process of filmmaking; and second, both were partiers rapidly succumbing to alcohol and drug abuse. To them, the idea of having to get up very early, put on costumes and makeup, and then be forced to sit in their trailer for hours before shooting a minute or two of material was tedious and led to finding any way they could to divert their attention. This frustration even led to Frehley taking off at one point during filming, leaving the production to use his tall and African American stunt stand-in to take his place for some shots in one of the fight scenes.

Saying that, Frehley comes off as one of the better actors of the group, blissfully unaware of the camera enough that he does rather well with his dialogue; and certainly better than Paul, who was handed more lines as the band's frontman but could never bring much emotional depth to his lines. Simmons is given the most to do, if not dialogue to say, and presents it with gusto. Criss, on the other hand, did not do nearly as well; a disappointment to himself, as he believed himself to be a natural actor and assumed he would shine when he appeared on-screen. Instead, according to those working on the production, his dialogue was redubbed by voice actor Michael Bell (known for his work in a variety of Saturday morning animated programs, including those for Hanna-Barbera) in order to make it effective for broadcast (some sources have the voice actor as Norman Alden, who was also doing cartoon voice work for the networks at the time). Criss was actually supposed to do the dubbing, but many witnesses, including the other members of the band, say that he never turned up to do it. Criss has argued both ways about this, claiming he had been there for all of the dubbing but in more recent interviews admitting he may not have been there after all. Either way, it was still a sticking point to him that more attempts had not been done to get his voice heard in the film instead of someone he feels did not sound at all like him. Oddly, his real voice appears briefly in the opening teaser trailer for the movie when it appeared before *NBC Saturday Night at the Movies* and eventually turned up on YouTube a few years back (although the promo used an undubbed version of the film for the edit). Odder still, Criss sounds perfectly fine in the promo, which conflicts with the legend that he sounded so bad that none of his original dialogue could be used.

Beyond the foursome's awkward transition to the screen, most of the other actors do what they can to bring some life to their roles (for example, Persky may be stuck playing a cliché biker chick but at least tries to bring some life to the character and attempts to show the fear Dirty Dee is experiencing when alone in the Chamber of Thrills). On the other hand, and unfortunately, the two main protagonists of the movie, Sam and Melissa, are played by actors who never really get a chance to show much range in their roles and would find limited success afterwards. Deborah Ryan, Melissa in the movie, would do a small number of television roles into the early 1980s before eventually moving on to other things.

Lobby card for the film.   *Courtesy of Tony Kazerrick*

Terry Lester, as Sam, would go on to work in a number of soap operas in the 1980s and 1990s before passing away in 2003 from a heart attack. Sadly, in many ways, their reputations as being bad in the movie are not of their own doing. Sam is given little to do once he is turned into a robotic zombie by Devereux except walk stiffly about the place; Melissa doesn't get an emotional moment until the last ninety seconds of the movie, which involve quietly pleading for Sam before shrieking at Devereux and then going back to a timid plead, as if Melissa had suddenly gone bipolar.

Editing in the film is also very confused. A quick look at the pool scene where the security guards confront the band shows one of many instances where there are odd pauses in dialogue, as if the characters are being too polite to talk over each other. Chunks of the movie also appear arranged in a haphazard way, with the band reacting as if they know something is wrong in the park during the pool scene when they have no reason to and another scene where they act exhausted while roaming the park long before their powers are taken by Sam. Some characters disappear midway through, and others have events happen to them off-camera to save time (such as the security guards being turned into Devereux's slaves). These scenes would be reshuffled and new scenes added to clarify things in the later theatrical cut, but for those watching the movie on NBC in 1978 (and later on video, but more about this a bit further on), it felt at times that the movie was edited just to get it done and with no concern for story structure.

The musical score also fell under criticism, but for reasons that may have been out of the control of those involved. Fred Karlin had gone into the production by first working on the fight scenes, with jazzy, funky material that would have been at home in a blaxploitation movie. Even ten years later, this may seem an oddity for the movie, but at the time it was not uncommon to hear in most action films and certainly in television shows (nearly all the detective series at the time seem to fall into this category). Perhaps with enough time and focus, Karlin may have driven the score in another direction. However, the July 1978 murder of his son found the composer leaving the production before completion. With Karlin out, Hoyt Curtin joined the production to complete the musical score. Curtin had scored plenty of television shows and movies, but he was best remembered for his work with Hanna-Barbera over the years and for creating most of the classic cartoon theme songs for the company, including those for *The Flintstones* and *The Jetsons*. The downside of that was that he had a very distinctive style that was readily associated with cartoons. Once one hears his score, used for incidental scenes beyond those of the few musical segments with the band, it is hard not to associate it with the cartoons Hanna-Barbera was doing at the time.

Even the KISS portion of the score is somewhat odd. Besides "Rock and Roll All Nite" being performed twice, midway through the film, the band gathers around Peter Criss and Paul Stanley as Criss sings a seemingly endless version of "Beth." What is peculiar is that Stanley is actually not playing the acoustic guitar part heard in the film (as per Criss, originally he was supposed to mimic the guitar part for the film but knew he would not be able to make it look convincing, so Stanley jumped in to do it—but not before a photo was taken of the band posed around Criss with the guitar, which was used on one of the Italian movie posters for the film). Instead it is a studio musician performing the part, most probably guitarist Dick Wagner, who had worked on the acoustic guitar part of the song when the band recorded it for the *Destroyer* album in 1976 (Wagner was an old acquaintance of *Destroyer* producer Bob Ezrin, having worked with him on albums for Alice Cooper and Lou Reed). Also, the "Rip and Destroy" song used to incite the audience to riot was actually the song "Hotter Than Hell" with lyrics rewritten by Paul Stanley on-set as the band had promised to write the song only to discover that no one had come up with anything when filming was ready to begin on the sequence.

Thus, the complete musical score is a weird mishmash of KISS songs, funky orchestration, and jazzy cartoon music. With the audience for the movie expecting to hear music in KISS's style, it felt as if someone was throwing anything on the screen when it came to the score without keeping it a coherent whole; which, as it turns out, was an unavoidable reality in order to get it ready in time for its October debut.

It is hard to judge how much of the occurrences behind the scenes were known by the band as they worked on the movie and after completing production. Many of the interviews with the band members before and just after it aired on NBC suggest that they were told either that anything they felt was not "right" would be fixed in post-production or that they were making the greatest movie in the history of cinema. It is also possible they felt they had to hype it as a great movie in hopes of getting people to watch even if they knew there were problems.

The reality of the situation came for the four members of the band when they finally saw the finished product just days before it was to air on NBC. The band's reaction was—to put the best face on it—mixed. While Peter Criss was upset to see his voice redubbed throughout the film, Ace Frehley reported later that he laughed all through the showing as if it were a very expensive home movie. As for Gene Simmons and Paul Stanley, the reaction was simply one of shock at how a movie put together by experienced, talented people that was supposed to propel them to the next stage of their career had turned out to be a half-baked kiddie action movie with bad special effects, wooden acting (especially and admittedly by themselves), and with a confused musical soundtrack. By that time, however, there was no turning back; the movie had been advertised for quite some time in connection with the solo albums ("Don't miss the Spectacular Action of *KISS Meets the Phantom*" read the ads), and NBC was enthusiastic about what they saw as a big ratings hit for them.

Which, according to legend, was exactly what happened—*KISS Meets the Phantom* supposedly was one of the biggest, if not the biggest, ratings grabber of the year for NBC—making it something for the fans to crow about even after everyone has a good laugh at the movie's expense. Yet a look at the ratings show that NBC's highest-rated program for the 1978–1979 television season was *Little House on the Prairie* at #14, and *KISS Meets the Phantom* could not outperform the one-two punch of *Rescue from Gilligan's Island* (with a 40 share one week) shown in two parts the previous two Saturdays before the KISS movie aired on NBC. Worse, *Variety* reported the week after the movie aired that "NBC had its worst Saturday of the year" in the ratings that October 28th (*Variety*, November 1, 1978, page 45). The comment in *Variety* is no wonder—NBC had preempted their popular *CHiPs* series to run *KISS Meets the Phantom*, and the movie ended up as a very dismal #45 in the ratings for that week. While the 10 o'clock program following it, *Sword of Justice*, may not have been doing well in the ratings, it most probably did not cause the whole night to tank for NBC. Thus, even with the many weeks, even months of hyping, the movie could not really be described as a success for the network.

Why was this? Two things: everything about the movie made it look exactly like what it turned out to be, an old-time horror/fantasy film with cheap special effects and featuring KISS playing some songs; and scheduling the program for Saturday night. High school kids, college students, and some older fans in their twenties were usually not watching television on a Saturday night; instead they were going out. Thus, the main audience that night was those who were home—kids allowed to stay up and watch the program and their parents. Even there, NBC had problems, with protests over the movie springing up around the country, including a station out in Minnesota, KSTP-TV, that had one hundred calls before the show from listeners of a local religious radio station that the movie was inappropriate for such a time slot and ultimately propaganda that would "encourage the worship of Satan."

Even with rather tepid results on the network, the film was set for a release in the UK and Europe in December 1978, and a preview showing was done for a carefully "selected audience" to gauge how the NBC cut of the film would play to a paying crowd. The results were dismal—a *Melody Maker* reviewer who had attended said that the audience tried to be respectful for the first reel, but it was impossible to do so after that, and the audience was soon convulsed with laughter. It was decided that work needed to be done, and the film was pulled just weeks before its release, causing an expensive ad campaign to be tossed out while those who had worked on it tried to figure out a way to save the movie.

To do so, three things occurred: editing of the film, editing of the film score, and a change in title. The first was the simplest, although it led to the most changes from what appeared in the NBC version in 1978 and what audiences saw in the theatrical release in 1979. Sam being kidnapped by Devereux and Melissa's search for him in the park are tightened so that she is already apprehensive about Devereux and his workshop before she arrives there. Devereux and the park owner have an extra scene early on to expand on Devereux's crumbling mental state and the owner's attempt to help him. After a loopy edit that has the band performing "Black Diamond" twice onstage, the audience sees

Melissa telling the band about Sam's disappearance before the scene where the Robot Gene destroys the cardboard Coke stand; thus, when the guards confront the band at the pool, the band already knows that something is up in the park and are not telling the guards. The band weakens after Sam grabs the talismans (instead of before); meanwhile, a new scene shows the converted Chopper and his gang as American patriots who gas the security guards and take them away to be made into Devereux's slaves as well. All of the band's mid-movie fight sequences appear one after the other at this point, with a lot of their dialogue cut in the process and quickening the pace to get to them becoming Devereux's captives. The rest of the film plays out in a similar way to the NBC version, with the exception that instead of Paul Stanley merely picking the resistor off Sam's neck like a bug, he uses his laser eye to cause it to explode (which probably would have caused more damage to Sam, but it looks flashier that way, so that is what mattered). As to the title, it became known as *KISS in Attack of the Phantoms*, although it sometimes would play as *Attack of the Phantoms* or just *Phantoms* in some theaters.

With these changes, the movie flows much better, with the logic of scenes making more sense. It is still a B-movie mad scientist plot, but at least the band appears more active in tracking down Sam and saving the park, rather than stumbling around the park until they run into things as in the NBC version. However, with the change in the structure of the film and editing of the fight scenes to make them more efficient, Fred Karlin's score no longer worked as featured in the NBC version.

Which led to the soundtrack changes that occurred in the theatrical edition. Fred Karlin's score was jettisoned outright and his name was taken off the credits, with Hoyt Curtin's material cut down to a bare minimum as well (but enough that his credit stayed on the film when it was theatrically released). Instead, the fight scenes and many other incidental sequences found songs from the band's solo albums being used instead, turning some scenes—like the confrontation with the Robot Werewolves/Apes using Frehley's "New York Groove" in the background for the fight music—into almost-music-videos. In some ways, such as the "New York Groove" sequence, it works nicely, while in others it falls flat— Simmons's "Mr. Make-Believe" works somewhat in a scene of Devereux walking away after being fired, but it does not sell the ending credits and end the movie with a bang the way that the NBC version used "God of Thunder." Nevertheless, in some ways it was an improvement, and the film was ready for release.

But first it had to find distributors, and so the revised version of the movie saw its first public appearance at the Cannes Film Festival in May 1979, alongside such films as *My Brilliant Career, Days of Heaven,* and *Apocalypse Now.* With that release came the first ads for the "theatrical version" of the movie, such as one that appeared in the Cannes-related issue of *Variety.* What is interesting about the ad are two paragraphs at the top stating "A few words about KISS . . ." that not only explain how popular the band is but also gives a bit of history on the superhero personas of the band members for viewers who were not familiar with

AN **AVCO** EMBASSY PICTURES Release

... A TOTAL INSANE - HORROR ROCK FILM THAT GOES BEYOND ALL LIMITS!

KISS ®

A GORDON HESSLER FILM

in **ATTACK of the PHANTOMS** A

Gene Simmons · Paul Stanley · Peter Criss · Ace Frehley

Released by BRENT WALKER FILM DISTRIBUTERS LTD.

UK Flyer for the film.   *Courtesy of Tony Kazerrick*

KISS's comic book history. Obviously, this was an attempt to cover for the movie never quite getting around to why the foursome has superpowers in the first place and hopefully persuading distributors to give it a chance.

The movie first saw commercial theatrical release in Europe—notably West Germany—on October 26, 1979. There also appeared to be a possible sneak preview in Lancashire, England, that same day in October, but the BBFC (British Board of Film Classification) shows March 17, 1980, as the date an A classification was given to the movie, so it appears that it did not hit theaters in England until after this date. November 1979 saw the release of the movie in Australia to strong box office, with ads from the Australian distributor making it into *Variety* in January 1980. The film would later see a successful rerelease in Australia on a double bill with Alice Cooper's concert film, *Welcome to My Nightmare*, while in some areas it played with the added bonus of the "music videos" made for the *Dynasty* album singles, "I Was Made for Lovin' You" and "Sure Know Something." Some American fans also remember getting a chance to see the movie (rated PG for no logical reason) on the big screen as well, which may explain the small number of American movie posters found for the film—posters that have given rumor to a possible run as a theatrical release before being given to NBC to show in 1978. But most reports state the posters come from 1979 or thereafter. From all accounts, the movie pulled in some money thanks to the theatrical runs, although not many found much good to say about it.

By 1982, the film had run its course in any guise at the theaters, just as home video was hitting its stride with movies being released on VHS and Beta for rental at video stores as well as for purchase by collectors. Hanna-Barbera jumped into the home-video market in the early 1980s by signing on with Worldvision for the release of their catalog of old animated cartoons and such, with the NBC cut of *KISS Meets the Phantom* in the collection. Worldvision would first release the movie on tape in February 1982 and later in 1986 (after the band had regained some of their popularity in the later 1980s) as *Hanna-Barbera Presents KISS Meets the Phantom of the Park*. With a retail price of $59.95, most fans passed on buying the videocassette, which came in a plastic clamshell case and featured artwork of Peter Criss and Gene Simmons, back to back above an image of Devereux at his robotic control panel. In 1988, Worldvision worked out a deal with Goodtimes Video, which released the movie once again, only this time solely on VHS (Beta had pretty much died out by that time), in a cardboard sleeve, and at $9. 95. It is this version of the video that most fans remember, as it was more accessible and certainly cheaper than the previous editions. Worldvision would also release the movie on laserdisc in 1992, which would come very handy in the DVD-era just around the corner, as multiple DVD editions came out from various companies that used this or other elements (sometimes even the old VHS Goodtime release) to package the movie again for sale to fans.

Besides all this, the movie appeared twice on the *CBS Late Movie* program in the mid-1980s, but in a condensed, edited form due to CBS cramming old 60-minute episodes of old television programs and old 90–120-minute theatrical and made-for-television movies into a 140-minute timeslot—with additional commercials to boot. Thus, the version that aired on CBS ran sixty-two minutes after all the editing, more than twenty minutes shorter than the original NBC version. Some fans were fine with this, as the edits eliminated most of the plot in order to get to the band sooner and show most of their concert sequences. The movie also had a limited run in a syndicated package of movies for television stations, but soon disappeared from that market after the video release in 1986.

Finally, in 2007, KISS released the theatrical version of the movie on the second volume of their *KISSology* DVD series. It is crystal clear, with plenty of KISS songs, more coherent and even closed-captioned for the hearing-impaired. It also killed the market for the bootleg releases on DVD of the earlier Goodtimes/Worldvision edition of the movie. While in many ways the theatrical cut is better, there is sometimes a bit more fun about the ragtag *KISS Meets the Phantom* edition that many of us saw as kids back in 1978. Or maybe it was partially due to the search for a good copy of the movie to show to friends that made the original cut so attractive to fans.

As for the players: Sherman and Buday followed up the movie with work on a script for a planned Dr. Hook movie that never happened and then went on to other projects before splitting off for projects of their own. Buday passed away in 2001. Gordon Hessler continued in television (including *CHiPs*, the show the KISS movie knocked off the schedule that Saturday in 1978) and some action films in the late 1980s and early 1990s. Fred Karlin continued working in movies for both television and the theater for many years until his death in 2004. Hoyt

Curtin carried on with his success with Hanna-Barbera into the 1990s before passing away in 2000. As mentioned before, many of the actors went on to busy careers as well. Most, if not all, have looked back on the filming of *KISS Meets the Phantom* as a one-of-a-kind experience in their careers and even if feeling a bit embarrassed about being in it, they do take some pride in being in something remembered so fondly by KISS fans.

KISS may still feel that the movie itself is not that great but that having done a movie at all was a great achievement in their careers. Plans for future movies died quickly after the mediocre results of this one as well as the uncertainty of the band's future after Peter Criss left and they struggled to find their footing again with the changing times in the early 1980s. KISS would try again to make a go at the movies and television soon enough. But that's a story for another chapter.

20

After the Phantom

Fifteen Other Important Television Appearances

K *ISS Meets the Phantom of the Park* may hold a special meaning as a
television event to anyone who knows the band (whether a happy,
sad, or delirious meaning is up to the individual of course), but it
certainly was not the only televised moment that propelled KISS into certain
directions of their career. Below is a list of fifteen appearances by the band that
were important in some way, such as a representation of the beginning of their
career, a closing of one door for another, or a reemergence after nearly disappearing from the public's awareness. Each had an effect on the band, in some
cases much more seriously than the television movie alone.

In Concert, ABC Network, Airdate March 29, 1974

The first national television appearance of KISS. That pretty much says it all.
KISS performed three songs on this program that would later evolve into *Don
Kirshner's Rock Concert* (for which the band would make an appearance in
support of the *Rock and Roll Over* album in 1977), and it is clear that they have
already fallen into the mixture that would suit them well for the next five-plus
years—Gene Simmons's tongue-waggling, Paul Stanley's jumping around, Ace
Frehley's unsteady movements combined with concentrated hands on the guitar,
the special effects (like Peter Criss's shooting drumsticks)—with Simmons,
Stanley, and Criss all getting equal chances to sing lead (leading to a humorous
moment of Criss belting out "Black Diamond" while the cameras stays focused
on Stanley in the assumption that he should be performing such duties).

What is interesting to note about the appearance (which can readily be
found in edited form on the first *KISSology* DVD set) is how attentive Simmons
and Stanley are to the television camera at such an early stage of their career;
focusing on home viewers in a way that was and is rarely seen by musicians in
mid-performance and usually discouraged by television directors as breaking the
"fourth wall" between the action on-screen and the viewers at home (one reason
why the cameras tend to cut away so quickly whenever one of the two looks into
them). While they obviously do well with the audience (many seem to be on
their feet and enjoying the show), it is clear that the band is already conscious

of the power of television and wanting to draw in the viewers in a visual manner beyond playing to the audience in front of the stage.

Mike Douglas Show, Syndication, Airdate May 21, 1974

On reflection, one can only say, "It was the seventies." What other time in the history of television would afternoon talk shows present acts like Iggy Pop, Alice Cooper, David Bowie, and others when the audience was predominantly bored housewives and grade-school kids home sick from school? Of course, today we have an all-too-common thread of talk shows with people discussing their disturbing afflictions that would make the peccadilloes of those artists of the 1970s "pure innocent fun," but it should be remembered that such programs today set up these individuals for ridicule as part of a freak-show atmosphere. Perhaps in some ways that was true of the '70s as well, but what was striking was how earnest the talk-show hosts were in creating a serious dialogue with their guests instead of treating them as someone to mock. Of the talk shows in syndication at the time—and there were several, with Douglas competing, and sometimes even sharing the same time slots on other channels, with rivals like Merv Griffin and Dinah Shore—Mike Douglas managed to easily obtain the services of a variety of rock artists. Securing the appearance of John Lennon and Yoko Ono in 1972 as cohosts for a week of shows no doubt helped, as it demonstrated to other rock performers that he would be more open to giving them a chance to shine without disdain. Certainly much more than the late-night alternatives; with the exception of Dick Cavett, most considered rock stars as individuals to be pitied rather than showcased, nor did they know how to record their musical performances for television for proper sound.

It is the Lennons' cohosting chore that brings up a point to be considered by viewers watching this moment in KISS television history on the first *KISSology* DVD box set: Douglas typically would have a famous person cohost the program with him during a week's run of five episodes (one a day during the workweek; airing at in the morning or afternoon, depending on when stations scheduled it). Comedian Totie Fields at that point and afterwards was a regular in the role, helping to introduce guests and interact with them, as she did in this appearance by KISS. This is why Fields interrupted so often during the interview; guest cohosts were expected to do that, so it was not some type of vendetta on Fields's part to dig at how Simmons appeared or Douglas being weak-willed in controlling the situation.

Not that the ribbing Simmons got was undeserved, although it is clear that he was doing the best he could under the circumstances. Told of the interview moments before the one-song performance, he attempted to stay "in character" as the Demon to only meager effect—mainly thanks to Fields wishing to have nothing to do with it. Fields—a Jewish comic who had been in the business long enough to see pretty much everything under the sun—made it plain that she wanted to deflect the "scary/disturbing" image that Simmons was projecting by pointing out that he was probably a "nice Jewish boy from Long Island," cracking that "you can't hide the hook." To his credit, Simmons took the comments in good humor, which allowed the audience to warm somewhat to him, even if they were still unsure of what to make of him—a moment Simmons respected enough to later thank Fields on his solo album as well as document it in his book *KISS and Make-Up.*

Nearly forty years on, it is easy today to look back on this appearance and wonder, beyond it being KISS at an early stage, what was the big deal. Perhaps the one thing fans watching these segments on the DVD set today have to remember is that all the trappings we come to expect from KISS—Simmons talking in character, the band performing "Firehouse" on a smoke-filled stage, the mild disdain of others shown by Fields—were brand new at the time. The only national television appearance before this for the band was in the March 29, 1974, episode of ABC's *In Concert,* a program that not only was aired during late-night programming on Fridays when mainly kids and college students would be watching, but also was not seen on all the ABC affiliates across the country (some stations dropped the show after the infamous premiere episode featuring Alice Cooper). Thus, the *Mike Douglas Show* was really the first chance most of America had to see the band in action, and no doubt that appearance did more to make people stand up and take notice of KISS than any other television appearance until . . . well, until our next entry.

Paul Lynde Comedy Hour, ABC Network, Airdate October 29, 1976

KISS had been on national television before by this point, but in niche market placement that saw them drawing a small segment of viewers. *In Concert* and *Midnight Special* were both late-night programming aimed at high school and college students, while *Mike Douglas Show* was mainly there for housewives and (possibly, depending on the local channel's scheduling of the program) kids coming home from school on a weekday afternoon. The *Paul Lynde* program, however, was on ABC at 8:00 on a Friday Night—thus making it the band's first prime-time performance.

For those curious, this was one in a series of specials that periodically replaced *Donny & Marie*—on which Lynde was a regular—during the season, which is why the program is entitled the *Paul Lynde Comedy Hour* and scripted for Halloween instead of a one-off Halloween special. A DVD of the episode has made its way to the public under the title of *The Paul Lynde Halloween Special,* however, so the episodes seems to be stuck with that title these days.

Once again, the *KISSology* release features an edited version of an appearance by the band, with only one song ("King of the Nighttime World") out of three making it on to the box set. (Both the *In Concert* and *Mike Douglas* appearances, as well as others included in the *KISSology* series, were edited to highlight certain moments only from longer segments.) By doing so, *KISSology*

PAUL LYNDE BREWS UP A HALLOWEEN FANTASY

Paul Lynde hates Halloween... until three "good" witches appear and change his mind. Helping Paul Lynde dress-up this new Halloween fantasy are guest stars **Tim Conway, Roz** (Pinky Tuscadero) **Kelly, Margaret Hamilton, Billie Hays** and **Billy Barty,** special guest star **Florence Henderson** and in a special appearance **Betty White.** The flash-rock group **Kiss,** makes its premiere on television and **Donny** and **Marie Osmond** are surprise guests.

BOO! HUMBUG!

THE PAUL LYNDE HALLOWEEN SPECIAL ⏱ TONIGHT 8:00PM ⑦

The infamous *Paul Lynde Show* with the "flash-rock group" KISS making their prime-time national television debut.   *Author's Collection*

sells the moment short in terms of how much exposure the band received in this prime-time hour. With three songs (the other two were "Detroit Rock City" and "Beth"), a jokey interview segment (which amazingly lets the band keep their dignity), and a brief appearance in the disco finale, the band dominates the hour. Thus, the *Paul Lynde* episode no doubt helped in their crossover with younger fans into the family-oriented image that had begun creeping into the band's agenda since late 1975.

It was also the first time that one member was emphasized over the others, thanks to the inclusion of "Beth" in the show. With Peter Criss being the singer and orchestration not involving the other members, there was nothing for Simmons, Stanley, and Frehley to do other than to standby (literally, as they are shown briefly at the end of the song, standing in the shadows as the camera pulls back from Criss) while Criss took center stage. There would be times to come where one member would be emphasized over the others, but up to this point the band had always been presented as four parts of a whole. Although purely done for visual reasons, in a sense this appearance shows that the "Four Musketeers" atmosphere of the band was beginning to unravel.

Don Kirshner's Rock Concert, Syndication, Week of May 28, 1977

Rock Concert was a spin-off—some would say continuation—of ABC's *In Concert* series that KISS first appeared on back in 1974. With an introduction by Kirshner—a courtesy he extended to most of the musical guests that was later famously parodied by musician Paul Schaffer on the original *Saturday Night Live* program—the band appears on a partial mock-up of their *Destroyer* concert stage to perform three songs: "I Want You," "Love 'Em and Leave 'Em," and "Hard Luck Woman."

For American fans, this would be the first national television appearance since the *Paul Lynde* episode a few months before and the last memorable one until the band's interview on the NBC news special *Land of Hype and Glory* in 1978. These segments were also some of the earliest "rare" video material in circulation among fans, being traded on videotape back in the early 1980s and before the glut released through various sources leaked to fans in the late 1980s and onward. Further, the clips allowed fans to see at least a portion of the *Destroyer* concert stage—a stage rarely seen in official material released by the band. This was ironic, as although *Destroyer* was a huge success for the band, photos and videos released in the 1970s of the band in performance tended to jump from the pre-*Alive!* stage to the *Love Gun/Alive II* stage, missing the "ruined-castle/moonscape" set so lovingly remembered by fans who saw it in person.

The three clips also show a tight emotional and professional harmony within the band. Everyone, with the exception of Ace Frehley (who would not sing lead on a KISS song until "Shock Me" from *Love Gun*, released later in 1977) gets a lead vocal, while he and Paul Stanley work together to give viewers a "surprise" ending to the "Hard Luck Woman" clip, thanks to their playing a double-neck guitar together. The *Paul Lynde* show demonstrated the band breaking out; the *Rock Concert* clips show them knowingly at the top of the world, with no fear of anyone knocking them down.

There are some oddities about this clip. Three songs are performed from *Rock and Roll Over*, including the first single, "Hard Luck Woman," but not the second single from the album, "Calling Dr. Love," which was still receiving random airplay in May 1977. Performed instead were two songs never released as singles. Speaking of dates, the band is shown promoting the *Rock and Roll Over* album in May 1977 when the follow-up album, *Love Gun*, would be released within three weeks of this appearance. Yet there really is not much of a mystery to resolve here: it was not uncommon for performers to film segments for *Rock Concert* weeks and sometimes months before their appearances made it to the air. The clips gives an idea of what other songs Casablanca and KISS saw as potential singles from the album (not to mention that "I Want You" would be covered in concert well after the *Rock and Roll Over* period, so it was obviously a favorite of the group).

These segments appeared on foreign television programs, from Europe to Japan to Australia, which is why KISS fans tend to refer to the three clips as "music videos" (more on this argument in Chapter 21). The most interesting thing about these foreign airings was the titling used for "Love 'Em and Leave 'Em" on the shows. While "Love Me, Leave Me"—as titled on one European program—could still work as lyrics for the song in some ways, the title of "No More People" used on a Japanese show makes the mind boggle as to what viewers thought Gene Simmons was describing in the song.

The Young Music Show, NHK-TV, Japan, Airdate Summer, 1977; HBO, USA, August 1979

As mentioned in Chapter 7, KISS made a spectacular tour stop in Japan in the spring of 1977, and there was talk was of releasing the recordings made during the tour as part of another *Alive* album. While production was done on such an album, the band eventually abandoned it (although at least some of the material made it to *Alive II*—see Chapter 14 for more details), that did not stop the airing of this fifty-minute special on Japanese television in 1977, taken from two concerts performed on April 2, 1977. With crisp live video of the band in action, KISS tears through a number of songs on the best-remembered stage set of their career to a enraptured audience. There were to be bigger shows and bigger audiences to come, but this was the highlight of the original foursome's live career, where everyone was working on all cylinders, and the cameras were there to record it.

The program, with some slight title alterations, would appear on the American pay cable channel HBO in August 1979. Short clips from it would also appear in other KISS-related material over the years (including a brief glimpse in the USA Network special *Yesterday and Today* in 1983), and multigeneration copies of both the Japanese and HBO versions circulated on video in the 1980s. But it really was not until 1992 that a cleaner copy began circulating through fandom. Eventually an eighty-one-minute version of the second concert from that day (without titles and credits) made its way to the first *KISSology* DVD box set. Nevertheless, the thrill of the chase for fans finally getting to watch faded, hiccupping copies on VHS back in the 1980s almost meant more than the show itself, as it was considered a holy grail for KISS fans at the time.

Land of Hype and Glory, NBC Network, Airdate January 19, 1978

The first news program (albeit a NBC special) to look at KISS in a serious vein tends to rile up some KISS fans for what they see as an attempt to discredit the band by focusing exclusively on the merchandising in a negative manner. To see it this way is to miss the point, although the edited footage found on the *KISSology* DVD set would understandably make some think otherwise.

Hosted by respected journalist and reporter Edwin Newman, the program's theme was a humorous review on the way hype—that is, over-eager promotion—was changing the landscape of many professional fields in the world, including movies, books, music, and even politics. KISS was an obvious choice to cover in the music segment for this reason, although certainly not the only one; the program focused on many other musical acts being just as motivated to sell trinkets with their names plastered on them. In the original broadcast form, Newman's point seems not so much that KISS was bad for focusing on promotional extravaganzas, but that at least KISS was honest about that side of the business, unlike many whose hypocrisy would have them publicly turn their noses up at merchandising while still taking their cut of the profits. Ironically, because the *KISSology* DVD is edited to only show segments of the program directly involving KISS, the impression is that they were the only artists being scrutinized, when all musicians were being poked by Newman's gentle ribbing.

From fans' perspective, what did appear of the band in the program gave them a chance to see some live footage (a rarity on video back in 1978) as well as a short interview with them on the *Love Gun* tour stage (photos exist of manager Bill Acouin also being present for this group interview, but he is only seen in separate interviews at another location in the program). Of the four, Gene Simmons is in best form (although a wide-eyed look from Peter Criss after

Newman throws out his first hard question is entertaining to watch). Simmons gave solid answers to Newman's questions and emphasized the band's career-long dedication to being entertainment first and not trying to solve the world's problems through their songs. He also has a great closing line to the segment ("What a way to make a living") that wraps it up in a nice little ball.

Entertaining as it is, the special does show that the tide was beginning to turn on the band thanks to their success. By early 1978, they had reached the summit of popularity and, as always with those who publicly skyrocket as the band did, they were going to find the media and public starting to swipe at them in order to knock them down a peg or two. While Newman did so with tongue firmly in cheek and obviously with an eye on the music business in general, many would view KISS as the poster child of rock-'n'-roll excess in the years to come. *Land of Hype and Glory* was there first in showing the turning point of the media's love affair with KISS, even if that was not Newman's intention.

Tomorrow Show, NBC Network, Airdate October 31, 1979

There is no doubt about it: Tom Snyder was an odd duck when it came to doing interviews. Improvising questions that rambled down long stretches of commentary having little to do with the interviewee, even sometimes appearing oblivious to who his guests were, Snyder nevertheless could be captivating when he and his interviewees clicked. As a late-night program done (until its final year) without an audience on an almost bare set, save for Snyder's beloved teddy bear off to one side of the chairs and tables, there was an intimacy about the proceedings that allowed guests to open up a bit more than typical of such talk shows. Then again, Snyder was a reporter and not a comedian, so his thought process was not about where the next punchline went, but how to make his conversation with the guests informative.

Meanwhile, in the late 1970s, there were not many outlets for in-depth coverage of rock music beyond the occasional late-night programming such as *Midnight Special* and *Don Kirshner's Rock Concert*, with *Midnight Special* being the only one of the two on a network, (oddly enough, replacing *The Tomorrow Show* on Friday nights in the NBC schedule). Rarely did these have interviews with the performers, instead filing their shows with musical performances only. Of the talk shows, beyond Dick Cavett (who had fleeting talk shows over the years), and Mike Douglas (see above), Snyder was one of the few to feature rock performers and even then usually for quiet sit-down talks rather than musical performances.

It was in that atmosphere that KISS appeared in the fall of 1979. If one looked at the various aspects of that interview—mistimed musical cues; an in-form hilarious Ace Frehley, with Peter Criss egging him on; a largely misinformed and at first indifferent Snyder; and an increasingly angry/nervous Gene Simmons and Paul Stanley—one would think the event was a disaster. Many fans still think so today. Nevertheless, as a whole, it was a classic moment for the band and certainly one of the funniest in many ways, thanks to Frehley (due to whatever it may have been that got him to that level) cackling in hysterics as he takes over the interview to the joy of Snyder and the crew watching him. Making dumb jokes, interjecting to destroy age-old stories by Simmons and Stanley, manhandling Snyder's teddy bear to turn it into Space-Bear, Frehley dominates the interview.

His domination is not only one of the first signs of cracks in the band's uniform front that made it appear it was "us against the world," but also a chance to see the four as real human beings instead of the invincible superheroes they'd spent the past four years building for the public. Stanley, although trying to stay serious to quell obvious resentment from Simmons over Frehley's antics, is still loose enough to tell a rather risqué groupie story dealing with an underage girl, while mentioning Frehley's tendency to tear up hotel rooms at the same time. Both Peter Criss and Frehley talk—or try to talk—about innocent hobbies, while Simmons uncharacteristically for the time fumes over what he sees as an interview with several foul-ups (watch his reaction to the wrong excerpt from "Beth" being played at one point), and Frehley seems on the verge of going over the edge. After years of telling fans that these four could do no wrong, they suddenly appeared all too human.

Some fans see this as the public point of no return for the original foursome, but beyond that, it is also a pinnacle of bare emotions for the band that was rarely seen before and never seen since.

Countdown, ABC Network Channel Two, Airdate September 21, 1980

KISS was about to embark on a tour of Australia, and the hoopla in that country for their visit would parallel and even rival the mania that the Beatles faced there sixteen years before (where 300,000 fans, nearly one-third of the population, had lined the streets of Adelaide to welcome them). In support of the tour, the music program *Countdown* aired a special KISS episode that featured several music videos as well as an interview with the band. Other programs would cover the KISS experience in that country before and after this, but *Countdown* was the big event in anticipation of the tour: an earlier interview on *60 Minutes* (an Australian adaptation of the American news program) was brief and featured only Gene Simmons and Ace Frehley, while the better-known *Inner Sanctum* documentary did not air until February 1981 and was mostly a concert film with short, humorous bits by Norman Gunston.

The interview was an introduction for fans to new drummer Eric Carr, but more importantly, it was a rare chance to see all four members together doing an interview where they appeared relaxed and having fun. Not much information was imparted, but the sense that these four guys loved every minutes of what they were doing shined through. There was the feeling that KISS were sitting on the top of the world; which would be proven right once they arrived in Australia. It would not last, but for a moment KISS appeared to be exactly as the fans thought them to be—having as much fun together as the fans did when watching them.

Fridays, ABC Network, Airdate January 15, 1982

This late-night variety series that was obviously patterned after NBC's *Saturday Night Live* is remembered for three things: 1) Michael Richards (of *Seinfeld* fame) and Larry David being involved; 2) a famous on-air incident with comedian Andy Kaufman that was staged to look like an authentic disruption of the show; and 3) the use of many popular, young musical acts to perform songs in-between sketches (whereas *Saturday Night Live* tended to use either more established or more experimental artists). It was in this environment that KISS appeared to perform material off their then-new album *Music from "The Elder."*

This was a major blip on the radar for American fans at the time. To them, KISS disappeared after the release of *Unmasked* and Peter Criss's departure, followed by stories about Eric Carr joining and a one-off show at the Palladium, and then nothing. Of course, at the time, KISS was busy touring Europe and Australia, as well as putting together the next album, but the world was a bit bigger in those days before worldwide information was instantaneously available to every part of the globe and being out of the country was really a case of "out of sight, out of mind." For some, KISS would not see a significant return until the beginning of 1983 and the *Creatures of the Night* tour, and even that mainly brought out the die-hards and the curious rather than the numbers they had seen in the past. It would not be until 1984, after the release of *Lick It Up*, that the band would start to catch the public eye again. Moreover, even with a new album out for months by the time of this appearance, publicity for the *Elder* album had been rather spotty—even the music video created for "World Without Heroes" did not get many airings on television, and certainly the single was not doing anything on the radio.

Now, to most fans unexpectedly, KISS was performing three songs live on a nationally broadcast television program. To the fans, it was their first real chance to see new drummer Eric Carr in action, as well as see the band in their new costumes and playing new material. While the performance on a small stage-space was certainly not on the level of earlier television appearances (even *The Mike Douglas Show* back in 1974 gave them more room to perform), this second lineup of the band was a thrill for fans to see. As fate would have it, it was also a rare chance, as Ace Frehley would be out before much longer. Thus, while a minor incident in terms of the events surrounding the band, it was a huge event for fans who managed to catch it at the time.

Festival di Sanremo 1982, Rai Uno, Eurovision Network, Airdate January 28, 1982

Festival di Sanremo is an annual Italian showcase for composers, with new songs in competition for a prize as the "best of the year" (the annual Eurovision competition was initially based on this festival). Although the focus has always been more on the writers and less on the musical talents, the television broadcast associated with the contest admits to needing a certain amount of Hollywood gloss to keep the audience's attention. Thus, popular musicians and vocalists appeared quite often throughout the program to entice viewers.

With this in mind, KISS was to receive an award from the festival in 1982 in exchange for performing on the program. Negotiations for the performance eventually became one where the band agreed to lip-synch the song "I" from *Music from "The Elder"* and say a few words of thanks to the festival via satellite from the recently reopened Studio 54 in New York. This gave the festival the international feel it was looking for, while allowing the band some much-needed publicity—both on American entertainment programs (which were covering the event as a news item) and in Europe—at a time when the media was showing little interest in KISS.

The only problem was that when it came time for them to emerge from a limo and run into Studio 54 to begin the performance, Ace Frehley was missing from the group. As fans later discovered, he had been on the outs with the others since the recording of *Music from "The Elder,"* which he had fought from its inception as being a misstep, and in terms of critical reaction and sales had been proven right. That and other incidents had led to signs that Frehley was contemplating leaving the band just as Peter Criss had done a couple of years before.

Even so, Frehley had always been counted on to put personal disagreements aside in order to keep up the public persona for promotional purposes of the band working together, and he would do so again to promote the *Creatures of the Night* album later that year. Also, to others within the KISS organization, the appearance was important to keep the band's name fresh in people's minds at a time when they increasingly needed it. To Frehley, however, it meant getting together with people he was not in the mood to spend time with, put on makeup and costumes that he was getting sick of, play-act a song from an album he hated, and all for a minor "make believe" award on a foreign program. It seemed to be a big waste of time, and so, even with a limo ready to take him from his home to the show, Frehley opted out.

To Stanley and Simmons, this was Frehley crossing the line. Frehley, on the other hand, saw the other three doing the lip-synch without him as the band readily accepting that they did not want or need him, not to mention an embarrassment to see. Management built up a story about Frehley being too sick to appear in hopes of covering any bad press about it, but it was clear that things were coming to a head.

The band would begin on their next album *Creatures of the Night*, within weeks of this situation, and attempts were made to smooth out problems between Frehley and the others (up to the tour beginning that winter with press releases stating that he was still in the band and would possibly join them on tour). By early 1983, fans accepted that Frehley was no longer in KISS, but the San Remo television appearance was the first public sign that he would be soon out of the picture.

KISS: Yesterday and Today, USA Cable Network, Airdate August 8, 1983

This hour-long special appeared on the USA Cable Network; known at the time by a number of music fans for airing occasional rock music specials and concerts, usually through their Friday/Saturday late-night programming block called *Night Flight*. *Night Flight* was one of the first national cable programs in direct competition with MTV, and one of the few that geared its programming toward an alternative from the generic pop-rock sound that MTV broadcast. Due to wanting to be an alternative, the music programming commonly seen on USA was a final refuge for the punk and new wave scene, while also providing a home for the emerging heavy-metal fan base (heavily covered in USA's weeknight music program, *Radio 1990*). Both *Night Flight* and *Radio 1990* were produced by ATI Video Enterprises for USA, an offshoot of American Talent International, Ltd. , the booking agency for KISS at the time.

Combine those elements with that of KISS having already established a relationship with ATI, and it made sense that the band would turn to USA for a special to help promote them. Oddly, the special would seem to be a natural to help promote the *Creatures of the Night* album, but it did not air until ten months after the release of the album and a little more than a month before the reveal of the band without makeup on—of all places—MTV. The program contains a series of clips of the band—the "I Love It Loud" video, a rare showing of the 1975 promotional film created for "Rock and Roll All Nite," and clips from both the 1977 *Young Music Show* from Japan and the 1980 *Inner Sanctum* special from Australia—peppered among segments of an interview with the band with Stanley, Simmons, Carr, and then-still-new lead guitarist Vinnie Vincent.

For many fans, it was the first time that the band had been given a chance to talk about their early days in a relaxed manner (the unedited interview shows that Eric Carr did much to keep Gene Simmons in a good mood as the interview went on, although it is obvious that Simmons and Paul Stanley are both cringing up when Vincent lets slip that he came from Bridgeport, Connecticut, instead of somewhere more "manly" like Brooklyn). With nearly thirty years of subsequent interviews that have explored the band's past, stories about Simmons setting his hair on fire or the KISS sign brightly flashing may appear to be old hat to many younger fans, but for those who witnessed it back in 1983, it was a rare chance to hear their heroes speak without an interviewer jumping on every word and asking the "same old questions" they were used to answering or steering them toward answering questions about a new album or tour.

Obviously, USA knew they had a good thing in their hands, as they aired bits and pieces of the interview on both *Radio 1990* and *Night Flight* so often that fans began to think of it as a bit of a joke. Bootlegs of the entire interview, as well as bloopers and station-identification greetings, also filtered into fandom—being traded extensively back in the 1980s when fans were still clamoring for the makeup period video material—even as the band was moving on to *Lick It Up* and *Animalize*. For although the makeup would be off within weeks of this program airing—proving that it was time to leave the characters behind (at least for a time)—many fans who grew up with the costumes and makeup saw *Yesterday and Today* as a last hurrah before the curtain fell on the first era of the band.

"KISS Unmasking," MTV Network, Airdate September 18, 1983

Even non-fans would likely have suspected the first television appearance of KISS without makeup—on the biggest cable channel of the 1980s—would be a momentous occasion, drummed up with multiple commercials and press releases. But such thoughts do not take into account the reality of the time. First, while MTV was steadily becoming an icon of the music industry and cable television, it was still rather early days for the channel, where a good chunk of the U.S. was still going without on their cable listings. Also, most programming on MTV was still an endless rotation of the same music videos, with other programming leaning toward edited versions of previously released concerts by certain performers in order to fill up hour-long gaps on the weekends. While the VJs (MTV's answer to radio DJs) were able to do some in-house interviews in the small studio used by the company, many were done without advertising and sometimes even without any type of announcement from the VJ doing the interview. In many cases, performers would seemingly magically appear to sit awkwardly next to a VJ on the MTV set for an impromptu interview, interrupted by various nonrelated music videos, before disappearing again within ten to twenty minutes. For many viewers, it was not uncommon to turn on the channel only to find themselves frustratingly halfway through an interview with an artist they liked.

Meanwhile, as MTV was taking baby steps to becoming a juggernaut in multiple industries, KISS was struggling to regain some of their lost popularity after the missteps of the early 1980s. As discussed elsewhere in this book, KISS could not argue that they had lost fans through their actions—especially in the U.S. after 1980 and a bit before that. Some fans had not been happy with the disco-like and pop sounds of *Dynasty* and *Unmasked*, and the departure of Peter Criss from KISS was a signpost to many that the days of the band were rapidly approaching a close. A tour of Europe and Australia kept the band busy in 1980, but with little media attention in the U.S., American fans wondered if they had folded or were shifting emphasis overseas because they could not draw many in America. The 1981 release of *Music from "The Elder"* split fans' expectations, with many believing the band was trying too hard for critical acceptance and the planned tour was scrapped when the logistics of a tour versus the money to be made became unfeasible. It should be noted, however, that while the follow-up album in 1982, *Creatures of the Night*, did not do well in sales, there was still a strong core of fans who were attending the shows, and KISS saw some renewed interest thanks to the "I Love It Loud" music video playing on MTV. Even so, by the time the band members had decided to release the next album without the makeup and costumes, there was a lot banking on *Lick It Up* being the make-or-break point for them.

Which leads to what occurred on that night in September 1983. While MTV heavily advertised a repeat of an edited Van Halen concert during the week leading up to it, information about the "unmasking" of KISS airing immediately afterwards was limited to brief mentions by the VJs and no other advertising. Also, an 11:00 p.m. airing on a Sunday

Beta release of the *Animalize Live Uncensored* concert video that originally aired in edited form on MTV.   *Author's Collection*

night (especially before a school week) hardly seems like the most prestigious location for such an important historical event for KISS, but MTV rarely aired any special programming except on the weekend, and typically only in late time slots. This also helps explain the visual staging of the event: a small table set up in front of a darkened MTV set, with little KISS name-holders in front of microphones so that viewers can associate names with the bare faces of the members. It has the look of a high school debate, or a press interview from the 1960s, yet at the time was all anyone was expected to do under the circumstances.

J. J. Jackson, a VJ who was well known in the music business and certainly the best to present the program, interviews the band for the program after first introducing a video of "Rock and Roll All Nite" that is a montage of them from many different years. After the montage, each member was introduced one by one, followed by an interview—naturally dominated by Gene Simmons and Paul Stanley, although Vinnie Vincent wins in the drinking-a-lot-of-water-just-to-do-something competition. The world premiere of the "Lick It Up" music videos and a further interview segment with the band members wrapped it up.

It should be pointed out that Jackson's intro to the montage and the clip itself are not included in the edited version of the special found on the *KISSology* DVD box set, nor are the promised airing of the "Lick It Up" video or the closing moments of the interview that appeared afterwards. Thus, it would be easy for fans to think that the MTV special was much shorter than its real duration, clocking in at less than eight minutes on the DVD set when the entire special ran closer to twice as long. It also omits a nice final moment where Simmons can be seen breaking character and having a laugh with Jackson as the camera slowly fades out.

Of course, it is obvious why this is such an important television moment for KISS, as this was announcing to the world the point of no return for the band. From that moment on, the protected mystery of what the four looked like without makeup was finally stripped away. With it came the time for the band to find a new identity, which would take them in many directions over the next twelve years before they decided to "come home."

MTV *Saturday Night Concerts*: "KISS Animalize Live," MTV Network, Airdate January 26, 1985

By 1985, MTV had expanded their programming to include a variety of shows as well as more concerts, sometimes even airing them during the week as well as the weekend. Typically, these were still edited version of various videocassette releases, but MTV would sometimes get the opportunity to air some of the footage before the commercial releases on VHS and Beta. As in the case of this broadcast, a fifty-five-minute version of what would eventually be released on April 1, 1985, as the videocassette *Animalize Live Uncensored.*

Although the MTV edit and the eventually released videocassette both suffered from some fan disappointment, mainly due to studio sweetening added to the audio mix (a method easily used on the live albums, but hardly to cover when the music being heard is not quite what is seen being played), the MTV version is significant for a couple of reasons. The *Lick It Up* album and tour that followed showed a groundswell of old fans returning to the fold as well as the gain of newer fans, but it was not until the *Animalize* tour that KISS could readily demonstrate that audience interest was beyond a random few only curious to see them without makeup. The concert was also a clear sign that the band members were beginning to get used to their new roles without the makeup or superhero costumes (although some would definitely state that the band still wore costumes of a sort, as discussed in Chapter 6), with Paul Stanley in particular enjoying the ability to be more active on stage, as his monologues grew longer between songs (to what some fans considered a ridiculous length by the end of the 1980s).

More significantly, this was also the first true public sign that Bruce Kulick was now a full member of the band, having "temporarily" taken over the role of lead guitarist from Mark St. John at the start of the tour. Heavily promoted as the new lead guitarist when *Animalize* was recorded, St. John had to sit out many of the early concerts on the tour due to suffering from a form of arthritis that kept him from performing, while Kulick was brought on to replace him. Thus, while some fans had heard rumors that Kulick was to permanently replace St. John, with the special ending showing Kulick in the credits as a member and no acknowledgment of St. John, it was clear who was there to stay.

MTV Unplugged: KISS, MTV Network, Airdate October 31, 1995

Continuing with the MTV/KISS relationship, with both sides having morphed somewhat in the ten years since the last significant television appearance of KISS on the cable network. MTV had reached maturity, moving past endless twenty-four-hour rotations of music videos to add in weekly and daily television programs—some dealing with music and some only vaguely doing so. Included among the programming was *MTV Unplugged,* a concert series featuring various artists typically doing acoustic versions of their hits for a small audience. The series, started in 1989, would help generate an interest in reinterpretation of songs by their original artists that still can be felt in the present marketplace, as well as allowing some performers a chance to discuss their music between musical numbers in a low-key manner without the typically nonmusical questions being directed at them by interviewers.

KISS was also evolving as the 1990s began. *Hot in the Shade* in 1989 and the tour that followed were only moderate successes for the band, while there were growing signs that the glitter age of heavy metal—once courted very heavily by MTV—was dying out to make way for alternate styles of music, similar in intensity but lacking in gloss. The illness and subsequent death of drummer Eric Carr also sent the band into a spiral, just as they faced producing another album for PolyGram due to contractual reasons. Pulling in drummer Eric Singer, the band recorded and released *Revenge* in 1991, at the same time staging a reinvention of their stage personas with less sparkles and happy anthems replaced by more black leather and angry attitude. However, even with merchandising surveys advising the band to make such changes, KISS saw only similar results to *Hot in the Shade* on the charts and a tour that folded after weak ticket sales.

Searching for a direction, they spent the next four years doing little more than variations of historical compilation projects—from a self-made "tribute album" (*KISS My Ass*) to three retrospective videos (*X-Treme Close-Up, Konfidential,* and *KISS My Ass*)—and peaking with a retrospective convention tour in 1995. The 1995 tour was very much in the same tone as nonofficial record conventions held in various parts of the country from the late 1980s onward and featured a museum, tribute bands, and, as a finale, the band signing autographs and performing acoustic numbers from their catalog on a small stage for the limited number of fans.

For a time, the concerts at these conventions involved more audience participation, but eventually the song list transformed into a set number of well-performed tracks (as fans typically would ask for the same songs on the tour anyway). With this in place, it was an obvious choice to go to MTV with what had been prepared and work out a deal for the band to appear on *MTV Unplugged* (even the flyers and postcards sent out to fans about the conventions made a point about the band playing "unplugged"). In response, there was some interest from the cable network, but only if the band went full tilt with the retrospective and could get Peter Criss and Ace Frehley to appear on the program as well.

This, contrary to popular thought at the time, was not that tough of a medicine for Simmons and Stanley to swallow. After all, even with the dismissive attitude about Criss and Frehley that the two tended to have in interview (certainly more than anything Criss or Frehley ever did), both had appeared with Frehley at one of his concerts in 1988, while Criss had performed with the others at one of the convention stops in 1995. Furthermore, with Criss and Frehley both being represented by the man who was also a former associate of KISS, George Sewitt, it was not that difficult to work out plans for them to join the then-current line-up of KISS (Simmons, Stanley, Singer, and Kulick) for the appearance.

The MTV version of the performance is only eleven songs long, with the official video release being longer and the eventual release as part of the third *KISSology* DVD box set even longer (and a bootleg of the entire recording session done in front of the cameras of course the longest of all). None of that really mattered, however, as the main thrust of most fans' interest was on the final segment of the program featuring the return of Frehley and Criss. With that, the ball began rolling for the reunion tour, making this television appearance a very important one in the band's history and leading directly to the next one on the list.

Thirty-Eighth Grammy Awards, CBS Network, Airdate February 28, 1996

With Frehley and Criss returning to perform with the band at the *MTV Unplugged* special, it was only natural for fans to wonder if the four would get back together for some performances or maybe even a tour. As rumors spread that something was in the works, it was still a surprise not only to see the foursome again on the Grammy Awards, being introduced by Tupac Shakur to present an award, but also to see them in makeup and costumes—the first time all four appeared together in makeup and costumes since the release of the "Shandi" music video sixteen years before. While it was little more than a brief appearance, with Paul Stanley doing the official talking for the group in announcing nominees and the winner (Hootie and the Blowfish for the category of "Best Pop Performance by a Duo or Group with Vocals"), it did not matter—their appearance was a highlight in the news about the awards show the next day, leading directly to the go-ahead for the KISS reunion tour that was officially announced on April 16, 1996.

XIX Olympic Winter Games, "Closing Ceremony," NBC Network, Airdate February 24, 2002

In 1999, KISS appeared during the pregame ceremonies of Super-Bowl XXXIII doing a performance of "Rock and Roll All Nite." Yet, even the number of people that watch the Super Bowl don't always watch the pregame festivities, and even those that do could not match the number of people that watched the band three years later at the closing ceremonies of the 2002 Winter Olympics in Salt Lake City, Utah.

Although the performance was a lip-synch (unavoidable in the precise staging needed for the event), it gave fans a rare chance to see the short-lived Stanley-Simmons-Frehley-Singer version of the band (Peter Criss had quit in 2000, only to rejoin the band for a short time after this). That is, if one could make out Singer behind the drums, as the cameras do a very good job of avoiding him through the televised performance.

It would also be the last performance featuring Ace Frehley. After this event, he left the band and was replaced by Tommy Thayer in his makeup and costumes. Once Criss left for good in 2004, KISS would consist of Simmons, Stanley, Singer, and Thayer and have remained as such to the present day.

21

Watch Out for Amazons

The KISS Music Video Landscapes

W hat is fascinating in retrospect about KISS is that for such a visual musical outlet, the band did very little in the way of promotional films for their singles in the 1970s and only really caved in to making them a priority for their singles once everyone else was doing so in the 1980s. Certainly for a band that heavily promoted its visual look, there is a certain disappointment that the films made for their songs are a handful in the 1970s and then two to three for each album from 1983 onwards, leaving KISS with a rather small number of music videos in comparison to the number of albums they have released and nowhere near the number done by bands that came after them and found success in the post MTV video explosion of 1981.

Yet the band's lack of music video/promotional films, especially in the 1970s, is proper to the standards of the time. In that decade, such clips were called promotional films for a good reason—they were done simply to help promote a single and a performer on programs. Since such clips were rarely seen outside of late-night television shows and/or one-off appearances on random prime-time variety programming, there was not much effort put into them. They were either in the "live in concert" vein, like all of KISS's promotional films of the 1970s, or "wacky" improvised musical-comedy numbers featuring the artists (which KISS avoided during that period). It was only with the 1980 release of "Shandi" that the band had a music video that could be clearly seen as storyboarded with a beginning, middle, and end like a small film.

A bigger issue about such videos (and I will refer to them from here on as music videos, as that is the most common term for these clips, even from an earlier period than when the term came into practice) on television in the 1970s is that they were seen as a poor substitute to having said performer on your program. When a television show announced that a famous artist was to appear, only to end up showing a music video, it was deemed a disappointment at best and a rip-off at worst. It was much more prestigious to have those performers appearing "live" on the show to interact with the host and perform, even if for a lip-synch of a single. The only time such videos were acceptable was when there was no alternative. For example, to use "Shandi" again, KISS released that single from the *Unmasked* in June 1980, right at a time when Peter Criss was no longer in the band and the others were still ironing out details for a replacement for a European tour in the fall. There was no option but to send out the video filmed for the song in order to help promote it, as the band certainly could not appear without a fourth member and certainly not the drummer (yes, some would argue that the band did appear without one member on television—see Chapter 20—but that was an exception that defines the rule). Thus, a television program could at least say they had KISS on and the band got to promote their single, even though it was not a live appearance. Such videos also helped to promote songs in other countries when there was no option for the band to perform "live" as seen by the number of clips found on foreign programming, such as those used in the *Countdown* special done in 1980 to promote the then-upcoming Australian tour, where only a short interview with the band was available otherwise.

Then everything changed come 1981 and MTV. Suddenly, music videos were not only a standard needed for all singles released by practically everyone (even Dean Martin and Frank Sinatra were doing music videos for MTV by 1984), the common perception by the music industry was that it was a necessity for sales and radio play. Beyond MTV, other programming sprang up that consisted mostly, if not 100 percent, of music videos. The few shows that did not—such as *Solid Gold* and *American Bandstand*—were eventually pushed into the new era as well, showing a good number of music videos mixed in with in-studio appearances by performers. Therefore, if KISS wanted to get radio play, sell albums, and make the record company happy, music videos were inevitable. Before that, however, the main thrust of promotion for the band was to appear "in the flesh," which is why there are many memorable television appearances from the 1970s but little that fit into the standard definition of the music video.

There have been arguments over the years as to whether the three songs done on *Don Kirshner's Rock Concert* in 1977 for the *Rock and Roll Over* album should be included in the list of music videos. After all, these clips—showcasing the band performing songs on a mock-up of their then-current concert stages—are very much in the same style as previous ones done for the *Dressed to Kill* album and later ones for *Dynasty*. Additionally, the three clips appeared on foreign television programming as promotional videos for KISS instead of being relegated to the one-off American airing. However, if one were to include these as music videos, then similar clips done exclusively for foreign television during the *Unmasked* tour—such as "Talk To Me," "She's So European" (both which appeared on the September 13, 1980, episode of the German series *Pop Rock*), and "Is That You?" (from the aforementioned program *Countdown* and filmed in Perth during a sound check while the band was touring there in 1980)—would also need to be included. This sets the net for inclusion so wide that one would be inclined to then add in the *Paul Lynde* clips from 1976, the *Alive II* promotional clip (featuring bits of "Rockin' in the USA" and "Shout It Out Loud" among other songs), and onward, which is beyond the focus of this chapter. Yet the final judgment has to come from official quarters:

the *Don Kirshner's Rock Concert* clips are listed as a single segment on the first *KISSology* DVD box set, with Kirshner's opening statement included, and not as separate music videos as with the *Dressed to Kill* and *Dynasty* promotional films, among others, that also appear in the DVD series.

While KISS is remembered more for their music videos from *Lick It Up* on, fans tend to forget that both "A World Without Heroes" (from *Music from "The Elder"*) and "I Love It Loud" (*Creatures of the Night*) got a fair amount of airplay in the very early days of MTV (thanks mostly to being some of the few clips available for MTV to use in those days when music videos were rather scarce and not because MTV was an early supporter of the band). In other words, KISS was remarkably ahead of the curve when it came to music videos. For a time, at least.

Between the 1975 release of *Dressed to Kill* and the start of 2012, there have been over thirty music videos created for public consumption. Somewhat ironically, the majority of the band's success in this area is due to MTV, as KISS fans typically tend to look at the music cable network as not giving much time or care to the band over the years. This, however, is based more on selective memory by fans of the public's depth of disinterest in KISS than on some dastardly plan on the part of MTV. As already mentioned, MTV did play "A World Without Heroes" and "I Love It Loud" in the early days of the cable network, and featured the band extensively during the heavy-metal craze of the later 1980s (including interviews, guest VJ appearances, and, of course, the "Unmasking" special in 1983 and the *Unplugged* special in 1995 covered in the previous chapter). Naturally, once the makeup came back on to enormous response, MTV followed through with more programming on the band through its own channel and its associate channel VH1—contrary to popular belief, the video for "Psycho Circus" did get plenty of airings on MTV before lack of public interest saw it dropped from rotation. After all, there was little sense in MTV pushing videos by the band at time when interest was not there, but even with the tepid response from buyers to the *Revenge* album in 1992, MTV still put the three videos created for that album in rotation (perhaps late at night, as in the case of the "I Just Wanna" video, but still in rotation). Thus, even if fans tend to dismiss what MTV has done for the band—as even I have done in the past in other books I have written about the band—in hindsight, the channel has been of great help over the years in promoting KISS.

It should be mentioned that there is at least one music video filmed and supposedly edited, but never released, which was for the *Animalize* single, "Thrills in the Night." While a conceptual video was filmed in Louisville, Kentucky, during December 1984 and a video supposedly edited together—with former Playboy Playmate Candy Loving as a frustrated office worker who has the members of KISS as associates in her office, including Eric Carr as her boss and Bruce Kulick as the custodian—the video eventually released features on the band onstage performing the song and none of the conceptual material recorded. Although some pictures from the filming have turned up in other publications, the video itself has never been seen by fans, even in the darkest corners of the KISS Army.

One final thing to mention before diving into the official releases is the music video done by KISS for the television comedy series *That 70's Show*. The video, featuring the band performing "Rock and Roll All Nite" onstage, is a conceptual video showing the cast of the series (which is centered on growing up in the mid- to late 1970s) at a KISS concert. The video aired as part of a half-hour VH1 special on August 30, 2002, to promote the series' syndication to local stations. Along with clips from various episodes of the series and the music video, the special included some behind-the-scenes footage of the making of the video. While this could be argued as being part of the official KISS catalog of music videos—in fact it is probably the most clear-cut argument for a full storyline being realized in a conceptual video starring the band—the video was done specifically to promote the television series and was not used for promotional reasons by KISS for any album, tour, or single, unlike the clips listed below.

Each of the music videos listed below falls into one of three categories in terms of its primary storytelling device: Concert, Conceptual, or Documentary. It can be argued that some videos cross over between one or more of these categories, and the Concert category even has subcategories that break down its format even further, but any video done by KISS since 1975 follows one of these three ideals.

Documentary

This category has the least number of musical videos but has been used often enough by the band over the years to stand on its own with many candidates. These videos typically try to present a "fly on the wall" view of the band either through montages of older film/video clips or behind-the-scenes footage. In doing so, the videos do not quite fit the ideal of a conceptual video, where there is a beginning, middle, and end to the storyline. Instead, they tend simply to demonstrate a desire to say either "these guys have a musical legacy" or, in the case of the first example below, "these guys are wacky . . . and have a legacy as well."

It should be noted that there have been at least three occasions where montages have been created for promotional purposes that could be argued as being music videos: The *Alive II* promo, which features footage of the band performing in concert as "Shout It Out Loud," "Beth," and "Rockin' in the USA" completes the soundtrack to the montage (typically only the "Rockin' in the USA" portion got used in programming at the time, such as in the case of the 1979 musical documentary *The Heroes of Rock 'N Roll*); a montage of live clips from various years used during the USA Network *Yesterday and Today* special; and a similar montage of clips for "Rock and Roll All Nite" that appears at the beginning of the MTV "Unmasking" special in 1983. Surprisingly, none of these

Disappointing official music video collection of only five videos
done by the band in the 1980s.   *Author's Collection*

appears on the *KISSology* DVD series, which is a shame, as the *Alive II* and MTV
clips are both rather good.

One interesting aspect of the videos listed below is that they all appeared
within a six-year period and all during the nonmakeup days of the band in the
late 1980s and early 1990s. This again shows that as the band moved forward
through their nonmakeup period, the emphasis was shifted back to the days of
the costumes and makeup.

"I"

Filmed for the single released in October 1981 from the *Music From "The Elder"*
album. Rumors flew around for years that Casablanca had created a video for "I"
that was to be a follow-up to "A World Without Heroes" from the *Elder* album,
but was then shelved when Casablanca decided not to release the song as a single

in the U.S. Then in the late 1980s, a video popped up in fandom that was supposedly the long-lost music video for "I." It opens with footage of the door from the front cover of the album that swings inward to show the table, candles, and chairs from inside the gatefold cover. It then ends with the door swinging close and a hand reaching up to the doorknocker just as on the front cover. This bookend footage is the only original footage used in the video, with the remainder of the video being a montage of clips of the band in action over the years.

Many fans were (and still are) on the fence about whether this is the true video, a loosely edited mock-up for a potential video, or a fan-edited fake made years later. The argument for it being real is that *The Elder* cover footage looks authentic, while the band was already known by this point for doing promotional clips that were montages of them in concert and would continue to do such in the future—both the *Yesterday & Today* special and "Unmasking" special from 1983 would feature such montages—as well as in a few official music videos as listed below. On the other hand, *The Elder* footage seen appears in the television ad for the album, and many of the clips of the band in action had filtered out to fans by the time the video made its way into fan quarters. Further, the video puts a large emphasis on the previous drummer of the band, Peter Criss, at a time when KISS was trying hard to both avoid mentioning Criss and promote their new drummer Eric Carr; thus making it out of step with the band's agenda at the time (then again, this could have been a deciding factor for it not being released).

More recent evidence has supported the fact that this really is a video created by Casablanca for airing in foreign countries where a single was released of "I" (namely those countries where KISS had a stronger recognition value, such as in Europe, Australia, and Japan). In Australia alone, it appeared on such programs as *Countdown*, *Rock Arena*, and *Wonderworld* with mentions that it was the new "video" and song released for KISS. Thus, only in the U.S. would there be room for such a rumor to develop in the first place. There are also photos taken of the band performing "I" on an ice-like stage in front of fans, which some have assumed for years to be a music video created and then shelved for the song from *Music from "The Elder."* Yet, if this was the case, one would think images of it would have at least turned up in the "I" music video that was eventually distributed.

Many of the following videos would take their lead from the "I" music clip as to how to present the band when it came to those that fit into the Documentary category, although with better production in each as well.

"Rock and Roll All Nite"

Released in May 1987 in support of the *KISS Exposed* videocassette and one of two official videos that gives a visual history of the band through its many phrases. This video contains a mixture of "comedy clips" from the *Exposed* video along with various clips of the band from in concert and earlier music videos.

"God Gave Rock 'N' Roll to You II"

Released summer 1991 to promote the soundtrack album for the movie *Bill and Ted's Bogus Journey*. With a song directly focused on the ups, downs, and determination of rock music to survive the ages, it is understandable that portions of the video focus on the band's history. While the first segment of the video—the last done with Eric Carr before his passing, although he did not play drums on the recording—looks to be that of the band performing on a wet (keep this in mind) airport hangar and therefore could readily fit into the "concert" category, the emphasis on the historical montage places it here. Ironically, the video is to promote a movie but does a better job of promoting the band's mark in music than the one done for their own video release of *KISS Exposed*.

There are two versions of this video—one that promotes the movie with a montage of clips and another that leaves the montage to only that of clips of KISS in action from over the years.

"Forever"

Filmed for the single released in January 1990 from the *Hot in the Shade* album. It is documentary in style, with a touch of the then-new *MTV Unplugged* look as, with the exception of Paul Stanley, the band sits and plays the song for the duration, while the camera swirls around them. Oddly enough, although there is nothing more to the video than a very relaxed group of guys playing a song in a room (even Gene Simmons avoids grimacing or spitting on the floor as he commonly would to show some form of disdain for the quieter songs in the band's repertoire), this is commonly picked as a favorite among fans of the band's music videos.

"Every Time I Look at You"

Filmed for the single released in September 1992 for the *Revenge* album. Very similar in style to the "Forever" video mentioned above, which makes sense as the song itself is in a similar melodic style with reflective lyrics about a relationship. Thus, seeing the band hopping around in concert or some type of conceptual folly involving postapocalyptic amazon warriors probably would not have been a great idea. While the song had some promotion efforts behind it at the time, it had only limited release as a single overseas, and thus it, as well as the video, tends to be less remembered than many in the music video catalog. And Paul Stanley needs a shave.

"Domino"

Filmed for the single released in July 1992 for the *Revenge* album. Hard to pinpoint what category this video could fall into. At one point there must have been a storyline planned for the video that concerned Gene Simmons cruising in his car until he spots his "domino," followed by some antics involving the woman of the song's title. Instead, it seems to be about Simmons going from one drive-through window to the next for large sodas until he gets gas (seriously, watch the video—one wonders what the pitch meeting was like that sold him on such a premise). Which is why it falls into this category instead of Conceptual, as the video is nothing more than the camera locked on Simmons driving in his car. Which brings us to the next category . . .

Conceptual

For the purposes of this category, the term *conceptual* is being used to showcase music videos that have either a storyline with a beginning, middle, and end, or images to generate an emotional response. In either situation, the main thrust of the visuals is to correspond with the music to create an overall effect, sometimes making it hard to untie the imagery of the video from the song. For example, it is hard to distance the final image of the teenagers standing in the street with their eyes glowing at the end of "I Love It Loud" from the message of the song of defiantly proclaiming a love for heavy metal, or hearing "Heaven's on Fire" and thinking of the band's antics while rolling around with the girls in the hotel room in the video created for the song. On the other hand, to use a video examined in the previous section of this chapter, there is nothing to tie the visuals from the "Domino" video to the song unless the message of the song is "Boy, Gene sure does drink a lot of soda, doesn't he?"

Such a definition also helps to filter out videos tailored to show the band performing in a concertlike atmosphere. For example, while videos for "Lick It Up" and "All Hell's Breakin' Loose" have the concept of the band in a posta-pocalyptic world, neither does anything with the idea beyond window dressing, ultimately settling into being footage of the band performing a song for an audi-ence (a crazed, murderous futuristic audience, but an audience nonetheless). On the other hand, although "Reason to Live" features the band performing the song as if during a concert, the video contains a storyline involving a woman wanting to take revenge on Paul Stanley for breaking up with her.

Because of the need for a message of some kind or of a storyline told, only a quarter of the band's music videos fall into this category. The remainder are videos specifically tailored to show the band performing in a concertlike atmo-sphere and appear in the third and final section for music videos.

"Shandi"

Filmed for the single released in June 1980 for the *Unmasked* album. The band's first true conceptual video is also one of their best examples of how a storyline in a video can enhance not only the song but the theme of the album as well. As discussed in Chapter 10, *Unmasked* features an album cover that tells in comic-strip fashion about someone trying to see the band without their trademark makeup. "Shandi" was the first single from the album and deals with a love affair gone wrong. The storyline in the video deals with a woman sneaking around as the band ventures from their dressing room to the stage. As they progress, Paul Stanley sings the song to the camera even before the band reaches the stage, extending it into the reality of the storyline instead of it being merely a song performed by the band onstage (as so many of the "Concert" music videos listed below are wont to do). In the end, the band returns to their dressing room and put on their street clothes. Upon leaving, the girl calls out to them and they turn around, only to reveal they are still wearing their makeup, thus tying in the video with the last image of the album cover (and poster enclosed within) while concluding the storyline of the video as well.

The video also manages to give good showcases to the other members of the band: Simmons's Demon appears to be solemnly tolerating the song at best; Peter Criss provides support while giving the camera knowing glances, as if he has seen it all before; and Ace Frehley is allowed some humorous touches as he directly addresses the camera. "Shandi" is a good example of how everything can come together in a music video to enhance a song rather than overpower it.

"A World Without Heroes"

Filmed for the single released in November 1981 for the *Music from "The Elder"* album. In many ways, this video is nothing more than the band performing the song in the spotlights of a darkened stage. Yet the focus of the song is on Simmons, or rather his Demon character, as he (or it) sings about a "world without dreams" where "you cannot look up to anyone," and ending with him realizing that he could not exist in such a world. Therefore, the video conveys a visual extension of the song's meaning, taking it outside the realm of the "concert" video (of the band performing on a stage) and into the conceptual.

The single teardrop from the Demon at the end gets a lot of ribbing from fans these days. It did even at the time of the release of the video (Paul Stanley jokingly introduced the clip during an interview with Flo & Eddie back in 1981 as being as powerful as the 1970s ad of a Native American seeing trash and crying a single tear). Nevertheless, it does get the point across that a lack of imagination, spirit, and goals can make for an unhappy life and world. Grade-school sentiments in both lyrics and visual forms? Perhaps, but fans' dislike at the time had more to do with Simmons's character suddenly expressing such an emotion after years of defiant anger than with any cliché critics wanted to pin on it.

"I Love It Loud"

Filmed for the single released in October 1982 for the *Creatures of the Night* album. As with "Shandi" and "A World Without Heroes," "I Love It Loud" once

CD and DVD collection that excited fans who thought it might contain
various older music videos of the band, only to discover it was a reissue
of *KISS Exposed* instead.   *Author's Collection*

again shows the band performing a song onstage—in this case, the tank stage
used for the *Creatures of the Night* and *Lick It Up* tours. This time, however, the
conceptual element comes directly from the band performing: a teenager sees
them doing the song on television while his zombified family eats dinner, until
the boy—his eyes glowing white-hot—finally leaves to join many other glowing-
eyed teenagers in eventually meeting up with the band in the street.

With the song an anthem for loud music, the video does a good job of
tying together several elements: the power of music video, the need for kids
to break out from the norm of family life, the introduction of the new concert
stage for the tour, and even the cover of the *Creatures of the Night* album cover

(recreated in the final moments of the video by the band, with their eyes also glowing). Like "Shandi" before it, "I Love It Loud" shows how a music video can successfully pull in many elements to promote a song, a tour, and an album all at the same time.

"Heaven's on Fire"

Filmed for the single released in September 1984 from the *Animalize* album. What at first looks to be a film on fire safety (kids, never set your hands on fire like Paul does, unless you want to whoo-whoo-whoo like him all the way to the hospital) soon shows the band performing for the camera onstage; intercut with footage of them "after the show" with a vicious swarm of groupies (okay, actually, no; but a couple look so plastic that you wonder if the Invasion of the Bee Girls had just occurred). While this video could be placed into the Documentary category due to its "you are there" aspect, obviously the intention was to produce a humorous exaggeration (or, perhaps to Gene Simmons, a dramatic reenactment) of what life was like for the foursome offstage.

The only video to feature Mark St. John, there were some censorship problems due to complaints about a shot featuring "two girls making out under a table," which—to Eric Carr's amusement—was actually him with one of the girls. This video did serve as a turning point in which the band began to look comfortable without their makeup in their music videos (compare with the previous two videos done for the *Lick It Up* album) and also willing to have some relaxed, silly fun.

"Reason to Live"

Filmed for the single released in November 1987 for the *Crazy Nights* album. The song is about regretfully breaking up with someone. The video shows KISS performing onstage while the jilted love of Paul Stanley's life resolves her conflict over his dismissal by setting fire to his car. It ends with her having a postcoital smoke and playing with a gun. Love is funny like that.

The video was the second of three done for the *Crazy Nights* album. The first, "Crazy Crazy Nights," appears in the Concert section, but while both "Reason to Live" and "Turn on the Night" feature concert performances, the latter two also showcase a storyline about a former lover who wants to take revenge on Stanley and KISS. It is never quite clear how the visuals fit the lyrics, and they are pretty much abandoned halfway through "Turn on the Night," so one is left wondering what the original pitch for this storyline was and how it was to end. The video does show how using a storyline can throw off the balance of a song, though: the lyrics appear to be missing the part where one wishes someone well after a breakup by setting fire to his car.

"Turn on the Night"

Filmed for the single released in February 1988 for the *Crazy Nights* album. As mentioned above, "Reason to Live" was the debut of a homicidal former love for Paul Stanley who burns his car and ends the video waving a gun around. She—or someone with shorter blonde hair—returns in the follow-up video for the third single off the *Crazy Nights* album to inflict further damage. Sneaking into the show by way of an anvil case, the woman wanders around the concert hall and attempts to cause damage, but only succeeds in making the show even better. She eventually joins in the fun with the audience as the song ends, making the whole exercise rather pointless for her. That or KISS music has charm to soothe the savage breast.

Strangely enough, the anvil case, the dark notions of love, and the need for retaliation are all elements used well on the *Revenge* album. It is as if the "jilted lover" storyline of the "Reason to Live"/"Turn on the Night" videos was four years too early—imagine how well it would have worked for the singles from that album instead of these.

"Hide Your Heart"

Filmed for the single released in October 1989 for the *Hot in the Shade* album. For a time, there was talk of an *Elder* movie where the band's music would work as a "Greek chorus" to the action. Such a departure from the standard usage of the band in their music videos comes into play in the video for "Hide Your Heart," which shows them filming the video for the song as the video cuts to the storyline about Johnny, Rosa, and Tito from the song. Johnny loves Rosa, upsetting her boyfriend Tito. The boys grab guns to have a shootout on a rooftop to end the rivalry (speaking of which, Johnny is rather sloppy there, what with bullets falling out of his gun like Barney Fife on a bad day). Rosa is horrified, Johnny is defiant, Tito is overacting, and Gene is phlegmy. The video ends with Gene Simmons closing the doors of the ambulance for the dead inside as the band plays on.

It is, of course, all a variation of *West Side Story*, with some serious overacting going on by the young cast, but the effort is there, and the band comes off well. It should be mentioned that Stanley and Simmons interact with the storyline only in its final moments, which seems out of left field in comparison with the rest of the video, and one wonders if perhaps the intention was to have them do more in that regard throughout the video. Even odder is that a version of the video appears on the videocassette *X-Treme Close-Up* minus the violent scenes, as if KISS fans might be offended by the use of guns in the storyline (although the suggestion has been made that this was due to a European version of the video—one with the gunplay censored for European sensibilities—used for the documentary by accident).

"Unholy"

Filmed for the single released in April 1992 for the *Revenge* album. The video is a series of images of children playing in bizarre locations intermixed with the band performing the song, all within a montage of various effects to give off a "spooky" feel to a song about endless evil in the world. To fans of the song, the video enhances its mood and certainly falls into line with other heavy-metal videos done at the time by a variety of different bands in 1991. The best aspect of the video is that the filmmakers managed to find a way for Simmons to reproduce his old Demon character from the 1970s without the makeup—using his scruffy beard and hair as a form of mask, combined with the rolling back of his eyes—which works well here.

"Psycho Circus"

Filmed for the single released in October 1998 for the *Psycho Circus* album. "Psycho Circus" was the second video to be released by KISS after the return of Ace Frehley and Peter Criss in 1996, but the previous video was a concert clip of them performing "Shout It Out Loud" at the June 28, 1996, concert in Detroit, Michigan. "Psycho Circus," on the other hand, was for the first album of new material from the band after the reunion tour. Sadly, it would be the last, as *Psycho Circus* was the only new studio album created by the reunited KISS before Frehley and Criss eventually left once again.

The video ties into the album's concept of a demented (perhaps demonic) circus and the album cover with an introduction featuring the camera zooming into the circus tent and curtain that were used for the cover. Once inside, the band appears in various stages of movement toward the camera—Simmons spitting fire and blood, Criss throwing a stick, Stanley repeatedly thrusting his hands forward and upward, while all three guitarists stick their guitars forward—intercut with various computer animation and scenes of succubae tempting the viewer and tormenting a man. The purpose behind all the movement toward the camera has to do with the 3-D concept of the album cover and tour (discussed in detail for each in other chapters), and the video was eventually released in cassette form with 3-D glasses so that fans could achieve the full effect of the 3-D work done within the video. Many of the computer effects seen in the video cropped up numerous times on the video screens during concerts on the tour, sometimes to the point of irritation (the skeleton on the hand, for example). The video saw limited airing on MTV, which only helped the downward spiral of the reunited foursome. With word that the album was more a venture for Simmons and Stanley than for the four, fan interest deteriorated and the album bottomed out. Within two years, Criss and Frehley would begin their departure from the band.

Concert

In many ways, one can say that KISS played it safe when it came to their music videos. Many, if not most, artists appearing on MTV in the 1980s attempted a few videos that make them look like they escaped from theatrical musicals or an episode of *The Monkees* rather than the standard "shut up and play your guitar" standards of promotional clips from the 1970s and before. KISS, or perhaps those putting together their videos, naturally stuck with what they knew fans loved about them—performing onstage. Even the clips listed above for the Conceptual and Documentary categories all have this element, with the band seen at various times in a live-performance setting. Some would say it shows the band's sad lack of interest in doing anything with the media, but at least one can say that KISS never phoned it in by not appearing in their videos (as many artists also did in the 1980s when they realized that they looked a bit silly as characters in their three-minute musicals).

Although the remaining videos fall into the arena (no pun intended) of concert performances, these clips can be broken down into three different types and will be described in more detail below: Faking It, Audience-Driven, and Fantasy-Land.

Faking It

The term is self-explanatory, although perhaps a bit confusing; after all, it is clear that most of these videos are done in the standard manner of having a band synchronize their movements onstage to a playback of the song. In other words, they really are "faking it" for the sake of the filming. Typically, filming occurs in two parts for such in-concert clips—the first with multiple camera setups onstage with the band, but without an audience, in order to get shots that may be difficult in live concert situations (such special effects being too dangerous to do with an audience or specific close-ups). The second is with an audience—either during a real concert or a mock-up of one done specifically for the filming—in order to give the illusion that the band is performing a song exactly as on the album live to an appreciative crowd.

However, the four examples given here deviate somewhat from these rules in that they do not include the second element of audience shots. Instead, they stick with footage of the band onstage (or at least a close approximation of the stages from their time periods). In some cases such as these (and in the *Dynasty* clips listed below, cheers and applause are then added to the sound mix to make it appear that the band is playing to an audience, even though the band members are merely going through the motions for the camera

To do it this way was actually nothing usual for the time and still is done in some cases today. The main reason for doing so is that it is quicker and cheaper to do one camera filming, where the band does not even necessarily have to be on their normal stage. For example, the *Dressed to Kill* clips were done on a mock-up of the stage, allowing the cameras to be on the same level as the band and move about freely instead of having to shoot up from below the stage and/or clutter it up for multiple reshoots by having cameras on the stage itself.

"Rock and Roll All Nite"
Filmed for the single released in April 1975 for the *Dressed to Kill* album. The first promotional clip ever done by the band for one of their biggest songs, "Rock and Roll All Nite," seemed to disappear for several years from fandom until early 1983 when it popped up on the USA Network *Yesterday and Today* special. Both it and the follow-up clip for "C'mon and Love Me" were filmed at the Michigan Palace in Detroit, Michigan, in May 1975, where the cover of the *Alive!* album was photographed.

"C'mon and Love Me"
Filmed for the single released in July 1975 for the *Dressed to Kill* album. The second of two promotional clips filmed for that album, "C'mon and Love Me" was the easier of the two to find in fan circles for a time in the 1980s. The video begins with some documentary footage of the band interacting with fans before cutting to them performing the song in the same setup as for the previous clip.

In the cases of both it and "Rock and Roll All Nite," the band performs as if to an audience. The emphasis will change a tad for the subsequent two videos listed in this section.

"I Was Made for Lovin' You"
Filmed for the single released in May 1979 for the *Dynasty* album. The song was a big hit for the band in 1979, leading to the video created for it seeing a lot of airplay on television that summer. The video shows the band on the *Dynasty/Unmasked* stage performing the song. Gene Simmons does get a good moment to address the camera; staying in character while at the same time playing his bass in time with a song that in other circumstances would not have fit the Demon character at all.

"Sure Know Something"
Filmed for the single released in September 1979 for the *Dynasty* album. As with "I Was Made for Lovin' You," the band appears on their *Dynasty* stage performing the song. There is a big difference here, however, as the band is used in a bit of camera trickery beyond that of simple editing—showing the four as floating heads in the darkness until finally the cover for *Dynasty* is momentarily recreated, and then the foursome begin to move. A very classic moment in one of their rarer music videos.

Audience-Driven

In contrast to the previous four music videos, the following seven videos listed are all cases where the emphasis was on the band performing in front of an enthusiastic crowd. Most of these, however, are still mainly composites of shots, with close-ups and certain special-effect moves done outside of the "concert footage" (for example, the intros/outros for "Rise to It" and "Modern Day Delilah" obviously were done outside the scope of the footage in front of the audience for their own unique reasons). In several cases, the concert footage consists of the band doing multiple takes to prerecorded music and not actual concert footage.

"Thrills in the Night"
Filmed for the single released in January 1985 for the *Animalize* album. This was originally to be made as a conceptual video featuring Candy Loving, a former *Playboy* model (January 1979 Playmate of the month), as a woman overloaded in her work at an office. The band members were to have played fellow coworkers, her boss (Eric Carr) and the janitor (Bruce Kulick) in her office, and it would then segue into her getting her emotional release after work as the band appeared onstage performing the song to a crowd.

All this footage—filmed in Louisville, Kentucky, on December 16, 1984, during the *Animalize* tour—was jettisoned in favor of a concert clip with no storyline attached. Concert footage was taken at two shows: audience shots in Cleveland on December 14, 1984, and performance footage in Louisville on December 15, 1984.

"Crazy Crazy Nights"
Filmed for the single released in August 1987 for the *Crazy Nights* album. As mentioned above for the other two music videos done for the *Crazy Nights* album, "Crazy Crazy Nights" is the only one of the three without a storyline. Instead, the video shows the band playing to a crowd and ends with them holding Paul Stanley up as he walks across the top of the crowd.

With the band not yet on tour for the album, the video was instead filmed with a small group of select fans at the Olympic Auditorium in Los Angeles for a multihour recording session. Footage of the filming has circulated in fandom.

"Rise to It"
Filmed for the single released in April 1990 for the *Hot in the Shade* album. The video begins and ends with a brief interlude into the past, as Gene Simmons and Paul Stanley are shown in "1975" preparing to go onstage for a show in full makeup and costumes. After Stanley suggests that someday they may go without the makeup—and idea Simmons abruptly brushes off—the camera cuts to the band as they appeared in 1989, sans makeup and costumes and performing for a crowd in a clublike atmosphere. The video then ends back in 1975 with the two in slow-motion heading out to the stage.

The video caused some internal conflict in the band, as Eric Carr reported at the time of its release. Carr felt shortchanged in having his back to the camera for the flashback segment of the video and stuck into the role of Peter Criss, when he felt they could have easily updated the timeline to 1980 and allowed him to be seen putting on his Fox makeup with Simmons and Stanley. In many ways, his disagreement channeled that of a small percentage of longtime fans who felt the video was more of a middle finger to the band's legacy than the tribute to the early days that Simmons, Stanley, and (emphasis here) most fans saw it. To those in support, the point of the video was that KISS was still KISS, with or without the makeup—still having fun onstage with an enthused fan base there to enjoy it. To the detractors, the "1975" footage was dampened by wrong costumes and makeup for the period as well as trying to pass off Bruce Kulick and Eric Carr as Ace Frehley and Peter Criss (insert obvious "Frehley/ Criss" replacement joke here). To those fans, it felt wrong and—more importantly—it felt as if the band saw their previous history in makeup and costumes as something to ridicule. Rather ironic in a way, for although the band appears to be paying tribute to their hardcore fans, it was those very fans—the ones anal enough to immediately note the discrepancies—who had a problem with it.

"I Love It Loud" (Live)
Filmed to promote the *Alive III* album in May 1993. The video shows the band performing the song to an audience during the *Revenge* tour and thus gives viewers a chance to see the stage used for the short-lived tour. The video premiered on MTV in April 1993, but only in limited rotation on the channel.

"Every Time I Look at You" (Live)
Clip from the *MTV Unplugged* special to promote the March 1996 release of the album. Although an MTV exclusive, due to the origin of the clip, this footage of the band performing from the special did get a fair amount of airplay on MTV/VH1, and many fans consider it part of the official group of music videos released for KISS. More information about the special itself appears in Chapter 20.

"Shout It Out Loud"
Filmed to promote the *You Wanted the Best, You Got the Best!!* album released in July 1996. Recorded at the June 28, 1996, Detroit concert that opened the reunion tour, this video was released to promote the compilation album released just days before the reunion tour started. As such, the video to promote the album is of a performance that is not on the album itself.

"Modern Day Delilah"
Filmed for the single released in August 2009 for the *Sonic Boom* album. Opening and closing with special-effects footage of Godzilla-sized band members walking through the Detroit cityscape to get to an arena, the majority of the video shows the band performing the first single from their *Sonic Boom* album. The single got some airplay on MTV and VH1, although the industry for music videos had changed much over the past twenty-plus years since MTV first started and ran almost exclusively music videos. For two decades, it was felt that music videos had to be done or else singles would not sell; by 2009, the tide had turned, and once again videos were done more as a promotional afterthought (with the exception of bigger "event" videos that were heavily advertised) than the end-all for the success of an album. With MTV having little focus on music videos by the early 2000s, the marketplace had changed.

Fantasyland

What separates these videos from those of the previous two categories under Concert are that they display the band performing songs in places that could not possibly be normal concert situations. The videos here involved postapocalyptic landscapes, Busby Berkeley–like musical numbers, fantasy stages unique to the videos themselves, and even white voids. None feature conceptual ideas beyond the premise of where the band is performing (with the possible exception of the *Lick It Up* clips, which quickly abandon any narrative for emphasis on the band playing on a stage of some sort), nor are they made to look as if the band is performing for anyone other than the camera or an obviously faked audience. Nearly all involve footage of female models and/or dancers in direct or greater ratio than footage of the band performing.

A multidisc DVD set that was one of three volumes. Although some fans were unhappy with the editing done on some segments, it at least allowed them to see some of the band's earlier music videos in excellent picture quality.   *Author's Collection*

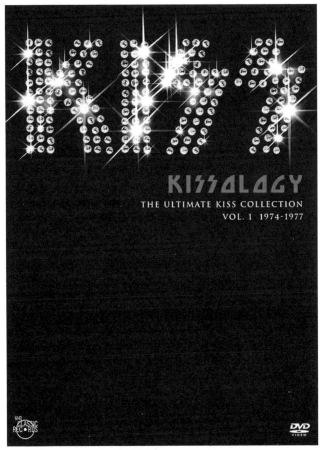

"Lick It Up"
Filmed for the single released in September 1983 for the *Lick It Up* album. The first video by KISS without their trademark makeup or costumes is the first to find them in an actual comic-book environment. Strutting their way into a *Mad Max*–like battle zone (a theme so popular in movies and heavy-metal videos in the early 1980s), the foursome meet up with a group of Amazonian Tupperware Ladies who force-feed them weird liquids until the band is immolated on a small fire-lit stage. The video ends with Paul Stanley's skull as an ornament on display for one of the happy saleswomen.

Okay, actually the above is not quite true—although there is an initial storyline presented with the Amazons meeting KISS, that all peters out midway through as the camera focuses on the band performing on a makeshift stage before ending with one of the women leaning next to a skull like some blood-thirsty model on *The Price is Right*. Hence, the video is a bit of a fake-out; what appears to be a conceptual video suddenly turns into one about the band showing their unmasked faces for the first time and how they would physically appear live on stage for the album's tour. In other words, grab the viewer with the girls, to lead them into the show for the big reveal.

The video is interesting to evaluate how well the four adjust to being without their trademark characters for the first time, with Paul Stanley immediately jumping into the role he would play for many years to come while still incorporating his role as emcee during shows and Gene Simmons having a hard time breaking away from the movements that were so much at the core of his Demon character. Simmons would need a tour under his belt before he finally broke away from the physical characteristics that he brought into his earlier role.

"All Hell's Breakin' Loose"
Filmed for the single released in February 1984 for the *Lick It Up* album. The second video from the *Lick It Up* album is also the second to feature the band without makeup, and they are once again seen in the barren post-WWIII world of the "Lick It Up" video. This time they run into a few circus performers, one of whom raps his displeasure with Paul Stanley's attire. The band then performs the song in a dark bar where two women have a sword fight until a sword is tossed up to Stanley and the band stumbles out into the night. In essence, as with "Lick It Up," an atmosphere is set up for the song, only for the band's performance being the focus, with no resolution to the storyline created.

The video is memorable for a shot of Gene Simmons clearly starting to laugh on camera as Stanley swishes his blade. The circus sideshow atmosphere from early in the video will reappear in the video for "Rock Hard" as well as being the motif for the *Psycho Circus* album, video, tour, and comic book.

"Tears Are Falling"
Filmed for the single released in September 1985 for the *Asylum* album. Once again, a narrative begins the video with a woman tearing down a bunch of dusty curtains in a house until she discovers a ghostly Paul Stanley standing in the

corner with his back to her (which makes the ending of *Blair Witch Project* a giddy moment to watch in retrospect). From there, while the girl in the video is referenced throughout in fantasy images and seen in the end lying on a dusty couch as it begins raining in the house, the video is mainly focused on the band playing on an islandlike landscape, with an exploding volcano and a set of palm-tree-size poles with televisions on top (the "Solid State Dancers," as Eric Carr referred to them in interviews). All sense of a dramatic ending vanishes as an insert shot shows Paul doing a windshield-wiper effect with his fingers.

Bruce Kulick plays his guitar in a rainstorm during the song (the first of two videos where he gets soaked), while reports at the time stated that Carr narrowly avoided a mishap with the explosions placed near him during the filming. The video is a clear sign of the band veering (some would say out of control) into the glam look that was so popular at the time in heavy metal, with the band members wearing broad shoulder pads in militaristic outfits, neon colors, and sparkles. It would get even worse in the subsequent videos from the *Asylum* album.

"Who Wants to Be Lonely?"
Filmed as a possible single for the *Asylum* album released in September 1985. Moving further away from a storyline, but still keeping a conceptual edge, the video begins with Paul Stanley strutting down an underground tunnel with industry piping and steam blowing. It all winds up in a vast area where the band plays as dancers hit the showers and Bruce gets soaked once again (thanks to a shower stall). Two versions of the video created—one with more footage of the dancers and one with more of the band. The one with the dancers won out—which shows where priorities lay—although the other circulated in fan circles.

As Eric Carr told me in a 1990 interview, by this time the music videos they filmed were starting to blur together in his mind, as they seemed to be all the same, with the band playing on a stage while a bunch of stuff happened around them. This is evident in the next video as well.

"Uh! All Night"
Filmed as a possible single for the *Asylum* album released in September 1985. Going full tilt into the musical number mode, this video features the band performing while a group of dancers dressed in skimpy outfits dance around a series of rolling beds. It is actually more fun than it sounds, with the band members peeping through windows and holes and giving a series of bug-eyed reaction shots to the girl, which works well with such a silly song. After this one, the band's costumes will begin to tone down.

Both this and "Who Wants to Be Lonely?" were filmed to help promote the songs once they became singles, but no commercial singles were released in the U.S. for either song. Even so, "Who Wants to Be Lonely?" got a good amount of airplay on MTV, while "Uh! All Night" struggled to do the same.

"Let's Put the X in Sex"
Filmed for the single released in October 1988 for the *Smashes, Thrashes, and Hits* album. The band decided to take a break after the *Crazy Nights* tour (one

that many fans at the time felt saw the band performing shows at a low emotional ebb), releasing the compilation album *Smashes, Thrashes, and Hits*. To help with sales, along with the controversial redubbing of "Beth" with Eric Carr singing, two new songs were added to the album: "Let's Put the X in Sex" and "Rock Hard." Videos were created for both songs, showing the band once again performing as a group of dancers were edited into the footage.

The video emerged as part of a lawsuit involving the office building seen at the beginning, with claims of defamation due to making the building out to be a "phallic symbol." The lawsuit had more to do with other issues, with the band's video being rather a small part of it, and was eventually settled out of court, although they used the notoriety to help promote the video.

This and "Rock Hard" are usually considered the two worst KISS music videos by both the band and fans. Neither appears on the *KISSology* DVD series, although they do appear on the *X-Treme Closeup* documentary commercially released in 1992.

"Rock Hard"

Filmed for the single released in March 1989 for the *Smashes, Thrashes, and Hits* album. The second of two videos filmed for this compilation album and the rarer of the two due to limited airplay on MTV. Interestingly, the video shows the band performing in a circuslike set and features Paul Stanley, as well as one of the women in the video, swinging on a trapeze. KISS would return to the carnival/circus concept for both *Carnival of Souls* and *Psycho Circus* in later years. Although this and "Let's Put the X in Sex" are considered the band's worst videos, the videos themselves are not much different from those done on earlier album, and their low ranking has more to do with the songs than with any visual issues fans have with the videos.

"I Just Wanna"

Filmed for the single released from the *Revenge* album in June 1992. The song, nearly a backwards homage to "Summertime Blues," was used during the *Revenge* concerts as a moment for a group of local strippers to come out onstage and dance with the band. The video finds the band in a white void, with Paul Stanley singing as the band plays and the camera doing a number of visual effects to keep the proceedings moving. A girl dancer is occasionally seen in brief flashes to show that Stanley is not stuck in the void and singing to the other three guys in the band. That certainly would be a very odd way to end the Fantasyland collection of videos. This was the last of the KISS videos to feature Gene Simmons spitting up phlegm on camera, which is good as he was beginning to do this so often in appearances that one began to wonder if he needed to go see a doctor.

22

It's the ABBA Movie, Only with KISS!

Other Attempts to Bring KISS to the Screen

t may be hard to believe, but *KISS Meets the Phantom of the Park* was not the end of the road for KISS when it came to transplanting the power of the band into another media. In the years that followed, there would be several other attempts to get something going on television or in the movies or even Broadway. With the exception of *Detroit Rock City*—a comedy that bombed at theaters and only sparingly used the band—none have come to fruition, however.

KISS Cartoons

As KISS was getting superhot in 1978, the cartoon studio Filmation took interest. Filmation had gained a name for itself in the 1960s for their series of action-oriented cartoons made for Saturday morning television that featured DC super-heroes like Batman and Superman. They also had a major success with *Archie* and the various spin-offs over the years based on that series, no doubt helped by the success of the song "Sugar, Sugar," which was written as if performed by Archie and his gang on the television show.

Filmation was riding high in the 1970s. Their *Fat Albert and the Cosby Kids* was going strong, and they had a good run of live-action shows for CBS featuring characters like Captain Marvel (*Shazam!*) and Isis, among others. With the ability to do live-action and animation both, it seemed logical for them to go after KISS, who were looking to expand into television anyway. A contract was signed between the studio and KISS, and several ideas were tossed around for the first special that was to be done to see if a possible series could be made out of it. Meanwhile, Gene Simmons had brought in some ideas for future episodes of the series if that would occur. However, after months of negotiations and preproduction, everyone agreed that it was not going to work out, and the special was dropped.

In 1997, KISS approached the Canadian animation studio Nelvana to put together a Saturday morning superhero cartoon series for the group. The studio had done the animation for the rock-fantasy film *Rock & Rule* in 1983 along with animation for *Star Wars*–related series like *Droids* and *Ewoks* and even an animated version of *Tales from the Crypt*, so it was not out of their area to try to do something with KISS. However, after talks over a period of years, the project was finally turned into the Gene Simmons–connected series *My Dad the Rock Star*, a comedic animated series that ran on Nickelodeon for two seasons of thirteen episodes each between 2003 and 2005. The year 2000 saw the first multipart "webisode" series from Brilliant Digital Entertainment called *KISS: Immortals* that could be played online and follows the band from the stage to fighting in an alien world with their "magical" instruments. Twenty-seven episodes were done for the series, which was created and written by Jeffrey Sullivan and Bruce Onder, with the final episode wrapping up the storyline. Unfortunately only the first nine episodes were included on the 2001 DVD release, leaving fans to pick through various video websites in order to find the rest of the story. The band initially did the voices themselves, but sound-alikes were soon brought in. Oddly enough for a series that was hyped as cutting-edge in technology at the time, most fans tend to jump right over it when discussing the band's TV/movie projects.

KISS has made animated appearances in other places, especially in a few guest shots on *Family Guy* (including an episode parody of what a KISS special back in 1978 probably would have looked like, with KISS saving Santa from dinosaurs, in the 2001 episode "A Very Special Family Guy Freakin' Christmas"). But on their own terms, such a KISS series or even one-off special has yet to appear on television.

KISS in Australia

As mentioned in the *Phantom* chapter, KISS was looking at all types of proposals for movie scripts before the movie aired on NBC. Then album issues and internal problems, along with the movie not measuring up to what anyone wanted, pretty much scuttled any potential movie projects. However, there was one discussed for a time in late 1980 that was given some serious thought. In October 1980, New York Production Company approached KISS and Aucoin Management with a seven-page proposal for a quasi-documentary of the band as they toured Australia in November of that year. The film would focus on pretty much all the clichés people think of when it comes to Australia in the form of a travelogue that would periodically pick up on KISS as they toured the country. The proposal had surprisingly very little footage of the band performing in concert, although the production company was requesting they write two songs for the film, which would end on a Maori child wearing KISS makeup.

In essence, it appeared to be a movie about Australia that happened to have KISS music playing over most of it. With the details on profit participation probably not found to be in favor of the band and Aucoin Management, along with a proposal for the script that seemed to take advantage of the band more than using them properly, it was understandable that the project never got any further.

The Elder

There was no doubt about it, the idea was to get what amounted to a soundtrack album out on the market for people to clamor over as a KISS album first and then a big conceptual motion picture second. As it turns out, *Music from "The Elder"* never went beyond that stage. The plot by Gene Simmons had involved some type of fantasy story involving a boy fighting against someone named Mr. Blackwell, while Morpheus would be the boy's guide to becoming a hero.

Not much is known beyond that about the project. It is known that the band was looking to get the project going as a movie in early 1982, with the concept that the band itself would only be working in it as a "Greek chorus" to the action through their music. In fact, it was quite possible that they would not have appeared at all in the film but merely have their music there to help set up the story.

The original deal would have seen the album as a double-vinyl release if things had gone the way Simmons had envisioned (others convinced the band that it would be better to tease the listeners with a bit of the story before giving them more in a follow-up album). Instead, the plans were to do the "War of the Gods" sequel after the sales for the first album died down. Then there would be the final movie soundtrack album at a later point, pretty much already done and delivered when the time came.

But, such a time never came. The album had bombed with fans, in sales, and—contrary to popular belief—with most critics as well. It was time to move on and be a band again, which lead to *Creatures of the Night* and eventually the discarding of KISS World, with the loss of the makeup and costumes in 1983.

KISS Biopic, or Something Like It

When the band returned to the makeup and costumes in 1996, Gene Simmons began spearheading a number of projects to push the band into movies or television. One of the first was mentioned in October 1997 when producer Gene Kirkwood (*Rocky; New York, New York*) approached Simmons about a theatrical biopic about the band with Keanu Reeves and Johnny Depp playing the parts of Simmons and Paul Stanley. The idea was tossed around for a while, but by January 1999, Kirkwood would tell the press that the deal was dead.

Then in 1999, there was talk of a CBS movie-of-the-week to be called *Rock and Roll All Night* that would be a variation on *Sleepless in Seattle* only with the couple meeting at a KISS concert at the end instead of the Empire State Building. That project also fell through.

For a time Simmons was looking into a project with Barnum & Bailey's Circus involving the band, as well as a lavish KISS production at one of the casinos in

Las Vegas and a Broadway musical about the early days of the band. None of these transpired either. The only thing that did seem to come to fruition was that of the Demon wrestling character for World Championship Wrestling, but that was deemed an embarrassment by wrestling fans, and after little interest was shown, the character was given a series of matches to lose to comical effect and finally dropped within eight months of first appearing.

Looking at the projects above, it is easy to say that springboarding off the band's image without their direct involvement has produced little. Yet when it comes to their success in music, in touring, and with videos, etc., it is clear that there is an interest in the band that is marketable. Just as long as the band is there to push it as well. With new talks beginning in early 2012 for a movie based on the band's experience in Cadillac, Michigan, in 1975 (see Chapter 7 for more details), it appears that their interest in some type of film project will remain for years to come.

23

Did the Band Peak with *Howard the Duck?*

A Look at the Comics

K ISS may never have realized the potential they thought to achieve in television and movies, but they did see some success in another visual media, comics books, even if that road has been a bit rocky or even forgotten at times. It certainly was an avenue of logical expansion for a band that had been compared to comic book superheroes since the days of the *Dressed to Kill* fumetti that appeared in *Creem* magazine (see Chapter 10 for more details). Besides, after the incredible sales success of both *Alive!* and *Destroyer*, it would seem unlikely that many entertainment enterprises would not have been looking at KISS with extreme interest including the comic book companies, if only for monetary and publicity reasons.

To many fans, as well as those outside of the industry, the idea of having real-life personalities such as KISS appear in comics seemed to be a first; yet in reality, their debut was continuing a tradition that had been in place since the early days of the genre. Biographies of famous actors, singers, athletes, and historical figures were always bankable for comic publishers, especially when the public grew anxious to read anything they could about an artist. Plus, comics had the additional bonus beyond providing historical information about a favorite personality of physically showing that person on every page of text, perhaps even in the form of pinups or posters to cut out and display—something that could not necessarily be done with books or other printed media. While many such offerings were one-time-only releases with no suggestion to continue as a series, there were plenty of attempts to create longer series based on such subjects, although some were more successful than others. Teenage heartthrobs, such as Bobby Sherman, Pat Boone, and David Cassidy are just a few to have short-lived comic-book series based on them. Overall, however, it has been comedic and action-adventure stars rather than musicians that have succeeded in having long-lasting comics, as it is much easier to write about cowboys saving a town in danger than having to come up with another story where David Cassidy avoids being chased by girls. Dell did well with books about western stars such as Gene

Autry and Roy Rogers, while DC Comics published both *The Adventures of Bob Hope* and *The Adventures of Jerry Lewis* for nearly twenty years each (and both featured issues finding the main character dealing with superhero antics long before KISS would do so in the pages of Marvel Comics). Even the Monkees comic book out of Dell in the late 1960s had the foursome at one time or another in their superhero roles as "Monkee-Men."

Nor were the two giants of the 1960s and onward—Marvel Comics (home of Spider-Man, the Hulk, and the X-Men) and DC Comics (where Batman, Superman, and Wonder Woman held court)—immune to bringing real-life individuals into their superhero books in a crossover fashion to draw readers. Marvel had the Beatles making a brief appearance with the Thing and the Human Torch in an old issue of *Strange Tales*, while Superman would later fight Muhammad Ali in a giant-size extravaganza in 1978 and Spider-Man would team-up with President Obama in 2009 for an issue of *Amazing Spider-Man*. Thus, such attempts to incorporate real-life individuals into the "universe" of these companies' superheroes may not have been an everyday occurrence, but was certainly not outlandish in the history of the publishers.

Of the two companies in the 1970s, many considered Marvel the "cool kid" in class, with an audience that tended toward older teenagers and college students, while DC had the image of being for younger children. Further, as DC was busy promoting *Super Friends* on Saturday mornings and pursuing the idea of turning Wonder Woman into a lighthearted weekly television series, Marvel's leader and creator/cocreator of many of their biggest heroes (Spider-Man, Fantastic Four, the Hulk, etc.), Stan Lee, was appearing for talks on college campuses, and monthly series such as *Howard the Duck* and *Conan the Barbarian* were seen as worthy of serious discussion by adults in the mid-1970s. Marvel even attempted to jump into the rock music genre a bit earlier than their successful usage of KISS by putting together a comic based on Alice Cooper's *Welcome to My Nightmare* album back in 1975 (and later finally producing a comic based on Alice's *From the Inside* album in 1979 as part of their *Marvel Premiere* series as well as a later miniseries in 1994). Because of these factors, longtime comic book fans, of which Gene Simmons was one, would not have found the idea of KISS in comics that unusual, and going to Marvel would have been considered a credible move. Not to say there were not those who objected to Marvel, as we will see in the first entry below.

What was once a marketplace for essentially two companies in the 1970s expanded greatly in the 1980s and 1990s with multiple publishers producing comic book titles. Many were fly-by-night operations, thrown together by fans and artists who hoped to catch on, but Dark Horse (established in 1986) and Image (1992) were two independent companies that succeed extremely well, and both would eventually do comic book series based on KISS. Platinum Studio Comics would attempt their own official continuing series starting in 2007, but after much hoopla would make the comic available only online after issue #6 and finally petered out after a year and a half midway through issue #10 in

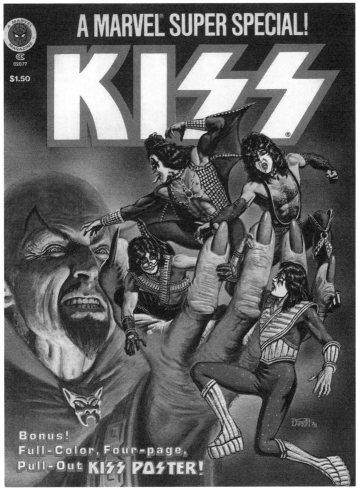

The second KISS comic, released at the height of mania for the band.

Author's Collection

2008. Since then there have been no more attempts to bring the band back to the world of comics; at least in the sense of an ongoing series (but more on that later in the chapter). Even so, KISS has a thirty-year history in the comic-book industry that makes them one of the longer lasting of real-life personalities to make it to the comic-book page.

Along with the many companies that have produced official comics based on the band, there are also comics that had an "acceptance/tolerance" from the band over the years, including those produced by the controversial company Revolutionary Comics that led to a few people connected to Revolutionary doing official work for the band. There are, of course, also a number of parodies and tributes, certainly many during the glut of independent black-and-white comics that appeared in the late 1980s and early 1990s that fans remember. Simmons himself would start his own short-lived comic book company in 2007 that produced a small number of comics before disappearing. Although none of his comics featured KISS, they appear in this chapter as well for fans who are curious.

While at times KISS has pushed aside the makeup era for album and tour projects, they never disregarded their heritage in comics. Drawings from the Marvel and Image comics have appeared in various merchandising over the years, and as a hardback collection of many of their comic-book exploits released in 2009 called *KISS Kompendium* (continuing the band's rather irritating grade-school practice of starting words with a K that would otherwise be spelled with a C, such as *KISS Konfidential*). The book is an accomplishment, reprinting not only the three major Marvel comics from over the years, but the Image and Dark Horse series as well. Yet even at a length of over 1,200 pages the book managed to do something similar to the *KISSology* DVD sets in editing material in such a manner that completists may find it frustrating. Not only are certain comics missing from the collection—the Revolutionary Comics are not considered "official" and therefore do not appear, even though Simmons and Paul Stanley were actively involved in their creations, while the Platinum Studio series was too recent at the time to be reprinted—some elements of certain issues have been edited to change the appearance of the original work involved. Recolored (some said rather badly) and reinked artwork created by Marvel for a 1995 reissue is used in the book, while pages of additional artwork featured but not part of the stories and articles from the editors and writers discussing the making of the comics have disappeared. Missing also are articles written within the *Psycho Circus* series (in both its original form and the magazine reissues that came later) that helped inform readers on the creation of the stories for the comic. Further, and more frustrating, beyond a couple of brief forewords by Simmons and Stanley at the beginning of the book, there is no explanation as to what these comics are, how they came about, or when they appeared, with the exception of an inaccurate article reprinted from the 1995 Marvel reprint giving some vague details on their creation (which also gives the impression that *KISSNation* was to be a regular ongoing series). On the other hand, at least said article mentions the names of Steve Gerber, Ralph Macchio (no, not that Ralph Macchio, but a writer/editor at Marvel at the time), and Alan Weiss, who wrote and co-plotted the first two Marvel comics, as the first pages of both comics (typically referred to as the splash page), which listed their names as creators, were edited out of the *KISS Kompendium*. It is a bit of a shame, for the material of the band's history in comics is nearly all there in the *KISS Kompendium* book in a spectacular fashion, but without the background given as to how the books came about, the band misses out on telling not only the history of said comics, but a bit about their own history as well.

Marvel Comics

As mentioned above, Marvel Comics had been toying with the idea of bringing in real-life figures to star in their comics for a while before they finally broke through with agreeing to produce a comic for KISS. Even so, they would achieve an even greater result—albeit in terms of a regular series and not one of long-lasting popularity—later in 1977 with the series *The Human Fly*, based on stuntman Rick Rojatt and advertised on the front cover of his comic as "The Wildest Super-Hero Ever . . . Because He's Real!" Marvel would attempt to entice other musicians and popular acts such as Elton John and the Rolling Stones to agree to do comics, but had little luck in that endeavor even after publishing an unauthorized Beatles bio in 1978. An attempt to revive such comics came with the "Marvel Music" line of the 1990s, which brought about the return of KISS to Marvel, but the results were short-lived.

That was all in the future back in the summer of 1976 when KISS and Marvel first shook hands on a deal that would bring the band into the comic world for the first time. Marvel's in-house fan magazine, *FOOM* (an acronym for "Friends of Ol' Marvel"), first announced the project in issue #15, but in tentative terms—stating that it was a possible venture to come in the future. On the other hand, the blurb printed in *FOOM* mentioned Steve Gerber as working on the project, so contractual concerns must have been in discussion already by that point. Even so, it would not be until be until the spring 1977 issue of the *KISS Army Newsletter* (volume 2, issue 1) that the band would make the official announcement: "After a year of planning, writing and painting, KISS comics will burst onto your newsstands this June. The all-new Marvel Comic, *KISS Men*, written by Steve Gerber of *Howard the Duck* fame, will feature, Gene, Peter, Paul and Ace as the superheroes we have

KISS's 1996 return to Marvel in the disappointing *KISSNation* one-shot. *Author's Collection*

known they were all along, each with a special secret power for seeking and destroying evil."

There's a reason for the newsletter to trumpet Steve Gerber writing the book: of the Marvel writers, getting Gerber was a bit of a coup. Gerber was not only an established comic-book author, but also highly in demand thanks to his work on such comics as *Man-Thing* and (especially) *Howard the Duck*, both of which broke out of common action/fantasy themes to delve into existentialism, making them popular reading for high school and college students. Gerber (who passed away in 2008) was also known for having a knack for taking very oddball premises and finding clever ways of making them work, as can be seen with such characters as a mystical swamp creature whose touch can burn if fear is shown and a book about a talking duck that could have all-text issues dealing with creativity and still be in context of the series. Although people who are not comic-book fans today tend to see *Howard the Duck* based solely on criticisms of the wrongheaded movie adaptation done in the 1980s, Gerber had nothing to do with the film, and the comic book series was much more serious in tone, much harder in its satire, and certainly different in style than the film.

The work began with Gerber and co-plotter/artist Alan Weiss at Marvel, and Sean Delaney and Allen Miller at Aucoin Management, in the summer and fall of 1976, with a plot synopsis delivered to Aucoin Management at the end of December 1976. Delaney would go on to be recognized by all concerned for coming up with some essential elements of the comic-book characters, such as the box of talismans that give the four their superpowers, but most of the work in the book are obvious Gerber touches, such as Dizzy—a man looking like an old barbaric roadie in shades—and the ceremonial debut of Dr. Doom to KISS, to name a couple, and the book seems to be mostly a work of those at Marvel rather than those at Aucoin. In March 1977, Marvel and Aucoin signed a final contract for the comic, although work had been proceeding on the issue since the beginning of the year. Much of the negotiation between the two came down to matters of simply understanding the nature of each other's business—at one point Aucoin was concerned that the magazine would not be out in time for a spring 1977 release, as they typically saw record sales go up during that time of year. Marvel—or at least Gerber in a letter to Aucoin Management—pointed out that sales for comics and magazines usually dipped in the teenage/college crowd in the spring because of concerns about school finals and other spring activities and that summer would make for a more logical release date. (A major bit of irony is that the band would not release their next studio album, *Love Gun*, until June 1977, making concerns about a spring release of the comic debatable.) Gerber (as per his letter to Aucoin in December 1976) also seemed flustered with storyline suggestions by people at Aucoin Management that he felt were detrimental to the comic, reminding them that the people at Marvel working on the book knew how to create "visually compelling" comics and should be trusted to do so.

While all that was going on, Marvel snuck a brief appearance of the band into the pages of Gerber's comic *Howard the Duck,* drawn by legendary artist Gene Colan. The final page of issue #12 (dated May 1977 but released two months before that and therefore written and drawn in February of that year) shows the band emerging as apparitions from the mind of a mental patient, Winda Wester. Issue #13 (dated June 1977; written and drawn March 1977) further features KISS in the first three pages of the story. Appearing before a dazed Howard in the halls of the asylum, the band advises him, "When you meet reality head-on, KISS it, smack it in the face!" before disappearing once more into Winda's mind. No more would be seen of the band in this variation of their characters until the March 1980 issue of the magazine-size comic *Howard the Duck?* (issue #4), which saw Simmons's face momentarily appearing with that of various other rock performers and even Julia Child as further ghosts from Winda's id. In essence, the band members appear as advisers to the hero to motivate him to do something later in the story. Coincidentally, this is somewhat similar to how the band will function in the *Psycho Circus* series—as more of a Greek chorus to the action than being the focus of the series itself.

The first KISS comic—dropping the rather awkward *KISS Men* title (although to be fair, this title never appeared in any Marvel documents)—came out in June 1977 as the first full-color, magazine-size comic book from Marvel, under the title of *Marvel Comics Super Special* #1 (Marvel had previously released magazine-size comics, but those had been with black-and-white interiors, as would most of their magazine series released outside of the *Super Special* series). Co-plotter Alan Weiss drew the forty-two-page comic in collaboration with Sal Buscema, John Buscema, and Rick Buckler, along with inks by Allen Milgrom, as well as doing the wraparound cover featuring KISS (with Marvel villain Dr. Doom pushed to the back cover, as per a request from Aucoin Management that no Marvel characters appeared with KISS on the front). Yet perhaps the most striking thing about the comic book that would immediately gain both KISS and Marvel notoriety was the claim on the front cover that the comic used "real KISS blood" in the printing ink. Whether that is quite true or not turns out to be a story in itself (and covered in Chapter 31), but with local Buffalo, New York, television stations filming the ceremony of the band members having their blood pour into the red ink at the printing plant, there certainly was an event made out of it that got the band and the comic press around the world.

The issue's story centers on a group of young men (Gerber's initial plot synopsis has them as fifteen-year-olds, although their ages are never stated and the artwork appears to make them college-aged at youngest) who are given what would later be referred to as talismans but in the first issue appear as miniature statues of the band members with the exception of Paul Stanley's (which appears as the star seen in the subsequent Marvel comic and the NBC movie). The talismans from the "Box of Khyscz" granted each of the four certain powers—Simmons with demonic fire-breathing and super-strength; Stanley with a laser he can shoot from his "starry" eye that can be used as a blunt

KISS Classics—a 1995 reprint of the two Marvel specials from the 1970s.   *Author's Collection*

force, pass on emotions to others, or used to read minds; Frehley with the ability to teleport and zap people with his fingers; and Criss with catlike powers—and transformed them into the makeup and costume versions of the band members' appearance onstage. With this action, the foursome becomes the target of Marvel super-villain Dr. Doom, who wants the powers of the box for himself, whether in the form of the talismans or through the four members. After a series of battles that sees guest appearances by several Marvel superheroes as well as demonic villain Mephisto, Dr. Doom gives up his quest for the talismans' powers, and the four realize they have a long way to go before they truly understand the powers they have been given.

Also included in the issue was the following: a two-page history of the making of the comic by Gerber, a one-page bio on Dr. Doom for readers with no background on the character, a six-page band history for readers with no background on the band, a four-page article showing the band getting blood drawn (which is reprinted in the *KISS Kompendium* book), a parody ad for Dr. Doom's homeland as a travel destination, a two-pager showing various magazine covers displaying the band, a centerfold of the band on the *Destroyer* stage set (in what appears to be a shot from the *Don Kirshner's Rock Concert* appearance from the time period), a questionnaire for fans to fill out on who they are, and, finally, a one-pager on the various people involved in producing the issue (including a comment that Sean Delaney was the originator of the "Box of Khyscz" concept for the comic. Ads in the issue featured one for Marvel, one for Casablanca (showcasing *Alive!*, *Destroyer*, and *Rock and Roll Over*, but oddly not the just-to-be-released *Love Gun* cover), and three for rock magazines: *Creem*, *Rock Scene*, and *Hit Parader*. As Gerber told the *Comics Journal* (August 1978, issue #41), such ads almost did not make it into the magazine, as some Marvel staffers were concerned about using KISS in one of their comics and compounding the trek to hell by publishing ads for rock magazines that did not "fit" the style they perceived Marvel to be. As Gerber pointed out in the same interview, Marvel did not even promote the magazine in its regular series of comics coming out at the time for fear of offending readers and parents who were already flooding the office with letters of concern about the release of such a comic book kids might see.

Such hysteria was fueled by an article written by columnist Bob Greene in the *Chicago Sun-Times* condemning the book sight unseen, which saw publication in numerous newspapers around the country. It would later lead to Gerber introducing a villain in the pages of *Howard the Duck* who was a journalist that got his arm cut off in a guillotine during a rock concert by a band he was determined to tear apart in a book (in a parody of Greene's biographical book about touring with the Alice Cooper group, *Billion Dollar Babies*) and would replace his arm with a clapper for a giant bell he now wore over his head. The character, Dr. Bong, would have a KISS-connection as well: Gerber had gone over to Gene Simmons's apartment to discuss the KISS comic when Simmons mentioned a fan letter he had received inviting him to visit a fan for "some bonging." Neither Simmons nor Gerber had heard the term before and began to joke about what it could mean, leading to the idea of someone holding a giant bell over their head and hitting the bell to cause dizziness. Strangely enough, even for all this silliness mixed in with a rather nasty attack on Greene in the guise of the character in the comic, Greene enjoyed becoming a comic-book villain and would later give Gerber a chance to discuss the KISS comics in his own words. Of course, that was long after the KISS comic had already hit the stands with threats of towns burning copies in bonfires.

Concerns about such threats by some within the Marvel staff were for naught. The magazine would be Marvel's best-selling comic for years to come, allowing the *Super Special* series to continue until 1986, although mostly as comic-book adaptations of various action/science-fiction/fantasy movies appearing in theaters at the time of publication. Ironically, the final issue for the series would be one for the *Howard the Duck* move in 1986 and, again ironically, the Marvel comic that finally outsold the first KISS comic (*Spider-Man* #1) was created by Todd McFarlane, who would go on to help produce the *Psycho Circus* comic in the 1990s. Because of the crossover audience of rock fans who were not necessarily comic-book fans being made available to Marvel thanks to KISS, Marvel was keen to have the band reappear in another issue of the magazine. This led to them appearing in the fifth issue, now called *Marvel Super Special*, in September 1978. By then, things had changed at Marvel beyond that of dropping the word "Comics" from the title of the magazine. Steve Gerber was gone, splitting from the company over disputes pertaining to deadlines and stories he wanted to write, and changes in the editorial department would soon alter the relationship between the band and Marvel. However, Alan Weiss would return to help co-plot the story, although with a relative newcomer, Ralph Macchio, who wrote the script. Macchio, who would go on to write and edit a variety of books for Marvel over the years, with long periods doing so on such titles as *Daredevil* and *Spider-Man*, had concentrated most of his time at Marvel at that point more behind the scenes than as a writer. However, with his previous editorial work on the Marvel black-and-white magazine comics at the time, the company saw him as a knowledgeable replacement for the book. Macchio certainly does attempt to continue where Gerber left off, not only with the KISS characters, but by introducing characters and situations seen in the same socially conscious manner as in Gerber's work: a world where leftover hippies believe a Victorian crime solver to be a "dinosaur" (and actually is a physical dinosaur in the story), a disco full of glassy-eyed dancers, and even the reappearance of a homicidal elf that Gerber had created for his run on *The Defenders* back in the mid-1970s. The final major difference between the first and second issues came with the artists on the book, as Weiss deferred this duty to John Romita Jr. (famous for his work on *Spider-Man* over the years) and Tony DeZuniga, along with well-known comic cover artist Bob Larkin painting the front cover of the issue and fantasy illustrator George Arthur Bush creating a poster of the band included in the center of the issue.

The second issue was smaller in page-count overall, but the story itself was actually two pages longer than its predecessor, thanks to the number of pages taken over by text pieces of ads being less. Such pages were broken down into four pages of biographies about various Marvel personnel involved with the comic, followed by a two-page article about the then-in-production *KISS Meets the Phantom of the Park* movie, a full-page ad for the magazine-size *Hulk* series, an ad for the KISS solo albums, and an ad for KISS merchandise. The story for the second issue is somewhat standard superhero material, with the foursome going off to battle an evil wizard, although his ability to feed on emotions created through musical events helps tie in the band a bit more than it would for other superhero characters. The talismans are drawn this time to appear more like those used in the *KISS Meets the Phantom* movie, which would see the band using superpowers in the same manner as in the two Marvel comics. While the main plot may appear to be generic in some ways, Macchio does move the conflict among characters due to their new superpowers forward, with friction developing between Simmons and Stanley due to signs of violence becoming more evident in Simmons's character. No doubt the growing distrust among the characters would have been advanced in the third issue of the comic—which was promised by editor Richard Marschall in a biography section of the issue as *KISS III*—but it was not to be, at least not in the form expected in 1978.

Instead, the corporate structure at Marvel was rapidly changing, and it led directly to KISS dropping out of another comic with them. At the time of the first contract in 1977, Aucoin Management had negotiated a deal where all copyrights and storylines about the KISS characters remained the property of KISS and not that of Marvel. This would continue into the second issue as well, but when the time came for a third possible issue—as Simmons told Rob Samsel in *Combo* #26 (March 1997, page 31)—Marvel demanded that they gain copyright control to the KISS characters in return. Seeing this as a very bad move, Aucoin Management bailed and decided to shop the idea of a KISS comic to other sources. There was some initial curiosity from DC Comics about jumping in to replace Marvel in 1979, but with demands similar to Marvel's and Simmons's hesitation about DC after the company began a legal battle with the creators of Superman over creative-rights, the two sides parted ways. Meanwhile, in 1979, Neal Adams—a famous comic book artist who had worked on many of both DC's and Marvel's most famous characters and who had gone independent by that time—approached the band through a company called Random Arts about a new KISS series. Aucoin Management took this up for a time, with even a budget of $5,000 contemplated to start work on the project, but it too failed to move forward.

It would be seventeen years before another official KISS comic would appear on the newsstands, and ironically, it would be from Marvel Comics. Or rather, from Marvel Music, a short-lived imprint of Marvel Comics that lasted from 1994 through 1995 by then Editor-in-Chief Mort Todd. The imprint was a stab at the type of popularity Revolutionary Comics was receiving for their series of unauthorized biographical comic books about different rock bands. The main difference from those for Marvel Music was that the artists appearing would have given authorization to Marvel to produce said comics, of which some were open-ended dramatic series instead of biographical. While it appeared that Marvel was riding the coattails of another publisher, the earlier KISS comics had led to the company trying for years to produce similar comics and was not a new step for them at all. However, not much had progressed in that area until Mort Todd created the Marvel Music imprint in 1994. The problem was that the musical-bio comic-book field was mined out by that point, and the frantic buying by some collectors of issues of the Revolutionary Comics during its hottest period of 1990 through 1992 was now dead. Thus, even with titles about Bob Marley and the Rolling Stones being issued, the interest was dwindling, and only one limited series—another Alice Cooper title, this one called *The Last Temptation*, which was written by famous fantasy writer Neil Gaiman—did well before the line closed after a year.

Before that time was up, however, Marvel Music did release a reprint of the two KISS comics from the 1970s titled *KISS Classics*. The two previous stories appear in full in the reprint, but there are obvious changes made to the material, starting with the artwork for the two earlier KISS comics that appears on the front cover of the reprint. As any KISS fan would note, Paul Stanley's star appears on the wrong side of his face on the second cover artwork due to it being flipped for visual reasons. More striking, however, is that additional artwork can be seen past the villain's head, suggesting that the original cover was also to have been a wraparound like that of *Marvel Comics Super Special* #1, but was cut in half to allow for the solo album ad to appear instead. In addition, updated computerized coloring replaced that of the original hand-drawn coloring, which unfortunately muddies the artwork, while shading to add texture along with some inking changes occurred. These revisions appear in the *KISS Kompendium* as well; in fact, with the removal of a couple of KISS-related ads in the middle of the second story (used to not only promote the PS10 Ibanez guitar and the KISS catalog of albums, but also to allow for two double-page spreads of artwork to appear in the proper order in the book), nearly everything is the same as in the latter reprint hardback book. This includes the eight pages of text between the two stories (one being an article about the KISS comics and the other being a reprint of the "printed in KISS blood" article that appeared in the first KISS comic back in 1977).

One vital piece of material curiously missing from the *KISS Kompendium* that does appear in the *KISS Classics* reprint is that of the splash pages for each book, which gives the names of writers and artists of each comic. The final thing missing from the hardback book that appears in the Marvel Music reprint is an editorial by Mort Todd where he promotes the upcoming *KISSNation* comic book with promises of it being one hundred pages of KISS-related topics and a comic written by Stan Lee and drawn by Nathaniel Palant. This makes sense once the full story is known about what happened there, as *KISSNation* appeared in November 1996 and was not quite what was initially expected

Fans first heard about *KISSNation* in 1994 with an ad promoting the book as a fanzine done by the band itself and published by Marvel. The three-part limited series was to include in each issue a forty-eight-page comic book depicting the band in its original Marvel superhero disguise, along with one hundred pages or more of articles, artwork and photos from fans. Eventually, the comic was advertised with artwork from *Destroyer* and *Love Gun* album cover artist Ken Kelly that was to be a wraparound cover for the first issue and depicting the band members in a parody of the first issue of *Fantastic Four* from 1963.

The final result was released with a lot of alterations, the first and most telling thing being that the book was no longer coming out under the Marvel

Music imprint, but had been incorporated back into the standard Marvel Comic line, as per the Marvel logo appearing on the front cover. Second, the Ken Kelly artwork had been demoted to that of "KISSNation Poster #1" in a foldout inside the front cover (and which, if not for a small appearance within the reprinted article about the Marvel KISS comics that had originally appeared in *KISS Classics*, would not have appeared in the *KISS Kompendium* book at all), while a similar cover with artwork by Dave Chlystek and Eric Lusk replaces it. Third, the forty-eight-page story became forty-five pages and featured the work of artist Nathaniel Palant for about half of the book before Chlystek and Lusk came in to complete the issue. Fourth, the issue had been cut down from the promised 148 pages to that of 100 (counting the cover), with only a small sampling of articles and artwork from the fans (Ron Frederick's rather gutsy probootleg article, for example), while the rest was filler written internally within the KISS Company (such as Spiro Papadatos's article about working on the KISS convention tour) or by writers such as *Metal Edge* editor Gerri Miller.

The most important thing, of course, was the comic, scripted by Stan Lee from a plot developed by editor Mort Todd and Gene Simmons. The story is a mix of crossovers, with the first being a world with KISS from the earlier Marvel Comics meeting up with the X-Men in a fight against monsters (a plot point Simmons insisted on to please his then seven-year-old son). It then shifts to "our world," where the 1995 version of KISS—with Bruce Kulick and Eric Singer—are meeting up with Marvel editors, writers, artists, and evidently anyone else in the Marvel office that could be packed into a two-page spread. This leads to the 1995 version of the rock band KISS meeting up with the superhero versions and the X-Men in a battle with the monsters that ends with the "1995 rock band" Simmons and Stanley driving trucks loaded with KISS stage equipment into the main monsters and destroying them. In the end, it all turns out to be a dream of a kid reading comics.

One can quickly see why Marvel had little interest in continuing the comic after the first issue. With Marvel Music's demise and its creator Mort Todd leaving the company, Marvel had little interest in putting out a magazine full of self-congratulatory articles for a project seen as the crowning achievement of Todd's visionary but short-lived and unsuccessful imprint. Further, the comic is an "everything but the kitchen sink" mess and written in a manner that does not suggest a sequel but namely a wrap-up to the Marvel version of the KISS characters; killing off any additional stories projected for them, since they appear to be merely a figment of a child's imagination. Todd's plea to fans to keep sending in material to use in subsequent issues appears on an ad page near the back of the book and looks like a quick afterthought that Marvel hoped fans would ignore.

Artists Nathanial Palant and Dave Chlystek (who was brought into the production after Simmons had seen his artwork at one of the 1995 KISS conventions) would go on to other projects in fields inside and outside of comics. Palant would work on a series of commissioned artworks for Michael Jackson (including a portrait of the singer that was later sold in 2009), while Chlystek moved on to directing and storyboarding a variety of animated television programs including *Batman Beyond* and *Venture Brothers*. Mort Todd would move back to *Cracked* magazine (which he had been editor-in-chief of back in the 1980s) for a time before moving on to other projects, including some animation work for the Playboy Channel.

Yet this was not quite the end for *KISSNation*. Not happy with the resulting Marvel Comics issue nor the distribution of the comic that saw it have limited success through mostly comic-book shops, the material for the issue was repackaged and reissued as part of a 234-page magazine from *Metal Edge* called *KISS Rocks the World*. The full-size magazine was released in spring 1997, with the first 124 pages of the book being that of interviews, photos, and various other articles about the band as they continued their "1996–1997 Reunion Tour," with the final 110 pages being the updated *KISSNation* comic. Although it was odd to see Marvel-controlled characters in a publication not published by Marvel itself (if KISS seemed concerned about their copyrights, Marvel was a hundred times more so, bringing lawsuits against those that used their characters without permission readily and often), there were logical reasons as to how this occurred. With Gerri Miller aboard on the original Marvel version of the comic, and with her as executive editor of *Metal Edge*—a magazine that KISS was regularly doing interviews for back in the 1990s—it was understandable how the deal would have been worked out among Marvel, KISS and the publisher of *Metal Edge*, Sterling/Macfadden (although curiously, there is no mention in the magazine's publishing credits of the KISS and Marvel characters being copyrighted to their respective owners).

The *KISS Rocks the World* magazine featured a version of *KISSNation* that was only altered in minor ways from the original: articles were repositioned to appear after the comic rather than breaking the comic up, while Miller's article about KISS cover band Cold Gin was replaced with several pages of "KISS News" (ironically, Cold Gin featured future KISS member Tommy Thayer as the "Ace" in the tribute band). Some additional fan letters, photos, and artwork also appeared, but ultimately the look of the material was not much different than had already appeared in the Marvel edition—only bigger and with a few more pages of fan material.

KISSNation was not quite the end of the band appearing in Marvel Comics. In 2002, Steve Gerber agreed to come back to Marvel to writer another *Howard the Duck* series, this time for their imprint called MAX, which did "adult-oriented stories" of which some were based on preexisting Marvel characters (as was the case with Howard the Duck). In the final issue of the six-part miniseries, Howard goes to a bar in hell to meet God. There at the bar was none other than Gene Simmons's Demon character from the original KISS Marvel comics, having a drink. Yet that was just an in-joke. After all, by 2002, the baton had been passed on to another. Twice over, in fact.

Image Comics

The switchover from Marvel to another publisher in 1997 was not very shocking. It was well known to fans at the time that the relationship between Marvel and KISS was dead in the water come 1996 after the release of *KISSNation* #1, as well as the fact that the band had signed on with McFarlane Toys for new action figures to be released. McFarlane Toys was a branch of Todd McFarlane Productions, operated by the famous comic-book writer/artist, Todd McFarlane, who had burst out in comics a few years prior while working for Marvel on several characters, but mainly Spider-Man. McFarlane's work on that character led to him getting a series to write and draw himself about Spider-Man, simply called

Ad for KISS: Psycho Circus: The Nightmare Child. The game was a direct tie-in with the *Psycho Circus* comic book, including the godlike KISS characters as well as cover artwork similar to that seen from the comic. Never missing a trick, the ad reminds readers to check out more details about the comic and action figures.   *Author's Collection*

Spider-Man, which, as per the previous entry, became the best-selling comic Marvel ever released, replacing the first KISS Marvel comic in the list. In 1992, McFarlane and several other comic-book artists broke away from Marvel (and DC Comics to a lesser extent) over creative rights to material and characters (much like the Superman legal fight in the 1970s that drove Gene Simmons from considering DC) to do independently owned comic books under the umbrella company title of Image Comics. In McFarlane's corner of the company, he developed the character Spawn (which would go on to huge success in comics, movies, and television, and continues in one form or another up to the present day) as a comic book, while also looking into creating a series of action-figure toys and statues for teenagers and older collectors who wanted something to display that did not look like it was made for grade-school children. McFarlane Toys was already doing toys based on Spawn when it looked to branch out into making figures based on movie characters (such as Freddy Krueger and Jason of the *Friday the 13th* movies) as well as famous rock musicians, with KISS being the first produced in summer 1997.

With KISS already looking to work with McFarlane on toys back in 1996, it made sense for reporters knowledgeable of the situation to ask if the band would be doing a comic with McFarlane. Such discussion was sidetracked in interviews, even by the usually quite vocal Gene Simmons, which indicated to some fans that there must be something to the rumor. Then in August 1997, the first issue of *KISS Psycho Circus* appeared in comic-book shops through Image. At a time when contractual obligations, production issues, and just plain missed deadlines by the creative staff caused many comics not to be released on time or without the same creative team for very long, *KISS Psycho Circus* had a strong continuous thirty-one-issue run with the same writer, Brian Holguin; inker, Kevin Conrad for all issues, with Jonathan Glapion helping out from issue #28 onward; and only two pencillers: Angel Medina for the first seventeen issues and some additional covers after that, and Clayton Crain from issue #18 onward.

Announced at the time as an extension of the studio album of the same name that the band was working on, that 1998 release would have little in common with the comic beyond that of a circus/carnival theme of the tour and album packaging (with the possible exception of "We Are One" on the album). In fact, the series borrowed more from the *Music from "The Elder"* album, with mention of "The Elder," Blackwell, and a "Dark Light" (all elements from that album). Nor would the series attempt to mimic established character history as set up by Marvel even though it appears that KISS owned the rights to those superhero personas; this was not a series that would see Paul Stanley using his "laser-eye" to mesmerize people while fighting cloaked supervillains. Instead, the series would display the group as "Four-Who-Are-One" of "The Elder;" elemental-like entities that protect the Earth while also involving themselves in the lives of ordinary people by directing them down paths of possible destinies. Surprisingly, the theme is very similar to the three-part miniseries released by Marvel Music back in 1994 for Alice Cooper's *The Last Temptation* album and written by Neil

Gaiman, which featured a carnival "showman" (aka Alice) who tried to steer a boy toward damnation through the various mystical devices available through his "dark carnival." Yet, then again, both borrowed themes from Ray Bradbury's novel *Something Wicked This Way Comes,* mining the same material in different ways and not simply copying the other.

Only rarely in the series are readers given a bit more insight behind the characters, such as issue #9, which digs into the background of the four carnival workers who make up the human alter egos of KISS: Blackwell, the Ringmaster, who is the Demon (Simmons); Fortunado, the clown, who is Starbearer (Stanley); Tiberius, the animal tamer, who is Beast King, aka Beastmaster (Criss); and Stargraves, the Stiltwalker, who is Celestrial (Frehley). Beyond the four, the series had two regularly appearing characters, Kismet—a girl who is the reader's point of view throughout the series—and Madam Raven—a fortune-teller that works as a liaison for the four. Even so, there were the occasional multi-issue storylines that stand out in putting the "Four-Who-Are-One" at center stage. "Destroyer," from issues #10 to #13, has the four fighting the "Nightmare King" (the genesis of which would go on to spark the computer game, *KISS: Psycho Circus: The Nightmare Child,* that had been in development for a time before finally being released in 2000), while the follow-up two-parter, "Year of the Fox," set in feudal Japan, paid tribute to Eric Carr's Fox makeup and character. Yet, for the most part, even stories stretched over many issues tended to fall within the realm of both victims and the guilty tampering with the Elder's domain and facing judgment of one kind or another.

Psycho Circus sold well at first, allowing for an expansion that saw magazine-sized reprints of the comic—usually two issues' worth in each magazine, although the premiere issue had the first three stories—that ran for five issues from October 1998 through April 2000. There were also three paperback collections of several issues released during that time (still a common practice for comic-book publishers once enough issues could be collected to throw four to six issues together in book form). However, even with the dedication of the creative team and a strong publisher behind it, interest in the series waned rapidly after the band had pretty much played out the Reunion/Farewell tours from 1996 to 2000 and the publishers were seeing some diminishing sales from comic-book fans in general. Price increases helped little by issue #30, and so all agreed to wrap up the series with issue #31, which saw the return of a character from issues #1 and #2 to conclude the storyline of the series. Planned later issues of the magazine and paperback reprints were also shelved.

Some KISS fans have different opinions about the series as a whole. Because the focus was not on the four directly, since they were manipulators of events for the characters seen in the spotlight of each issue, some fans who had expected something more like the Marvel comics felt disappointment with the series. Other fans embraced the series and enjoyed it, which certainly shows in the fact that the series lasted nearly three years and thirty-one issues. McFarlane would continue an association with KISS through the action figures, but the year 2000 would see the end of the band's *Psycho Circus* comic, nearly two years after the album it was connected with had been released and quickly disappeared.

Dark Horse Comics

For a time it appeared that Image Comics would become the number-one comic-book company in the U.S., with sales beating out both Marvel and DC at times. Then the comic-book market—which has always been a bit fickle ever since the "collectors" became the focus and it grew into a buyers' market—shifted, with readers looking for other comics beyond what Image was offering. Dark Horse had been around since the mid-1980s and had seen ups and downs enough to have grown from experience and survived where many other publishers had fallen off due to bad marketing and poor sales. Because of this ability to thrive, Dark Horse was gathering some of the readership that had moved on from Image as the new millennium began.

With this came the start of a new KISS comic in July 2002 from Dark Horse, this one simply titled *KISS*. The series began with a three-part origin tale, "Rediscovery," by former *X-Men/Superman* writer Joe Casey and drawn by Marvel/DC artists Mel Rubi and Derek Fridolfs in a style that changed the grit of the Image Comics version into something cleaner and more in an animated style. The story itself is a mixture of both the Image series, the darker "Four Who Are One" characters ,and the Marvel series, with the characters being Gene Simmons and Paul Stanley in recognizable costumes who are superheroes fighting supervillains (typically in this series as part of a group called the Outer Dark). Note that there are characters dressed and acting like Ace Frehley and Peter Criss from the previous comic, but they are never referred to by their names as Simmons and Stanley are, instead being referred to by the names of the Celestrial and the Beast King given them in the Image Comics. Since by this point Frehley and Criss were no longer in the band and Tommy Thayer and Eric Singer had taken over the "roles," it made a certain amount of sense to avoid using the names commonly associated with the comic-book characters.

The origin story was followed by another three-part story from the same creative team based on the Devereux character from the *KISS Meets the Phantom of the Park* movie. Issue #7 saw Marvel associates Scott Lobdell and Peter Vale take over the writing and drawing chores of the book, with Julio Ferreira providing inks. From here through the final issue, the stories become a bit more one-off and traditional in nature, with KISS meeting up with other characters that have some association with the band's musical catalog (a superhero called Mr. Speed and a girl with special powers called Christine 16, for example). The series continues with well-known creator Mike Baron (*Nexus, The Badger,* and several other series) taking over the writing, as Mel Rubi and Derek Fridolfs finish off the series' run as the artists. The series wraps up in issue #13 (released in September 2003) after a four-issue story with the foursome and their newfound friends fighting against "The Unholy." All thirteen issues would be reprinted in paperback form, three issues each except for the final one featuring the four-part finale. Although the series would conclude on an open-end note for possible future stories, it would be another four years before KISS would return to comics.

Platinum Studio Comics/KISS Comics Group

Platinum was another comic book company that kicked off in the later 1990s and had thrived on finding properties that not only sold well with comic-book fans, but also could be sold as projects for both movies and television. (*Cowboys & Aliens* with Harrison Ford and Daniel Craig is an example of one of their projects.) KISS joined the company in March 2007 for the release of a new superhero comic-book series about the band, this time called *KISS 4K*. A big promotional push came with the agreement, with Platinum releasing the first issue in a variety of forms, including a "Destroyer Edition" that was proclaimed to be the largest comic ever produced at a dimension of thirty inches by eighteen inches (making it a bit larger than what had been commonly seen as the world's biggest comic, *Wham-O Giant Comic* #1 from 1967, which was twenty-one by fourteen inches in dimension).

Ricky Sprague wrote the first four issues, and Daniel Campos drew all four along with Kevin Crossley on the first three. Fred Van Lente would take over writing on issues #5 and #6, with Clint Hilinski and Andrew Dalhouse doing the art. And then, things got a bit weird. In March 2008, Platinum announced that, although the comic was selling well, the book would no longer be available for sale at comic-book stores. Instead, every issue from that point on would be posted free on their website www.drunkduck.com with artist/writer Adam Black taking over all duties. Black would complete three issues and most of a fourth before announcing on the website that he was leaving the series due to financial issues.

The premise of the series took a little from all that came before and yet started something brand new as well. With the band finding that they had a destiny to save everyone as superheroes, the four members of KISS began to get used to their powers as they encountered a variety of villains and would eventually try to control an entity called The Unholy (in a similar fashion to that seen in the Dark Horse series). In the web-released issues, the comic brought back both the old wizardlike mentor, Dizzy, from the first Marvel along with Madam Raven from the Image Comics in a storyline that would span the vast storylines created for all of the former comic-book companies. Although the series died before the final storyline could conclude—resulting in nothing else being produced under the KISS Comics Group comic line (a joke name created, no doubt, to parody Marvel and their "Marvel Comics Group")—it does show that even with all the hiccups and dead ends that KISS has seen in their comic book form, in the end they had a long and rich history in the industry.

Meanwhile (as comic-book captions would undoubtedly put it), various others tried their hand at bringing KISS to the printed page.

Revolutionary Comics

The 1980s saw an explosion of black-and-white comic books published by a variety of companies. It is hard to explain in retrospect, but for a time, comic-book fans were looking at such comics as potential investments they could resell for hundreds of dollars years or even just months later. Such speculating came with the mega-success of a comic parodying the then-current storylines in Marvel's *Daredevil* and *X-Men* series called *Teenage Mutant Ninja Turtles*. With its success, many people thought that comic publishing was a goldmine and several companies jumped in, only to quickly find themselves struggling to survive and losing a lot of money in the process when the fan base for such comics quickly burned out due to an abundance of mediocre comics being released.

One company that did well was Revolutionary Comics, which found a niche soon after starting in 1989 by focusing a majority of their efforts on unauthorized biographical comics based on famous rock bands. Of course, with such a setup, it was understandable that KISS would soon become a target for the company, and in March 1990, issue #9 in Revolutionary's *Rock N' Roll Comics* series was released. Written by Robert V. Conte (misspelled as Conti in the credits), with

Revolutionary Comics ad promoting the band's involvement with the comics.

Author's Collection

pencils and inks by Greg Fox and additional inks by Mark Mazz and Mitch Waxman, the issue was titled "KISS—Their Rise to Greatness—And Beyond!!!" and as expected was a brief overview of the band's history in thirty-two pages. Conte would go on to actively work for the band a few years later, helping to put together the remasters of the early KISS albums in the late 1990s as well as contribute to various writings about the band (including one in Metal Edge's version of the *KISSNation* comic).

The issue sold well, seeing two additional reprints as well as a beefed-up, magazine-sized reprint as *Rock N' Roll Comics Magazine* #1. Then in July 1992, Revolutionary did a sequel for their *Hard Rock Comics* line entitled "KISS—Gods of Thunder" on the splash-page, although the front cover states it is "KISS—Tales of the Tours." The comic, written by Spike Steffenhagen and drawn by Scott Pentzer, drew upon information collected through an interview with Gene Simmons and Paul Stanley, which was seen by some fans as a means for the band to help control the content of the unauthorized material being released rather than because they were fans of the company. The issue sold well enough at a time when even people within Revolutionary considered KISS to be a group long forgotten by the public at large, and so the company went ahead with additional interviews for a three-part series—once again created by Steffenhagen and Pentzer—about the band's history that was released from April through July 1993 under the title of *KISS: Pre-History.*

Additional comics were advertised that would come out with the band's acknowledgement (if not handwritten permission), including a one-off adaption of the *Music from "The Elder"* storyline that was to have been released in September 1993, followed by a three-part continuing history of their years out of makeup to be called *The Revenge of KISS* for release starting in October of that year.

Then came the big announcement in *Goldmine* magazine (October 15, 1993) of a huge three hundred-page book from the band that would include one hundred pages of comics, a free CD of rare KISS outtakes, and the band's autograph inside that would be published by Revolutionary Comics. As it turns out, there was some type of miscommunication between the band and Revolutionary on the book, and with the advertisement coming too soon for their taste, KISS pulled all of their agreed-upon work with the company, leaving *KISStory* to sit until 1994 when the band published a similar book themselves to sell to fans. That book would feature a thirty-page biographic comic by the Steffenhagen/Pentzer team, although outside of Revolutionary (which had essentially shut down after the still-unresolved murder of its publisher, Todd Loren), while their Elder comic would eventually pop up in a 1998 Metal Edge special called *KISS Psycho Circus Tour* magazine. With that, the "some say official, some say not" relationship between Revolutionary and KISS ended. But the slew of unauthorized comics did not end nor even begin there.

Other Unofficial Comics

Parodies in comics about KISS were nothing unusual—certainly the popular satirical comic magazines covered them, from *Mad* to *Crazy* (Marvel's parody magazine) to *Cracked* and back to *Mad* again ever since the mid-1970s. Doing a parody as a regular feature, however, was something no one would have touched even with a ten-foot lawyer around. Thus, while a few comedic jabs at the band were present even in comic strips from the daily strip *John Darling* to *Pandora's Box* in *Kerrang* magazine, no one would do so on a regular basis with the exception of the popular Mexican weekly comic *Simon Simonazo*, which ran from 1979 through 1986. Several issues presented a parody of the superhero version of KISS called Chiss (a variation of the word Chis, meaning "piss" in Spanish), which lasted for several issues and was known of and accepted by the band (with rumors that Gene Simmons even collected the issues). The characters, who change into their superhero personas when they urinate, would go so far as to include parodies of Vinnie Vincent's Wiz and Eric Carr's Fox characters in the comic and even have their own special issues before the parent magazine finally ended in 1986.

Still, *Simon Simonazo* was a good example of an exception that proved the rule. It was one thing to do a short satirical comic in the back of a foreign comic and another to try to do something up-front and in a more serious tone in comics, especially with comic-book creators knowing that Marvel had produced a couple of comics using the band's image and possibly that KISS was very particular about how their image appeared in various mediums. Still, with the success of Revolutionary and their rock-music comics, many other companies felt the coast was clear to jump onboard to do similar projects in the early 1990s (including Marvel with their Marvel Music line, which leads right back to the beginning). Two companies that tried to repeat such a success were Rock Fantasy Comics and Personality Comics.

Rock Fantasy tried to play with the concept a bit by creating a fantasy universe for its characters based on rock musicians, turning them into either superheroes or wizards in a multi-issue storyline. KISS would appear in two issues of the twenty-one-part series, #10 and #18; the first entitled "KISS Fights the Shadow of Death." Written by Michael Valentine Smith and drawn by Don Rinehart, Dave Deffner, Ron Hall, Bob Kerr and Sante White (along with Smith), the issue made little sense on its own. A second feature was also included called "KISS This," written and drawn by Peter C. Knight, which was more a parody of Marvel superheroes with KISS appearing rather than a parody of KISS. The second issue, published in April 1992—also written by Smith but drawn by Jerry Minor—was called KISS II" and featured the band finding that their robot twins were destroyed and having to face the Shadow of Death on their own. There was also a second story called "KISS In: Stoned," written and drawn by James Harmon that was a continuation of the "KISS This" second strip from the first issue and showed the band facing off with a villain who wants to use their powers.

Personality Comics released five KISS comics in 1992, two biographical issues under their parent company name, two others under a subdivision name of the company called Celebrity Comics, and a spoof of the band done for another subdivision called Spoof Comics. The first was *Personality Comics Presents KISS* #1 in April 1992, followed in June of the same year with #2. The first, written by Mark Stanislowski and drawn by Joan Pineda, Kelly McQuain, Bob Dignan, and David Rowe, covered the history of the band up to 1991 and Eric Carr's death. The second, written by Amy Wasp-Wimberger, with Ron Fattoruso and Sven O. on the artwork, is a retread of the previous book, starting around the time of the *Lick It Up* album and moving forward to 1991 once again. The second series was called *KISS: Satan's Music?*, and it too lasted two issues. The first issue is rather odd for a comic book—seventeen pages of biographical text about the band, written by Richie Prosch, mixed in with illustrations by Nora Tapp and Kenneth Becker, and thus it does not read like a comic at all, bur more like a children's illustrated book. The issue also came with a series of cutout trading cards that use the illustrations from the book. The second issue was the return of Mark Stanislowski to the writing chores, with no name listed for the artwork. It also is in the same style as the first issue and—remarkably—covers the same material as the first. The final Personality Comic is *KISSES*, which came out in December 1992 from their Spoof Comics line and featured a number of superhero parodies that made the main male character female; and this KISS satire was no different. Writer/artist Allan Jacobsen sets the tone with names such as "Lace Freely" and "Patricia Criss," and the humor never gets beyond that level, but with inks from Mike Halbleib, Kenneth Becker and Keith Quinn, the issue does look the best out of the four, with some solid storytelling. It is unclear is this is the same Allan Jacobsen who would go on to write *The New Invaders* series for Marvel in 2004 as well as become a director for the animated series *King of the Hill*, but if so it would make a certain amount of sense.

With the comic-book industry becoming more sporadic by the mid-1990s, most of these companies were gone. Thanks to Marvel popping back up with the KISS reprints and *KISSNation* in 1995–1996, as well as Image taking off with *Psycho Circus* in 1997, it was no surprise that no one else tried to follow up in their wake, making all of these unofficial comics a very small corner of the KISS universe for many comic-book collectors and KISS fans.

Simmons Comics Group

Although not part of the KISS comics run in any form, the Simmons Comics Group is worth a brief review here with all the other comics related to the band. While Gene Simmons contributed a storyline for an issue of the Simpsons Comic, *Bart Simpson's Treehouse of Horror*, in 2004 ("Bart Simmons: God of Thunder," which has Bart turning out to be the "thunder godchild" of Simmons), the comics listed here are ones that he created the characters in order to go to series under a publishing line. In 2007, just as the band was starting the KISS

The final issue in the four-part miniseries featuring the superheroic KISS with the Archie gang.   *Author's Collection*

Comics Group over at Platinum, Simmons was working with IDW (as mentioned above with Dark Horse as one of the few independent comic book companies to compete well with Marvel, DC, and Image) to create a line of comics under the name of Simmons Comics Group. The line was to start with four comics, three created by Simmons: *Dominatrix, Zipper* (listed as *Gene Simmons' Zipper*), *Gene Simmons' House of Horrors;* and one by his son Nick Simmons, *Skullduggery.* IDW held off on publishing *Skullduggery* after seeing artwork that Nick would later admit was not up to the level it needed to be. Two years later, Nick would redo the artwork for release as a three-issue miniseries known as *Incarnate* through Radical Comics, a comic-book studio cofounded by former KISS photographer

Barry Levine. That series would later face some charges of plagiarism in early 2010 from fans of manga (Japanese comics), with Simmons saying the series were "homages" to said comics and not to be taken as merely copying what had been done before. Nevertheless, Radical canceled a planned paperback reprint of the issues after the accusations went public.

Of the three released through IDW, two lasted six issues and the other only three before being canceled. *Zipper*, about an alien landing on Earth who must stay within his exo-suit that makes him look like a gimp, was written by Tom Waltz and drawn by Casey Maloney. It lasted from November 2007 through April 2008 for six issues and was later reissued as a paperback reprint. *Dominatrix*, written by Sean Taylor and drawn by Flavio Hoffe for the first four issues and Esteve Polls for the final two, is about a professional dominatrix who gains super-powers and becomes a superhero. That series went from August 2007 through January 2008 for six issues and was also collected in a paperback edition. The third, *House of Horrors*, was done on a quarterly basis and ran only three issues between July 2007 and February 2008. It too was released as a paperback reprint. Finally, IDW released a collection of all fifteen issues published by the Simmons Comics Group in December 2009 as the *Simmons Comics Group Omnibus*. With that, the line has issued no other comics.

Even if the Simmons line did not do well, IDW felt strongly enough about the relationship with Simmons to pursue a new comic with the band in 2011 to be released sometime in 2012. Whether the new series lasts as long as *Psycho Circus* or not, one thing is certain: there really will be no end to KISS in comics. No doubt someday another writer will pick up the mantle and the characters of the Demon, the Starchild, the Catman, and Space-Ace and come up with another inventive way to bring them back in the form of comics, even long after the band itself is no more. It is all just a matter of time.

Archie Comics

In June 2011 came the official announcement that deals had been made for the band to return to comics in the next several months, one from IDW Comics that would be an ongoing series, with the part again returning as superheroes to fight evil, and the other a four-part miniseries within the pages of the regular *Archie* series under title "Archie Meets KISS." To some this seemed outrageous, but Archie Comics had been down that road before. Back in 1994, they had done a one-off special edition that saw Archie and his gang meeting up with ultraviolent Marvel character the Punisher. So compared to that (actually quite fun) mashup, Archie meeting KISS didn't seem so strange.

The four issues came out between December 2011 and March 2012 (issues #627–630), with a script by Alex Segura, pencils by Dan Parent, and links by Rich Koslowski. Parent also did covers in the traditional *Archie* style, while alternate covers showcasing the band's makeup were done by artist Francesco Francavilla. Segura no doubt had his hands full while writing the scripts, what with introducing KISS into the series, four villains, reasons for Sabrina the Teenage Witch to be there and a variety of *Archie* characters new and old (probably as an attempt to introduce new—or long-ago—readers to characters from the Archie line while they had an opportunity to do so). Still, Segura throws in enough KISS references to keep fans happy, and Archie and his friends are given enough to do to help defeat the bad guys with the help of KISS. In all, it walked the tightrope of both franchises without doing harm to either.

Perhaps the biggest irony, however, was on the back of the final issue. Appearing there was an ad for a new comic line through *Archie* to arrive in March 2012: Stan Lee Comics. It appears KISS can never quite escape their Marvel beginnings.

24

Toys and More

Fifteen Pieces of KISS Merchandise You Can Put in Any Crazy Pose You Want!

No matter whether a person loves or hates KISS, one thing everyone can agree upon is that the band certainly released a lot of merchandise over the years. Whether that has been a good or bad thing is also a topic of conversation and not just with people who wish to use it as a rather weak argument against the band's success. After all, most popular music acts have had merchandise of one kind or another released that goes beyond simply music on an album—from concert T-shirts to posters and even such items typically thought of only in the KISS camp, such as action figures and lunch boxes. The only difference, as KISS members and the fans have pointed out over the years, is that KISS has always been more honest about it than those who raise their nose at the concept while still accepting the checks. Plus, as stated by Paul Stanley in more than one instance, if fans want to buy a toy with the band's name on it, why is it a crime to make them happy by creating such an item with the band's assurance that they are getting their money's worth? Bill Aucoin also mentioned in a 1980 interview with Pat Bowring for *Scene* that the band had little choice but to get involved when they began seeing people making money off their name and images. This was not only because of worries that fans would think inferior products were being okayed by the band, but also because they realized that if they did not take control, they would soon legally not be able to do so. Thus, best to make sure of what was coming out and making some money, rather than losing out in all ways by not doing anything at all.

Still, hardcore fans are just as likely as those who smirk at KISS to ask at one time or another if maybe the band has pushed the whole merchandising thing too far, especially in the late 1990s when Spencer's (an adult novelty shop in many malls) had so many oddball KISS-related items filling shelves it seemed at times they were not selling anything else. There would even be attempts to create an official physical store for KISS items; the first being KISS World, located for a brief time in Melbourne, Australia, and lasting less than a year due to reasons outside of the band's influence, followed by a KISS Coffeehouse in South Carolina that sells KISS merchandise and continues to bring in fans after five years in existence. Not even the band has been immune to the idea that they may be oversaturating the market with products, with Gene Simmons himself stating in the mid-1980s that they were spending too much time going into warehouses to review new products instead of recording material, and they had lost their focus as a band in the process.

Which may help to explain the lack of merchandise in the 1980s. In the 1970s, the popularity of KISS made them "family entertainment." True, the songs were still material like "Plaster Caster" and "Love Gun," but the parents were not paying that close attention, and the kids did not really care that much either way. Thus, when the eight-year-olds wanted KISS merchandise and the band had no qualms about giving the audience what they wanted, the boom for toys, games, and other kid-friendly items was the way to go. Then the fan base changed in the early 1980s, with many of the kids of the 1970s moving on to other interests just as KISS seemingly disappeared between 1980 and 1984 (that was not quite the case, but as seen in previous chapters, it was an unavoidable image fans had at the time). When the band came back without the makeup and costumes, the fans remaining were teenagers who wanted to break away from being seen as kids and were not interested in lunch boxes or jigsaw puzzles. The band also did not have their comic-book personas to use to advance merchandise ideas, and there really was no want or need for a Bruce Kulick action figure. Thus, the band's merchandise in the 1980s is rather scarce beyond typical concert-event items like T-shirts, posters, and tour books. Even the examples given in the list below from that period are remembered today as a mistake rather than something "cool" or "fun." Besides, as the band was struggling to find a musical direction in the 1980s that would keep their careers going, they realized that there had to be more concentration on getting strong musical material out rather than merchandise.

Which is exactly what occurred . . . until the early 1990s when people within the KISS Company realized how much fans were willing to pay at KISS and record conventions for the makeup-era merchandise. There were also problems in getting new studio albums released due to issues with the record company as well as internal adjustments being made. PolyGram had ongoing reorganization issues throughout the 1990s that had the band bouncing around for a time on various labels within it; meanwhile, after the death of Eric Carr and the tepid reaction to their 1991 release *Revenge*, the band was a bit lost as to what, where, and when new material could be done. Which is why there was a growing tendency of the band to reflect on their past with the tribute album *KISS My Ass* and various video projects as well as the 1995 convention tour rather than focusing on new material—it simply made financial sense. This led to many items released with the makeup personas on them in the 1990s and peaking with the ultimate sales item based on the past—the original foursome getting back together in 1996.

In some ways, the push for more merchandise in the 1990s spelled the end of an era for longtime KISS collectors. What motivated fans to attend KISS conventions in the second place (the first was to see former band members and other KISS-related individuals in person, of course) was a chance to scrounge

Ad for the heavily promoted KISS jackets. *Author's Collection*

around the dealers' tables in hopes of finding the one thing missing from their collection. Once the onslaught of new merchandise came out—from "Black Diamond Lip-Balm" to Christmas ornaments to baby clothes—the dealers at the conventions began filling their tables with leftover items that even Spencer's could not sell. Eventually the conventions would see mostly newer items that held no interest for the fans because they already owned them and/or every other table at the shows had the same things so there was no sense of needing to buy them. With the lack of rarer sale items, the interest in attending such events dried up, and what was once a thriving industry of expos around the country has become relatively rare (although a handful continue to thrive, thanks to bringing other hard-rock acts into the mix of guests).

Still, even with the glut of memorabilia in the past twenty years, there are still many items that stand out on their own for good and sometimes bad reasons. It has certainly been enough to see the release of three different KISS price guides over the years to help define what is available and how much such things are worth, and for KISS to make the merchandise the focus of their second "big" book, *KISStory II* (a book, like many others by the band, that is tantalizing with visuals but lacking in details). It is no mystery about the longevity of KISS collecting; even the most diehard music fans of KISS who concentrate their collection on the vinyl and CDs wishes to have one piece of unique merchandise that they can show off to other fans. Some are instantly recognizable as being collectible; some need a bit of explaining to show what was special about them. Either way, a dig through the clutter turns up the following twenty items that most fans remember from collecting KISS merchandise over the years.

The Gene Simmons Bong

Never an official item released by or for KISS, but you certainly saw enough of these in the late 1970s up to even today. Some are crude-looking bongs with Gene Simmons's face painted on them; others have been huge glasswork contraptions that involve massive extensions for his tongue (usually as some type of holder). Some people may have assumed that KISS would have gone that route at some point, and while the band have certainly danced around with drugs through their music (see Chapter 16 for more details), they never went the route of making official drug paraphernalia. Besides, the business of making bongs for sale in head shops was always a "ground-level" business at best (and sometimes even underground at worst), so worries about copyrights or trademarks were of no concern to people who produced such items. More so, Simmons—a strong and vocal antidrug advocate—would not have gone for doing such anyway.

Legal drugs such as wine and beer, on the other hand, were A-OK for the band to endorse once the reunion tour started, however. This has included a KISS Wine from Celebrity Cellars between 1997 and 2007, hip flasks from various companies since 1998, several shot glasses, and even a one-off KISS Beer in 1996. One would think that putting the makeup back on was driving people to drink.

The Barry Levine Posters

One area KISS always excelled in for merchandise during the 1970s was that of posters. This was not that unusual of a concept at the time—most bands had deals for such posters—and KISS had a handful that were common to see hanging on the walls of the fans. Many of these were collages of photos of the band performing, but two posed photos became the best known of the posters. The same photographer, Barry Levine, also created both.

Fans know the first as the "Spirit of '76" poster, which was used to promote the band's 1976 summer tour. In keeping with America's Bicentennial, the concept was to parody the famous *Spirit of '76* painting created by Archibald MacNeal Willard, only with the four members of KISS instead of the three battle-worn players seen in the painting. At least that was the idea. Instead, the poster is rather more silly than respectful. Paul Stanley looks the best of the group—defiantly marching with his guitar—while to his left is Peter Criss, who looks as if he is not aware that this shot would be the one used. Gene Simmons looks as if he is about to do one of his "angry demon" poses, but his eyes to heaven give off a "God give me strength" look to them, no doubt thanks to a grinning Ace Frehley holding on to him for balance as he looks off-camera. The story goes that Frehley was so tipsy that he had to hold on to Simmons in order to stand up long enough for the picture to be taken, which may further explain Simmons's reaction.

Thus, the whole thing is a bit sloppy, and yet the image is pure rock 'n' roll, with the sense of being patriotic mixed in with a rock rebellion stance and a level of goofy fun that sells the foursome as characters rather than just four guys in a rock band. It became a familiar image for the band in the years following (enough that when it appeared in the pilot episode of the CBS comedy series *WKRP* in 1978—about an easy-listening radio station changing to rock music—it was a plot point of the program and not just for show) and would eventually make it to the cover of Levine's *The KISS Years* photo book in 1997.

The other famous photo by Levine that became a poster is also from 1976 and features the band in full makeup and costume at the top of the Empire State Building. Thinking they would shoot the picture on the main level tourists get to use when visiting one of the tallest buildings in the world, the band were surprised when they were offered a chance to go a level higher with an unobstructed view of the city. From there, Levine had them pose on a ledge that looked to be a much farther drop than it was (a second larger ledge was five feet below where the band posed, so there was no fear of falling to their deaths . . . although a fall probably would not have been much fun anyway). The photo used for the poster and shot on that cloudy day in New York has the black-and-white motif of the band blend in with the city skyline behind them, making it look as if KISS were monsters above the city, unafraid and powerful. The poster released a few months later would become one of the most remembered posters of the band, so recognized that it was eventually used for the cover of the official KISS biography, *Behind the Mask*. Both posters in various sizes and shapes are still available today for fans, showing the durability of the images over the past thirty-five years and how influential Levine's photos were to the band's legacy.

"I Was There" Button

While some fans may not have known that the Cobo Hall shows back in 1975 were being recorded for use on a possible live album (or, for that matter, fans at the other cities where *Alive!* was recorded; see Chapter 14 for more details), the process had changed a bit by the time KISS decided to recorded a follow-up. Ticketholders arriving at the Los Angeles Forum on August 26 through the 28, 1977, received a black metal button that said "I Was There," with the "S" written in the same lightning-bolt font used in the KISS logo. The button, of course, was to let fans proudly announce to others that they had attended the recording of the new live album (which was dependent on people knowing what the button meant, but anyone curious enough to ask would certainly find out soon enough). Many official buttons of the same size or bigger were released in the late 1970s, some even promoting particular tour events, but because this one was for the album and because so many people attending these shows eventually would throw out their buttons or pass them on to other fans, the "I Was There" button has become quite a collectible.

KISS Poseable Figures/Action Figures

In 1978, KISS went full-swing into getting products out for the younger fans. Many of the better ones appear below, but the most memorable of them all and the one fans clamor the most to find in complete form, is the KISS Poseable Figures, commonly referred to as the KISS Dolls. Some of these items (such as the lunch box) were reinvented in the 1990s, but none had the longevity of that of the action figures in various forms; beginning with Mego, a company probably best remembered for their series of poseable six- to eight-inch dolls in the 1970s of various superheroes from both Marvel and DC Comics. The company had done well with their expansion into more such dolls for generally a boy-friendly audience, and would soon obtain deals to make dolls based on television characters (like those from *Welcome Back, Kotter, Star Trek, Happy Days*, and *Dukes of Hazard* as well as movie properties like *Planet of the Apes* and *The Wizard of Oz*). Around 1975 the company also began creating dolls based on pop stars, such as the Captain and Tennille, Sonny and Cher, and Diana Ross (coincidentally, both Cher and Ross would become well-known girlfriend of Gene Simmons in the late 1970s; which probably was not the reason he dated them, but did make "fantasy doll-time" with the Gene doll and those of Cher and Ross more interesting for kids).

KISS seemed a natural for the company. They were famous pop stars, had a great visual look for such figures, were popular with kids, and even had a movie coming out where they possessed superpowers. What really sold the deal for Mego to pursue the band was that some of the executives' kids were hoping to see KISS dolls, so there were personal reasons as well as professional ones to obtain KISS for the line. However, once everyone agreed to the concept, there were still things to be done before such a line could be put on the market—mainly getting approval from the band members of how the figures looked. Mego at first thought they could go with identical heads and bodies for the over twelve-inch dolls, as it would make them cheaper to produce, but the band was not happy with the idea—especially Simmons, who wanted his doll to have the tongue sticking out in order to make it more unique than the others. Eventually Mego agreed to use new sculpted heads for the members, with the exception of Paul Stanley, who got the same head sculpt for his doll as was used for the Captain in the Captain and Tennille set (admittedly, with the makeup on, it looks close enough to Stanley that not many noticed anything odd about it). The bodies for the figures were also a common "skinny" model used for most of the "real people" figures produced, and thus the first shipments of the dolls found the four with the body of Sonny Bono and Paul Stanley with the head of the Captain. Some people at Aucoin were not happy with the rather anemic bodies for the dolls, and eventually the figures were retooled with muscular bodies, making the value shoot up over the first produced figures (and explaining why collectors sometimes refer to the earlier versions as the "skinny" KISS dolls).

The hardest part for Mego was not the bodies, or even the costumes—which were variations of those worn by KISS at the time and commonly referred to as the *Love Gun* costumes—but rather the makeup on some of the faces. Peter Criss's was the most complicated of the four to do, with white, black, green, red, and silver to be painted in various places on the face. Peter's figure was also the least produced of the four; not due to time-consuming paint jobs, but due to Mego hedging on producing a large number of Peter Criss dolls after hearing rumors that he would soon depart the band (he would, but it would be a couple of years later and mostly after the doll line had run its natural course).

Each doll was sold separately in boxes featuring a photo by Barry Levine that shows the band standing on clear pedestals; the photo also made its way to becoming a poster (see first entry above for more Levine-created posters). With the packaging looking the same, a small window was carved out on the right side of the box so that buyers knew which doll they were buying of the four. Drawings of guitars and a drum were also printed on the packaging for kids to cut out and put with their dolls.

Some fans have gone as far as creating and/or finding proper-sized replicas of instruments for the band to hold that look more authentic, but Mego never went beyond the four dolls for KISS. Not that they did not try. The company came up with a few ideas and even prototypes to help extend the line of KISS accessories while contracted with the band, but none were ever released to the public. This included KISS Bendables—small bendable versions of the band members—as well as walkie-talkies with the KISS logo on them and a camping set for the dolls (including an inflatable tent, four sleeping bags, what looks to be a guitar but would have been about the size of a ukulele for the figures, and a raft . . . because who would not want to shoot the rapids in makeup in platform shoes). Still, although the line started and ended with just the four figures, it was still a solid success for Mego and even warranted a television commercial, which told kids to pose the figures in "any crazy pose."

But the high of that period would soon dissipate, and by the early 1980s, not only was the interest in kid-friendly merchandise dying out with KISS fans, but Mego was struggling to survive after passing up the chance to get the *Star Wars* franchise in 1977. Soon, the Mego dolls were turning up on remainder shelves for $1–$2 each. Of course, as is sometimes the case with collectibles, what was once found so cheaply is now hard-to-find, and the dolls go for hundreds of dollars if complete and in the original boxes, and ironically with the $2 stickers still on them. After Mego and the taking off of the makeup, the interest in more figures died out, although some fans would eventually begin making customized version of the Mego dolls of future KISS full-makeup members like Vinnie Vincent and Eric Carr in order to "complete" the series.

Ad for the action figures done in the 1990s for KISS by
McFarlane Toys. (Paul Stanley's poodle not included.)

Author's Collection

The 1990s renaissance for KISS in makeup saw a return of the band to the
area of poseable figures, or action figures, as they are commonly called today.
KISS had started a relationship with Todd McFarlane by 1997 (see Chapter 23
for more details about McFarlane) that would eventually lead to the long-lasting
Psycho Circus comic-book series from Image Comics, but the bigger goal at
the time was to put together a set of new KISS figures, most of which were six
to seven inches tall. The first series, released in June 1997, has the four band
members in similar outfits to those for the Mego dolls, but as if from an alternate
universe where the band evidently would go on dangerous safaris in order to
play gigs. These came with a number of accessories for each figure—mostly
of a sharp, stabby kind (spikes, swords, etc.) for the members to wear, as well
as a block-formed letter in each package to form the KISS logo (some editions replaced these with miniature solo albums in either gold or black for the
"records" included).

In 1998 came a sequel series, with each member appearing as his counterpart from the *Psycho Circus* comic book along with a figure that was the character's "human" counterpart within the series. More dangerous weapons appeared as well: Gene Simmons had a dragon's head that shot a fireball, Peter Criss came with a ferocious cat and a whip, Ace Frehley shot spears out of his armbands, and Paul Stanley had a poodle. (With makeup on its face. Okay, Stanley had a sword as well, but it was hard to get past the whole poodle thing.)

A third series came out in January 1999 that featured the band in new costumes similar to the ones they wore on the *Psycho Circus* tour, hence the series being called the "Tour Edition." Each member had accessories that were guitars or drums, and each had a facial expression that made him a bit more menacing. A stand-alone twelve-inch Simmons figure was also created at the time in the same style as the series, and another twelve-inch Simmons would be produced for the subsequent series released in September 2000 that shows the band as they appeared on the cover of *Alive!* (although it would be October 2001 before the twelve-inch *Alive!* Simmons figure appeared on the market).

July 2002 saw the release of the next series, which was called the "Creatures" series, although the figures, costumes, and makeup were based on what the band wore at the Palladium in 1980, which would place it during the *Unmasked* period. Eric Carr in an early version of his Fox makeup replaces Peter Criss in the lineup for the figures, making it the first time Carr was represented in any of the action-figure series. A deluxe edition was also released that had all four figures together with musical equipment included in the separate boxes. A twelve-inch version of the Gene Simmons figure came out just as with the previous two series, this one in August 2002, while six-inch head busts of the original foursome appeared in March 2002.

After this, the sets became a bit more restrictive, but still innovative, with August 2004 seeing a box set of the foursome appearing as they did on the cover of *Love Gun* and with three females groupies at their feet. October 2005 saw two three-piece sets released, one for Simmons and one for Stanley, featuring them in various costumes and poses—mainly the same ones from the previous three sets. As could be guessed by fans at the time, no such three-packs appeared for Frehley and Criss, as those members were long gone from the band and not seen as marketable. After that, McFarlane and KISS severed their relationship, and the KISS line through McFarlane ended. Other companies have done figures during and since that time—a couple of twelve-inch sets of the band from *Destroyer* and *Love Gun*, along with "jack in the boxes" that all came out of Art Asylum between 1998 and 2001, three-inch set of figures released in 2009 by Super Stars, and twelve-inch figures of Simmons and Stanley from a company called Medicom in 2010—but action-figure sets of the four members have yet to be revived once McFarlane stepped away.

That still leaves McFarlane with an eight-year legacy of toys for KISS, which lasted much longer than the one Mego had with the band. However, it is the Mego dolls that everyone remembers and clamors to obtain. Some may say this is due to the first few McFarlane figures being a tad on the silly side ("Look! Paul has a poodle!"), but this is mainly due to how the collectibles market has changed since the 1970s. Back then, the only buyers were a handful of oddball KISS collectors and a majority of kids who actually played with the dolls, lost parts, blew them up with firecrackers, etc. Since the 1980s, people have collected items mainly for resale purposes, which created short-term demand for them when they first appear, but little interest in the resale market because everyone has at least two of each in their own collection. Thus, the McFarlane toys are still pretty easy to find in good shape and even in their original packaging, while the Mego dolls are elusive to find complete, much less in their boxes.

The Lunch Box

In 1953, the Thermos Company hit upon a creative idea for the metal lunch boxes they were producing for kids to use at school each day—why not put popular characters on the containers so that kids can show off their interests? Their first release with Roy Rogers that year was a huge success and kicked off what would become the norm for Thermos and other companies producing lunch boxes ever since: media-related lunch boxes.

Renamed the King-Seeley Thermos Company in 1962, the company made a deal with KISS to produce the first KISS lunch box in 1977. Another Barry Levine photo—again from the clear pedestal *Love Gun* shoot also used for the Mego KISS dolls—was used for the front of the box, with a picture of the band on the *Love Gun* tour stage on the back and pictures of each member

The KISS lunchbox—one of the first pieces of KISS merchandise kids got in the 1970s.   *Author's Collection*

along the sides. Included with the lunch box was a "roughneck" thermos (so called because they were supposed to be unbreakable, unlike earlier lunch box thermoses) featuring drawings of the four along with the KISS logo. King-Seeley also produced a backpack for school-aged children in 1977, featuring the same Levine photo used on the front of the lunch box and which is also very collectible (and no doubt harder to find than the lunch box).

Back in the early 1980s, truckloads of these lunch boxes turned up at discount department stores like Big Lots in mint condition and usually for around $3. This explains why so many of them are still available today in great condition on the collectors' market—having never been used and thus not suffering from the rust common on such collectibles after years of having liquid and other food products in them—although prices can still be a bit steep for them.

NECA (National Entertainment Collectibles Association), which specializes in creating various merchandise for movies, musicians and others, produced at least seven different KISS lunch boxes sold through music and comic-book shops in 2000. Some of these included thermoses with the theme of the boxes reproduced on them, which were sold with or separately from the lunch boxes. These lunch boxes and thermoses still turn up regularly in the collectibles market for both KISS and lunch boxes. As with the action figures listed above, it is the 1970s variation that the collectors really seek to buy.

Toy Guitar, Amp, and Microphone

Carnival Toy Manufacturing Corporation of New York was a company that lasted for several years making a variety of inexpensive plastic toys—both of a generic kind and those related to famous names, such as Disney. In the 1970s, Carnival produced a toy guitar featuring a photo (once again a Levine picture) of the band on the guitar's body and a KISS logo on the head in some cases (other times the head was left blank). The KISS logo also appeared down the neck of the guitar on a few produced by the company. The guitar came with a pick and either in a box or on a card that was shrink-wrapped in plastic.

Of the toys released in the 1970s for the band, this 1977 item is one of the rarest. In fact, it was not unusual for many diehard fans to have never seen one up close, much less heard anything about the toy back in the 1970s. The guitar was followed up with a KISS "Microphone and Amp" set that was essentially a cheap plastic microphone attached to a little speaker with a KISS logo on one corner of the "amp." A catalog from Carnival at the time showed pictures of a complete "Concert Set" available, which had the guitar, microphone, and amp together in one box and ready for use by fans. Although one catalog ad showed a plug-in for the guitar and amp, the guitar body appears to have never been built for such a plug-in.

Record Player

Tiger Electronics had just opened shop when it got the deal to produce a kids' record player for the 1978 Christmas season. The player was a suitcase-shaped box with a picture of the band onstage that was the same photo as on the back of the lunch box from King-Seeley that opened up to reveal a large sticker inside the lid. The inside sticker was a large KISS logo and four pictures of the band members from the *Alive II* album cover. The player was pretty much standard-issue for such products made for children: a turntable made for 45s, but with large enough clearance in the box to accommodate larger vinyl and with two speeds for 33 1/3 and 45 RPM records.

The player remained on shelves for only a short time before being retired, although why appears to be lost in the ether. Tiger would go on to create a number of electronic toys and games after that, including the well-received Furbys as well as toys for movies and famous characters. Yet, because of the brief public marketing of one of their first toys, KISS fans still clamor to find the record player—especially one that is still in good working condition—in an era when most people do not even have any vinyl in their collections.

Colorforms/Rub n' Play Sets

It is easy for people to get these two toys mixed up—both Colorforms and Rub n' Play were produced by the same company (Colorforms Corporation), and both were in some ways similar in that they involved sticking pictures of people and objects onto other surfaces. They also came in similar-sized boxes, although the Colorforms one features the Levine *Love Gun* picture once again, while the Rub n' Play set used artwork to show what the toy was meant to do.

While the Colorforms are easier to find in the collectors' market, they are also more fun to play with than the Rub n' Play set. The Colorforms were pieces of vinyl shaped like characters and objects that can be stuck onto a polished surface, such as the box-sized card inside the packaging that showed a scene—in this case a mad scientist lab where a guitar-shaped laser is zapping a "KISS Tonight" sign on top of a building in a city. The little booklet with the set states that the person playing has to "help KISS defeat their evil enemy, the Mad Rock Promoter."

The Rub n' Play set from 1979 has a drawing of Ace Frehley, Peter Criss, and Gene Simmons watching as Paul Stanley goes about rubbing the pieces of paper onto the cards included within the box. The point of the set is clearly explained on the box—the buyer gets eight cardboard figures that they can punch out from the boards within the set, and each figure is blank in areas where you then rub the transfers from paper sheets included within the set in order to finish creating the KISS figures. You then can stand the figures up and . . . look at them. Maybe pat yourself on the back for a job well done.

So it is easy to see why the Colorforms set was more fun to play with. Of course, both were quickly made less than mint for collectors by anyone who actually played with the sets (which, after all, is the whole point of buying any toy or game). Pieces were quickly lost in the Colorforms set, and there was no way to do anything with the Rub n' Play set without making it nonmint in value, which is another reason why both are considered quite collectible in complete form by fans.

And we managed to get through all that without one observation about KISS and the term "rub n' play." Until now, that is.

Remote-Control Van

Another true rarity among KISS collectors is this 1977 release from Azrak-Hamway, who produced a number of both simple and more sophisticated toys under their name and that of Remco (Remco released the very collectible *KISS Your Face* makeup kit in 1978). The radio-control van is red or shocking orange-pink with an orange strip on the top that has the KISS logo on it and a decal showing the band from the cover of the *Destroyer* album on both sides of the van. The plastic exhaust pipes on the side and the rear bumper had a tendency to fall off the van after some use, and thus are sometimes missing on ones sold in the collectors' market. This came with a handheld pinkish transmitter to get the battery-operated van to move forward, backwards, and make turns. Packaging sometimes mentions the three available directions of the van ("3 Function Van") or just says it's a "Radio Controlled Van" (a Canadian edition of the van also appeared with info written in French). Some of these sold in their original box have a stand-up tag on the back of the box that displayed a picture of the band (once again, a Levine photo) and the legend about the "3 Function Van." This allowed for the plastic window into the box to show more of the van than in the "Radio Controlled Van" box, which showed the band in the same picture on the top of the packaging and with a smaller window for the van.

Combined with the scarcity of the product (as with the Toy Guitar, a lot of fans never even saw one of these until the 1980s when they began popping up at the KISS conventions), the tendency of pieces to fall off, and the van simply not functioning after a certain amount of time, it is considered a real achievement to get the van in a collection. With that in mind, it is easy to see why it was not a big seller at the time—it is an ugly, remote-control van with only the KISS stickers on it to make a connection with fans and was priced out of the range of kids at the time of release. Although collectors may clamor today for the item, none of the reasons seem to suggest that the item represents fun to anyone then or now.

Radio

This was certainly not a flashy product when it came out. The pocket (so called because it could easily fit in a shirt or pants pocket) transistor radio was released in 1977 through a mail-order campaign of magazine ads, flyers that came with certain KISS albums, and television ads. There is very little information in the packaging for the radio with the exception of a copyright notice from KISS/ Aucoin Mgt. Co. on the radio and the box it came in. The packaging and the radio have the same photos—the Levine *Love Gun* picture once again—used on one side and some separate shots of each band member on the other side. The KISS logo also appears on both faces of the radio as well as on the sides, and the controls at the time (giving the buyer the choices of volume and tuner) say simply, "KISS RADIO."

Because it was mail-order-only, many fans never got around to buying one, which is why it is so collectible today. Those same fans, however, do remember the cheesy ad for the radio that used to run on television stations during cartoon shows and after-school programming. The ad was nearly as cheap-looking as the one done for the following item on the list.

Jacket

A few clothing items that were not typical concert T-shirts made their way to the fans in the 1970s, such a bedsheets and pajamas, but the KISS jacket was unique in that—as with the KISS radio listed above—it was sold exclusively through mail order, including very cheap television ads. The jackets came out in 1978 from Atex USA, which these days creates specialty protective clothing for a variety of professionals dealing with hazardous materials. The material used for the jackets were a DuPont-created material called Tyvek (again, used in short-term hazard protection these days) and were bright, multicolor affairs suggesting flames with the KISS logo on the front and back and additional drawings of the four members on the back. A 1979 follow-up had a black jacket with red lightning bolts on one shoulder and flames around the cuffs. The back shows a drawing of the band. A 1980 edition done for the Australian market has Eric Carr on the back instead of Peter Criss.

As with the KISS radio, because sales were mail order, many fans never got around to buying one. Of course, the style was so cheap-looking and tacky it was an easy thing to resist at the time. Still, although KISS would come out with other jackets over the years, including incredibly silly ones for the KISS Army in the 1990s that gave you a choice of either a raised fist or raised finger on the back as a demonstration of "defiance," perhaps it is just as well that the Atex jackets are the best remembered of the bunch.

On Tour Board Game

This board game is another piece of 1970s memorabilia that somehow got past many fans at the time. It came in a blue box with Ken Kelly's artwork from the cover of *Love Gun* appearing (at least it was a break from the Barry Levine photo for once on merchandise). American Publishing Corporation, who released the game in 1978, produced a number of games and puzzles based on various licensed books, movies, and stars (a board game based on *The Hobbit* animated television special that ran in 1976 and a Superman sliding puzzle are a couple of examples of their work). American Publishing also produced two 200-piece jigsaw puzzles—one of the *Destroyer* album cover and the other of the *Love Gun* artwork—that same year in boxes roughly the same size as the board game's.

The game was very bare bones when it came to its layout and pieces. Generic plastic pawns for the players' markers, dice, and various cards to pick when landing on certain spaces came in the box for a game board resembling a star. Most fans find the game interesting to play once. Once. Thus, another item where having the item is of more interest than the item itself. There would be other puzzles—especially the better-known and also collectible Milton Bradley jigsaw puzzles of each band member that came out in 1978—and other games, especially after the 1996 reunion, but the American Publishing products hold a special place in the hearts of collectors.

The KISS radio—an AM/FM radio with the band's picture and logo slapped on it.   *Author's Collection*

View-Master

Back in the days before home video became the norm, or even possible, if someone wanted to watch any type of visual presentation in their own home, they either had to get a movie camera and projector or go the other route of having slides made to show on a projector. Besides making for various uncomfortable get-togethers to show off the latest vacation snaps, it also allowed people to see pictures from special events, movies, and television. Added to this was the concept of stereoscopic photography, which allowed a viewer to use a device to look at pictures in such a way that it created the illusion of a three-dimensional image. Usually these appeared as cards holding two images to be slid into a device for viewing. View-Master came up with the idea of created a circular pattern of pictures for a device so that, with one click, the viewer could see a number of images in 3-D.

Like so many other KISS products at the time, View-Master had licenses with a number of companies to produce such "reels," with KISS just being one more in the bunch. View-Master did manage to get three different items released within a year's time in connection with the band: the View-Master Three-Reels, a Double-Vue cartridge, and the Show Beam cartridge. The Three-Reels (copyrighted 1979) is the best known of the trio, as not only is it common to see for sale in the collectors' market, but also it is easier to obtain the equipment in order to watch it (since View-Masters are still being made to this day). What is also intriguing about these reels is that they contain pictures of the band not commonly seen in various magazines, etc., as they were photographed in order to show up the 3-D feature of the slides. These pictures also contain one of the first images of an "Axe Bass" for Gene, although the pictures show an early prototype and not the one that would become more well known from the *Dynasty* tour onward (in consequence, the bass, created by Steve Carr, is referred to at times by fans as the "View-Master Bass"). Thus, there is much interest in seeing the pictures as well as making the reels part of a collection.

The Double-Vue cartridge released in 1979 was for a device called the Double-Vue Movie Player. It was a movie-camera-like device with a slot allowing for a cartridge that contains two strips of film to rotate in loops. When viewers finished one loop, they could pop out the cartridge, turn it over, and watch the other film, hence the "Double Vue." The KISS cartridge included footage of the band live onstage on one loop and the film made for the "I Was Made for Lovin' You" music video on the other loop. Neither had sound, but that was a small price to pay for being able to watch KISS footage any time one wanted.

The final View-Master release was the Show Beam cartridge in 1980. This was a small boxlike cartridge that could be put into a flashlight device called the Show Beam, and then images from the cartridge could be shown on any surface, much like a handheld slide projector. The thirty images within the cartridge appear to be drawings of the band in superhero action.

Both the Show Beam and Double-Vue sets are harder to find as the interest is somewhat less since they require special equipment to play.

Trash Can

The Trash Can from 1977 actually was much more common in fans' collections than some of the other items listed here, as it was readily available and certainly of practical use. On the other hand, like the metal lunch box released, many of these trash cans shows signs of rust and wear after having been used for their true purpose as trash receptacles.

The manufacturer, P & K Products, an aluminum company that makes a variety of metal products such as flag and traffic poles, also creates novelty products for sports and entertainment figures, including hardhats and trash cans with emblems and pictures of popular personalities. Like similar cans from the company over the years, the KISS trash can features a number of photos of the band, including two large ones that wrap around it: one of the band in a stage pose that was also used for the cover of the record player, and the other a posed shot of the band from the same session that created the "Evolution of KISS" booklet in the *Alive II* album. The only problem with the second photo is that it is reversed, giving Paul Stanley his star over the wrong eye—a mistake perhaps common to magazines at the time but rarely seen on merchandise released for the band. Even so, it is an item fondly remembered by fans, although it may seem a tad strange for a trash can to be an objective of a collector.

Platinum Express Card (1987)

This entry does not refer to the Visa Platinum card released in the late 1990s that featured the band and allowed owners to get special "privileges" connected to the band, such as the *Second Coming* video documentary and discounts on merchandise at Spencer's. Nor does it refer to the "Feed the Children" cards given out at the time of the *Psycho Circus* tour that promoted the band's charity and using never-issued KISS Visa Platinum card faces on the front. It also does not refer to another Visa card released in 2007 in connection with the band. This is instead about the Platinum Express card released in conjunction with the *Crazy Nights* tour of 1987–1988 that turned out to be a rarity in many ways. First, it was one of the few band products during the nonmakeup era not related to the makeup era; second, it was a product, not a tour item in the sense of the word typical of that period; and, third, it was a promotional-only item, of which very few were released. It would also prove to be one of the biggest headaches for the band, the KISS Company (which received numerous confused calls about it), and fans who paid good money for one. A headache that still pops up even today.

The concept was simple: The KISS Company decided to create a gimmick that would attract people in the industry to check out the band on their next tour—which would have been the 1987–1988 *Crazy Nights* tour—and give KISS a good word in the press, etc. The concept worked like this: The recipient would get an envelope from the KISS Company that contained a small white folder inside featuring a faux American Express card on the cover of the folder. The card pictures a frowning Beethoven wearing shades inside of a circle-slash at the center, with the words "KISS Platinum Express Lifetime Member" and a 1-800 number to call printed on the card's face.

Inside the folder was a placement holder for a real metal card with the same design as seen on the front cover of the folder, along with the recipient's name and a serial number embossed. There was also text to the left of the card holder that butters up the person, saying the card is "good for two tickets to any KISS concert . . . anytime . . . anywhere in the world." Upon passing along the name and serial number given on the card, two tickets and backstage passes would be saved at the box office for the person—or someone else they wanted to pass them on to—for the show of their choice.

This, as could be expected, was a casual, even jokey, invitation to get industry people to see the band perform. It was pure hype to many but a nice gesture, nevertheless. Moreover, one has to remember that during this period the band was very receptive to meeting people backstage before a show (or, at least, allowing people to come backstage and perhaps meet a member or two). After all, fan club owners and fanzine creators at the time knew that a call to the KISS Company would commonly get them passes and tickets if they asked, so there was a friendly attempt to "meet and greet" people before a show. Yet, as the people in fandom realized, the main concept was strictly, "This is nice, but don't expect it to go on forever." In other words, the thinking at the KISS Company was, "If anyone uses their card, it will be once, and then they will throw it away."

That is not how it worked in reality, however. True, a majority of these sent out to industry people went straight into the trash, as a good number had no interest in bothering with getting tickets to see the band. The KISS Company itself ended up sending out far fewer than originally expected (rumor is that less than a hundred left the company), leading to an avalanche of folders eventually working their way into the collectors' circle, as cards were eventually destroyed or never produced. The few that survived made their way to "friends of friends" or were sold on the open market to KISS fans. Even that would not have been a huge headache (beyond that of the KISS Company having fans calling the number so they could "see if Paul or Gene were there," but then again their number was easy to find for resourceful fans anyway), but fans misunderstood the nature of the card.

Perhaps such a mistake was understandable. Nowhere on the card or in the folder does it state that the recipient could only use the card once, or even that it had a limited life span. Having the face of the card state "Lifetime Member" also gave rise to the thinking that there was something eternal about it. To fans who heard about the card, it seemed like a "golden ticket," one that would allow them to repeatedly see KISS, forever and ever. As long as they held on to the card and called the number—boom! Two fresh, free tickets and backstage passes to see KISS! Why, some fans would pay anything to get something like that.

And they did. Cards began selling for hundreds, even thousands of dollars from the original recipients to fans. Fans would then call the number and try to obtain tickets. For some of them, this worked fine, as the card had not been used and therefore two tickets were obtained for shows. Some early owners even got the chance to use their card more than once (this was especially true during the *Crazy Nights* tour itself). That was not the case for everyone, though. Soon people at the KISS Company decided that a few fans who managed to use the card more than once—simply due to oversight—were looking to abuse the system. Worse, it was setting up a scenario where people that KISS did not want to see backstage at shows (and KISS did have some crazed fans like this) could end up repeatedly showing up before concerts and causing disruptions. Thus, the KISS Company made clear that from that point on that the cards were one-time offers and then would no longer be available for reuse.

This caused a bit of a rift for fans who had received the card—they had counted on going back again and again to get such freebies from KISS but now found they only got a limited chance to use the card (and in many cases only once). That was still better than the fans who paid high prices for cards already used. As could be expected, such individuals wanted to find someone to blame for this and concluded it was the band ripping them off, but this made little sense. The band had sent out the cards free to people with no suggestion that they could be used multiple times or could be sold to someone else to be used. There was also no guarantee on the card or folder that the cards would be some magical passkey to a KISS show from that point into infinity. One could even say that the KISS Company was kind enough to bother allowing some fans to use the card when it was clear they were not the intended owners or had used them more than once in some cases.

Still, the rumors circulated about the "free KISS tickets" Platinum cards for many years until the band felt forced to make an official announcement at the time of the reunion tour in 1996–1997 that the cards were valid for one-time use only and warned fans not to buy the card from others if they expected to use it. Some later recipients of the unused cards found that KISS at least still allowed the card to be valid for tickets (but not backstage passes) even into the postmillennium tours, so one could say that the band did their best to deal with the problem in the most positive way possible.

Still, for a product that was done mainly as a promotional gimmick to entice the "right people" to the shows, it ended up sending the wrong message to some fans, with only the sellers who had found suckers to pay large amounts of money for them gaining anything out of the deal. A small connection on the other side of the fence to this: Ace Frehley had created a Rock Soldiers fan club for his solo appearances where members who paid a certain amount got a chance to go backstage and meet him in person. Once the reunion tour happened, some of these Rock Soldiers members thought it would mean they could go backstage at the KISS shows to meet at least Frehley if not the others. They quickly found out that such membership freebies were long-gone; another case of "special privileges" certain fans felt they had that became void in the wake of the reunion tour.

Autographed "Award Plaques"

The 1990s saw a revival of interest in the 1973–1982 masked version of KISS, and—understandably—with it came increasing attempts by the KISS Company to make some money from it. Some of these items made sense; T-shirts with the old album cover images, the *KISStory* books (the first, a pictorial history of the band; the second, a history of merchandise), even collectible plaques showing the official trademarks for the band's makeup stand out as things that could interest fans.

Then in 1995, KISS began selling Gold and Platinum Award replicas for the albums *Alive!* and *Destroyer*. These were different from later official and unofficial releases from KISS, which mimic the look of such awards in only vague ways, while the two released in 1995 were certified replicas acknowledged by the Record Industry Association of America (RIAA) who normally present such awards to musicians and others. The plaque on the award makes no mention of any individual and states that each was a "commemorative limited edition" and then gave the number of the award in the series made. A Certificate of Authenticity that came with the awards stated that a limit of 10,000 of the Platinum Awards and 5,000 of the Gold Awards were available, although it is clear that the band did not release that many of these.

The reason why is pretty simple—although they looked to be rather good replicas and official ones at that, KISS was selling the Gold Awards for $500 each and the Platinum Awards for $550 each. Of course, fans did have the opportunity to get the awards signed on the glass by the current members of the band for $100 on the Gold Awards and $150 on the Platinum. Which was the catch—it was the band lineup of 1995, which included Bruce Kulick and Eric Singer. It would have been one thing to have the four sign an award for *Revenge*, which featured all four members, or even an album like *KISS My Ass*, which at least came out in their era. Asking fans to pay $700 for an award replica signed by two members who did not even perform on the albums the awards were for seemed to either be very shortsighted or a symptom of seeing fans as suckers. Another reason why so few made their way out into the marketplace, even after the band attempted to sell a few on the reunion tour the following year.

Trailer Hitch

As mentioned earlier in this chapter, the reunion tour saw a heavy load of new merchandise released for the band, most of which were variations of products from the 1970s. What made the trailer hitch that came out a few years back was that it was a replica of an earlier product while at the same time not the same product. Novelli Creations, which makes metal products, put out many items for the band—shot glasses, jewelry, flasks, and even belt buckles that showed either the KISS logo or the KISS Army logo. Those last two were also turned into trailer hitch covers, which made a nice way to protect such a hitch on a truck or car while at the same time throwing in some nostalgia value by having the hitch cover look like the old belt buckle released in the 1970s for the band. Not everything released had to be something outrageously new or fancy, and this showed a bit of ingenuity in making a product to put the band's name on.

Condoms

There is an old line from *West Side Story* that goes, "From Womb to Tomb," and the following two items pretty much get that point across. KISS is no stranger to condoms as the band has used such products for publicity reasons since the late 1980s for certain singles, albums, and videos. It was 2002 when commercially available condoms connected to the band came out (yeah, yeah, go ahead, there is no way to avoid these puns when writing about the product) through Global Protection Corporation. The "KISS Kondoms" (yes, with a K for the C) came in three styles: "Love Gun Protection" (with the "Spirit of '76" Levine picture returning to KISS merchandise once again), "Studded Paul" (showing Stanley with studs on his outfit), and "Tongue Lubricated" (guess who). Three condoms, or Kondoms, were included in each pack.

As expected for a novelty series—which Global Protection would do for any company interested in selling condoms with their company's name on them—the product died out quickly. In 2011, another company—this one called Condomania—announced a new series of KISS Kondoms that also feature a cartoon drawing of Gene Simmons in makeup with a large tongue printed right on the condom itself—which the company claims makes it a first in having full-color printing on condoms. Ones featuring Paul Stanley were to come out sometime in the summer of 2011, although it is not known if those will be studded or not.

Coffins

For those who bothered with the KISS Kondoms and died of humiliation there was the lucky break of a "KISS Kasket" (yes, again with the K instead of a C) that became available in 2001. The casket featured large images of the band members on the top and the words "KISS Forever" on the side that could then be buried deep within the earth and never seen again. A casket company called White Light—creator of various novelty caskets—made a limited number of these for sale through KISS's official mail-order company. Reports were that the number to be sold was limited to 2,500, but most believe that only a handful of them made it out into the public, especially as the coffins cost $5,000, making them too pricey for many people to be used for their proper purpose. It is known that

Pantera guitarist Dimebag Darrell requested to be buried in one, at least. Gene Simmons did do some promotional appearances with the casket, often advising people that it could be used as a cooler for beverages if one did not want to use it for its intended purpose (a suggestion strongly advised against by casket makers, who stated such coffins were not made to hold liquid in such a fashion and doing so would destroy the integrity of the box for "further use").

In 2011, new caskets were created by Eternal Images, Inc., who also planned to make urns, memorial cards, and more with the KISS logo on them. Two styles were created for the new caskets—a premium model that has the KISS logo on the side and a picture of the post-2000 version of the band on the top, and a standard one that is more sedate with a black finish and the KISS solo album pictures on the top. Both for under $4,000 as well. Between the condoms and the caskets, KISS managed to come up with products that have embarrassed more fans over the years than anything else they have produced.

Sunglasses

A rather clever idea for a product rejected by the band back in the 1970s was sunglasses shaped in the style of the makeup. At least the concept certainly made it easier to dress like KISS without going through the trouble of the makeup (such as that included in some of the 1970s *KISS Your Face* makeup kits—a rarity in itself—that was nearly impossible to remove and led to threats of lawsuits). Surprisingly KISS passed on these at the time (and included them in the early pages of their *KISStory II* book as samples of merchandise "beneath them").

In late 2010, a company called Costumes Galore sold very similar sunglasses done in the style of Gene Simmons's makeup. Called "Demon Shades," they were released through the band's official merchandising arm. Of course, such an idea is a universal one, and no doubt someone came up with the same concept years later and suggested it again to KISS with them agreeing to it the second time around. Shame that they never expanded the line to add the other makeup characters, however.

Pinball Machine

There have been many things considered crowning achievements for collectors to have in their KISS swag. Certain autographed albums, a piece of costume worn by the band onstage, rare videos or albums, pieces of a guitar Paul Stanley smashed on stage, or photos taken with the band are just a few of the unique items that a fan can show in his collection to impress other fans. Yet each of these items is one of a kind items that can only be obtained in rare circumstances. Of the mass-produced items made in connection with KISS there is one piece of merchandise considered the "holy grail" of any KISS collection: the 1979 Bally KISS Pinball Machine.

Bally is a famous name in pinball machine history, creating a variety of famous machines over the years and—as with many other manufacturers listed in this chapter—not one to shy away from incorporating famous people into their products. Machines based on *Star Trek, Playboy* magazine, Evel Knievel, *The Six Million Dollar Man*, and others were common for the company. Machines based on rock-music themes were normal as well—such as the *Tommy* machine, based on the movie version of the Who's rock opera, as well as one for the Rolling Stones and (one of the most sought-after machines of the 1970s) the Elton John/*Tommy*-themed *Captain Fantastic* machine of 1975. With the breakout success of KISS, it simply made sense for Bally to go after the band, and it certainly made sense for the band to agree to the product.

A total of 17,000 machines were made of the KISS pinball machine, which was designed by Jim Palta (designer of the *Playboy* and Rolling Stones machines among many others, including the fondly remembered *Centaur* machine of 1981). Palta's name appears in the artwork of the backglass of the machine—on the head of Ace Frehley's guitar—which was created by Kevin O'Connor, who did pinball artwork on many other machines, including the 1979 *Star Trek* and the 1980 *Flash Gordon* machines. The design of the machine was very straightforward, as the common perception in the trade was that people played such machines because of who or what it was about and not because of fancy ball play or additional gimmicks within the game itself. Nevertheless, fans love the sleek style of the game, which allows for clean objectives of the player in the game (besides not losing the ball, lighted scores led to special bonuses, including free balls and free games). Of course, one cannot help but note that the simplistic scoring in the game led to high scores and free games, which made many fans feel they were "pinball wizards" and certainly did not hurt bringing people over to the game to drop quarters into it.

The game could be programmed for three to five balls per game and included a relatively new feature for dollar coins. It also had a slightly different backglass for the German release, with the revised "backward Z" logo used to avoid issues pertaining to the lightning-bolt "SS" part of the name (see Chapter 5 for more details). The main thing, however, is how everything about it is simply KISS. The frame of the machine has drawings of the band members, the playing field inside has various pieces of artwork showing the band, the machine lights up with the band's name several times, and of course there is the backglass. It is an overload of brightly lit KISS nostalgia and defiance all wrapped into one, and thus makes for a centerpiece to any KISS collection that cannot help but draw the eyes. Bits and pieces of the machines are collectible as well, with the operating manual and posters released to promote it going for a good deal of money among fans, just as the machine can go for thousands today if in good working condition.

Some fans may recall seeing a *Smashes, Thrashes, and Hits* KISS pinball machine that turned up at a few KISS conventions in the late 1980s and early

Information showing the artwork for the "holy grail" of KISS merchandise items: the KISS pinball machine.   *Author's Collection*

1990s. But this was one created as a custom-built machine for a fan and was never an official prototype or released machine for the band. Still, it was a very nice-looking machine that is probably still sitting around in someone's home today.

It was announced on the band's official website, kissonline.com, in 2006 that a company was considering putting together a new KISS pinball machine. Artwork was shown to display what the new machine would look like, with promises that it could be out as early as 2007. While this did not occur, it was interesting to note how much the playing field of the new version looked like that of the original in many spots. This actually was a common theme in many retreads of KISS merchandise after the reunion tour occurred in 1996—many products were brought back from the 1970s, and many were more or less variations of the old look. Just goes to show that the styles created nearly thirty-five years ago have remained with fans and could not really be bested with new designs, only improved upon or modernized.

Rumors had circulated for years that Bally had thought about putting then-new voice recordings into the machine (this became quite common for machines soon after, including the *Flash Gordon* machine mentioned earlier). As reported by the website *Internet Pinball Machine Database* (http://www.ipdb. org/machine.cgi?gid=1386), one prototype actually was made that featured such an addition to the machine. Displayed at an Amusement and Music Operators Associations (A.M.O.A.) show in Chicago in 1979, the machine told the player to show certain letters on the board and the band's name when a row of letters was completed, as well as saying "Too much Rock and Roll!" when the machine was tilted. Only the prototype was ever produced and supposedly was put back into storage after the one-time display. Where is it now? Hard to say, but the person who has it must know that he or she has the "holy grail of holy grails" for any KISS collector.

25

Ten Possible Fifth KISS

Those Connected to KISS That Fit the Role

There is a tradition among Beatles fans to look back on all the people who have worked with that band over the years and determine who would be considered the "Fifth Beatle." Was it Pete Best, who played with them for a time before Ringo joined? Billy Preston, who recorded with them? Perhaps Brian Epstein, their manager, should be considered the fifth? And so on and so forth.

The same holds true for KISS fans. There have been plenty of individuals who have helped KISS over the years, either in the studio, in concert, or behind the scenes, and in many cases more than once. None of them quite got the recognition for their work with the band outside that which comes from knowledgeable fans, but all had some influence over the direction of the band; some in ways that they probably still do not realize. Thus, after Gene Simmons, Paul Stanley, Peter Criss, and Ace Frehley, who would the fans consider to be the "fifth member"?

This game of picking someone for such a role has to sidestep the obvious answer, of course—that there were enough guys who became official members of the band over the years to form another band or two: Eric Carr, Vinnie Vincent, Mark St. John, Bruce Kulick, Eric Singer, and Tommy Thayer. Each one of these automatically is officially a "fifth members of KISS." Even so, such a conversation between fans commonly makes mention of something whose importance to the band's legacy is sometimes neglected. Without their help, KISS would never have quite gone down the path that they did.

Bill Aucoin

To take the Beatles analogy one step further, many KISS fans have noted that KISS and the Beatles share some similarities when it came to their best-known managers. Just as Brian Epstein was a gay man working in a music-related industry when he first took over management for the Beatles, so too was Bill Aucoin when he first became intrigued with KISS. Aucoin started his career in television production, working at PBS in their early years on programs such as *Julia Child's French Chef* and *Folk Music USA* when he branched out into other productions, looking to find a hit show he could call his own. While producing a short-lived syndicated rock-music program called *Flipside* with Joyce Biawitz (who would comanage KISS for a time and later marry Casablanca Records owner Neil Bogart) and Howard Marks (who would become the business manager for KISS through most of the 1980s), Aucoin was getting repeated invitations to see KISS perform. Tired of the drain he felt in television, Aucoin wanted to do something in the music industry and—after seeing the band in an August 1973 performance at the Hotel Diplomat—decided that he would take his case to the band to do just that.

Aucoin's version of the meeting was that he felt so strongly about the band that he signed on to be their manager with the promise of finding them a record deal within two weeks (some versions of the story have the time as a month). However, others who were working with Neil Bogart on the planned Casablanca label state that Bogart already knew about the band—Simmons was hustling tapes to everybody, not just Aucoin—and had mentioned his interest and desire to start his own label to his girlfriend and future wife, Joyce Biawitz. Nevertheless, it still means that Aucoin, along with Biawitz, had to sell the band to Bogart and managed to get KISS a deal within the time period he told the members he would.

Aucoin would push the band to be distinctive and yet united in much the same way the Beatles were—with a uniform look that also spoke of the individual personas each member displayed onstage. With this in mind, he was constantly trying to come up with new schemes for them, such as spitting fire and levitating to the ceiling (both big standards of Simmons over the years in concert) and trying new effects. He felt so strongly about them that he even maxed out his American Express card in order to keep the band on the road while they searched for their audience in the first couple of years.

By 1977, KISS was very much in the spotlight, and with that came interviews. The band did several, but under supervision, with most featuring Simmons doing the talking since he was the most reliable to sell "the product." Thus, it was not uncommon for Aucoin himself to do interviews in support of the band, and as the only unmasked representative then in the public eye, his face became synonymous with KISS—much as how Brian Epstein had become famous for his management of the Beatles. Fans may not have known what the four members looked like when the band was in town, but they certainly knew Aucoin, making the manager a focal point for the KISS Army and giving him a popularity that most managers do not achieve in the business. His association with such a hot act as KISS also brought other artists to his attention, including Billy Squier's early band Piper, Starz, and Spider (which featured KISS session musician—and future *David Letterman* drummer—Anton Fig and writer Holly Knight), but Aucoin never quite clicked with these bands as he did with KISS.

By 1979 the golden days of the band were fast disappearing. Aucoin would later acknowledge that the *Dynasty* tour did not do as well financially as anticipated, and attempts to bring the band back after Peter Criss's departure with *Unmasked* failed to raise hopes. Eric Carr once stated that the business of KISS was also running like a well-oiled machine by that point, and decisions needed for the band were handled by others, without Aucoin getting much input because he was not needed to do so. The attempt to push the band in a new direction with the Simmons/Stanley–driven *Music from "The Elder"* album proved to be a critical and financial disaster and Aucoin was left to take the blunt of the blame. Soon after, Aucoin and KISS mutually agreed to split, with KISS taking on their business managers Carl Glickman and Howard Marks (who appears as the father in the "I Love It Loud" video) as the decision makers for them, while Aucoin moved on.

Aucoin immediately jumped back in the game, looking after Billy Idol and his emergence from his band Generation X to that of a solo artist, but the two split by 1984. After that, Bogart would occasionally pop up working with other bands, such as Flipp and Lordi, but just as with the bands besides KISS back in the 1970s, lightning never quite hit twice for him. In the 1990s Aucoin began making occasional guest appearances at some of the KISS conventions, while also producing a spoken-word CD, *13 Classic KISS Stories*, about his time with the band. Keeping in touch with the band members over the years in minor ways, Aucoin eventually reconciled with them for some things connected to the reunion tour and after, including interviews for the official biography, *Behind the Mask.*

Bill Aucoin died on June 28, 2010, while undergoing surgery due to prostate cancer. At the time of his death, Peter Criss referred to him as the "Fifth KISS," and many reports had no qualms in reporting the same about Aucoin. Gene Simmons readily stated that it was due to Aucoin's pushing the band to be over the top that got them noticed in the first place. While KISS would have found some notice in music at some point thanks to the band members' efforts, without the right man looking out for them in the beginning, they may not have ever been the phenomenon they would become.

Neil Bogart

Usually there are two men outside of Gene Simmons, Paul Stanley, Ace Frehley, and Peter Criss that fans think of as the brains behind the success of the band in the 1970s. One, of course, was Bill Aucoin; the other was Casablanca Records mastermind Neil Bogart. Ironically, though, KISS was not his legacy—they were just one act in an overall amazing career in music.

Bogart started his career as a teen singer, using the name of Neil Scott, with a minor hit called "Bobby" in 1961. He continued to try to make a go as a performer but soon found himself advancing through the business side of the industry. A job with *Cash Box* magazine led to work at MGM Records and then a big

Solo album by Sean Delany, who worked extensively with the band in
the 1970s.   *Author's Collection*

break for him at Cameo-Parkway Records in 1965. It was at Cameo that Bogart
succeeded in releasing ? and the Mysterians' big hit "96 Tears," but a dust-up
with Allen Klein (later a manger for the Beatles, another Beatles link for KISS)
led to him moving on to Buddah Records, where Bogart became known as the
king of bubblegum music—a style of strongly orchestrated rock music backed
with light, kid-friendly lyrics—in 1968, with acts like the Ohio Express, the
Lemon Pipers, and the 1910 Fruitgum Company.

Just as KISS was starting to pull itself together in late 1972/early 1973, the
same was true with Bogart and his idea of a new independent record label. It
would be a risk, as the industry ate up new labels quickly, but he had several
old associates from previous and current work relationships to help get things
started for the company. KISS would be the first act signed to the label in
November 1973, just as Bogart worked out a distribution deal through Warner
Brothers.

The first few years of the label were a bit rocky, and some of that was due to
Bogart's allegiance to his first act. When he discovered that Warner had issued a
memo from their promotional department to not bother pushing KISS's second
album, *Hotter Than Hell* in 1974, he demanded his label be released from the
distribution deal he had managed to get with Warner. The Warner deal had
been one that many labels starting out would have killed for, and several would

have no doubt buckled to the distributor's demands that KISS be let go, but Bogart saw it not only as a disservice to the act but as a challenge to his authority over the label. So, Casablanca went independent. This was a bigger risk as he continued to pump money into albums and singles from acts like Parliament, Fanny (a well-known all-female rock band of the era), the Hudson Brothers, and T-Rex while sales continued to disappoint.

Things were not perfect among him, Aucoin, and the band either. Bogart held back money promised to the band, leading to Aucoin demanding they start getting proper accounting or else the band would look for another label. This was a worry to Bogart as KISS had been a prime image for the label; to lose them would mean showing that he could not keep his acts. Further, he knew that the "KISS gang" (Simmons, Stanley, Criss, Frehley, Aucoin, and the producers of the first two albums Kenny Kerner and Richie Wise) were close to staging a coup and signing with Atlantic Records, who had been paying attention to the increase in sales the band had gotten over their first two albums. This would eventually led to Bogart attempting to oust Aucoin as the band's manager in favor of himself, while also firing Kerner and Wise in order to produce the third album, *Dressed To Kill*, himself. The band's loyalties to Aucoin and Bogart were so strong, however, that they never considered such a defection from their manager or the label, and eventually contractual concerns were settled to a mutual agreement by all.

An attempt in late 1974 by Bogart to push a double-vinyl collection of moments from *The Tonight Show* in 1974 (see more details in Chapter 30) almost killed the company and left Bogart near-suicidal (as he later reported to *Rolling Stone* magazine), but perseverance led him to keep pushing the company until things began to turn around in 1975. This was due to excellent results from acts brought in that did well in the growing disco craze of the later 1970s—such as the Village People and Donna Summer—but KISS had always been the label's flagship, and when the both *Alive!* (1975) and the follow-up album *Destroyer* (1976) became blockbusters, it was a public sign that both KISS and Casablanca Records were making it.

With the company finally going into the black, Bogart poured money into KISS while also always making sure that any review of the label meant a review of their success with KISS as well (another reason why Aucoin was seen so often in interviews at the time, as he was promoting not only KISS but Casablanca as well). While his company had many successes beyond that of KISS, Bogart also saw then as a metaphor for Casablanca's struggle in the early years, whether a band wearing makeup and using special effects or a record label hiring acts deemed uncommercial and finding them winners with the public.

KISS as the symbol of the company's success also worked in the opposite manner when both saw their power slide at the end of the 1970s. As the band began to pour more money into their tours to weak return, saw members leave, and began looking for the "new sound" that would help them progress, so too were Bogart and his team for the label. With PolyGram's investment in the company in 1977, and their concerns about control over Casablanca's financial bottom line, Bogart soon found himself on the outs with the company in 1980, just as KISS found themselves trending water with their label going into the new decade.

Bogart would bounce back with a company called Boardwalk that had signed Joan Jett just as she was about to burst on to the scenes with "I Love Rock and Roll," but cancer saw Bogart pass away on May 8, 1982. PolyGram struggled with what to do with KISS after Bogart left Casablanca, leading to the band bouncing around between labels within the company come the 1990s. Although Bogart may have always had more irons in the fire than just KISS, he pushed for the band as well as protected them. His death was the resounding sign of the party being over, and soon KISS would abandon their makeup and fantasy-world characters for the real world in the 1980s.

Sean Delaney

Delaney was a musician who found himself in the unusual position of being an "everyman" to KISS during their years of struggle and through their flight of success in the 1970s. As Bill Aucoin's partner both professionally and personally, Delaney knew many of the events occurring behind the scenes for both the band and Casablanca, going back to hearing the original tape Gene Simmons had sent out to prospective managers and labels back in 1973. Delaney was also there when Aucoin saw the band perform at the Hotel Diplomat in August 1973 as well as their showcase tryout for Casablanca soon afterwards.

Yet being a witness to the band's history was only the starting point of Delaney's involvement with them. With a background in off-Broadway musicals and rock music, Delaney had an understanding of stage choreography, costuming, and makeup that would be vital to the band's education in presenting their over-the-top personas onstage. It would be he who helped with minor details to makeup, hair, and costumes that were overlooked by Aucoin and the band members, as well as practicing with the band in rehearsal to get their look as tight as possible for a strong presentation to the audience. Delaney would jump in to also cowrite songs with the band members (on *Rock and Roll Over* and *Alive II*), offer suggestions in the studio for other songs, remix songs for the *Double Platinum* album, and help produce Simmons's and Peter Criss's 1978 solo albums. Nor did it stop there—Delaney was also involved with original concepts for the superhero KISS characters and motifs used in the Marvel comics and *KISS Meets the Phantom of the Park* (mainly the talismans that give the band their power, as well as the individual powers each received). In fact, it is nearly impossible to find something done by the band in the 1970s where Delaney was not involved and his name somewhere in the credits, be it album, film, or books. Nor were the band and Aucoin shy about making reference in interviews to Delaney for his hard work making KISS as good as they could be. On the other hand, Delaney was known for taking others' ideas and extending them to their limit—thus, while several people who had worked with the band have supported his role as a huge factor in the band's look, they are also quick to state their own involvement in such ideas. This has led to many interviews with people in the KISS circle that start with "We came up with . . . " rather than "Delaney came up with . . . " This would irritate Delaney years later when he discussed his KISS days while guesting at KISS conventions or doing interviews, as he felt his involvement was being unfairly ignored. He would also touch upon some of this resentment in his autobiography released in 2004, *Hellbox*.

Delaney's involvement with the band diminished just as Aucoin's direction for them subsided in the very early 1980s. Eventually Delaney would move on to other musical projects over the next twenty-something years, including a solo album and two albums with a band called the Skatt Bros., but he will always be remembered by the KISS Army for his work with the band in those golden days, even if sometimes they don't quite see how much influence he had with them.

Bob Kulick

Bob Kulick, brother to KISS guitarist (1984–1996) Bruce Kulick, was one of the other guitarists who tried out for the band back in 1972. As a matter of fact, the guy sitting, watching, and waiting to try out after Bob was none other than Ace Frehley (covered in more detail in Chapter 4). From all reports, Kulick went over well with the three members of KISS, but balked at the idea of putting on makeup once the concept was broached to him. Of course, Frehley's tryout and consequential acceptance of wearing makeup and costumes onstage would see Kulick passed over, but that was definitely not the end of his association with KISS.

Keeping in contact, the band returned to Kulick when they began working on the new songs to be recorded for the fourth side of *Alive II* in 1977. Numerous stories have been told as to why Frehley was not used, but the results were the same: Frehley was unavailable for at least three tracks out of five recorded for the album, and Kulick was called in to play guitar instead, with a request that he imitate Frehley's sound as much as possible. He returned to do similar functions on the foreign-released *Killers* album when two new songs were required for the compilation ("I'm a Legend Tonight" and "Down on Your Knees") and Frehley was unavailable. In that case, he was asked to play in his own style and not worry about sounding like Frehley. He would subsequently return for the follow-up studio album *Creatures of the Night* to play lead on "Danger," as well as "Keep Me Coming."

Kulick also worked on solo projects for Paul Stanley, playing on both his 1978 solo album and performing with Stanley on his solo tour in 1989 (with the future KISS member Eric Singer on drums). Over time fans have discovered that other musicians have played instruments in the studio for KISS albums, but fans seem justified is suggesting that the man who nearly became the fourth KISS should be thought of as the fifth for these reasons.

Bob Kulick front and center with his band Skull.   *Author's Collection*

Stan Penridge

When Stan Penridge joined the band Chelsea in 1970, he had no way of know-ing how his world would interconnect with one of the most popular bands of the era in the years to come, or how such a band would not be the one he was a member of. Chelsea was a rock band that had already recorded an album set for release that fall and looked to be on the threshold of big things. However, internal problems in the band would eventually see the band fall apart until it became a threesome called Lips (see Chapter 1 for more about how that name is relevant) and then finally a duo, with Penridge on guitar and the drummer a man named Peter Criss.

Splitting off in different directions, Penridge joined a "Texas Swing" band called St. Elmo's Fire at the same time Criss hooked up with two guys named Gene Simmons and Paul Stanley for what would evolve into KISS. The parting was cordial, and the pair kept in touch as well as former musicians usually do, but then things changed when the band began working on their fourth studio album, *Destroyer*. With *Alive!* drawing in new fans, KISS was anxious to keep the interest growing with exciting material on the new album. They were also working with a new producer, Bob Ezrin, who had driven the Alice Cooper band and Alice as a solo artist to huge success with a series of albums through most of the 1970s. Ezrin's work on Cooper's 1975 album, *Welcome to My Nightmare*, had also opened up Alice's career by including the ballad "Only Women Bleed," which nearly broke the top ten. Thus, KISS came into the *Destroyer* sessions with Ezrin ready to present anything and everything to see what could work.

One of the songs Peter Criss brought in was an old one that he and Penridge had thrown together back in the Chelsea days called "Beck." Oddly enough, the song was originally written as a joke response to a fellow Chelsea member, Michael Brand, constantly having to stop rehearsals in order to talk to his wife on the phone, with his phone responses being worked into the lyrics. Criss, finding the song, tossed it Ezrin's way, and with some slight alterations to the music and a name change from Beck to Beth (a decision made either by Ezrin or Simmons, depending on which one is speaking), the song would go on to be one of the biggest singles ever for the band.

Understandably, with that success Penridge came back to work on more material with Criss for the next two follow-up albums with "Baby Driver" (written back in the days of their band Lips) on *Rock and Roll Over* and "Hooligan" on *Love Gun* in hopes of another hit. Things were moving along with Penridge becoming a regular contributor of music for the band when things got very hectic in 1978—Criss found himself short of material for his solo album due to come out with the others in September that year. Although he had started work on the album in the spring, he had only four tracks somewhat ready before he had to hold off thanks to production ongoing with the television movie and then was involved in a car accident that left his hands badly injured.

Hunting around for songs to use, Penridge suggested a number of songs he had written for a possible Lips album back in 1972. Digging through them, they picked six for the solo album, with Criss and Penridge splitting ownership 50/50, making Penridge a partner in Rock Steady when all was said and done. The other band members also appreciated Penridge saving the project, with Simmons even sending him a Christmas card telling him that without his help on "Beth" and the solo albums, the band would have been in trouble. Penridge would help contribute one more song to another album ("Dirty Living" on *Dynasty*), breaking away from the band at the same time Criss did, but during the makeup years of 1973 through 1982, Penridge would be one of the band's

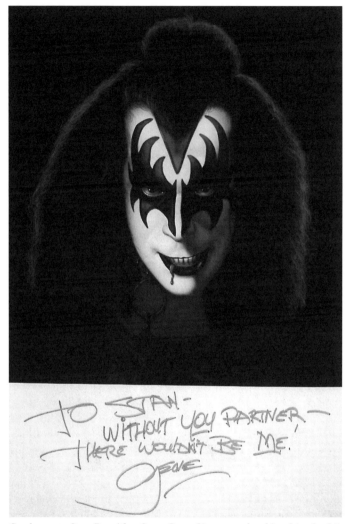

Card sent to Stan Penridge from Gene Simmons thanking him for his help with the band during the "solo albums" recordings.

Courtesy of Nell Penridge

most consistent song contributors and cowriter of the band's most popular song from the 1970s.

Penridge worked with Criss on his first solo album after the band, *Out of Control,* and attempted a run as a band that would be best known as the Criss-Penridge Alliance, but eventually personal differences took their toll. Penridge split from Criss in the fall of 1984 to do things outside of the music field as well as producing bands and even starting his own label out of his studio in Texas. He was involved in a lawsuit to obtain royalties for his work with the band that got caught up in red tape after Criss sold off his catalog of songs published under Rock Steady in 1985, which also led to the two never speaking again and also a legal mess that was still being straightened out when Penridge passed away in May 2001 from a heart attack. It was only after his death that a settlement finally occurred.

Bob Ezrin

In the early days of the band, the concept of KISS was usually defined as "four Alice Coopers onstage." So when the band got a chance to have Cooper's producer Bob Ezrin work for them, how could they pass it up?

Ezrin had cut his teeth as a producer with the Alice Cooper group back in 1971 when they began work on their third album after the first two failed to do well on the charts. Ezrin was fascinated with a song by the band called "I'm Eighteen" and would help orchestrate an album with the band that would not only deliver their first hit single with "I'm Eighteen," but turn *Love It to Death* into their first album to break the Top 40. Ezrin continued to work with Alice Cooper, with each succeeding album doing well on the charts, while also producing the controversial but later critically admired Lou Reed album *Berlin*. Looking for other projects, Ezrin had heard about KISS and decided to check them out. Of course, with the Ezrin-produced *Welcome to My Nightmare* being Cooper's biggest album yet at the time, everyone knew who Ezrin was and were happy to have him come onboard to guide them in the studio.

The album he produced with KISS would become *Destroyer* and be a hotly contested piece of work for fans over a number of years. Featuring orchestration and production quite different than the naked garage-band sounds of the first three studio albums, the album made some fans at the time feel that KISS had lost their street cred as a hard-rock band, while others thought it was an exciting extension of the whole otherworldly image the band was increasingly cultivating as the '70s progressed. With Paul Stanley's "God of Thunder" essentially giving Gene Simmons's Demon character a theme song, one of their biggest hits with "Beth," and a number of songs that would become staples of their live performances for years, the album is considered a classic by most KISS fans today. Not at the time, however, as it was controversial enough that the band would be seen as backtracking with the next album *Rock and Roll Over*, which was recorded "live" with their *Alive!* producer Eddie Kramer.

Ezrin returned in 1981 to produce the band's conceptual album *Music from "The Elder"* and once again found himself and the band at the mercy of critics and fans who split between either really liking or hating the album. With Ezrin's work on conceptual albums and having just come off the huge success of Pink Floyd's *The Wall* in 1979, it was again understandable why the band would turn to him to help guide such a project as *The Elder*, which was viewed as the basis for a possible movie as well as a couple of subsequent albums to complete the story. It was also seen to be a momentous career-changer for KISS, pushing theatrics to a new level for them, but instead it burned out fans and even members of the band—both Ace Frehley and new drummer Eric Carr had several discussions with Stanley and Simmons that the album was a sure misfire, only to be told to mind their own business—who felt it was not the direction the band should go.

Ezrin once again moved on to other projects but returned to produce KISS once more for their 1992 album *Revenge*. *Revenge* found the band again looking to remake themselves with a harder album after the party-friendly style of their *Asylum/Crazy Nights/Hot in the Shade* days. With a darker look to their image and a darker tone in the album's music and lyrics, Ezrin once again joined the band as they reached a crossroad. Even with their effort, however, KISS soon looked back to the days of the 1970s and the makeup for their journey into the new millennium.

Ezrin was only involved with three full albums with KISS over their career, but those albums were signposts of changing directions in tone, attitude, and musical styles. The band trusted Ezrin enough to bring their efforts out in the productions and shatter earlier concepts of them. All three have been the most controversial albums in the band's career, a fact that is due to Ezrin's production.

Eddie Kramer

Eddie Kramer was already a solid legend in the music business by the time KISS got hold of him. What may surprise some fans is that the band had known him long before Kramer came in to help put together their first live album, *Alive!* In fact, he was there since nearly the very beginning.

Kramer was known as an engineer who had worked with the Beatles, Hendrix, Traffic, and Led Zeppelin. He had been there to record Woodstock and lend his skills to popular live albums and had branched out into producing while working out of Electric Lady Studios in New York. As it turned out, Stanley and Simmons were given some recording time at the studio in exchange for providing backing vocals for an album by an artist named Lyn Christopher. Knowing Kramer was there and knowing how much his name attached to any recording they did would help boost interest by listeners, the two asked Kramer if he would record KISS for some demos they wanted to send out to labels, etc. Kramer, after hearing the band perform live, decided to give them a shot and recorded a five-track demo that they then circulated to various people in the business. Four of those songs—"Strutter," "Deuce," "Cold Gin," "and "Black Diamond"—would eventually turn up rerecorded for the first KISS album, with "Watchin' You" making it to the second.

When Casablanca allowed the band to record a live album in 1975, they knew they wanted Kramer to do the job, as his past experience in getting the raw energy of other bands for live albums, as well as his earlier work on the demos for them, proved him to be an excellent choice. Kramer completed work on *Alive!* and then was asked to return to record *Rock and Roll Over* in a near-live atmosphere at an empty theater in Nanuet, New York, as a "return to form" for supposedly deserting fans after the heavily orchestrated *Destroyer* album.

Kramer returned to help produce two further live albums for the band, *Alive II* and *Alive III*, while also producing a few of Ace Frehley's solo albums over the years, including his 1978 solo album with the band. This may seem as if Kramer has only been involved in a small way to some, but as KISS has always depended on their live sound to win over listeners, Kramer's influence on the band is as big as or perhaps even bigger in some ways than that of other producers they have used over the years, making him a vital part of their personality.

Anton Fig

Anton Fig was already making a name for himself as a hired studio musician in the mid-1970s when he was asked to help cut some drumming tracks for the Kramer-produced *Alive II* album. His work there led directly to Kramer using Fig for Ace Frehley's 1978 solo album, which got Frehley to know Fig well enough to remember him when it came time for KISS to record *Dynasty*. With Peter Criss still recuperating from his car accident of '78, along with beginning to distance himself from the others, the band decided to bring in Anton Fig to record drums on most of the album (with the exception of Criss's "Dirty Livin'" track). This went over so well that Fig was brought back in for the follow-up album, *Unmasked*, which he recorded drums for in its entirety, as Criss was already working on his *Out of Control* album in a different studio from KISS. In fact, KISS's management did not even hide the fact that someone other than Criss was recording drums for *Unmasked*, going so far as to flatly state so in an Australian newspaper article in May 1980.

Unmasked was Peter Criss's last official outing with the band (even with Fig playing drums on it instead of him), and the search soon began for his replacement. When pressed if the "studio musician" was to remain in the band as Criss's permanent replacement, the band's spokesperson stated that it was a strong possibility. Considering Fig's strong personal relationship with Frehley and his professional attitude recording with the band—they certainly would not have invited him back to record a second album if it were not so—it probably was a big consideration at one time. However, knowing that Fig was still with his band Spider at the time, and had been seen publicly on the cover of the Spider album as well as other places, the band probably decided that Fig was too exposed to be made a member.

Fig continued to work with Frehley through the 1980s as part of his Frehley's Comet band and beyond, and it was not unusual to see the two perform off and on through the years after that as well. Meanwhile, Fig has had a very successful career working with Paul Shaffer first on *Late Night with David Letterman* and later on *The Late Show with David Letterman* as well as continuing to do studio and live gigs when the opportunities arise. Still, for one moment in 1980, Fig came very close to actually fulfilling the role of the "Fifth KISS Member."

Gary Corbett

KISS had usually shied away from keyboards on tour for many years, but there was no way to avoid them completely in the music they produced in the 1980s, and by the time of the *Crazy Nights* tour they knew it was either introduce the instrument onstage or radically change several songs in the set list. This was accomplished by giving Bruce Kulick a keyboard to run to for some songs during the tour, but fans readily recognized that keyboards were eerily being played at points in the show where no one was near the instrument onstage.

As it turns out, this was accomplished either by record playback in shows or—more than likely—by the addition of a keyboardist backstage or below stage playing with the band. That man performing like a true KISS phantom was Gary Corbett, a studio musician who had worked on a number of albums for various artists in the 1980s by that point. When it was feasible to do so, Corbett was brought in to play "behind the curtain" and allowing the band to perform songs without having to resort to recorded playback or not play the songs at all.

After serving this function during the 1987–1988 *Crazy Nights* tour, Paul Stanley invited Corbett to join him on his 1989 solo tour of various clubs. Corbett would then return to do a number of shows on the *Hot in the Shade* tour in a similar fashion before Derek Sherinian replaced him in a similar role on the *Revenge* tour. As was typical for any hired-gun musician, it was just one job of many in the business, but for a time on a couple of tours Corbett really was the "Fifth KISS Member."

Ed Kanon

Ed Kanon had worked with Peter Criss since Criss began working on getting a solo album together in the early 1990s. When the time came for the Criss to rejoin KISS, he asked Kanon to become his drum tech for the tour, a job Kanon held until Criss left the band again in 2003. For many, that would have been a good enough connection with the band to make him important to some fans, but things did not stop there.

As mentioned in Chapter 17, the April 5, 1997, show in Columbus, Georgia, found Criss unable to perform and the band deciding to go on anyway thanks to Kanon being available to replace him for the night. Wearing Criss's makeup and outfit, Kanon was the first musician to "play the role" of one of the four for a concert. He never got another chance to do so, but while Eric Singer and Tommy Thayer would go on to take over the makeup and costumes of previous KISS members in the tours to follow, Kanon had been there first. Ironically, although it may have been a one-shot deal, Kanon can say he was not just a fifth member of the band, but for one night, he was the fourth.

26

Four or Five Thousand

As someone who has written about KISS in the past, I sometimes get asked questions about the band and its members. Usually they are about the "urban legends" centering on them, including one that people are not really sure if it is a legend or not—that of Gene Simmons's number of conquests over the years. Back in 2009, I was contacted by *Esquire* magazine to give my opinion on the numerous reports (of which many came from Simmons himself) about his adventures with several thousand women over the years. Of course, "adventures" and "conquests" do not refer to wins at Tiddlywinks tournaments (well, maybe they could; it may be Simmons's preferred icebreaker for all we know), but rather to having sex with so many women.

How many women are we talking about here? Hard to say—Simmons has never been very definitive in the count, with the number already in the 5,000 range back in the 1980s when he first began boasting about his "efforts" in interviews, and nowadays down a bit to 4,600. (Evidently if he ever gets to 5,000, confetti and balloons will fall from the ceiling, and he will have to hand off a big cardboard check to the woman, so he is holding off on that as long as he can.) Whether this means he thought 5,000 was just too unrealistic compared to 4,600 or he had spent a couple of nights away from such pursuits to actively count up the true number is hard to say. Sadly, it may be the second option, as Simmons told *USA Today* live chat in 2002 and other sources since that he had actually determined the exact number to prove his point. To some that may seem a bit of the old "protesting too hard" to be believed; myself, I prefer to imagine him sitting all night in front of one of those old-fashioned adding machines with the crank on the side and ripping off the paper tape to verify his numbers. It is more wholesome that way.

Is it possible that he had done this? As I told *Esquire* for the article, "A famous, rich rock star is able to score with a variety of women during the most explosive moment of sexual freedom of all time? Yeah, it sounds feasible." One has to remember that the 1970s were much different when it came to sexual freedom and experimentation. The worse things people thought could come from sex were an unwanted pregnancy, crabs, or getting an STD treatable with a shot from a doctor. Admittedly, not everyone was like that at the time—truth to the contrary, the 1970s was not a huge orgy of drugs and sex, it is just remembered that way by people who do not remember it or never lived it—but to be famous and rich at the time did mean certain privileges were available without any concerns for tomorrow. The music business certainly had a good number of female fans, otherwise known as groupies, who would be happy to spend time with a famous rock star and no doubt kept their own tallies in a similar fashion to Simmons. After all, this was not Gene Simmons, the English teacher down the street with 2.5 kids and a car payment, this was GENE SIMMONS—the flashy rich rock star—and bedding him or any other member of the band was a notch on the belt for a groupie. Plus, one should remember that other famous stars of the day have come forward with similar or higher numbers, such as basketball great Wilt Chamberlain, who claimed to have had sex with 20,000 women (a number some scoff at, but others who knew him believed could have been possible). It was a revolving turnstile for many celebrities during the 1970s and early 1980s, with everyone looking to rack up the numbers for their own reasons.

Even so, could it be physically possible? Simmons states in his *Kiss and Make-Up* that his first groupie was in Edmonton, Alberta, Canada, in 1974. Yet it has been reported elsewhere that he was running into groupies back when Wicked Lester was recording, and no doubt he was not one to remain "pure at heart" for long when he ventured into the music scene back in the 1960s. He has frequently stated that the reason he picked up a guitar in the first place was for money and girls, and with a career in music since the late 1960s, he probably would have seen a side of that type of life long before 1974. Simmons has also made it clear that he was not one to make racking up one more in the tally a long process, with dressing-room quickies being just as fine as anything more "romantic." With that, and his claims of being able to move out one girl from his room in order to bring in another or more, the number would quickly shoot upward. Further, as pointed out in the same *Esquire* article by mathematician John Allen Paulos, if one thinks about a forty-year career, it means that Simmons would have slept with an average of 115 women a year, or just a little over two a week. Definitely in the range of being physically possible.

However, there are problems with the forty years calculation. Such numbers stem from the idea that there would be no breaks within that period in order to allow Simmons to have at least two to three women a week. The main roadblock is that he was known for his involvement with several famous women over the years such as Diana Ross and Cher (his conquests supposedly include actress Liv Ullmann as well, and several other names have been dropped over the years by Simmons and others). Women with such strong personalities probably would not have stood happily by while he was rolling up the numbers on the ol' odometer. This surely would put a dent into the overall figure, as would his long relationship with actress Shannon Tweed, which was supposedly monogamous for many years and has gone on since 1984, although a sex video showing Gene with a model seemed to suggest that there may have been a few times here and there where he wanted to sow some wild oats. Second, a lot of these numbers would be women he met while on tour, which would be many during the first few years of the band, but there have been periodic breaks in touring after that—some as long as years—that would play with the numbers as well. However, even with such breaks, the number is still approachable—one could easily reach the same number by simply one partner a night in a little over twelve years, after all.

If so, how do you keep track of such a number in the first place? If Don Juan could not even remember the names of his conquests, could Gene Simmons be counted on to do so? In his favor, his friends and KISS fans have long heard the stories about him keeping photo albums full of Polaroid instant snapshots of his various conquests. And to show how much time has changed, it should be mentioned for younger fans out there that Polaroids were a way to get quick instant photos in front of you instead of using a camera with film that would have to be developed and then transferred to photo stock to see the final results. Instead, it was a simple click of the shutter button, waiting for the photo to be released, and waiting for the chemicals to form the picture of what was taken. The downside was that such photos tended to turn off-color very easily and could not be copied very well. Yet, if you were in a position (no pun intended) that you wanted physical proof of something without the need of developing photos (or having someone develop them for you, which could be an issue for photos such as those Simmons was taking), Polaroids were the way to go. Of course, nowadays one would simply use a cell phone to do all the work and keep the results on a computer, which probably lessens the fun in a way. (One can hardly imagine Simmons impressing anyone with a cell phone in the same manner he could with the big black binders he had for the "series.")

Thus, Simmons and Number so-and-so would have their bit of fun, and then he would snap a Polaroid of her for his records. He stated in 2010 that this involved the woman holding a hotel key, but earlier comments from him have suggested that such individuals were posed in various ways and in some circumstances in ways that would suggest such women would not be able to hold hotel keys (such as dangling naked from a flagpole outside of a hotel room window . . . seriously . . .). He would then put the photos into binders to show off to others.

Which he certainly did, and proudly so. There have been several interviews over the years with individuals who have seen the photos in the binders, and I personally saw a number of them (admittedly without opening them) that he used to keep in his formal office in New York during the late 1980s and early 1990s. (No doubt kept there for purely business reasons.) There was even a story from back in the 1980s about someone stealing one or two of the books, although there are confused reports if he ever got them back (no doubt a police report about them would be interesting to read: "Victim states binder is of old, yellowing pictures of Numbers 326–580 in a series of nude poses . . . ."). How many binders would that be? Well, Polaroids were big clunky things, so you usually could not get more than four photos to a page. Eight photos, front and back on one page of the binder would mean 575 pages and thus probably three to five binders at most and not really hard to count through. Could he have had some doubles or even triples in there? Hard to say, but who would remember them that well after so many?

Nevertheless—in as serious of a tone as can be mustered here—he definitely had sex with a lot of women, and he gets a certain amount of the jollies out of telling people about it. But the point is, what does this have to do with the history of KISS? Absolutely nothing. No one is a KISS fan just because of Gene Simmons's escapades with women. A few might get a hoot out of the stories, but no one ran into a record shop demanding the new KISS album because "Gene's been with 4,600 women!" Band members have found the numerous attempts by Simmons to turn band interviews into showcases for his tally a bore as well, with a famous leaked video of Simmons and Paul Stanley being interviewed for a 1994 Dick Clark special (*American Bandstand's Teen Idol*) where Stanley cut into Simmons for doing so and the two arguing before resuming the interview. For the fans, it is knowledge that "everyone" has heard, so why focus on that when there are other interesting things to discuss about the band, like a new album or tour.

Which is the irony of the whole 4,600 thing Simmons brags about—whether it is an urban legend or not, it does not drive anyone to become a fan of the band. No one thinks Mama Cass had a great voice because she supposedly choked to death on a ham sandwich (and, no, she did not). No one listens to Keith Richards tear it up on the guitar just because he "changes his blood" every 2,000 miles. And no one is a KISS fan just because of the number of women Gene Simmons slept with . . . although it at least gives nonfans a topic to discuss when they are stuck trying to make conversation with someone from the KISS Army.

27

From *Runaway* to Cameos

Gene's Acting Career

B esides Gene Simmons's dedication to photography, as seen in the previous chapter, he has made no bones over the years that he really wanted to stretch out into other aspects of entertainment as well. This had led into work within the music industry as both a producer and manager for other entertainers, as well as twice throwing together his own record label for possible projects. It has also found Gene working with others on books—namely autobiographical tomes—as well as a short-lived comic book imprint called Simmons Comics Group, and even producing his own magazine called *Gene Simmons' Tongue*, which lasted five issues before folding.

One area that Simmons has often said he wanted to venture into was acting. Even in the mid-1970s he was seeing his future in films, going so far as to suggest that he would be perfect as The Thing in an adaptation of the Marvel comic *The Fantastic Four*. One hindrance, however, was that he was in KISS—this band that had a gimmick where no one was seen without their makeup. Simmons was a strong protector of that mystery to the band's image and therefore had to balance his yearning to perform for the cameras with that of carrying on the mystique of the band. This also explains why he would readily would bring up playing The Thing, as it could easily have been made a role where he performed behind a mask the entire production and thus not affect his KISS persona.

All this easily plays into why Simmons could be argued into taking the makeup off in the early 1980s: It was a chance to be get his true face out there in public and start picking up roles in the movies. Note here that the discussion has been strictly on movies, as Simmons made clear early on that he had no interest in doing acting for the stage. He told Jim Steranko in *Prevue* magazine in 1984 that he had been training under acting coach Alice Spivak starting in 1981 and even attended a few of her classes to perform onstage, but did not care for the technique involved and preferred the more technical and "close-up" look of screen acting to performing for a live audience. This may sound ironic from someone who had spent years playing a "demon" during rock shows, but perhaps having done pantomime for so long to crowds, he may have simply felt the need to do something a bit different. Also, it has always been clear that Simmons's first love was horror movies and comic books, growing up writing fanzines about such movies and becoming quite an expert on classic horror films and cartoons. So it was natural that he would want to move in such a direction.

Appearing in movies before the makeup came off was no doubt a trial for Simmons, as the offers were certainly out there. Some obviously because of his fame, but some were certainly legitimate movies that got theatrical release and some quite popular. *Variety* reported in 1982 that he had been up for the lead role in the film *Running Brave* (about real-life Olympic athlete Billy Mills), which eventually went to Robby Benson, as well as for Michael Nouri's role as the male lead in the 1982 film *Flashdance*, which Simmons supposedly turned down because he did not want to be in a "disco movie." He was also considered for a role in the Ron Howard comedy *Night Shift*, which would catapult Michael Keaton into film stardom in the 1980s. Other films that he reportedly was asked to do but turned down were Howard Hesseman's role as a pimp in the Dan Aykroyd comedy *Doctor Detroit* and the James Woods role in Sergio Leone's *Once Upon a Time in America*. However, these last two films were produced while the band was still in makeup in 1982; while many actors were considered for the part he was to play in the Leone movie, other factors kept Simmons out of these projects instead of just him turning them down.

With the makeup finally off in 1983, he began more actively looking for roles and in March 1984 auditioned for two films set to go into production: *Sea Trial*, an action movie to have been directed by *Exorcist* author William Friedkin and that eventually saw Michael Nouri getting the role before the movie fell through, and another that would be his debut in movies.

Runaway

It is a jump ahead into the future, where minor tasks are carried out by robots and everyone has one in the home. Tom Selleck plays a cop whose job is to take care of malfunctioning servant robots (aka "runaways") that could pose harm to humans. Gene Simmons plays sociopathic scientist Charles Luther, who is killing off people who stand in his way of profiting from a computer program he plans to sell on the black market. His method of murder is through the use of robots, in particular spiderlike robots that can inject acid from a needle built into their bodies and special bullets that can be adapted to seek out individual people as their targets.

Michael Crichton will be forever remembered for having written the novel on which the movie *Jurassic Park* was based. The film version of that book, directed by Steven Spielberg in 1990, would go on to be a huge success and lead to Crichton getting many other movie projects in the works, but he was no stranger to movies before that. His novels—many of which played with current-day activities involving "day after tomorrow" technology gone wrong (much as how *Jurassic Park* is laid out)—had been adapted since 1969, starting with *The Andromeda Strain*. By 1973, he was directing movies, starting with *Westworld* (featuring a score by *KISS Meets the Phantom* composer Fred Karlin), and

Gene Simmons as the villain Charles Luther in his first movie, *Runaway*. Because of the role, Simmons would have to wear a wig for the *Animalize* tour.   *Author's Collection*

many of his films, such as *Coma* and *Looker*, deal with technological madness. Continuing with that theme would be his 1984 movie, *Runaway*.

Runaway was set to be a big winter film for TriStar Pictures. Crichton was a known name, and the star was popular television actor Tom Selleck, who filmed *Runaway* during off-time from his television series *Magnum P. I.* Joining him in the film was Cynthia Rhodes, a dancer who was building a name for herself as an actor after appearing in *Stayin' Alive* and—another Simmons connection—*Flashdance*. Also appearing was Kirstie Alley, who had broken through with her work in the movie *Star Trek II: Wrath of Khan*, but was still a few years away from success on the television series *Cheers* when she took over for Shelley Long. Simmons tried out for the role as the main villain, Dr. Charles Luther, and got the part upon convincing Crichton that he could appear menacing by changing the look on his face.

Production began in the summer of 1984, with Simmons cutting his hair short for the role. This led to him having to wear a wig on the 1984–1985 *Animalize* tour (held in place by a band around his forehead) that many fans commented on at the time (he can be seen wearing the wig on the *Animalized Live Uncensored* video). It also found him away in the state of Washington and Canada while the band was trying to complete the *Animalize* album—leading to Paul Stanley doing most of the production on his own, having Jean Beauvoir play bass on several track, and completely remixing the album after Simmons had departed for filming. This explains in part why the album lists Stanley as producer, while Simmons only got an associate producer role in the album credits.

The movie was looked to be a solid holiday entry for Tri-Star and was released on December 14, 1984. Also released that day were *Dune, Starman,* and *The Cotton Club,* while *Beverly Hills Cop, The Terminator, A Nightmare on Elm Street, The Karate Kid,* and *Ghostbusters* were still eating up a lot of ticket sales at the theaters. *Variety* listed *Runaway* as an $8 million production, and the final take after six weeks in theaters was a dismal $6.7 million, even with heavy promotion on the entertainment programs and in ads. Most critical reviews found the movie rather silly (Siskel and Ebert joked on their television program about the illogic of Luther's bullets that could seek out people but were so slow you could dodge them), but gave merit to both Selleck and Simmons for doing their best with what they were given. Selleck would move on to other movie projects, but never quite reached the level of success one would assume was heading his way in the movies and has instead concentrated on various movies for television. Meanwhile, Simmons would make brief cameos as bad guys on two television programs—*Miami Vice* and *The Hitchhiker*—before seeing the release of his next film.

Never Too Young to Die

John Stamos is the son of a famous spy (played by one-time-only James Bond George Lazenby). When his father is killed by the evil genius Velvet Von Ragner (Gene Simmons), the son meets up with his dad's partner (Vanity) to defeat the villain. Oh, and Ragner is a hermaphrodite.

This was Simmons's second film and his second as the main villain. He did a bit of promotion for the movie as it was being filmed, even talking to *Entertainment Tonight* while dressed in the showgirl outfit he wears in his musical number from the movie (yes, musical number; and check out Chapter 30 under "Lynda Carter" for more details about that outfit). The movie was produced by Paul Entertainment from a screenplay by Lorenzo Semple Jr. (best remembered for writing many of the *Batman* television episodes of the 1960s) and Steven Paul. John Stamos was becoming a hot property at the time, while Vanity was already known for her music work with the franchise of acts working with rock star Prince, as well as appearing in several films up to that time.

Filming took place from August through October 1985 in Los Angeles, once again just as the band was putting finishing touches on a new studio album in New York (in this case, *Asylum*). Fortunately, in that situation, most of the work was done during the summer, so the production was more evenly split between Stanley and Simmons than when *Animalize* was being put together.

The film had some problems finding a distributor, even with ads running in *Variety* for the picture from March through May 1986. The ads themselves are interesting, as one featured Simmons in his second role in the film, Carruthers— an agent who is secretly Ragner in disguise—and with no mention of his villainous alter ego in the picture. Another ad featured Stamos and Vanity in a pose similar to what was used for the movie poster, but with an added drawing

ULOGE: JOHN STAMOS   VANITY   GENE   SIMMONS
SCENARIO: LORENCO SEMPLE   KAMERA: DAVID WORTH
DAVID PAVL   REŽIJA: GIL BETTMAN

Simmons in his role from *Never Too Young to Die*, wearing a copy of the same outfit Lynda Carter wore in her 1980 television special when she sang "I Was Made for Lovin' You."   *Author's Collection*

of Simmons in facial makeup to make him appear somewhat demonic. Finally, the ad campaign concentrated on Stamos and Vanity in the pose used for the video release of the film as well.

The $5.2 million movie finally opened in seven "hardtop" theaters (as *Variety* reported) during the second week of June 1986 and eventually was pulled after a run of three weeks with diminishing returns. Other films released to theaters that summer were *Top Gun; Karate Kid, Part II; Labyrinth; Maximum Overdrive;* and *Howard the Duck.*

Never Too Young to Die would see video release in 1987 through Charter Entertainment, where it has picked up a bit of an audience who "love to hate it." Even so, it was not the worst break for Simmons—at one point he said jokingly that being in the movie was the darkest moment of his career. Besides, he had two other movies that would come out soon and both were being expected to be big hits.

Trick or Treat

Eddie, a high school nerd (Marc Price) who loves heavy metal, is upset over hearing about the death of his rock idol Sammi Curr (Tony Fields). Visiting a radio DJ (Gene Simmons) who knew Curr, the DJ gives Eddie a copy of Curr's last recordings. Eddie soon discovers that the recording allows Curr to return from the dead and start killing and that the recording will soon be played by the DJ on his radio show. Eddie must stop the music unless Curr is able to return for good from the dead.

This film, billed as a "rock and roll horror comedy" when looking for a distributor, was directed by Charles Martin Smith, who had played a nerd himself in *American Graffiti* in 1973. The film was produced from May to June 1986 in North Carolina. Oddly enough, although this would come during a bit of a break for KISS (their next album, *Crazy Nights*, would not be released until 1987, and touring had just been completed for the *Asylum* album, giving them some free time), Simmons only has a small cameo in the film. He has reported that he was asked to play the Curr part but declined, stating the script was not very good, although he probably was sensitive to the idea that he would be playing a demon rock-'n'-roll performer, which may have hit a little too close to home. (W.A.S.P. frontman Blackie Lawless has also gone on record as saying he was to play the role before it went to dancer Tony Fields.) Instead, Simmons plays the DJ who tries to convince Eddie that sometimes entertainers can carry their "act" too far and should not be worshiped. Strangely, the film seems to point toward Simmons's character reappearing near the climax of the film, and his voice is heard from the radio to kick in the final act, yet he is never seen again after his one brief appearance early on.

The film would feature Ozzy Osbourne in a small role as a preacher seen on a television talk show discussing the evils of rock music and being attacked through the television screen by Curr. This has led to the movie being boxed on video and DVD with both Simmons's and Osbourne's pictures on the cover, although both only appear briefly and in roles that are not villainous.

The $8 million movie was released to theaters on October 24, 1986 through De Laurentiis Entertainment Group. Also out in theaters at the time were *Crocodile Dundee, Children of a Lesser God, Stand By Me, Top Gun* (still packing them in), and the just-released *Soul Man*. The movie seemed to have a decent if slightly soft start when released, but business soon fell, and the movie ended up making only $6.7 million before finally being pulled from theaters.

Wanted Dead or Alive

Nick Randall (Rutger Hauer) is an ex-CIA agent turned bounty hunter who is asked to track down a terrorist, Malak Al Rahim (Gene Simmons).

This New World production was promoted as being based in part on the 1950s television series *Wanted Dead or Alive* that starred Steve McQueen. The original series was set near the beginning of the twentieth century and was a western, but the concept of a bounty hunter was retained with Hauer's character being mentioned in ads and in the movie as a descendant of McQueen's character. The film was produced in the summer of 1986, which as mentioned in the previous entry was a period when KISS was taking some time off from touring and recording, so Simmons's involvement in the Los Angeles-based production did not interfere with the band activities.

The small-budgeted movie would gross $7.5 million after its release on January 16, 1987. Also out in theaters at the time were many of the same features playing when *Trick or Treat* came out a few months before, as well as *Star Trek IV, Platoon, Little Shop of Horrors*, and *The Golden Child*.

The movie's director, Gary Sherman, would go on to direct Simmons in his "Rock Against Drugs" ad, as well as work with Simmons on the pilot for the comic-book-based action series *Sable*. The show was based on a long-lasting comic book from First Comics produced by writer/artist Mike Grell, which had a mercenary whose secret identity was that of a children's author under a fake name (thus a slight switch on the normal way alter egos in comics were handled).

Terrorism has never hit home until now...

Promotional flyer for *Wanted Dead or Alive*, which gives away the ending of the film.   *Author's Collection*

Simmons helped develop the project as well as star as Sable in one of the pilots done for the series. Sherman later stated in an interview that ABC loved the series but did not care for Simmons in the lead and asked for it to be recast. To let everyone down easy, Simmons announced that he would be too busy to work on the series anyway thanks to things happening in KISS, although the band was still on its long break in action and would not ramp up things until late in 1987. *Sable* ran for seven episodes on ABC before being canceled but at least had the opportunity to do a wrap-up episode that allowed for the series to have a natural ending in January 1988.

One similarity for the series to that of *Wanted Dead or Alive* was the opportunity for Simmons to play the hero for once, just as it was a chance for Hauer—best remembered at the time for his role as the replicant trying to kill Harrison Ford's character in *Bladerunner*—to play something other than a villain in the movie. At least Simmons's next movie would give him a chance to play something of a good guy. But there would be one last tempting offer to play a villain before that.

Red Surf

Remar (George Clooney) is one of a group of surfers who deal drugs to make some money. In a convoluted story, the surfers decide to exact revenge on a drug lord for killing one of them. Simmons plays Doc, an older surfer dude, drug dealer, and Vietnam vet who helps the group with weapons as well as taking part in the revenge.

In the spring of 1988, Simmons was offered a chance to be part of a major motion picture, the new James Bond movie, *Licence to Kill*. The movie would have found him playing the villain, Franz Sanchez, a deadly drug lord. However, he passed up the chance, stating prior commitments with KISS would have made it impossible. This was true—production began on the Bond movie in September 1988 while KISS was looking to do some final dates on their *Crazy Nights* tour, including the famous *Monsters of Rock* shows in the UK. Then again, the tour was over by the end of that month, and the band would take a break again until late 1989. Thus, there may be also a hint that he was getting tired of playing drug lords and bad guys by this point—Simmons had been linked to such roles in *Rock and Roll High School Forever* (1991) and another episode of *The Hitchhiker* series—and wanting to do something a little different. Strangely enough, if he had taken on the role, one of his henchmen was played by *KISS Meets the Phantom* costar Anthony Zerbe.

Instead, Simmons's next role would be a Vietnam vet who is a surfer who sells drugs on the side. Which does not really seem like typecasting for Simmons. However, it did give him a chance to play a good guy who is out to get a drug lord instead of the other way around. Production began in the spring of 1989 in Los Angeles for Academy Entertainment and featured Simmons with his hair pulled back in a style that would be quite common for him through the 1990s.

Simmons's role is actually pretty minor and just as well—the movie sat on a shelf until June 1990, when it was finally released to a total of six theaters before being pulled, earning a total of $13,000 for the production. The film would eventually be released to video, playing up Clooney's involvement although he disappears two-thirds of the way through the film and doesn't play a very likable character.

Still, for Simmons, even though it was a small part, it was a final chance to play a feature role in a theatrical film. He did try to get a series produced for his housemate Shannon Tweed called *Delta Tenn*, based on a short-lived comic-book series of the same name. Although NBC took a serious interest in the concept, they finally passed on it. There was also talk about producing a movie based on Gerald Frank's book *The Deed* in 1989, but this also fell through after some initial interest from Warner Brothers. From here on out, Simmons's appearances would be cameos and in documentary footage. These would include quick appearances in *Decline of Western Civilization Part II: The Metal Years, Detroit Rock City, The New Guy, Wish You Were Dead, Extract, Expecting Mary, Rush: Beyond the Lighted Stage,* as well as television series such as *Third Watch* and *Castle.* In nearly all he would be presented briefly as himself or play someone much like himself.

Which of course gets us to *Family Jewels,* a scripted "reality series" featuring Gene Simmons playing a version of himself along with his entire family, much in the spirit of *The Osbournes* on which it is based. The series, which aired in America on the A&E cable network since 2006, has proved to be the biggest success of Simmons's acting career, an ironic ending for someone who went into acting to get away from his role in KISS only to find his best success playing off of that very image he was trying to shed.

28

Producer, Songwriter, Solo Artist

Paul's Projects Outside of KISS

W hen people talk of someone from KISS doing projects outside of the band, there is an immediate tendency to think of Gene Simmons. This is no disrespect for the other members of the band; it merely shows how hard Simmons has worked to promote himself and his various activities over the years. After all, if any member of KISS is going to pop up in the news, it is commonly Simmons because he thrives on getting his name in the news. Doing so, however, can sometimes give the impression that everyone else in the band merely sits around for months at a time, waiting for his call to do another KISS project.

Of course, that is not the case for any of the band members, past or present, as all have used their "free time" to deal with other ventures. Most typically, this means writing or playing some music for other performers live or for use on albums. Paul Stanley has certainly gone this route as well, but he has done a variety of other things that have put him in the limelight—away from KISS and away from Simmons. Stanley himself made the point in interviews for his *Live to Win* album that what mattered when dealing with press was being able to promote his latest project and nothing beyond that. Thus, he tends to keep most of his private life exactly that—private—while Simmons talks about most anything public or private if it will help draw attention to what he is currently doing. Yet when one sees how often Stanley has done work released professionally over the years—acting, painting, producing, and contributing songs and performances to other artists—he has shown himself to be nearly as active as Simmons.

Solo Artist

Many fans and acquaintances of the band acknowledge that KISS became Paul Stanley's band during the 1980s. Peter Criss was essentially gone before the 1980 album *Unmasked*, and Ace was out the door even before *Creatures of the Night* was released in 1982 (although they attempted to make it look otherwise). Meanwhile, after the bashing *Music from "The Elder"* got from critics and fans, and the dismal returns on *Creatures*, Simmons began focusing more of his time on kick-starting his acting career (see Chapter 27 on how that all turned out), managing other bands, producing other acts, and even starting his own music label. With Simmons's attention elsewhere, Stanley jumped in to keep the ship sailing for KISS from 1983 through 1989—a situation that even Simmons has acknowledged in his book *Sex Money KISS.*

Looking back on those years (from *Lick It Up* through *Smashes, Thrashes, and Hits*), it is clear that Stanley's peppier, anthem-oriented, more pop-driven style of music was setting the direction of the band, as well as in costumes and stage designs. However, when Simmons returned from his "exile" in 1989 to focus on KISS again, with *Hot in the Shade* and *Revenge*, the music turned back toward story-based and mystical themes again. The costumes and stage designs also changed to feature a more fantasy-world element (such as the ruined New York landscape of the *Revenge* tour and even the laser eyes of the sphinx for the *Hot in the Shade* tour), after years of flashy glamlike costumes and bare steel stages of the Stanley-centric years.

Just before Simmons's proactive "return" to the band and years after turning down outside projects such as producing albums for other artists in order to focus on KISS, Stanley finally took a chance to do something on his own, a solo tour in early 1989. The tour, sometimes referred to as the "Who Dares Wins" tour due to the title being listed on some of the official T-shirts sold at the shows, would last roughly seven weeks from the middle of February to the beginning of April 1989 and feature Stanley with Bob Kulick on lead guitar, Eric Singer on drums, Dennis St. James on bass, and Gary Corbett on keyboards. Playing in a number of bigger clubs on the East Coast and a few in California, Stanley went through a number of KISS songs as well as songs from his 1978 album and even "Hide Your Heart," which would eventually appear on the *Hot in the Shade* album but had been circulating in bootleg form among fans before the tour had started. (Stanley would even tease the audience with the chorus of the song first in order to see what type of reaction it got. Usually a strong, positive one, proving how quickly bootleg material would circulate among fans.)

While some fans wondered if the tour meant that Stanley would soon break off from KISS for good, it appears everyone in the band knew it was more a case of wanting to do something as a solo performer (or, as Eric Carr told me in 1990, "A chance for Paul to get his rocks off."). Even so, the coincidence of Simmons's refocus on the band after this tour is rather interesting to see. As such, KISS would get back into the studio in the summer of 1989, and Stanley would put his solo musical career on hold for another fifteen years.

After several years of having put back on the makeup and costumes of the 1970s KISS, Stanley decided to go into the studio and record a new solo album in 2006 called *Live to Win*. The album featured ten tracks all written by Stanley, with some help from previous cowriters from the KISS days such as Desmond Child and Holly Knight. He followed up the release in October 2005 with a small number of live shows that month and into November, along with a few in Australia during April 2007. The band included Jim McGorman and Rafael Moreira on guitars, Sasha Krivtsov on bass, Nate Morton on drums, and Paul

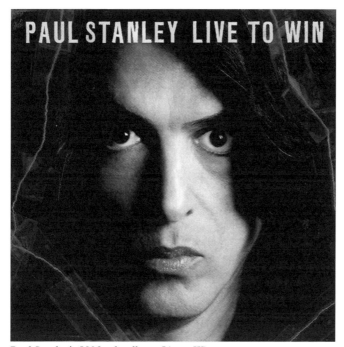

Paul Stanley's 2006 solo album *Live to Win.*

Author's Collection

Mirkovich on keyboards. A live DVD and CD was released in 2008 of the November 6, 2006, show at the House of Blues in Chicago called *One Live KISS.* Since that time, Stanley has returned to focusing his attention on KISS, although his other interests have also begun to take up some of his public life in a variety of ways.

Producer

Obviously all four members of the band had some input into the recording of their albums in the 1970s, but for the most part they allowed control to be in the hands of those they felt knew better as to what to do than they. Of course, when said producers were people like Eddie Kramer and Bob Ezrin, it made sense to defer to their control. However, it was only natural that Paul Stanley's first credit as a producer on an album sleeve would be with his 1978 solo album (see Chapter 7 for more detail on this and the other solo albums), and both Ace Frehley and Gene Simmons did the same with their albums. After all, with a chance to go in their own directions with the solo albums, it only made sense that they would want to be the ones making the final decisions for their chance to show the world their "true selves." With the success of the band, their manager, Bill Aucoin, was starting to branch out his management company to obtain other acts. One of those bands was New England, who had impressed Aucoin after a couple of sets he saw in 1978. In getting the band a deal with Infinity Records, Aucoin made the suggestion of having Paul Stanley produce their first album. The members of New England thought it was worth a shot, and after some rehearsal time with Stanley agreed to have him produce the album.

 Stanley is listed as coproducer with Mike Stone, who at that point was mainly known for his work with engineering the early Queen albums. Stone had also recently worked with Paul Stanley on his 1978 solo album as well as mixing KISS's *Double Platinum* album that year, so they obviously had a good understanding of how each other worked. *Billboard* magazine in May 1979 stated that Stanley's role as producer was merely to help the performance side of the band while Stone dealt with the technical side, but this makes it sound as if all Stanley did was make sure they looked good in their clothes. Hirsh Gardner, drummer of the band, told the New England fan website newenglandrocks.com that Stanley's role as producer dealt more with making sure the band sounded good while Mike Stone concentrated more on the technical side of the production (Gardner even makes a point of stating how good a producer Stanley was, just as Stone was a brilliant engineer for the album).

 Paul Stanley can also be heard on vocals for the song "Don't Ever Wanna Lose Ya," their first single of their debut album, *New England*, which was released in May 1979.

 The song reached #40 on the *Billboard* chart, helped by the band touring with KISS in 1979, but for some reason the act never really caught the attention of listeners at the time. In a bizarre coincidence, Gardner and bandmates Gary Shea and Jimmy Waldo would spend some time trying to start a band after New England called Warrior in 1981 and 1982; working on several demos with their new lead guitarist, a man named Vinnie Cusano before the guitarist got a job and a new name as Vinnie Vincent in KISS. Perhaps both Warrior and New England were cases of being just a smidge too early to break through, as both Shea and Waldo would finally move on to bigger success with their band Alcatrazz in the 1980s.

 Over the years, rumors have popped up of Stanley agreeing to produce albums for other artists, but things would never quite gel. Some choices that seemed obvious at the time were Ratt, Poison (for their *Open Up and Say . . . Ahh!* album), and Warrant (who had opened for Stanley on his 1989 solo tour), but typically these came just as KISS was about to record a new album or go on tour, and thus Paul would have to pass. Two that were closer to actually occurring were Cher for her *Heart of Stone* album in 1989 and the 1985 Girlschool album, *Running Wild* (featuring their take on "Do You Love Me?"), but neither came to fruition. Stanley was also in the running to produce Guns N' Roses' *Appetite for Destruction* album, which was nixed after he and the band split on the song "Welcome to the Jungle"; according to Slash in his autobiography,

Stanley thought the song could work as an uplifting anthem—a direction the band did not think would be right.

Stanley did go back into the studio to help produce the first album from a band called Crown of Thorns, which he and Gene Simmons were managing for a time. Leading Crown of Thorns was Jean Beauvoir, a guitarist who had worked with Stanley on music for both *Animalize* and *Asylum*, while also playing bass on some of *Animalize* as well. Stanley would produce tracks for the band that would pop up on several releases over the years, with the largest number appearing on a three-CD box set from 2004 called *Crown Jewels*, although most of the tracks were recorded in 1991. Paul also cowrote two songs for the band, "Winterland" and "Dirty Walk, Dirty Talk."

Dynasty tour ad showing the band Stanley produced, New England, opening for them. *Author's Collection*

Since the run of production work for KISS in the 1980s and his work for Crown of Thorns, Stanley has taken a more hands-off approach to recording, allowing others to produce the KISS albums and focusing more on writing and performing. His last producer credits are for his own 2006 solo album *Live to Win* and his live album follow-up *One Live Kiss*.

Songwriting

In the late 1970s, both Ace Frehley and Paul Stanley wanted to spread their musical wings a bit while still being connected with writing and playing with KISS (Gene Simmons would also go this route, but a tad later in the 1980s). Besides the number of artists that have rerecorded KISS tracks written or cowritten by Stanley, there have been several times where Stanley has worked with other artists to create original songs. In some cases, like "Hide Your Heart" and "Sword and Stone," songs originally written for KISS (both songs went as far as demos for the *Crazy Nights* album, and "Hide Your Heart" finally appeared on album and as a single for the *Hot in the Shade* album in 1989) were picked up by other artists instead. In many cases, such writing came about while working on material that has ended up on KISS albums with other performers (such as Stanley's work with Andreas Carlsson while putting together material for his *Live to Win* album).

"The Fight"—Desmond Child and Rogue, *Desmond Child and Rogue* (1979). The trio of singers who made up Rogue also sang on Paul Stanley's 1978 solo album. More important, Desmond Child, would cowrite "I Was Made for Lovin' You" with Stanley for the 1979 KISS album *Dynasty* and continue to write material for KISS with Stanley in the 1980s. Child would become a very hot writer/producer in the 1980s as well, creating hits for many artists.

"It's My Life"—King Kobra, *III* (1988). Carmine Appice's band recorded in 1988 their own version of this song that also appears on Wendy O. Williams's album *W.O.W.* from 1984 (see Chapter 18 under "Plasmatics" for more details on this and other songs from that album). King Kobra had opened for KISS on the *Asylum* tour a couple of years before.

"Sword and Stone"—Paul Dean, *Hard Core* (1988) and Bonfire, *Shocker No More Mr. Nice Guy The Music* soundtrack album (1989)
    Dean is the lead guitarist of the popular early 1980s band Loverboy and cowrote the song with Stanley and Desmond Child. Meanwhile, Child produced the soundtrack album for the Wes Craven horror movie *Shocker*, with the band Bonfire doing the song.

"Hide Your Heart"—Bonnie Tyler, *Hide Your Heart* (1988); Robin Beck, *Trouble or Nothin'* (1989); Ace Frehley, *Trouble Walkin'* (1989); and Molly Hatchet, *Lightning Strikes Twice* (1989). Tyler got the drop on this song thanks to Desmond Child producing her album, although it would be covered by four other artists within a year, and both by a former KISS member (Frehley) as well as KISS for their *Hot in the Shade* album. Beck's album was also produced by Desmond Child, which would make the song a rather surprising choice considering Child had just produced it for another artist for whom Tyler named the album after the track as well. Considering the animosity starting to emerge between KISS and Frehley (as well as Peter) Criss by the late 1980s, it felt strange to some fans to see Frehley pick Stanley's song to record, but his argument came down to knowing a catchy song when he heard one and not letting any hard feelings get in the way.

"A Lover Like You"—Voodoo X, *The Awakening Vol. 1* (1989) and Craig McLachland, *Hands Free* (1992). Song cowritten with Jean Beauvoir, who—as mentioned earlier in this chapter—had worked with Stanley on material for a couple of 1980s KISS albums.

"Clock Strikes"—Wild Side, *Under the Influence* (1992). Stanley connected with the band after their manager, Barry Levine, who had photographed the band many times in the 1970s, asked him to check out the band.

"Hang Me Up"—War Babies, *War Babies* (1992). Columbia, War Babies' label, thought the band would be helped in sales if Stanley were brought in to help write a song with them and perhaps perform on the album as a guest artist. This led to Stanley cowriting "Hang Me Up" as well as him playing twelve-string guitar on the track "Cry Yourself to Sleep."

"Jump the Gun"—Jeff Paris, *Lucky This Time* (1993). Stanley cowrote this song with Jeff Paris back in 1987 and sang backing vocals on the recording. Paris had worked as a session player for a number of years while writing songs for a number of other performers like Alias, Mr. Big, and Vixen.

"If We Ever"—Stan Bush, *Higher Than Angels* (1996) and *The Child Within* (1996); "If We Ever Get Out of This Place"—Eddie Money, *Shakin' with the Money Man* (1997). Song cowritten with Curt Cuomo and Stan Bush. Cuomo had written several songs with Paul Stanley and Bruce Kulick for the *Carnival of Souls* album and two songs cowritten with Stanley for the *Psycho Circus* album. Cuomo also produced Stan Bush's album. Bush has done a lot of movie and television soundtrack work, but is probably best remembered for the song "The Touch" that was used in the animated movie *Transformers: The Movie*. Robin Beck also made an appearance on this album, although not on this particular track. *The Child Within* is a European release of the *Higher Than Angels* album with some slight changes. The song was reworked for Eddie Money's album in 1997, with a slightly longer title and also produced by Cuomo.

"I Was Wrong"—Stan Bush, *Higher Than Angels* (1996). Cowritten by Cuomo and Bush with Stanley. When the album was reworked for a European release, this song was dropped from the reissue.

"You're Gonna Be the One"—Lenita Erickson, *Lenita Erickson* (1996). Curt Cuomo produced this album and cowrote all of the original songs on the album. Stanley cowrote this track with Cuomo, and Tommy Girvin and played guitar on the track. Cuomo would go on to perform with Bruce Kulick and Eric Singer in a band called ESP Kulick would also help out Lenita Erickson for a short promotional tour done for the album in 1996.

"Game of Love"—Garbo Talks, *Garbo Talks* (1998). Cowritten with Bob Held, this is rather unique as the recording used has a demo created by KISS at the base. Stanley recorded this song with Bruce Kulick and Eric Carr back in the 1980s, and Carr's drums as well as Stanley's and Kulick's guitar and vocals can be heard on the track.

"Machs Dir selbst"—Silbermond, *Verschwende Deine Zeit* (2004) and "Bloodtype R"—Bad Candy, *Bad Candy* (2006). Cowritten with Andreas Carlsson, who would work with Stanley on his *Live to Win* album. The Silbermond version has new lyrics written by the German band, which is why they have a credit for the song.

"Angel to You (Devil to Me)"—The Click Five, *Greetings from the Imrie House* (2005). Stanley cowrote the song with Ben Roman of the band.

"Timeless"—Erik Gronwall, *Between a Rock and a Hard Place* (2010). Cowritten with Andreas Carlsson.

Studio Appearances

Besides those listed above for Jeff Paris, War Babies, Lenita Erickson, and Garbo Talks, Stanley has also lent his support to other performers by assisting in the recording of their albums, typically in the form of backing vocals (much as he did for the *New England* album he produced). Paul was also involved with the recording of the 1984 Wendy O. Williams album *W.O.W.*, which is covered in more detail in Chapter 18.

"You're Out of Love"—Alessi, *Driftin'* (1978). Stanley became friendly with this band made up of twins Bill and Bob Alessi in 1978 through mutual friend and songwriter Pepe Castro (aka Peppy Castro, aka Emil Thielhelm, who had been in the band Barnaby Bye with the Alessis). The Alessi brothers had a UK hit with the song "Oh Lori" in 1977 and were working on a second follow-up album when Stanley suggested he add some "KISS guitar" to one of the tracks. He also provided backing vocals for the song. Castro would perform on two songs for Stanley's 1978 solo album ("Hold Me, Touch Me" and "Ain't Quite Right") while also cowriting "Naked City" for the *Unmasked* album.

"Falling in Love"—Balance, *Balance* (1981). Stanley did backing vocals for this track. Balance was made up of Pepe Castro, longtime KISS studio support Bob Kulick, and Doug Katsaros.

"Shocker" and "Shocker (Reprise)"—Dudes of Wrath, *Shocker: No More Mr. Nice Guy—The Music* soundtrack album (1989). Stanley sang lead vocals with Desmond Child on the title track for this Wes Craven horror movie. Stanley's cowritten song "Sword and Stone" also appears on the album by the band Bonfire.

"Save Up All Your Tears"—Robin Beck, *Trouble or Nothin* (1989). Stanley sang backing vocals on this track for the album produced by Desmond Child. The album also featured one of the various versions of "Hide Your Heart" that came out between 1988 and 1990.

"Johnny's Got a Mind of His Own"—House of Lords, *Demons Down* (1992). Stanley sang backing vocals for this track off the third album by the band (the first not produced in part by Gene Simmons or released under his Simmons Records label). House of Lords was created by Greg Giuffria, former keyboardist for KISS's "opposite" in the Aucoin Management group of bands back in the 1970s.

"Love Her All I Can"—Anthrax, *Black Lodge* (1993). Stanley sang co-lead vocals on this remake of an old KISS song along with Gene Simmons.

"Brite Lites"—Kuni, *Fucked Up!* (2000). Stanley played bass guitar on this track along with Bruce Kulick and Eric Singer.

"I Will Be with You"—Sarah Brightman, *Symphony* (2008). Stanley sang co-lead on this duet with Brightman.

"Cut the Wire" and "Kukaracha"—Pushking, *The World as We Know It* (2011). Stanley sang lead vocals on these two tracks for an album released as a series of duets with a variety of performers.

Acting

Stanley never showed as much interest in going into acting as Simmons did, nor does it appear he put as much time into studying the field as Simmons had in the late '70s and early '80s. Still, even after the ridicule Stanley got for his work on the *KISS Meets the Phantom* movie (which he has readily admitted he was pretty terrible in), he was not deterred from at least investigating acting as an avenue for his talent. The results? Unfortunately, a lot of film on the cutting-room floor and appearances as himself for documentaries and even mockumentaries.

Attempts at cameos in movies started back in 1982 when word went around in KISS fandom that Stanley had filmed a bit for the *Airplane!*-like spoof of medical dramas and soap operas called *Young Doctors in Love*. He would have appeared only briefly as a singer who gets a microphone stuck in his mouth or throat. Some sources have this listed as Stanley appearing as himself in his KISS makeup, which, considering KISS was still in their makeup at the time the film was produced in early 1982, would make sense if this were the case. However, this was never been confirmed by any photographic evidence or interviews with other cast members.

In 1983, there were rumors that Stanley was to appear briefly in the Dan Aykroyd comedy *Doctor Detroit*. This came from the fact that Stanley was dating Aykroyd's costar Donna Dixon around the time the movie started filming. As fans later learned, the two had broken up by that time, and if Stanley had bothered to film anything, it too was edited out of the finished film. Dixon would go on to marry Aykroyd, while stories swirled that Stanley wrote "I Still Love You" for the *Creatures of the Night* album based on the broken relationship—a song that was never released as a single but became a standard for KISS concerts during the 1980s. For those keeping track, Gene Simmons had been offered a role in *Doctor Detroit* but had turned it down.

While *Doctor Detroit* remains a rumor, there was solid evidence that Stanley had filmed a cameo for the movie *American Anthem,* released in 1986. A drama about young athletes training for the Olympics, with several montages set to a rock score full of popular artists—a common trait for teenager-aimed dramas in the 1980s—it remains unclear as to what his bit in the film would have been. Still, even with his part being scuttled, Stanley helped promote the movie by appearing for a brief interview about the film for its MTV-filmed premiere in 1986.

After the *American Anthem* situation and Stanley's real concerns about keeping KISS afloat, he took a long break from seeking acting work. From 1986 forward, if he made any type of appearance on television or in movies, it was typically for documentaries discussing music and/or KISS; typically with Gene Simmons somewhere in the mix. These include *The Decline of Western Civilization, Part II: The Metal Years; The History of Rock and Roll; Gene Simmons' Family Jewels;* and *Rock N' Roll Fantasy Camp,* among others. This makes his appearance in the 1986 mockumentary *The Return of Bruno* logical. The HBO special is a supposed documentary about an influential musician named Bruno (played by Bruce Willis), with Stanley among many real artists who discuss on camera the man's influence on their careers. In some ways, one could say it was an acting job, but in many ways, it seemed typical of the type of thing Stanley was doing at the time with only a smidgen of acting added to the mix.

Yet brief moments of acting were really what Stanley was geared for over the 1980s and 1990s. At most, these involved performing a line or two in skits for television shows and typically with the other members of the band standing alongside him (two appearances on *Family Guy,* various commercials, an episode of *MadTV,* etc.). One venture that did allow him to do more acting than normal, even though it involved the whole band, was an episode in 1998 of the supernatural detective series *Millennium.* The episode, ". . . Thirteen Years Later," was a tie-in with Fox Network's coverage of the band's *Psycho Circus* tour just starting at the time (the band's stint on *MadTV* occurred as part of the promotion on Fox, as well as bits from the band's L.A. live concert performance to kick off the tour) and featured them both as KISS performing for a movie and as individual members appearing as other characters in heavy makeup. Peter Criss and Ace Frehley's moments in the episode were brief, while Simmons gets a moment to act like something other than a drug dealer or mafia don (and instead does a variation of his *Rock Against Drugs* character). Stanley, on the other hand, gets a chance to do the most acting in the episode in the first few minutes as a movie producer who ends up getting killed.

Ironically, Stanley's last real stretch as an actor came with performing in something connected to a phantom, only instead of the 1978 *KISS Meets the Phantom*, it would be the musical *Phantom of the Opera*.

The Pantages Theatre in Toronto, Canada, had become a home for the Andrew Lloyd Webber musical in 1989 and remained there for ten years, to the point that some felt the musical was actually killing business for the theater. In the later stages of the run, the theater actively sought out new performers to do their take on the main character, which some critics saw as a case of desperation in finding ticket sales. Paul Stanley signed a ten-week contract from May through August and then come back for five more weeks at the end of September to October of that year. Reviews were mixed for his run, but most simply had problems with the musical still playing at the theater more than with Stanley's performance, and most gave him credit for attempting such a part with respect. After the run, Stanley toyed with the idea of signing on to appear in a musical version of *Jekyll & Hyde* for a time before finally putting the idea on hold as the band began looking to tour again in 2000.

Manager

In 1987, Gene Simmons took another step away from KISS by venturing with Howard Marks into managing other performers (one being Liza Minnelli) under the name of Monster Management. Not wanting to be left behind, Stanley soon looked into doing the same with his company, Paul Stanley Entertainment, Ltd. Although heavily promoting the endeavor in interviews, only two bands were noted to have signed up with Stanley and both in 1988: a young band called Racket and a band called Unchained (featuring Benny Doro, who would go on to perform in the KISS tribute band Black Diamond, which played at some of the official KISS conventions in 1995). Yet neither got past the demo stage as the huge success of heavy metal in the mid- to late 1980s was quickly dying out, leaving Stanley to pull the plug on most of his managerial pursuits, although he did comanage the band Crown of Thorns for a period in the early 1990s with Gene.

Painting

Although already creative and having gone to school to become an artist, there had been little of Stanley's art on display over the years. Typically, fans' knowledge of this area of his talent is mostly his work on the KISS logo and some early concert poster art he did for the band. In 2006, however, he began exhibiting his paintings throughout the country, many of which are abstract, although he has done some portraits of himself and the other KISS members in their makeup and without. Although exploring his possibilities away from the band, it has been hard for Stanley to get completely away from the connection.

29

From Out of the Void

K ISS has an unfortunate habit of seeing former members as "out of sight, out of mind." While there have been many official histories of KISS, these usually stop discussing the musicians once they leave the band, only for them to usually and mysteriously reappear years later with something associated with KISS. It is not just with official sources either—unofficial reference guides and biographical studies tend to disregard the work of the men who made up KISS as soon as they are out the door.

Peter Criss

Criss was already recording his first post-KISS solo album, *Out of Control*, with Stan Penridge when KISS was working on *Unmasked*. He would do a number of interviews for the album when it was released in October 1980, but the album and single "By Myself" did not do well on the charts. Criss would reemerge in October 1982 with a new album called *Let Me Rock You*, without the participation of Penridge and a harder sound (including a song by Gene Simmons, "Feel Like Heaven" and featuring Steve Stevens, who would work with Billy Idol). This album also performed poorly and was never released in the U.S. Criss blamed the band and the record label for this, but since KISS was already a bit unsure as to how they were doing with *Creatures of the Night*, Simmons and Stanley probably had little say in such matters even if they wanted.

Criss formed a band with Penridge in January 1983 and did a series of shows at clubs around the country under a number of names that ultimately became known as the Alliance but was normally listed in ads as "Peter Criss." The band lasted close to two years before it broke up over personality issues. After selling his rights in the KISS company back to KISS in 1985, including his makeup, Criss began talking about writing his autobiography, *A Face Without a KISS*. In 1986, he played for a brief time with a band called Balls of Fire and then in 1989 with a band called the Keep, before hooking up with Mark St. John and his brother Michael Norton to work on demos in 1990 and 1991.

The publicity surrounding an imposter who appeared on television and in the gossip magazines helped get Criss some exposure, and he began working on an album that would be released in 1994 as *Cat #1*, with his band called Criss. As he worked on material for a follow-up, he joined Ace Frehley for a

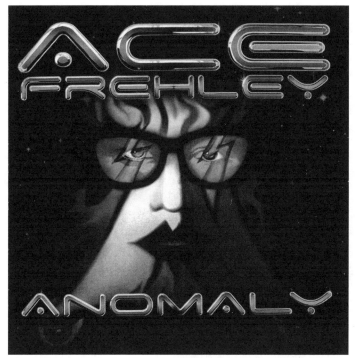

Ace Frehley's 2009 solo album *Anomaly*.   *Author's Collection*

coheadlining tour called the *Bad Boys* tour in 1995. In some ways it was to help them prepare for the reunion with Simmons and Stanley that would come in 1996.

After leaving the band again in 2000, Criss appeared on the HBO series *Oz* in 2002 and released another album, *One for All*, in 2007. Since then he has been working on another album and finishing the autobiography that has been in the works for over twenty-five years. The book is to be released in 2012.

Ace Frehley

Frehley was under contract until 1984 and laid low for a time as any project he worked on would have been co-owned by the KISS Company. After the contract ran out, he began putting together a band with Anton Fig called Frehley's Comet. Their first album was released on Megaforce in 1987. Frehley did two more albums under the Frehley's Comet name, but Megaforce was pushing for him to go solo as they felt they could promote him better that way than as part of a band. He did this reluctantly for his 1989 release, *Trouble Walkin'*, but then Megaforce was beginning to feel the money crunch associated with the general audience's declining interest in metal and cut ties with him soon after the album was released.

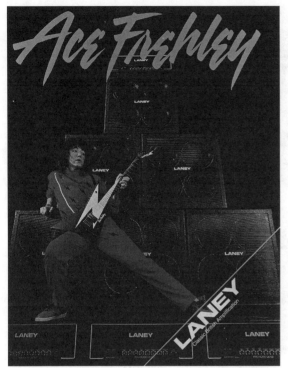

Mid-1980s ad featuring Ace Frehley without makeup for the very first time. With this, all four original members had officially left their makeup personas behind. But not for good.   *Author's Collection*

Frehley occasionally did solo tours after the dismissal from Megaforce before signing up to tour with Peter Criss for the *Bad Boys* tour in 1995. After leaving KISS again in 2002, he again started doing occasional touring while working on new material. He released an album in 2009 called *Anomaly*. He is looking to release another album in the near future, and his autobiography, *No Regrets*, came out in November 2011.

Eric Carr

Carr did some side projects while in KISS, including his cartoon series concept *The Rockheads*. He helped produce demos for an all-female band named Hari Kari in 1988 and 1989 and demos for a band out of South Carolina called New York in 1988. Nothing further

A 1999 CD release featuring material Eric Carr had worked on for possible use in KISS and his *Rockheads* project.   *Author's Collection*

happened in either situation. After his passing in November 1991, a number of Carr's recordings from before and during his time with KISS have surfaced on various albums and on video. A book about his life, *The Eric Carr Story*, by Greg Prato, was released in 2011.

Vinnie Vincent

Vincent would have a very strong comeback after leaving KISS, thanks to a lucrative deal with Chrysalis Records that paid him millions for producing eight albums over a ten-year period. Looking at first to reform Warrior, Vincent instead created the Vinnie Vincent Invasion and produced the first album in 1986 while opening for Alice Cooper that fall and Iron

Post-KISS autographed photo of Vinnie Vincent.

Author's Collection

Maiden the following spring. This was followed up with the 1988 release of *All Systems Go* and the band doing a music video for the latest *Nightmare on Elm Street* movie for the song "Love Kills." But then things went sour, and the band broke up in August 1988.

Stickers promoting the first Vinnie Vincent *Invasion* album.   *Author's Collection*

The singer of the band, Mark Slaughter, and the drummer, Dana Strum, went on to strong success as the band Slaughter. As Vincent picked up the pieces and began putting together another band, Chrysalis decided to terminate his contract. With lawsuits from former associates soon to follow, Vincent ended up filing for bankruptcy.

Vincent signed with Enigma in 1990, only for the label to fold soon after. With his bankruptcy still ongoing in 1991, he met up with Gene Simmons, and the two decided to let bygones be bygones and work on some songs for the next KISS album at the time, *Revenge.* The relationship did not last long, however, and Vincent was soon on the outs with KISS again. He began releasing some material on his own through his Metaluna Records, although a planned multitape box set never became a reality. He also sued KISS more than once in the years since over royalties and other issues. The murder of his ex-wife in 2000 led to further seclusion for Vincent, although he has popped up every so often to mention working on a new project.

Mark St. John

St. John left KISS to join his brother in the band White Tiger, which released one album in 1986 and had demos for a second that was to have been released in 1988. After struggling for a time to get noticed with a band he was working on with Peter Criss, St. John supposedly spent some time going back to his job of teaching guitar, while making some appearances at the many KISS expos

Mark St. John's short-lived band after leaving KISS.

Author's Collection

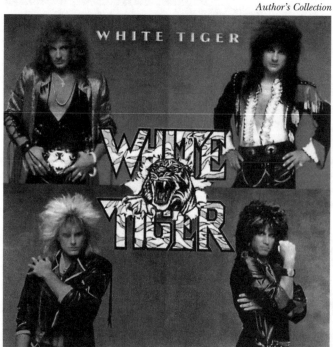

Ad for Bruce Kulick's post-KISS band Union's second album.   *Author's Collection*

around. He released an EP in 1999 called *The Mark St. John Project* and then a full album in 2003 called *Magic Bullet Theory.*

Mark St. John died of a cerebral hemorrhage in April 2007.

Bruce Kulick

Kulick continued to work with a variety of artists while still with KISS in the 1980s and 1990s. He also started a band in 1996 with former Mötley Crüe singer John Corabi called Union. The band continued through October 2000 with two studio albums and a live album to their credit. After releasing his solo album *Audiodog* in 2001, Kulick linked up with Eric Singer to perform for a bit as part of the Eric Singer Project (ESP), and the two spent some time going between that and a form of Union that Kulick had revived. Kulick also teamed up with Grand Funk Railroad for touring and released another album, *BK3*, in 2010. He has also done a lot of guest work on a variety of albums, including KISS, since going on his own in 1996.

Eric Singer

Singer had a similar career upswing upon leaving KISS in 1996, doing tours and albums with his band Eric Singer Project, a number of tribute albums, and working with Alice Cooper off and on on album material and touring. Things did not even slow down once he came back to KISS in 2003, with a large number of guest appearances still popping up for him whenever he has free time away from KISS.

Tommy Thayer

Thayer has worked on a few outside projects, including a number of Black N' Blue collections, since joining KISS on a permanent basis in 2002. For the most part, though, he has concentrated on working on projects related to KISS, including the *KISSology* box sets and other historical packages for the band.

30

From Dylan to Carson

Ten Surprising People Associated with KISS

I t is easy to see how certain people would be connected with KISS over the years, mainly due to being on the same record label or through the various projects the band members have been involved with. However, here are a few names that people may recognize but not normally think of as having a KISS connection.

Katey Sagal

Coming from a show business background (her father, Boris Sagal, had many television credits as a director and also directed Charlton Heston in *The Omega Man*, which costarred future *KISS Meets the Phantom* star Anthony Zerbe), she started her career as an actress before switching to a musical career in the mid-1970s. During this period she was asked to sing backing vocals on Gene Simmons's 1978 solo album. In the 1980s, she went back to acting, doing very well in the part of Peg Bundy on *Married . . . With Children*. For a Hollywood premiere of the Fox series, both Simmons and Stanley appeared to support Sagal.

Along with occasional ventures into singing, Sagal has kept busy with acting, including memorable roles in *Lost, Sons of Anarchy*, and as the voice of Leela on *Futurama*. She also sang backup on Olivia Newton-John's 1985 *Soul Kiss* album, which produced a music video featuring future KISS drummer Eric Singer.

Johnny Carson

When Casablanca first broke away from Warner in the fall of 1974, Neil Bogart had put himself in debt, while banking that a new acquisition would put the company back on top: a two-album compilation of interviews and skit segments from *The Tonight Show* called *Here's Johnny: Magic Moments from The Tonight Show*. Bogart heavily promoted the album to distributors, allowing Casablanca to push a million copies out the door when it was released in November 1974.

The problem was that the audience for such audio collections of television shows was not as big as Bogart had thought. Although *The Tonight Show* had plenty of fans, many preferred watching the show at night to listening to

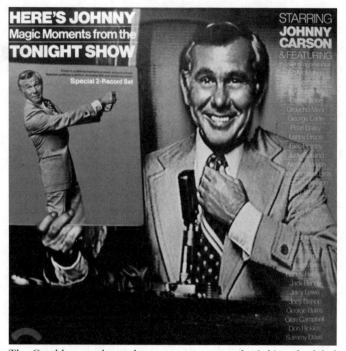

The Casablanca release that many saw as nearly sinking the label
before KISS took off with *Alive!*   *Author's Collection*

excerpts from earlier episodes. While the company sold an impressive half-
million copies, they had plenty sitting in record bins unsold. The distributors
eventually sent back the unwanted copies, forcing Casablanca to eat them and
giving the album a reputation as a dud. This was the album that created the
famous saying of a record "shipped Gold and returned Platinum."

This damaged Casablanca's reputation at a time where they had none to
really build on, even though for a brief moment the company had an influx of
money thanks to advance sales on the collection. Bogart later told *Rolling Stone*
that he was near-suicidal after the failure of the album made headlines in early
1975 and figured the company was dead in the water. Then KISS and some of
the other acts on Casablanca began moving when signs appeared that the band
was beginning to sell albums and singles. The year 1975 was the turnaround
moment for Casablanca, but for a brief moment it looked like Johnny Carson
was going to cause the end of the company.

Bryan Adams

The famed Canadian singer-songwriter who is more commonly thought of today
for some of his ballads had a fine career going in the 1980s as a rock musician
with such hits as "Cuts Like a Knife" and "Summer of '69." In the early 1980s,

he was working with Jim Vallance on songs and submitting them to other artists. In 1982, the pair submitted two songs—"War Machine" and "Rock and Roll Hell"—to Michael James Jackson, who was about to produce the album *Creatures of the Night* for KISS and was looking for material that would suit the band. Gene Simmons took the material and transformed it into the songs known from the album (there has been the suggestion that Adams was never even in the same room with Simmons when the changes were made).

Adams also worked with Paul Stanley and Mikel Japp on the song "Down On Your Knees" for the *Killers* album. Meanwhile, Eric Carr worked with Adams and Vallance on a song called "Don't Leave Me Lonely," which appeared on Adams's *Cut Like a Knife* in 1983, his breakout album.

Bob Dylan

Legendary singer-songwriter of enough distinction that it would be impossible to list his credits here. Back in 1992, Simmons arranged to spend time with Dylan and work on some material, namely so he could say, "I worked with Bob Dylan." Simmons took what was done and later created a song he initially titled "Laughing When I Want to Cry."

Bryan Adams's *Cuts Like a Knife* album, with a song cowritten by Eric Carr. *Author's Collection*

When working on his 2004 solo album, *Asshole*, he brought in the song for possible recording. It was reworked into "Waiting for the Morning Light" for the album.

Karen Carpenter

Singer and drummer for the brother-sister act the Carpenters. Simmons at one time mentioned that he had met up with Karen at a club when both the Carpenters and KISS were touring in Indianapolis at the same time in 1976. He would go on to say that the two spent the night in her hotel room, although he was quick to say that nothing happened and the two had talked all night, which for someone always ready to claim his post notches means that this probably is exactly what happened.

Lynda Carter

Actress best remembered for her role as Wonder Woman in the 1970s series of the same name. Carter also was a singer, and in a 1980 CBS variety special sang "I Was Made for Lovin' You" in a feathery, sequined costume while dancing around four thin gyrating men in KISS makeup and costumes. The clip would be a favorite among KISS fans, even if it was a bit nauseating to watch.

Later, when Simmons filmed the movie *Never Too Young To Die*, he wore a duplicate of Lynda Carter's outfit from the special in a musical number. It has never been confirmed if this was his idea of a joke, someone playing a joke on him, or just a huge coincidence.

Lou Reed

Another famous singer-songwriter, who had first won notice in the band the Velvet Underground. Bob Ezrin produced Reed's controversial *Berlin* album in 1973 and was asked to help throw around some ideas during the recording of *Music from "The Elder."* Reed came up with the title for "A World Without Heroes" and worked a bit on the song. Supposedly there is also video of Reed in the studio singing the song.

Reed also cowrote "Mr. Blackwell" with Simmons for the album as well as some additional lyrics to be used if there was to be a second album in the series. Speaking of Reed . . . .

John Cale

Another founding member of the Velvet Underground. Cale played viola on a track for the 1971 album for Peter Criss's band Chelsea.

Laura Nyro

Singer-songwriter known for her many songs that became hits for other artists. Lyn Christopher, a backup singer for Nyro in the late 1960s, recorded a self-titled debut album in 1972 that featured Gene Simmons and Paul Stanley singing background (and supposedly Peter Criss with some additional hand-clapping, although only Stanley and Simmons are credited on the album). The recordings led to KISS being able to get a five-track demo down at Electric Lady Studios with Eddie Kramer producing in exchange for payment on the Christopher sessions. The demo tape then led to Neil Bogart and Bill Aucoin taking notice of the band and signing them on in 1973.

Vinnie Vincent played guitar on Nyro's 1978 album *Nested*.

Michael Bolton

Bolton became a superstar in the 1980s for his many ballads and in the 1990s, but before that he was struggling to make it as a hard-rock singer under the name of Michael Bolotin. He met up with guitarist Bruce Kulick and formed a band called Blackjack that released two albums in 1979 and 1980. After the band broke up, he changed his last name to Bolton and tried to kick-start his career by writing for other artists (he wrote "I've Found Someone" that would later be a hit for Cher) and continued to get noticed as a hard-rock singer, but it was his 1987 remake of "(Sittin' on the) Dock of the Bay" that drew attention to him, and from there he went on to success by concentrating on ballads and remakes of other classic pop songs.

31

Legends Never Die

The Rumors

W hen you have a band that hides their faces and past as they become hugely successful, it is natural for all types of rumors to be created to help explain things. KISS was no stranger to rumors and have had plenty over the years. Some have been so silly that they can be dismissed without much knowledge of the band (case in point, one stating that Ozzy Osbourne was the lead guitarist in KISS, a rumor that gained momentum in the 1980s but still pops up once in a while even today). Of course, some of the ones listed below may seem very silly indeed, but that doesn't stop them from being memorable. Here are some of the better ones that still pop up today.

Ace Interrupted Bob Kulick's Tryout in 1972

A story perpetuated by the members of KISS as much as fandom, the story goes that when Bob Kulick was auditioning for Gene Simmons, Paul Stanley, and Peter Criss in 1972, Ace Frehley walked in and either plugged into his own amp and started playing along, or ripped out Kulick's lead and plugged in his own to take over. While it makes for a good story, it appears to be only that.

Further, it appears to have been a bit of a thorn in Kulick's side as people have remembered it and would ask about it many times over the years. However, considering the type of New Yorkers these men were—struggling in a dog-eat-dog world to make enough to live—most probably if Frehley had done such a thing, as Kulick himself said years later to me in an interview, Frehley would have been wearing his guitar around his head a minute later.

From less thrilling tellings of the tale, it appears that Frehley did interrupt while Kulick was with the others, but not in such a forceful manner. Rather, he had walked in while the others were discussing the band, was deemed to be rude, and was nearly kicked out for interrupting them all while they were still talking to another applicant.

Yet it is one of those stories that will never go away.

The Photo on the Back Cover of *Alive!* Is a Phony

As mentioned in a previous chapter, the back cover of *Alive!* shows two young KISS fans with their makeshift sign. Fans loved the picture. They thought it showed how the band had a connection to the fans, and the only vague rumor that came out of it for years was from really silly people wondering if one or both were girls.

Then former KISS associate Sean Delaney dropped a bomb. In an interview with Steve Stierwalt Jr. for his fanzine *KISS Freaks*, Delaney passed on the news that not only was the photo of the two teenagers not from a KISS show, but he had created the sign himself for kids to hold up. For years this story would escalate into one about how Delaney got a photographer (usually Bob Gruen, as that is who Delaney remembers as taking the photo) into either a Bob Segar, Styx, or someone else's concert, slapped the poster in front of the two young men, took a picture, and used it for the back cover. The point of telling such a story is, "Who would know?" while also making it sound like Delaney once again was a major force behind what the band did in the 1970s.

However, in 2005, the fanzine *KISS Kollector Online* interviewed Fin Costello, who went into detail about taking the picture seen on the back cover at the Cobo Hall KISS show—just as everyone had assumed for years before Delaney made his comment. He also provided photo contact sheets showing when the photos were taken, as well as additional photos of the boys with their sign with other fans at the concert. The two men in the photo have also discussed the concert and situation of ending up as icons of KISS fandom as well in plenty of interviews over the years, so there is obvious evidence that Delaney's statements were incorrect. Costello went on to state in his interview that he believed Delaney was misremembering what had occurred with the inner gatefold photo for the Rainbow album *Long Live Rock 'n' Roll*, where a photo taken of the crowd at a Rush concert had a large banner for Rush airbrushed out so it appeared to be a large crowd at a Rainbow show.

Thus, while things have been done in the industry to make Delaney's story sound like there could be truth to it, in this particular case, it appears to be a case of mistaken memory.

Sports Illustrated Printed in "REAL KISS BLOOD!"

One of the most brilliant stories ever told about the band. As everyone seems to know, the first Marvel KISS comic in 1977 stated on the front cover that it was printed in "Real KISS Blood." To commemorate the event, photographers and a television station camera filmed the dumping of each band member's blood into a drum of red ink at the printing plant to prove this was the case.

However, the story goes that after completion of the ceremony, the printer found that they needed to get the new issue of *Sports Illustrated* done first. In the rush to complete the print run, the sports magazine accidentally used the blood-tainted red ink for printing before the Marvel comics were done. Thus, a run of *Sports Illustrated* features "REAL KISS BLOOD" in the ink.

Information about the situation was hard to come by—naturally, it is not easy to locate such information thirty-five years after the fact. People I spoke with at

Marvel and *Sports Illustrated* seem to have never heard of the rumor (not that they didn't enjoy hearing about it), and the printing plant closed in 2011 after decades in service. However, thanks to former employee Hal Lane, who was working at Arcata Graphics (the plant that printed the comic) at the time, I was finally able to track down more details.

While it is true that the band poured blood into a drum of red ink at the plant for the press, one must consider the ramifications of having to switch drums of ink for a specific project. The method of printing, heatset offset, required the use of oil-based inks that took time and money to switch when necessary. Considering the cost of doing so just for the KISS comic, and the fact that Arcata had a wide variety of magazines and books each day to print, it did

The First KISS Comic, *not* printed in REAL KISS BLOOD. *Author's Collection*

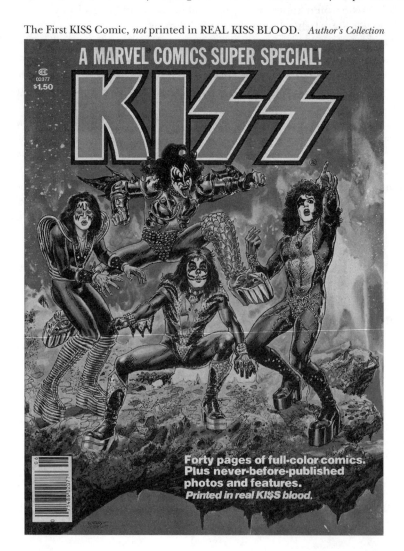

not make sense to stop the presses and change the drums around for just one job. When Lane joked with fellow employees later about whether the second printing of the comic would also need "REAL KISS BLOOD!" in the magenta ink, he was told that the first was not done that way either, so it didn't make any difference.

Besides, who was to know? It was not as if fans would be able to get all *CSI* on the comic and verify that blood was in the ink. It was enough to see the pictures and read the news articles about the event to be convinced of its authenticity. Therefore, the first printing of the comic went out with normal magenta ink, while other publications got the ink with "REAL KISS BLOOD!" in them. As for the second pressing of the comic, it too used normal red ink (as that print job occurred long after the blood-infected ink had been used). Thus, it appears that none of the copies printed has "REAL KISS BLOOD!"

So what did end up having "REAL KISS BLOOD" in it? Hard to say. Arcata (now known as Quebecor) printed a variety of items at the time, among them *People, Reader's Digest, Time, Easy Rider,* "various skin mags," comics, and *Sports Illustrated* as well as Harlequin Romances and other paperback novels. So if it really was *Sports Illustrated,* which issue would it be? While it is fun to think it was the June 6, 1977, issue, which featured Mark Fidrych (who played with the Detroit Tigers; rather fitting for KISS) posing with *Sesame Street*'s Big Bird, it would most probably be the issue before that, dated May 30, 1977, with Dave Parker on the cover. However, the true details of the situation make it even more fun to think there are a bunch of cheap romance novels out there somewhere printed in "REAL KISS BLOOD!"

Paul Being the Son of the "2,000 Flushes" Inventor

When it was discovered that Paul Stanley's real name was Stanley Eisen and the man who invented the 2000 Flushes toilet-bowl cleaner was named Al Eisen, people assumed that Paul was Al's son. This was usually in relation to Paul either helping finance Al's start in his business or vice versa. As it stands, however, Paul's father's name is William.

Destroyer Tour Featured Car Being Blown Up Onstage

This was a concept thought up while everyone was throwing ideas around for the tour, and some sketches showing such a thing in the show made their way into one of the rock magazines of the time, but the band never did such a thing during the tour as the cost and insurance needed made it impossible.

KISS Stands for Knights in Satan's Service

This rumor seemed to take hold in 1976 among some Bible thumpers who were looking for hidden meanings in anything related to rock music that proved they were devil worshippers. The rumor has been one of the most persistent of those centering on the band (although sometimes the wording would be Knights in Service of Satan) no matter how many times the band has denied it over the years. Other versions of it include Knights in Service of Satan and Kids in Satan's Service, and a bunch of variations in between. At first, the band tried to correct them—especially Peter Criss, who found them troubling—but soon enough they ignored the rumors, along with many others about their supposed satanic dealings.

Peter Criss Refused to Do Show on 1979 Tour and Was Replaced

There have been rumors for years that Peter Criss refused to do a show on the 1979 tour, and the band had a roadie or someone from the audience replace him for the night, announcing the imposter as Criss and forcing him to realize that he had to clean up his act or would be easily replaced. Although an incident did occur in the reunion tour where Criss's drum tech replaced him, and there certainly were incidents on the 1979 *Dynasty* tour that would seem to fit for such a thing to occur, this never happened. Or at least no one has ever come forward with proof, which is surprising if it had actually occurred in front of a crowd at a concert.

Gene's Tongue

Gene Simmons supposedly had a cow's tongue grafted onto his own, or had the little cord underneath the tongue cut off in order to make it look longer. The other story was that he had the tip of it split so that he could make it look more like a snake's tongue. The real story—he just has a long tongue and certainly has never had it split. Rather dull when you bring it down to Earth, isn't it?

Assault on Andy Gibb

The story goes as follows: Andy Gibb is backstage at either an awards ceremony or a KISS show when he starts causing trouble and hitting on women. KISS, seeing this, surround him and begin beating him up with their guitars and drum-sticks in order to teach him a lesson. Sometimes the story goes on to make it so that each member formed a queue to assault Gibb.

For some reason, it is pretty easy to see that this never happened. Why KISS would be used as heroes saving women from the dastardly Andy Gibb is a question that remains unanswered, however.

Ad for *Alive!* showing the back cover photo that became part of a well-known KISS rumor.   *Author's Collection*

Gene's Blood

Simmons's blood-spitting has been a part of the stage act for KISS since their early days. For years all types of guesses have been made as to what exactly he was spitting up during concerts. The wildest, of course, was that it was real animal blood, but in actuality it was a variety of concoctions over the years, from a synthetic fake blood (which never looked quite right) to a mixture of eggs, yogurt, and cottage cheese. One thing for sure, it was never real blood he was spitting up in concert, no matter what the cool kids told each other in school.

Gene's Hand Gesture Being Satanic

Simmons has told a variety of stories as to how he came by the hand gesture he used while costumed as the bat-demon. The most innocent and logical of these was that one night he wanted to wave to someone in the audience without losing his pick. By cupping his two middle fingers in, he kept the pick in place while extending the thumb out and proceeded to form the hand gesture.

Simmons has also stated that he recognized the symbol as the same one used by two popular Marvel Comics superheroes (both originally drawn by artist Steve Ditko)—Spider-Man and Dr. Strange. With such a reference in his head, it was easy to start using the symbol constantly while in character.

For those wishing to see the band as satanic anyway, the gesture was immediately jumped on as being an invitation to Satan, symbolizing his head and horns. This merely led to even more kids doing it just to scare the older folks denouncing KISS and other heavy-metal and hard-rock bands, and it became increasingly difficult to separate the gesture from that connotation. It should be pointed out that Simmons would nearly always extend his thumb out when doing the gesture, which was different than the one that was supposed to be some type of Boy Scout salute to Satan. In American Sign Language, his hand gesture means "I Love You" (which may have even been where artist Ditko was going with the supernatural Dr. Strange using the gesture), but the naysayers simply took that to mean "I Love Satan," so it was a no-win situation. After the makeup came off, Simmons usually resisted using the hand gesture.

Peter Criss Was to Be Replaced by a Female Drummer

This grew out of a simply misunderstanding when it was announced that the new drummer's name was Eric Carr. Someone misheard this as Erica and reported it as such, leading to a brief double take by the KISS Army, who wondered if the new drummer would still be able to sing "Beth" onstage.

"Flash and Balls" Ad

For years the band would claim that their *Village Voice* ad to find a lead guitarist stated they were looking for someone with "flash and balls." That held until fans actually found the original ad and discovered it said nothing of the kind. The band's response was that they wanted it to say that, but the *Voice* refused to use the word "balls" in an ad. However, knowing the type of very liberal reporting and advertising appearing in the *Voice* in the early 1970s, it would seem odd that such usage would have been a problem.

Eric Singer Received Three Million Dollars to Rejoin KISS in 2001

For some bizarre reason, fans tend to think rock bands have a lot more money to blow than they do in reality. The story stands that when Peter Criss left in 2000 and negotiations broke down, KISS was in desperate need of a replacement for the Japanese tour already booked for early 2001. They immediately went to Eric Singer, knowing he knew the material and had played with all of them before. Singer's reaction was that he had been fired once and would not get burned again, and he demanded three million dollars to sign up. Simmons and Stanley, broken, and having been taught a lesson by Singer, bowed their heads in shame and agreed to pay up.

This mostly comes out of the rumors that Singer would take over but that there were some delays in signing him up. Most of this, however, was due to figuring out when and how he could leave his current tour with Alice Cooper in order to help KISS out and not due to monetary demands. When I mentioned this story to someone in Cooper's management back in 2001, he found it hysterically funny. So at least it gave someone a good laugh.

KISS II

In 2008, Gene Simmons began telling reporters that the band planned to have a reality show soon that would be done to find replacements for himself and Paul Stanley. That band—KISS II—would then go on to record albums and tour under their supervision for years to come.

At the time, many fans rolled their eyes at this bit of news, as it was typical Simmons. Anything to get a reaction from the reporters, they figured. That did not stop some from wondering if the story might be an inkling to what Simmons and Stanley plan to do with the band at some point in the future.

It is clear that KISS is now structured not around the four musicians in it but around rather the personas they inhabit. The Demon, Starchild, Catman, and Spaceman are who the songs are written for, the makeup is applied to, and the costumes inhabited by. Once Eric Singer and Tommy Thayer adopted these disguises and were given reasons to do so by Simmons and Stanley that were accepted by the fans, the old rules no longer applied. Now it is accepted that at some point Simmons could leave and another man could be put into the costume and makeup and be the new Demon. The same holds true for Paul Stanley and the Starchild. It may be some time before it happens, but both men are in their sixties, with ailments becoming more frequent (Stanley has stated this his two hip surgeries have been due to having danced around in platform shoes for too many years). Then again, the other two members of the band are in their fifties, and they are considered the "youngsters" of the band.

KISS II is not so much a rumor as something that will probably happen. But will it be accepted? A number of fans still look at the band as it is today and see only Stanley and Simmons and two other guys. Even after Thayer and Singer have proven themselves by years of touring and now two albums of new studio material, even when plenty of other bands have resorted to being only half or even less full of original group members, the image is still "KISS is half a cover band." It may be an unfortunate label to give them, but it persists nonetheless. Thayer plays lead guitar on *Sonic Boom*, but fans say, "he is just trying to copy Ace." It is a trap that cannot be avoided.

But with Stanley and Simmons's presence still there—and with most in agreement that they have always been the leaders of the band—many can see KISS as still being KISS. Once they are gone, however, will fans still be interested in the band? Can it continue when the band seems to be in a time loop that sees them endlessly repeating the stage shows and music of the 1970s? People are buying albums like *Sonic Boom* and *Monster* because Simmons and Stanley are there, but once they are gone, will KISS be viewed favorably if the "next generation" produced an album without Simmons and Stanley's presence? Would they even want that? Better yet, if nothing new can grow in that vacuum, can KISS continue to attract the attention of the fans?

For the moment, KISS II is just a silly rumor. Nothing to worry about, as KISS is planning a new album release in 2012 and a summer tour with Mötley Crüe, and there will no doubt be another tour and more videos and books and homages to come.

For the moment.

A good example of why people came up with so many rumors about Gene Simmons's tongue over the years.   *Courtesy of Tony Kazerrick*

Selected Bibliography

Books

Abbott, Waring, Gene Simmons, and Paul Stanley. 2002. *KISS: The Early Years*. New York: Three Rivers Press.

Duncan, Robert. 1978. *KISS*. New York: Popular Library.

Floren, Ingo. 2004, *The Official Price Guide to KISS Collectibles*. New York: House of Collectibles.

Gebert, Gordon G. G. and Bob McAdams. 1997. *KISS & Tell*. Fleetwood, NY: Pitbull Publishing.

Gebert, Gordon G. G. 1998. *KISS & Tell More!* Fleetwood, NY: Pitbull Publishing.

Gooch, Curt and Jeff Suhs. 2002. *KISS Alive Forever: The Complete Touring History*. New York: Billboard Books.

Holm, Anders and Dave Thomas. 1988. *KISS Still on Fire*. London: Caroline Publishing.

KISS. 1994. *KISStory*. Los Angeles: Kisstory Ltd.

KISS. 1995. *KISStory II*. Los Angeles: Kisstory Ltd.

Leaf, David, and Ken Sharp. 2003. KISS: Behind the Mask: The Official Authorized Biography. New York: Warner Books.

Lendt, C. K. 1997. *KISS and Sell*. New York: Billboard Books.

Lesniewski, Karen and John Lesniewski. 1993. *KISS Collectibles Identification and Price Guide*. New York: Avon Books.

Levine, Barry. 1997. *The KISS Years*. Westbury, NY: Studio Chikara.

Prato, Greg. 2011. *The Eric Carr Story*. Greg Prato.

Sharp, Ken. 2009. *Kiss Army Worldwide! The Ultimate Fanzine Phenomenon*. Beverly Hills, CA: Phoenix Books.

Sherman, Dale. 1997. *Black Diamond: The Unauthorized Biography of KISS*. Updated Edition. Ontario, Canada: Collector's Guide Publishing, 2009.

Sherman, Dale. 1998. *Black Diamond 2: The Illustrated Collector's Guide to KISS*. 1998. Ontario, Canada: Collector's Guide Publishing.

Simmons, Gene. 2002. *Kiss and Make-Up*. New York: Three Rivers Press.

Simmons, Gene. 2006. *Sex Money KISS*. Beverly Hills, CA: Phoenix Books.

Swenson, John. 1978. *Headliners: KISS*. New York: Tempo Star Book.

Tomarkin, Peggy. 1980. *KISS: The Real Story*. New York: Delilah Press.

Websites

http://www.kissonline.com—Official website for KISS. Has official news about KISS and a number of exclusive photos and videos of the band, as well as a merchandise area.

http://www.kissfaq.com—Website by Julian Gill (and not connected with the publication of this book) that is an update of an earlier 1990s FAQ created by others. Gill covers a lot of information within one site, from tours to albums to news and many things fans forget about. It is a good first site to check for information of any kind. Gill has also self-published a series of books about the band and their history over the years.

http://www.genesimmons.com—Official website for Gene Simmons. All four current members have official websites, but Simmons typically is the most actively involved of the four. More advertising than needed (is any fan surprised?), but it also contains a letters area where Simmons will reply to certain e-mails.

http://www.kissasylum.com—Longtime unofficial website for KISS. These days it is mostly a showcase for merchandise and news items that do not get picked up by the official website, but some older features still remain for fans to view.

www.kissarmywarehouse.com—Large collection of KISS merchandise, both new and rare.

http://www.necramonium.com—Excellent website that includes a multimedia history of the band with videos and rare photos.

http://www.kissnews.de/NewsUSA.htm—Website with current KISS news and merchandise. Has pages dealing with minute details about costumes and staging of the band over the years.

Index

THE FAQ SERIES

Lucille Ball FAQ
*by James Sheridan
and Barry Monush*
Applause Books
978-1-61774-082-4
$19.99

**The Beach Boys
FAQ**
by Jon Stebbins
Backbeat Books
978-0-87930-987-9
$19.99

**Black Sabbath
FAQ**
by Martin Popoff
Backbeat Books
978-0-87930-957-2
$19.99

The Doors FAQ
by Rich Weidman
Backbeat Books
978-1-61713-017-5
$19.99

Fab Four FAQ
*by Stuart Shea and
Robert Rodriguez*
Hal Leonard Books
978-1-4234-2138-2
$19.99

Fab Four FAQ 2.0
by Robert Rodriguez
Hal Leonard Books
978-0-87930-968-8
$19.99

Led Zeppelin FAQ
by George Case
Backbeat Books
978-1-61713-025-0
$19.99

Pink Floyd FAQ
by Stuart Shea
Backbeat Books
978-0-87930-950-3
$19.99

Star Trek FAQ
by Mark Clark
Applause Books
978-1-55783-792-9
$19.99
(June 2012)

**Three Stooges
FAQ**
by David J. Hogan
Applause Books
978-1-55783-788-2
$19.99

U2 FAQ
by John D. Luerssen
Backbeat Books
978-0-87930-997-8
$19.99

Neil Young FAQ
by Glen Boyd
Backbeat Books
978-1-61713-037-3
$19.99

HAL•LEONARD®
PERFORMING ARTS
PUBLISHING GROUP

FAQ.halleonardbooks.com

Prices, contents, and availability subject to change without notice.